MABOU MINES

MABOU MINES

Making Avant-Garde Theater in the 1970s

IRIS SMITH FISCHER

THE UNIVERSITY OF MICHIGAN PRESS

ANN ARBOR

First paperback edition 2012
Copyright © by the University of Michigan 2011

Published in the United States of America by
The University of Michigan Press
Printed and bound by CPI Group (UK) Ltd, Croydon, CR0 4YY

2015   2014   2013   2012   5   4   3   2

A CIP catalog record for this book is available from the British Library.

Library of Congress Cataloging-in-Publication Data

Fischer, Iris Smith.
    Mabou Mines : making avant-garde theater in the 1970s / Iris Smith
Fischer.
      p.   cm.
    Includes bibliographical references and index.
    ISBN 978-0-472-11762-8 (cloth : alk. paper)
    1. Mabou Mines (Theater group).   2. Experimental theater—New York
(State)—New York—History—20th century.   I. Title.
    PN2277.N52M33   2010
    792.02'22—dc22   2010040238

978-0-472-02898-6 (e-book)

ISBN: 978-0-472-03518-2 (paper : alk. paper)

Acknowledgments

The process is the romance.
—LIZA LORWIN

Mabou Mines: Making Avant-Garde Theater in the 1970s attempts the impossible: to capture and describe the work of an avant-garde theater company that set out to create indescribable performance.[1] In 1970, when Mabou Mines took shape as a project of Ellen Stewart's La Mama Experimental Theatre Club in New York City, its members' purpose was to explore whatever interested them through performance. The evanescence of performance and the dynamics of group work attracted them; the traditional process of play production did not. Like other performers in the late 1960s and early 1970s, most of Mabou Mines' early pieces were not recorded. Once the experience ended, for both performers and audience, any written account seemed superfluous, inaccurate, and intrusive.

My first encounter with Mabou Mines' work came through Lee Breuer's publication of *The Red Horse Animation*, first in 1977, then in 1979.[2] In the mid-1980s I discovered the full-color rendition of the play's staging in Lee Breuer and Ann Elizabeth Horton's comic book format. By the early 1980s Mabou Mines had become perhaps the best-known avant-garde theater company in the country, its membership had more than doubled, and it was touring extensively both in the United States and abroad. Yet the texts of the Animations retained much of the company's early character. From the stream of consciousness lines it was difficult to imagine the intimate arena in which the action of *The Red Horse Animation* (1970) took place. The text carried no stage directions, although photos conveyed something of the three performers' interactions. I was drawn in, though, by the lures of the pun-filled language, the humor of the Red Horse's mock heroic circumstances, the romance of "his" motion, and the challenge of approaching a work whose performance origins remained mysterious.

The decision to write about Mabou Mines' early years came later, after I had seen several shows of the 1980s—*Cold Harbor, A Prelude to Death in Venice, Sueños, The Warrior Ant*—whose production histories were much more widely known and better documented in the press. By this time the company had sought to draw attention to its earlier productions, and my project—then conceived as a history of the company to the present day—was welcomed. I am grateful for their support. The present volume would not have been possible without the long memories of current and former company members, associates, and critics, some of whom have shared documents with me as well. This book represents only a fraction of the work I have done, interviews conducted, and materials organized on Mabou Mines, but it also represents the best choice: to account for the least documented of the company's productions, those of the first ten years, 1970–80, and the prehistory that brought those productions, and the company, into existence.

This book is dedicated to the members, current and former, of Mabou Mines. Much of the "romance" of their work—that is, the work process at its heart—remains to be recounted, from the perspectives of the artists I fervently hope, or of those who were in the audience. I am indebted to those I interviewed for this volume, some many times, for the generous gift of their assistance. Particularly helpful have been founding members JoAnne Akalaitis, Lee Breuer, Philip Glass, and Ruth Maleczech, and longtime member Frederick Neumann. David Warrilow, also a founding member, kindly spoke with me once before his death in 1995. I am also grateful to current members Julie Archer, Sharon Fogarty, and Terry O'Reilly, as well as associate artists Honora Fergusson, Clove Galilee, Karen Kandel, and David Neumann. Former members, all of whom graciously allowed me to interview them, include L. B. Dallas, Ellen McElduff, Greg Mehrten, Bill Raymond, and B.-St. John Schofield. Associates and colleagues who spoke with me include George Bartenieff, Herbert Blau, Beverly Brown, Ruby Cohn, Tom Finkelpearl, Richard Foreman, Marion Godfrey, Jill Godmilow, Jane Gullong, Sabrina Hamilton, David Hardy, Linda Hartinian, Cynthia Hedstrom, Mimi Johnson, Patricia Spears Jones, Candy Kodish, Marian Koltun, Ellen Levy, Bill Longcore, Liza Lorwin, Martin Lucas, Bonnie Marranca, John McGrath, Mary Overlie, Gail Merrifield Papp, Rosemary Quinn, Gerald Rabkin, Stephanie Rudolph, Richard Schechner, Don Shewey, Ellen Stewart, Robin Thomas, Jed Wheeler, Dale Worsley, and Alison Yerxa. I am grateful to the company's current general manager, Joe Stackell, and his predecessors while this project was under way, including Frier McCollister, Jennifer Greenfield, the late Anthony Vasconcellos, Sharon Fogarty, Martha Elliot, and Alia Rose Connor, who helped me locate people and information. At the Mabou Mines office, where I viewed scripts, production files, correspondence, publicity, photos, and other materials, I am indebted to Stephen Nunns, Allison Astor, Andrea Fishman, and numerous interns for their assistance. Any omissions are unintentional and much regretted.

My colleagues at the University of Kansas have been warmly supportive of this project as it has grown and changed. Five chairs of the Department of English—Michael L. Johnson, Richard F. Hardin, James W. Hartman, Dorice Williams Elliott, and Marta Caminero-Santangelo—have provided encouragement and assistance. The Department of English supported the acquisition of illustration rights and copies with a Klemmer Research Fund Award, as did the American Society for Theatre Research, which chose *Mabou Mines: Making Avant-Garde Theater in the 1970s* for its 2010 Brooks McNamara Subvention. The University of Kansas College of Liberal Arts and Sciences awarded me three Graduate Research Fund summer grants (1990, 1992, 1994). The Hall Center for the Humanities provided two travel grants (1990, 1994), and a Keeler Intra-University Fellowship in 1997 underwrote a semester of hands-on experience in play directing. Two sabbatical semesters, in 2001 and 2009, supported the writing and revision of the manuscript. Students in my courses in comparative drama, avant-garde theater, literature of the 1960s, and U.S. drama and performance always challenged me to look deeper and farther in the material.

Among the archivists and librarians who provided access and advice were Marvin Taylor and Ann Butler at the Fales Library/Special Collections of the Elmer Holmes Bobst Library (New York University), which now holds the Mabou Mines archive; Robert Taylor of the Billy Rose Theatre Collection at the New York Public Library for the Performing Arts; Doris Pettijohn and Ozzie Rodriguez at the La Mama Experimental Theatre Club; and Mary Ann Jensen and Adriana Popescu in the Department of Rare Books and Special Collections, Princeton University Library. Other organizations that provided access to archival materials were Theatre for the New City and the Guthrie Theatre. On my visits to New York, Rose Edwards made it possible for me to be located close to the Mabou Mines office.

The following sources kindly provided copies of illustrations and/or documents: Mabou Mines; the La Mama E.T.C. Archive; The Fales Library and Special Collections, Elmer Holmes Bobst Library, New York University; Department of Rare Books and Special Collections, Princeton University Library; Richard Landry; Bill Longcore; the Estate of Peter Moore/VAGA; Frederick Neumann and Honora Fergusson.

Excerpts from Samuel Beckett's letters to David Warrilow (30 April 1978); to Frederick Neumann (19 December 1977 and 14 January 1978); and to JoAnne Akalaitis of 1976 are reproduced by kind permission of the Estate of Samuel Beckett c/o Rosica Colin Limited, London. (© The Estate of Samuel Beckett.) My thanks to Joanna Marston and Lisa Gilbey at Rosica Colin for their assistance, and Enoch Brater and Lois Overbeck for their advice. Permission to reprint quotations from Samuel Beckett's published texts *Play and Two Shorter Pieces for Radio, The Collected Shorter Plays, The Lost Ones, Mercier and Camier,* and *Disjecta* has been requested from publishers Faber and Faber Ltd. and Grove/Atlantic, Inc. Permission to quote from "A Bunch Manifesto" has been granted by Richard Schechner and Richard Foreman, as well as the Princeton University Library, which houses the document in the Richard Schechner Papers and *The Drama Review* Collection, Manuscripts Division, Department of Rare Books and Special Collections.

Publication of earlier versions of selected passages and related articles on Mabou Mines is gratefully acknowledged. "Mabou Mines' *Lear:* A Narrative of Collective Authorship" (1993) framed this 1990 landmark production in the context of its development and touring. My account of Breuer's writing and directing as an "autographical" body of work appeared in "The 'Intercultural' Work of Lee Breuer" (1997) and, when his book *La Divina Caricatura* appeared in 2002, in an *American Theatre* review. I published an earlier version of a portion of chapter 3 in *Text and Presentation 2006,* after delivering the paper at the Comparative Drama Conference.[3] I presented two papers related to this volume at Memphis State University, thanks to Lesley Ferris, and developed material in papers read at meetings of the International Federation for Theatre Research, American Society for Theatre Research, Association for Theatre in Higher Education, Semiotic Society of America, American Comparative Literature Association, and Midwest Modern Language Association.

I would like to thank friends and colleagues who read all or parts of the manuscript, or articles and conference papers related to it, and provided valuable feedback: Vicky Unruh, Marvin Carlson, Joan Lipkin, Henry Bial, Janet Sharistanian, Jeanne Klein, Mary Ellen Lamb, Mary Karen Dahl, J. Edgar Tidwell, Jenny Spencer, Bill Worthen, and the members of the Performance and Culture Seminar, sponsored by the Hall Center for the Humanities, and the Lifewriters' Group, both at the University of Kansas. Thanks to those who transcribed tapes, checked facts, gathered permissions, and did word processing: Michelle Bradley, Gwen Claassen, Paula Courtney, Susan Dunn-Hensley, Katie Egging, Karen Hellekson, Pam LeRow, Patrick Phillips, the late Lynn Porter, and the late Anne Turner.

This book, long in development, would not have appeared without the spectacular faith, patience, and support of my editor, LeAnn Fields. She is a true friend of theater scholars and scholarship. The insightful comments of the University of Michigan Press's anonymous reviewers have strengthened and clarified my narrative. My thanks also to Scott Ham, Marcia LaBrenz, and Michael Kehoe at the Press for their generously helpful answers to my questions.

As my first, always perceptive reader throughout this project's several incarnations, my husband, Hans J. Fischer, must have experienced at times the second half of "for better or for worse," but he never let on. For my mother, the late Ethel R. Smith, whose support was constant in the face of a topic that seemed inscrutable, I can only be grateful.

—Iris Smith Fischer

Contents

Illustrations following page 98

Mabou Mines: The Avant-Garde, Gender, and Community

In 2003 the New York-based theater company Mabou Mines, founded in 1970, captured new audiences with its adaptation of Henrik Ibsen's *A Doll House*. As Margo Jefferson wrote in the *New York Times,* director Lee Breuer and performer Maude Mitchell created "a passionate allegory that works—and plays—on many levels."[1] *Mabou Mines Dollhouse* drew audiences into the fun house of the twenty-first century. It was not just that Ibsen's drama of Nora and Torvald Helmer's marriage still works but that Mabou Mines brought to this classic its unique ability to play skillfully with serious drama and to move audiences to places they never expected to go. In this case, Nora's house was shrunk to the size of the male characters—Torvald, Krogstad, Dr. Rank—all played by actors no more than four and a half feet tall. Nora—like Kristine and the maid, almost six feet in height—had to crawl through her own front door and kneel in order to look up into her husband's face. Each scene brought new, contemporary insights into the power dynamic. Even those who had only read news accounts of the production seemed to enjoy the visual irony. Framing *A Doll House* with a strong visual metaphor might have led to a mere satire of the play. The key to success lay in Mabou Mines' approach to theater. Fun to watch, this production at the same time moved beyond the director's or actor's interpretation of Ibsen to a new kind of "play."

Watching the New York premier at St. Ann's Warehouse, I recognized Mabou Mines' rethinking of the actor as creative agent rather than interpreter. The work involved three elements: emotional engagement, estrangement, and "personalization."[2] I was moved when—to take just one scene—Nora recalled sadly the exact day of her father's death. I snapped out of it an instant later when actor Ricardo Gil, throwing his arms wide, sprang Krogstad's trap on Nora, catching her unawares. "Which brings up a rather curious point I simply cannot explain," Krogstad cried, flourishing the paper with the famously forged signature. "The curious point, madam, is that your father signed this document three days after his death!" The lines were Ibsen's, but the mode was

Mabou Mines'. Breuer showed the audience not just the melodrama but ourselves looking at it and back to it. The production surrounded the dollhouse
onstage with rows of boxes occupied by puppet-spectators, husbands and
wives in late-nineteenth-century evening clothes. Breuer was drawing on major innovators of twentieth-century theater to bring Ibsen into our time. In the
shadows of this dollhouse-theater, the figures of Stanislavsky, Artaud, Meyerhold, Brecht, and Grotowski might have been just visible. But Mabou Mines
went beyond these influences to its own conception of the fun house. While
the estranging visual distortion of male and female relationships kept the audience off balance, the emotional texture given to Ibsen's words toyed with us,
drawing us in and slapping us around. I leaned forward to breathe in Kristine's
pronunciation of Nora's name—"Nuuura"—extracted from the Norwegian of
Ibsen's day. The language, like the characters, was both tragic and comic. The
impersonal brutality behind the smooth surface of Nora's middle-class life
emerged like Artaud's image of dolphins levitating themselves out of a placid
sea; at one point, when Nora exclaimed that she could tear herself to pieces,
Mitchell clawed at her body savagely. The moment was moving and memorable and completely of our time. I had no trouble seeing what she saw: the
"bloody stumps" of Nora's married life, which Ibsen's language suggests and
she will take with her when she closes the apartment door. For this fun house
became Mitchell's world—and ours. We, like Nora, play out the culturally conditioned scripts in our heads. Ibsen, says Breuer, leads us to think about every
movement and how it is created.[3] *Mabou Mines Dollhouse* turns acting upside
down. The performers do not interpret Ibsen; rather, Ibsen's text interprets
them.

   Mabou Mines Dollhouse demonstrates why and how this avant-garde theater company has produced pathbreaking work for forty years. Breuer's conception for *Dollhouse* highlights the company's working methods and thematic interests. "The work" is an idea of performance as a way of life, the
actor's return to the self by juxtaposing performance art's "cool" with the
"warmth" of theatrical emotion.[4] To do so the artists use their own lives as material. The work is also an idea of artistic independence, actor-managers working for themselves—at their own pace, according to their needs—and of work
and play as indistinguishable. Not surprisingly, Mabou Mines has stated on its
Web site, "Years before 'performance art' was popularized, Mabou Mines was a
performance company, taking as its first principle the idea that life is performance, that the study and practice of one [are] the study and practice of the
other."[5] In many ways unique among the companies that emerged from the

combustible performance experiments of the 1960s and 1970s, Mabou Mines is still innovating after forty years.

This book tells the story of the company's first ten years and the prehistory that brought the artists together as early as the late 1950s. Articles and reviews have documented the history of Mabou Mines in piecemeal fashion, but no one has attempted to tell the company's story in detail, with attention to the work process, from each piece's conception to its workshops, staging, and continued revision. In choosing to focus on the artists' first twenty years together, I have sought to make visible the work that is the least documented and account for the events and decisions that established Mabou Mines' defining ideas and methods, particularly their devotion to collaboration with artists of varying backgrounds and disciplines. While the current volume ends with 1980, it demonstrates that Mabou Mines' work has played a crucial role in shaping contemporary cutting-edge performance.

The Spirit of "The Work"

It all began in December 1969 when two young people, writer and director Lee Breuer and actress Ruth Maleczech, stepped off the freighter that had brought them back to the United States. They had spent the previous five years living, traveling, and working in Europe. Now New York beckoned. Maleczech and Breuer wanted to live in an English-speaking city where experimental, interdisciplinary work in the arts would be tolerated, perhaps even welcomed. In lower Manhattan an exciting arts scene had developed, a community where they could collaborate with other directors and actors and also with painters and sculptors, dancers, poets, and musicians. This scene had been under way for at least ten years beginning in the late 1950s when Beat writers, jazz musicians, and abstract expressionists offered the latest ideas. In the early 1960s, the artists of Greenwich Village spread to the East Village and south to Soho and created alternative communities of like-minded individuals. Here Maleczech and Breuer found groups and individuals engaged in work similar to their own. The Performance Group, founded by Richard Schechner, had begun in January 1968 as a workshop of *The Bacchae* conceived as a project, not a production.[6] Similarly, Breuer and Maleczech had spent 1965–66 in Paris working privately with friends on Samuel Beckett's *Play* without concerning themselves with performing it before an audience. Recognizing that similar work went on in the Village and Soho created a powerful lure. JoAnne Akalaitis and Philip Glass had settled there after two years in Europe and subsequent travels in India. After having seen the Living Theatre, Grotowski's Theatre Laboratory, and the Berliner Ensemble on their travels, Paris in 1969 seemed almost stodgy to these young people. On the other hand, New York now housed venues such as the La Mama Experimental Theatre Club, Judson Church, 112 Greene Street Gallery, Andy Warhol's Factory, and Caffé Cino and featured performances by an astonishing variety of groups, of which the Open Theatre, Fluxus, and the Bread and Puppet Theatre were only a few. Come to New York, Akalaitis urged. Here we can be part of a community or invent one. Here we can work for ourselves.

Mabou Mines was established in January 1970. Though based in Greenwich Village, it was named for another village, a working-class coal-mining town on Cape Breton Island in Nova Scotia, where members of the new company rehearsed their first original piece, *The Red Horse Animation,* that first summer. They chose a name that had the mystery and edginess of those given to genre-breaking rock music bands. Mabou Mines' five founding members (the fifth, David Warrilow, arrived later in the year) were joined in 1971 by Frederick Neumann. The group had worked with both Warrilow and Neumann in Paris. The troupe became first a project of La Mama, whose founder, Ellen Stewart, had offered space and support to many playwrights and performers since the club's beginning in 1961. In 1970 the East Village and Soho were low-rent districts attractive to young artists for their affordable housing and working space. As the children of older residents fled to the suburbs and businesses left the industrial warehouses and factories once vital to the city's growth, empty buildings and condemned tenements became available. This seeming wasteland, though, offered an "empty space" for youthful experiments in performance. Bill Raymond, a friend from California, joined these experiments in 1974. Younger artists, some coming straight from college or even high school, began to work with the company. Those who became members include Terry O'Reilly, Ellen McElduff, L .B. Dallas, Greg Mehrten, and B.-St. John Schofield, and later Julie Archer and Sharon Fogarty. None of the members of Mabou Mines had grown up in lower Manhattan or any borough of New York City; it constituted a new frontier, a place where they could continue to invent themselves.

Mabou Mines quickly became part of the downtown arts scene. Its work included both original productions and adaptations of nondramatic literary texts, both usually performed in art galleries and studios. Projects involved an extended period of development rather than a predetermined schedule of rehearsals. A piece might continue to change while being performed. When asked what appealed to him about collaborating with the company, writer

Dale Worsley said, "There was a spirit of exploration, of open-ended thinking. There was tremendous humor, energy, irony, passion, commitment, honesty."[7] This spirit of artistic generosity and dedication to the work, and its emergence from a very specific time and place, is the spirit of Mabou Mines.

In 1970 the members of Mabou Mines, like many artists, were seeking to rethink the conventions of "traditional" theater (or painting, music, etc.) in order to create a "genuine" experience for both creators and audience. The Performance Group, for example, sought to break down the distinction between actor and spectator, theater and ritual, in productions such as *Dionysus in '69* (1968–69), *Makbeth* (1969), and *Commune* (1970). Environmental theater surrounded the audience and immersed them in the action. Some groups also sought to politicize their audiences or expose them to performance that questioned basic cultural and political assumptions. The earliest of these groups, the Living Theatre, had left the United States for Europe in 1964 but returned in 1968–69 and toured many college campuses, where opposition to the Vietnam War, the draft, and the "establishment" in general seemed to offer receptive audiences. The Living was at that time a commune; its members lived and worked together for the most part. Akalaitis, Breuer, Glass, and Maleczech had seen the Living perform in France. They did not seek, however, to create the same sort of communal theater but rather a collaborative one. Like the Open Theatre, founded by Joseph Chaikin, a former member of the Living, they intended to shake up audiences and retool their perceptions.

Recent intercultural performance—that is, performance marked by the "self-conscious practice of 'modeled differentiality'"—owes a debt to the group work of the 1960s and 1970s.[8] Mark S. Weinberg points out that "collective theatre" of the late 1960s provided "a model for the reenfranchisement of marginalized groups and the revitalization of indigenous cultures,"[9] which developed (not coincidentally) with a civil rights struggle that empowered blacks and women and the Vietnam War, which galvanized student movement and the counterculture. If these theater groups were not explicitly political, their demand for the freedom to experiment and their expectation of personal rather than career development increased the likelihood that all members would have access to decision making and the opportunity to explore new ideas and techniques.

From the first, Mabou Mines' working methods were based on such assumptions of participatory democracy. The members of Mabou Mines were (and still are) its artistic directors and executive board. Although Breuer has been the company's most visible writer and director, they did not create a hierarchy, preferring to remain a company of equals. Products of postwar liberal arts educations rather than professional theater programs, they approached performance, in a sense, as generalists engaged broadly in the arts. At the same time, they were part of that youthful movement to break open conventional, hierarchical, "uptight" behaviors and redefine personal relations. As James M. Harding and Cindy Rosenthal note, "Making theater was in this respect as much an experiment in the practice of radical democracy as it was an exploration of the possibilities of theater as such."[10]

While Mabou Mines developed work in a variety of ways, *The B.Beaver Animation* (1974) demonstrates the attitudes that underlay the company's early practices. *B.Beaver* grew out of writing Breuer had done in 1968, then abandoned for a time. In the early 1970s the company improvised on a sculpture created by Tina Girouard at the 112 Greene Street Gallery, and Neumann and Warrilow briefly explored with Breuer the possibility of doing the piece as a two-hander. By the time *B.Beaver* premiered, however, it had developed into a five-member cast, each of whom contributed material—comic bits, costuming, props, ideas of all sorts—for the show. It is true that Breuer wrote and directed. Neumann provided *B.Beaver*'s most prominent voice. But it is equally true that everyone wrote, directed, performed, and designed. The process was messy, laborious, and energizing.

By the mid-1970s Mabou members wanted more—or perhaps less. The utopian approach to theater as participatory democracy began to change as a result of internal pressures and external demands. Glass left the company in 1973 to concentrate on work with his own music ensemble. Mabou Mines left La Mama's shelter when Breuer found outside funding to keep the work going on *B.Beaver*. In 1975 Mabou Mines began to receive attention in the theater world. The troupe performed for the first time at a well-known theater venue, the Public Theater, home of the New York Shakespeare Festival, and began a long and productive relationship with its director, Joseph Papp. At about the same time, Breuer began to chafe at a lack of recognition for his accomplishments as a writer and director. Several members were coming to a point where they wanted to work with artists outside the company. Akalaitis had begun to direct in 1975; a few years later Neumann and Maleczech developed their own productions as well. By the late 1970s Mabou Mines was becoming a company of "co-artistic directors," as they sometimes have described themselves. The company's dedication to collaboration did not change; to workshop a production still involved lengthy discussion and argument, a process that has marked, more clearly than genre or method, the character of Mabou Mines. But as the group added members external funding did not keep up, and internal competition to stage projects increased. The National Endowment for the Arts (NEA) and the New York State Council on the Arts had become the company's most reliable sources of grants, while those from private foundations often came with strings attached. Even public money began to be directed toward arts organizations that hired the artists and thus took a slice off the top for administration. As Richard Goldstein noted in the *Village Voice*, the artists faced an impossible choice: the freedom to do the work or the means. In 1979 downtown artists were raising families on annual incomes averaging 6,500 dollars. Goldstein reported that the Performance Group paid its members 5,000 dollars per year and was 50,000 dollars in debt. After staging two shows in a single year, Mabou Mines owed 20,000 dollars. While the company managed to pay its eight members 200 dollars a week as the work was going on, sometimes it could not provide a salary, and members took outside jobs to pay the bills. Some downtown artists had unique sources of support: Robert Wilson, for example, had begun to develop work in Western Europe, where patrons and funding were easier to acquire. Mabou Mines benefited from its relationship with Joe Papp, who over a ten-year period contributed Public Theater resources to individual shows and made several loans to the company. In general, though, its members struggled like everyone else to find the money to do the work.[11]

Papp was a charismatic producer with definite ideas about theater, but he generally did not interfere with Mabou Mines' productions. Clashes among the strong, independent personalities within such groups, though, sometimes radically changed them. Harding and Rosenthal note, "The workshop . . . serves as an apt metaphor for the difficult internal negotiations that group theaters undertook in an open-ended process of collectively plotting the course of their theater while simultaneously being drawn to charismatic figures of creative authority from within their own ranks."[12] While Joseph Chaikin remained the Open Theatre's director until he dissolved it in 1973, R. G. Davis, with whom Breuer and Maleczech had worked after he founded the R. G. Davis (later the San Francisco) Mime Troupe in 1959, had already been ousted by his collective in 1970. Richard Schechner's Performance Group disbanded ten years later after several of its members formed the Wooster Group. In effect, by 1980 these companies were struggling to retain the *communitas* or spirit of community that they had set out in the 1960s to create.[13]

Another factor was gender. The 1970s was an era of identity politics, after the civil rights movement segued into more militant forms of action and the women's movement took shape. Women active in theater groups were becoming aware that while their companies created work collectively the female members did not always see their own realities represented. In some ways collaborative work that developed as an alternative to established hierarchical theater practices still impeded women's individual artistic development. Roberta Sklar of the Open Theatre, for example, later reflected:

> *The Mutation Show* was about domination and submission [in societal roles], and what did that have to do with gender? I remember having dinner with [Jerzy] Grotowski and Joe [Chaikin] and Joe said to Grotowski, "Roberta is very caught up in women's liberation. What do you think of it?" Grotowski responded that he was too busy with men's liberation. Neither Joe nor I countered Grotowski's statement. There was so much ambivalence. This period was a boy's club.[14]

Similarly, Mabou Mines' work together was inflected by women members' increasing attention to gender relations. While initially the company dealt with practical issues, such as finding or developing material that would include roles for women or sharing the costs of babysitters for the members' children, by the mid- to late 1970s gender had become prominent as a theme in the work, particularly for *The Shaggy Dog Animation* (1978) and *Dressed Like an Egg* (1977). The most visible thread in Breuer's ideas on "cultural biology" examines the forces at work in gendered behavior.[15] It has also been central for Maleczech, whose *Song for New York: What Women Do While Men Sit Knitting* (2007) was just as focused on women's experience as was *Vanishing Pictures* (1980), her first full production as director. The public discussion begun in the 1970s of women's lives (and the even less visible lives and sexualities of gay men and women) prompted investigations of gender difference that continue in the company's work today.

The Avant-Garde as Community

Mabou Mines was a crucial part of the avant-garde in the 1970s. I make that statement knowing that for many readers the term has lost its meaning. Arnold Aronson, for example, maintains that the avant-garde artist looked to a utopian future, a sensibility that U.S. artists seem now to lack. He writes, "The so-called avant-garde no longer exists in opposition to established culture; it is a dynamic subset within the culture. The *raison d'être* of the avant-garde has fallen away—evaporated—leaving behind a kind of exoskeleton of style and form that has been subsumed within aspects of thriving popular culture." Recalling the European origins of the term *avant-garde* in its military usages—a vanguard of shock troops—Aronson cuts the ties between contemporary downtown work, which he describes as "a subgenre typified by an edgy, glossy, hip style with elements of the grotesque and perhaps a slightly jaded, distanced, ironic attitude or point of view" and the historical avant-garde of the earlier twentieth century, when artists "strove toward a radical restructuring of the way in which spectators viewed and experienced the very act of theatre."[16]

Aronson identifies the avant-garde in the United States as largely a postwar phenomenon extending from the 1940s to the early 1990s. Mabou Mines, like other artists and groups that began in the 1960s and 1970s (Aronson focuses primarily on the Performance Group, the Open Theatre, Jack Smith, Robert Wilson, Richard Foreman, the Wooster Group, and artists who did happenings, body art, and performance art), began in a time of communal effort. These artists did their most important avant-garde work early on, Aronson claims, when it was possible to "exist in opposition to established culture." Then the downtown avant-garde began its long, losing struggle to keep that oppositional attitude and community spirit as the deteriorating economy of the mid-1970s made housing and work space more difficult to find in lower Manhattan and artists began to scatter to other parts of the city. Aronson rightly links the waning of community to the development of identity politics and performance art in a new era of competitiveness and self-interest inspired by, among other things, a necessary turn to public and private grant funding. The avant-garde had already begun to "become a kind of cultural establishment" replaced by a "downtown aesthetic" that had more to do with that hip, ironic style.[17]

Aronson's adherence to a nineteenth-century definition of *avant-garde*, though, limits his analysis and perhaps his ability to see how artists continued to resist and remake conventional values in their new circumstances. Richard Schechner, as one of those artists and also as a scholar, has perceived a proliferation of avant-gardes where once he, too, declared the movement dead and the term meaningless.[18] In a 1997 interview, he notes that these avant-gardes can be linked more legitimately by being "against the grain" rather than "in advance of" it. He sees the theater groups of the 1970s as part of the historical avant-garde, that is, "the burst of naturalism through various other movements (symbolism, futurism, dada, surrealism, etc.) until around 1980." At the same time "the avant-garde is a tradition . . . handing something down, taking something from an elder. Tradition suggests that whatever you are doing someone else did it before roughly in the same way." The avant-garde is part of the tradition of rebellion that Schechner traces back through the French and American revolutions to "the Renaissance idea . . . that ordinary people, forces from below, the vox populi, could overthrow established authority." Also the avant-garde has been itself a tradition, tracing its own lineages in terms of art as "handicraft," artists passing on "techniques and values" one person or group at a time.[19]

In 1986, the performer Louise Steinman had already put the term *avant-garde* in a similar perspective.

> In work that is considered experimental or "avant-garde" because it doesn't fit into traditional categories, one is very likely still to find the values that are at the root of traditional art forms. The playwright Ionesco has commented that "to be avant-garde is not to be 'far out,' but to return to our sources, to reject traditionalism in order to find again a living tradition." This living tradition is rooted in our first breath, in the transformation of childhood and dream, in the acknowledgement of our ancestors and our animal selves. It is this living tradition that new performance addresses.[20]

Being "against the grain" does not preclude reconnection with performance techniques and concerns that revitalize both the earlier work and the artist who has rediscovered them. Steinman identifies the characteristics that many artists have shared since the 1960s: questioning identity, returning to sources, and searching for a living tradition.

Artists of the 1950s had already conveyed this attitude to those who founded Mabou Mines. For example, Michael McClure, reflecting on the Beats' desire for a living tradition, said in 1995:

> We knew we were poets and we had to speak out as poets. We saw that the art of poetry was essentially dead—killed by war, by academies, by neglect, by lack of love, and by disinterest. We knew we could bring it back to life. We could see what Pound had done—and Whitman, and Artaud, and D.H. Lawrence in his monumental poetry and prose. . . . We wanted to make it new and we wanted to invent it and the process of it as we went into it. We wanted voice and we wanted vision.[21]

Much of this desire remained in the 1970s, although Walt Whitman and Ezra Pound were perhaps less immediate as forebears than William Burroughs and John Cage. The defining element of the avant-garde in the 1970s was its search for living tradition through the shaping of community, which brought together like-minded artists "outside" the ideology of mainstream culture. The community characterized its activity as a generous artistic and personal exchange that seemed to offer the possibility of escape from the conventional subject positions of writer, director, designer, actor, dancer, sculptor, painter, and musician. In an ironic yet utopian gesture, avant-garde artists threw themselves, often with a certain self-conscious humor, against forces and institutions seen as responsible for the selling out and commodification of both the work and the artist. This avant-garde attempt to undermine the individual's embedded response to a culturally imposed identity—a process described by Louis Althusser as "interpellation" or the "scene of hailing"—involved the creation of a different scene of hailing. There the artists and the audience (at first made up largely of other artists) realized a more complete human identity for themselves than they could find or create elsewhere.

How did these artists "hail" one another in the 1970s? The first clue is offered by actor and writer Spalding Gray, who explained in *Swimming to Cambodia,* "I wanted to live on an island off the coast of America."[22] This attitude— that the United States seemed too large and its taste for anti-intellectual entertainments too unwelcoming—was shared by Breuer and Maleczech when they answered Akalaitis's hail to come to New York. The forming of community in this time and place thus involved two moves, an implicit refusal to turn at the hail of mainstream culture and a mutual recognition of one another as those who have refused to turn. That recognition also involved a willingness to provide mutual support; in the absence of funding, the artists would underwrite one another. As with any segment of society that buys its freedom with its *labor,* the primary sacrifice was (and is) the artists' time, or lack of it, to do the *work.*

So how did Mabou Mines characterize itself at the end of the 1970s? As part of a forum devoted to Schechner's assertion in 1981 that the American avant-garde was dead, Maleczech wrote a brief response that alluded to what the company had already accomplished and what it was passing on in Re.Cher.Chez, its studio for emerging artists. "I suppose it becomes a question of stamina," Maleczech wrote. "It's not important to look backwards or ahead, not important to create for anything outside of the need to create. . . . Two tasks[:] to become responsible—to Re.Cher.Chez, a group of artists who must rely on the

tradition of oral teaching to know, to whom I am committed to bind their future to my history[;] and to remain passionate—to Mabou Mines, whose creativity gives me the room for my future, for my personal unknown."[23]

Akalaitis chose a different way to continue answering the avant-gardist
hail. In the late 1970s she became interested in developing projects with artists
outside the company while still directing occasionally for Mabou Mines.
Rather than being involved with Re.Cher.Chez, which was run by Maleczech
and Breuer, she took the collaborative attitudes and methods she had developed with the company to that work outside. In 1996, as a widely known independent director, she made clear that she had maintained the avant-garde
stance developed twenty years earlier.

> [As a director] I don't want to know anything too well. . . . I never could stand
> up to a company of actors at a first rehearsal and say, "This is my vision. This is
> what the play is about." . . . I think that practice is something we inherit basi-
> cally from a male, European theatre tradition. . . . I like to do certain movement
> exercises with a company that I've developed over the years—when people
> move together they understand each other in an irrational, communicative,
> deep way that provides for a kind of bravery and communication in the re-
> hearsal room that is important to me.[24]

Akalaitis brought this attitude with her when she became Joe Papp's successor
at the New York Shakespeare Festival. But what did this notion of community
and communication mean in 1991 when the notion of an avant-garde already
seemed quaint and few theater groups that had answered that hail were left?
Akalaitis announced that she wanted to make the Public Theater a place where
artists, particularly writers, could find a home. She had come to reject the
downtown/uptown distinction; she wanted, she said, only to foster good theater. But some writers balked. "I don't want to be part of a community," announced playwright Jon Robin Baitz.[25] And in fact Akalaitis's notion of offering artists a place to work and financial support did not pan out as the idea of
community she herself has deployed as a director.

When Akalaitis was fired in 1993 by the festival's board of directors, Frank
Rich of the *New York Times* characterized her as alternately timid and arrogant,
unfocused and too narrowly focused, too big for her avant-garde britches and
too small for the charismatic role of commercial producer—polemical state-
ments that a variety of respondents later revealed as largely inaccurate or distorted. Rich went beyond this personal critique of Akalaitis, though, to attack

the "theatre community" for allowing the supposed decline of "what once was the most influential theatrical institution in the country" to go unchecked.[26] But which community was Rich himself hailing? Each use of the term was designed to appeal to a certain faction, whether Broadway producers, the Dramatists' Guild, Theatre Communications Group, or some other body. Akalaitis pointed to real achievements during her tenure: "It was such *hard work,* such *good work.* I feel I revitalized that theater. We commissioned $80,000 worth of plays. We altered the playwrights' deal. We raised the artists' pay" (emphasis added). Porter Anderson comments that unfortunately these concerns "made little sense to the executive committee that deposed her." Akalaitis's refusal to be a commercial producer, and her preferred self-image as a fellow artist working to benefit a community, was a hail the board could or would not recognize. Maleczech commented, "It seems to me that the Public's board feels [that] ownership of the theater runs the theater. Maybe I'm naïve. And our little Mabou Mines is different, I know. But at least an artistic vision runs our theatre."[27]

How do avant-garde artists live and work in the United States today? How do they "become responsible . . . and remain passionate," as Maleczech has urged? Perhaps the answer lies in fostering a developmental relationship among the artists and between artists and audiences. In 1977 Schechner and Richard Foreman had urged such a developmental relationship in an unpublished manifesto.

[T]he center and focus of the work is displaced inward toward itself, toward the community of artists, and toward a consideration of the *oeuvre:* the whole trajectory of a given artist or group. . . . [T]he passionate spectator . . . has to look not only at the relationship between art and social structure but inwardly at the relationship between the work and previous works of the same artist. This way the world-version of this artist is seen developmentally, and new spheres of experience open.[28]

Today it is rare to sit in an audience that shares the "world-version" of 1970s avant-garde artists. Foreman and Schechner were summoning a kind of passion that comes to life only when both personal memory and cultural memory are actively involved. If the concept of the avant-garde still has a role to play in theater, it lies in the artists' vision (of the grain they work against) and the spectators' openness to that vision—in other words, a shared belief in the community they form, however briefly.

"The Two-Handed Gun": The Inside/Outside Role of Play

The American theater has never found a way to integrate its avant-garde artists into the larger world of theater the way Europe did, by giving them a place in their major institutions after they've proved their worth, nor even the way that the film, literary, and art establishments/industries have done here. In theater, the avant-garde spirit is made perpetual outcast.

—BONNIE MARRANCA

French cultural theorists and American theater critics may rarely agree, but on the cultural position of the theatrical avant-garde editor and critic Bonnie Marranca might be paraphrasing Pierre Bourdieu.[29] In 1992 Marranca saw contemporary American avant-garde theater as economically dominated ("made perpetual outcast") but symbolically dominant ("they've proved their worth"), a distinction Bourdieu draws for the nineteenth-century avant-garde in his essay "The Field of Cultural Production." Had 1970s avant-garde artists come to maturity in Europe rather than the United States, as Marranca notes, they might have been running major theaters (like the Public), as Heiner Müller did the once edgy but now canonical Berliner Ensemble. There are exceptions. Sam Shepard, David Byrne, and Julie Taymor, for example, have had success in high-budget films, popular videos, and Broadway shows. Akalaitis has run the theater program at Bard College and continues to direct at well-known theaters while Glass has become familiar to global music audiences for his continuing productivity as a composer and his extensive touring, collaborations with other artists, and popular film scores. Breuer's *Gospel at Colonus* (1983), which moved to Broadway, was filmed for the Public Broadcasting Service (PBS), and continues to be staged by groups around the world, has made his name widely visible to audiences and contributed to his selection as a MacArthur fellow in 1997. Even as he celebrated being out of debt for the first time in his life, though, Breuer revealed his desire to "push the envelope on the definition of opera." While *Gospel at Colonus* is, as he says, "accessible to American audiences,"[30] much of Breuer's work (like that of Glass and Akalaitis) is best received by those who are developmentally prepared for it. For most of the artists Marranca mentions, the confrontational avant-garde stance is accompanied by an ongoing struggle to be understood.

Being understood has its ironies too. In his 1991 article "The Two-Handed Gun: Reflections on Power, Culture, Lambs, Hyenas, and Government Support for the Arts," Breuer outlines this situation. In the early 1960s, he felt that the artist was solely defined by his aesthetics—"Give me a metaphor or give me death"—but he came to see the cultural context shaping that attitude as American, Calvinist, and capitalist.[31] While art was removed to an elitist, privileged realm, the artist-individual was situated as capitalist producer. If not as useful a commodity as a toaster, his or her product could at least be assigned to "high" culture, a safe realm in the doxology of bourgeois capitalism. And *doxa,* as Roland Barthes noted, sticks.[32] Breuer soon learned that art could be seen alternatively as a field of cultural production or, in 1960s terms, a field of struggle, the artist with his art, yes, but also with other artists and institutions, including government, corporate sponsors, and the press. Already in the late 1950s, as young Breuer turned to directing with the R. G. Davis Mime Troupe and the San Francisco Actor's Workshop, he had found that theater collaboration was, unlike many forms of artistic struggle, healthy for the individual artist. Among other benefits, it uncovered new ways of working and thus new ways of seeing.

As Bourdieu points out, cultural production is contained within larger fields of power and class (and, I would add, gender and race) relations, wielding little influence in those realms yet retaining relative autonomy. These are not absolute relations of control. Bourdieu notes how several prolific and popular nineteenth-century playwrights were discredited in their own time as "hack" writers while the poètes maudits, the "bad boy" bohemian artists of their day, earned relatively little but were held in great esteem.[33] As a college student identifying with transgressive writers such as Camus, Breuer had plugged into the lingering romance of the bohemian. By the late 1960s he was invested in a more complex image of the artist as both author and director. The techniques and cachet of postwar films such as *8-1/2* (1963) by Federico Fellini or *Touch of Evil* (1958) by Orson Welles added auteur to the ideological mix of the avant-garde. In the early 1970s the downtown idealizing of Mabou Mines as a "collective" competed with the larger culture's call for Breuer to fill the more conventional role of auteur. Breuer answered obliquely. By the later 1970s he was casting himself as a writer who directs, a configuration that has allowed him to play in several fields of cultural production. Even today Breuer prefers to be called a writer rather than an author.

In the late 1970s Breuer seemed to struggle to find directorial approaches that worked both within and outside the company. By the mid-1980s, though, he took a Barthesian stance as a writer who does not claim patriarchal authority but returns to the text as a guest, in this case as a director who listens, negotiates, and translates.[34] Directing *Gospel at Colonus,* Breuer translated his vision as librettist to the company; he and composer Bob Telson also worked collaboratively, exploring different "takes" on a given moment. Breuer's authority in rehearsal involved both "absorption in and detachment from" his collaborators' work.[35] By means of a distinctly avant-gardist lack of closure, they sought to involve the audience in the interactive, intercultural catharsis Breuer has called "Artaud without the cruelty."[36] Here an inclusive, intercultural aim replaced the "high-culture" tone of earlier pieces such as *The Red Horse Animation* (1970) or *The Lost Ones* (1975).

In "The Two-Handed Gun," Breuer shows that he clearly understands the many ironies involved in the position of avant-garde artists as economically dominated and symbolically dominant. He complains that while corporate philanthropists, state agencies, and the NEA made possible the brief blossoming of arts festivals in the 1970s and 1980s they sought to create an upper-middle-class avant-garde that perpetuates a conservative European tradition of elitist art. He sees Glass and Wilson as two early beneficiaries and yet admits that he, the self-styled "working class intellectual," has also sought and received funding from these organizations.[37]

> In the Endowment mirror I can see myself to be a fake. I play the counterculturalist, but . . . hey! . . . I taught at Yale. I'm a cultural pluralist, but . . . hey! . . . I'm white and I'm male and I even, at age 53, love my mother. I rail against fat institutional felines . . . when I am a willing, unduped party to the system one plateau down. Buddy Holly will rise from the grave singing "That'll Be the Day"—"the day" the Institutional Radio Choir or Moods Pan Grove get an Endowment grant. No, the so-called plurals of cultural pluralism that I work with are funded through me. Hey! I'm a two-handed gun.[38]

Later in the article Breuer's metaphor for the artist morphs from gun hand into a Janus-faced dog that bites the institutional hand that feeds it: "Why? Because a dog is a domesticated animal, with the pent-up rage of the wolf that sold out and came in from the snow—a rage of self-hatred." This two-handed gun roams U.S. culture only in extended metaphors. Aware that the NEA "ministers to real need," he checks his guns at the door.

Avant-gardists' passionate belief in the work often, but not always, goes hand in hand with this ironic awareness of its place in the socioeconomic food chain. Certainly, in the early 1960s, when some artists followed Artaud in seeking an unmediated sense of presence in the theater, the future members of Mabou Mines were playfully exploring the complex visions of writers such as

Beckett, Genet, and Brecht. James M. Harding and Cindy Rosenthal, looking back to the Open Theatre, note that when members demonstrated a "feminist orientation" a questioning of presence was already in play. They conclude that "the legacy of presence within theaters like the [Omaha] Magic Theatre and the Women's Experimental Theatre is marked by a dialectic in which the very suspicion [of presence] is subsumed."[39] Perhaps play, not presence, is the key. Sally Banes argues that downtown artists' passion for presence usually carried an ironic, transgressive quality. She finds that the downtown notion of "the village in the city" emerged from the artists' belief that "art was meant to be made not for profit but for people, and community was felt to be remodeled and regained." In 1963 (the year on which Banes focuses), artists were using "art as liberating play."

> To pose art as play was a positive value because it was transgressive in two ways. It bucked the values of mainstream culture that considered high art serious business, and at the same time it challenged the pomposity of the previous generation of avant-garde artists (the generation of the Abstract Expressionists, modern dancers, and realist theater) by returning to an avant-garde "tradition" of pleasure of the 1920s and 1930s.

Living variously in California, New York, and Europe in 1963, the future members of Mabou Mines already had adopted such an approach. Performance was not *like* play; it *was* play. As such, it was subtly yet thoroughly subversive both socially and culturally. Yet it must be noted that Banes's notion that "both work and play were reinstalled as unalienated labor and as uninhibited revelry" remains within what she calls "the ethos of the period." If "art was seen as a social space that united work and play to produce freedom," it is also important to remember the price of that freedom.[40]

Mabou Mines' attention to Brecht in the 1960s, and then to Grotowski as the decade ended, may have been early factors in its approach to the work as play. Breuer has provided the best explanation by addressing the company's playful juxtaposition of techniques. In an often-overlooked 1977 article, he announced "the advent of the conceptualizing actor." Motivational acting, he wrote, whether indebted primarily to Stanislavsky ("emotion produces expression") or Delsarte and Meyerhold ("expression produces emotion"), allows the actor to "feel . . . something during performance analogous to the character's emotional stream." Brecht's actor "'say[s] something' in performance over and

above the simple elaboration of character." Brecht "solves" realist style by taking an "objective" stance visibly juxtaposed to it. But Brecht didn't go far
enough in Breuer's opinion.

> [N]o matter how proficient acting became, it never questioned its "role" as a
> technique to interpret given material.
>
> Brecht didn't question it either. He just gave more material to interpret. . . .
> But [the actor] *was* asked to have a point of view on his role, and in this task,
> the actor as *self* took a first step on stage.
>
> The idea of the actor as creative artist began with Grotowski a little over a
> decade ago. Along with his highly publicized physical technique (an elabora-
> tion of biomechanics utilizing hatha yoga) came a few wonderful ideas:
>
> 1) The idea that . . . Brecht's solution to "style"—objectivity—was not the only
>   one; that beneath emotions visible in terms of social psychology, i.e., "real-
>   ism," lay others that became visible in images akin to styles of greater abstrac-
>   tion; that there is neuro-muscular "surrealism," "expressionism," etc. . . .
> 2) The idea that an actor's creative input was as important as a writer's, direc-
>   tor's or designer's—that a theater could exist where the director's, de-
>   signer's and writer's work was to "interpret" the actor instead of the reverse.
> 3) The idea that the most important part of Stanislavski was "personaliza-
>   tion"—an actor understanding experience, to be represented literally or
>   metaphorically, in terms of his own. The implicit statement was: Actor,
>   your life is your material.[41]

The "conceptualizing actor" makes visible the "texts" of all the artists involved
in the work. Breuer notes that Spalding Gray (whose performance in *Rumstick
Road* prompted him to write this article), Elizabeth Lecompte (Gray's director), Meredith Monk, Robert Wilson, Richard Foreman, and Charles Ludlam
engage in this "evolved" form of performance in which the "dance mind," the
"painting mind," the "architectural mind," and the "writing mind" are variously in play.

It should be noted that in 1970 Mabou Mines had adopted no statement of
principles or company aesthetic other than a spirit of exploration through
performance. Breuer's account of the evolving role of the performer best suits
his own plays. There his theoretical considerations take the concrete forms of
styles and tempos juxtaposed, resulting in arresting, sometimes moving moments. Arthur Sabatini puts it well.

I can think of many instances in Breuer's work with Mabou Mines where the story and succession of media and bodily images stop and a richly felt moment transpires, usually with a rock and roll soundtrack and crisp lighting effects. In short, this is Breuer's method as a writer and director: to have a scene gallop along rapidly and then instantaneously freeze everything in order to convey the vivid emotional center of the situation or to reveal a character's feelings.[42]

Other members of Mabou Mines have revealed that they, too, use their own and each other's lives as material. That is, their work in the 1970s documented the historical shift from a focus on the self as a known quantity, a stable Cartesian identity presumed to be white, male, and heterosexual, to multiple culturally and biologically constructed subject positions.

Breuer's continuing interest in the construction of subjects living in a society marked by dynamic cultural and ethnic shifts has its origins in the conversation on gender that began in the 1960s and gathered momentum in the 1970s. As Charles C. Mann notes:

Breuer is of the generation closest to [the feminist] struggle, and a good deal of his art springs from the sweaty grapple with the self that feminism entails. "Although anybody who works with black artists [Breuer says] had better be aware of what color means to this society, the liberation movement that for me hit closest to the bone was feminism. You're dealing with attitudes that may be even deeper than racism, and any male has got to feel ambivalent about it. The position of power was sweet, and that's why we held on to it for so long."[43]

Breuer may have been ahead of other male directors in realizing that feminist issues forced men as well as women to reexamine their gender roles. Breuer's work does exhibit techniques associated with a variety of feminist approaches such as the double-voiced narrative and ironic stereotyping.

Mabou Mines' importance as a theater company rests in part on its early recognition of the constructedness of gender. Despite claims that the early twenty-first century is a "postfeminist" era, the discoveries made in feminist theory and gender studies still inform the vocabulary for public discussion not only of gender but of national identity, postcolonialism, and intercultural matters as well. Even as the members of Mabou Mines were performing their own experience as gendered subjects in the 1970s, radical-feminist psychoanalysts Julia Kristeva, Luce Irigaray, and Hélène Cixous "were challenging the male-oriented tradition of Freud and Lacan to seek a ground for a literary and artistic woman's voice," as Marvin Carlson notes. Each rejected in her own way the assertion that women are incapable of operating as subjects or that reason and feeling are gender-segregated realms. Radical or essentialist feminists sought to give female-associated affective knowledge a subject position. Combining psychoanalysis, cultural theory, and semiotics, Laura Mulvey, Teresa de Lauretis, and others tried to rewrite the cinematic roles of a male subject gazing at a female object. A decade later materialist feminists brought these debates to theater studies. Barthes had already noted in 1963 that Brecht had developed his own cultural semiotics by arguing for the malleable character of both the theatrical sign and the culture to which it refers. Gendered behavior is conditioned, not natural or inevitable (a point Breuer has made repeatedly since the 1970s). Feminist theater, said Elin Diamond, could "interrupt and deconstruct the habitual performance codes." In lesbian performance, argued Sue-Ellen Case in 1989, "butch femme seduction . . . transforms all presumed realities into 'semiotic play.'"[44] Mabou Mines had already engaged in such play over ten years earlier.

Increasingly, the search for ways to deconstruct subject and object has morphed into a playful, post-deconstructionist "tacking." Julia A. Walker suggests that post-Derridean thinkers should "tack" like sailboats between affective or experiential (inside) knowledge and analytical (outside) knowledge.[45] Tacking, though, is a form of triangulation, a playful negotiation (or a fierce struggle) with wind and waves. I suggest that to take full account of Mabou Mines' creative engagement in play it is necessary to separate the affective from the experiential and include a third kind of knowledge, one produced by the intuitive or hypothetical sense. Thus revised, Walker's metaphor of a lateral movement among multiple subject positions is akin to the shifting modalities in which Mabou Mines' "conceptualizing actor" has performed since the 1970s. In the "fun house" of *Mabou Mines Dollhouse,* the performers tack playfully among emotional engagement, estrangement, and personalization.

I have a favorite photograph of Mabou Mines actors at work—or is it "at play"? In this photo Lear, played by Ruth Maleczech, is surrounded by her family: her two sons, played by Bill Raymond and Ron Vawter;[46] Edmund in the person of Karen Kandel; and in the background composer Pauline Oliveros, accompanying the action on her accordion. Maleczech as Lear is speaking happily to Raymond; Kandel and Vawter smile on the twosome; Oliveros observes impassively, like a *raisonneur* or a chorus. This shot, of the 1987 workshop production of *Mabou Mines Lear* done at the Theatrical Outfit in Atlanta, is faintly blurry, as though all the principals are in motion, as, indeed, they are throughout this opening scene of the play. Yet there is a tremor in the way the photo communicates: is this moment "real" or "playful"? Is it part of the production or an unstudied moment in rehearsal? The tremor is appropriate, suggesting the essence of Mabou Mines' work, formed in the risky interplay of techniques and genres and the equally risky collaborative dialogue of friends and colleagues whether in rehearsal, performance, or everyday life.

Chapter Summaries

This book sketches the arc of the work's development and the corresponding arc of the company members' working relations. I have anchored my account in the plays, clustering several in each chapter and working out from that discussion to broader issues. I characterize the work process and the resulting performance as seamless parts of the collaboration among colleagues and friends. It may be objected that I have not shed much light on the personal lives of the participants. This is true; just as Mabou Mines has left identity politics to the politicians, I have left biography to the biographers. Perhaps a company member or faithful follower will document the private stories behind the public work. Having had no opportunity to attend these early productions, I have taken another tack, seeking out participants and observers in order to gather their memories and reconstruct works that often had no scripts or physical record. I have made use of archival material such as scripts, publicity, reviews, and correspondence. Many gaps in our knowledge remain. In the company's freewheeling early years, it did not seem important to document the work. In fact, documentation ran counter to the spirit of living and working in the moment that many company members, current and former, still espouse. More than once, feeling like an archaeologist, I have had to supplement my subjects' contradictory or incomplete memories with other types of evidence. The result is a somewhat literary account of the plays in performance and the company's development to 1980, one that is, I hope, both reasonably accurate in fact and true to the company's spirit.

Mabou Mines is divided into five chapters. Chapter 1, "Coming Together: San Francisco, Paris, New York," outlines briefly the activities of the artists during the 1960s and discusses the formation of the company in 1970 as a project of Ellen Stewart's La Mama Experimental Theatre Club. The process of working together really began in San Francisco, though, where Maleczech and Breuer met Raymond, Dawn Gray, and Akalaitis, and continued in Europe, where Breuer and Maleczech reencountered Akalaitis and met Glass. In both locations the founding members of Mabou Mines made valuable connections with artists they admired and walked the streets of San Francisco and Paris with the sources of their inspiration, some living, others present only in their work. Each location held the promise of inspiration, creativity, and a chance to grow and learn in an atmosphere of tolerance for avant-garde work. Only when the founding members decided to return to the United States did they situate their company in New York. This chapter explores the freewheeling, generous artistic community that Mabou Mines became part of in 1970. Performing first in art galleries, the company created a unique combination of the cool of performance art, well understood in this community, and the heat of motivational acting, usually felt only in productions mounted farther north, on Broadway. The character of Mabou Mines coalesced in these early years as a theater that sought to collaborate with visual artists in a search for new, defining techniques in American performance. Incorporating brief accounts of its members' backgrounds, chapter 1 shows how this collection of strong egos came together and discovered the work in the process of its making. Here I sound the book's paramount theme: the company's passion for the work as a continuing process involving first the performers and then, eventually, the audience.

Chapter 2, "Form, Force, and Flow: *The Red Horse Animation, The B.Beaver Animation,* and Other Early Pieces," accounts for the first two-thirds of the Animations. Although among Mabou Mines' earliest productions, these two (much more than the slighter pieces discussed here, *Arc Welding Piece* [1972] and *Send/Receive/Send* [1973]) set out themes and techniques that the company has used repeatedly. I discuss these two Animations as choral performances structured around narratives whose filmic linearity forms their primary psychic lure. *The Red Horse Animation* tells the familiar story of a young rebel looking for "some form to hold me," while *The B.Beaver Animation* riffs comically on the figure of the becalmed middle-aged professional overcome by the apparent gravity of his situation. These first two Animations mapped the forms and forces at work in the artists' lives, particularly those that stop the creative flow. The artist, trapped in human desire, struggles to break out of self-destructive cycles. Both the horse and the beaver are comic myths in the sense Northrop Frye reserved for the ironic mode—characters whose power of action is visibly outmatched by their circumstances.[47] In confronting familiar myths, Mabou Mines engaged cultural narratives in a confrontational manner reminiscent of the "traditional" avant-garde. The taboo that turns myth back on itself is the actor, who evokes and violates an originary moment. *Red Horse* and *B.Beaver* both worked through and organized experience, demonstrating how human beings are animated variously by our illusions of self, specifically the false heroism of what has been called the West's current philosophy of "spiritual materialism." As Mabou Mines' actors worked through the first two Animations, they began to explore a notion that I call "forgetting the self and following the other," a line of thinking that comes to some fruition in the third production in the series, *The Shaggy Dog Animation* (1978), discussed in chapter 4. Nowhere, however, did Mabou Mines adopt a particular philosophy. The Animations were irreverent and ironic, with comic-mythic figures who dissolved into the performers' various "takes" on the characters. These multiple interlocking layers of stage business sometimes obscured the narrative, rendering each Animation a uniquely dense, evocative experience. Through the performers' extensive collaboration on each piece, the "animated" figure, whether horse or beaver, took on a life of its own and became magical. The collaborators themselves imbued these filmic narratives with their own preoccupations, performing their subjectivities by taking on the images, postures, and utterances of a comic other.

Chapter 3, "*Play, Come and Go, The Lost Ones:* Staging Beckett, 1965–1975," backtracks to the company members' early years and the development of their interest in the work of Samuel Beckett. Here I discuss the short drama *Play* (1967, 1971), the "dramaticule" *Come and Go* (1971), and the narrative *The Lost Ones,* which Mabou Mines adapted for the stage. Beckett's work encouraged the actor to undergo "a radical self-denial" in which he or she loses the distinction between human consciousness and the external world. At the same time the members of Mabou Mines were drawing on what Maleczech and Akalaitis had learned from Grotowski, to free themselves from authorial intention and use themselves as material. These seemingly contradictory purposes came together in their work as they developed Beckett's texts under the gaze of their fellow artists. Although their early experiments with Beckett did not encompass the work fully, in 1971 the company restaged *Play* and added *Come and Go,* first pairing the two and then joining them in 1975 with a third, the adapted text *The Lost Ones,* for an evening of Beckett that remains one of the company's signature events. While the works explore their own "author"-ity in postmodern fashion, the journey taken by players and spectators led them to consider human attachments, specifically how others are often appropriated for the formation of a sense of self. The work offered no transcendence other than its own pleasure and difficulty. As noted by Barthes, such work is "a series of intellectual acts profoundly committed to the historical and subjective existence . . . of the man who performs them."[48] Mabou Mines' work on

Beckett contributed to their later examination of the cultural construction of the concept of the self, explored in *Dead End Kids* (1980), *Cold Harbor* (1983), *Through the Leaves* (1984), and other shows in the 1980s. Chapter 3, as a result, traces a seminal line of thinking from the company's prehistory, through its early years as a group supported by Ellen Stewart's La Mama and into the transition period of the later 1970s.

Chapter 4, "'See yourself as a heavyweight': *Cascando, The Saint and the Football Player, The Shaggy Dog Animation, Dressed Like an Egg*," traces this exploration of the narrated subject into the crucial realm of gender, where two distinct sensibilities emerged. While Breuer led the company in the extended exploration of *Shaggy Dog Animation* (begun in 1974, premiered 1978), Akalaitis undertook *Dressed Like an Egg* (1977), based on texts by the French author Colette. Juxtaposing her useful forgetfulness with Breuer's master narrative of tenacious, unrelenting memory, Akalaitis took the audience into a different sort of theatrical moment, the "fettered freedom" of emotional commitment, by replacing Breuer's gendered stereotype with gender ambiguity. Before outlining this bifurcation in Mabou Mines' sensibility, I begin with a discussion of Akalaitis's 1976 production of Beckett's *Cascando,* her first foray into directing. Wanting to get back to characterization, Akalaitis ended up instead creating a tapestry of miniature actions that suggested rather than represented the constrained environment of Woburn, the central figure of Beckett's text. As with several of Akalaitis's later productions, *Cascando* had a distinctly feminine sensibility and an unexpected sense of humor. It played with a type of associational logic reminiscent of the films of Yvonne Rainer but most immediately introduced in the production by choreographer Mary Overlie.

Akalaitis's desire as a director is to do the work of rehearsal and then leave the piece to be performed. Breuer, on the other hand, had already established himself as a director who stayed in the work, blurring the distinction between rehearsal and performance. *The Saint and the Football Player,* for example, burgeoned from a small art gallery piece in 1973 to a Superbowl-sized pageant that sought to communicate a concrete poem by Jack Thibeau to a broad audience via the choreographed imagery of football action. At once a fantasy, a parody, and an evocation of sports as modern religion, *Saint* became Breuer's first large-scale piece, a precursor to his vision of an American choral theater on a grand scale.

The Shaggy Dog Animation began to realize that vision and in itself brought writer Breuer the first public recognition he had received since his student days. It became the first piece of a much larger work, *La Divina Cari-*

catura (which Breuer had originally called *Realms,* then *Animation*), which he continues to assemble. *Shaggy Dog* first presented the epic's archetypal characters and theme of attachment encompassing romance, sexual attraction, interaction with other species, and the intertwining commitments—personal, political, and economic—that hedge in the life of the contemporary U.S. artist. As a lengthy, highly abstracted performance piece, *Shaggy Dog* challenged audiences to follow two "tracks": a sound track to which the performers would lip-synch romantic songs in modified Brechtian fashion and an image track that tried to disrupt the narrative logic of the romance. The electronic filtering of sound in *Shaggy Dog* prefigured more elaborate uses of electronics in later shows, such as *Mabou Mines Lear,* and represented a second step (the first being the voice and body work in *The Red Horse Animation* and other early shows) in Breuer's efforts to create a choral theater rooted in American popular culture. Using gender parody to liberate his alter egos Rose and John from their prison of romantic stereotypes, Breuer led the company in a highly ironized production that became itself a staging ground for a kind of dissent against Breuer's own subject and methods. David Warrilow's early departure from the piece prefigured his departure from the company in 1979. Saying that the piece glorified women's sexual slavery, Akalaitis stayed and seemed to make her dissatisfaction part of her performance.

If *Shaggy Dog* brought to the foreground gendered differences within the company, *Dressed Like an Egg* may have provided the safety valve of a new sensibility. Akalaitis began rehearsals while *Shaggy Dog* was in development. Rather than romance as attachment, Akalaitis wanted to explore romance as an inheritance of romanticism, a legacy the culture remembers well even as individuals lose themselves in it. Akalaitis communicated Colette's ability to render in words a woman's experience and explored gender roles in beautiful, startling images. Without providing explanations, either in performance or in person, Akalaitis's production seemed to slow time, but rather than alienating the audience's affections these techniques drew them closer. The source of the fascination proved to be the very issue Breuer wrote to escape: attachment. Perhaps for this reason Akalaitis used many techniques drawn from work she had done with Breuer and the rest of the company such as the Animations. Working once again with Mary Overlie on choreography and Nancy Graves on the set, the company riffed on Colette's texts in order to perform the gender ambiguity about which Colette wrote.

Ultimately, Breuer and Akalaitis were not in opposition. In making this pair of works, they began the company's change from collaborative theater to a company of directors. With those ranks joined soon by Maleczech and Neumann, Breuer and Akalaitis also began to freelance, translating their public visibility into grant funding and turning more often to outside projects. Chapter 5, "A Company of Directors: *Vanishing Pictures, Mercier and Camier,* Re.Cher.Chez," articulates the company's gradual transformation to a collective of "bosses" with their own projects who also appeared in the others' work. The intimate group that had created Mabou Mines with the assistance of Ellen Stewart had evolved, in association with the New York Shakespeare Festival, into a larger, more freewheeling company whose members met and decided on projects to be funded and in which they still joined together to explore new project ideas and learn new skills but which they now occasionally left to do work in other circumstances with other artists. In these last years of Mabou Mines' first decade, Breuer, Maleczech, and Raymond also founded Re.Cher.Chez, a studio for the performing arts designed to foster the work of emerging artists and diversify the skills of experienced performers.

In the midst of these changes, Maleczech and Neumann began to direct. In chapter 5, I first discuss *Mercier and Camier* (1979), which Neumann received permission from Beckett to stage. While as an actor Neumann had always contributed strong motivational acting, as a first-time director he allowed staging concepts to shape performance choices. *Mercier and Camier* sought to create the immediacy of sensation suggested in Beckett's early, detailed narrative, but it also distanced the audience from those sensations, creating a piece that seemed to look back to early-twentieth-century Ireland through the filtering scrim of Beckett's language. Despite its complexity of staging and movement, unique among Mabou Mines' Beckett productions, its intimate, filmic quality resembled *Shaggy Dog,* as did the sculpting of sound and photographic effects that "acted" alongside the performers onstage. *Mercier and Camier* examined the interior landscape of two wanderers whose memories appear on the alternately transparent, translucent, or opaque scrims that surrounded the audience. Each character creates, in a sense, the other's reality, a relation whose comedy Neumann underscored by harking back to traditions of clowning. A lack of rehearsal time hampered the success of the production's comic elements, but the photographic projections created a powerful flow picked up in the performers' movements. This first production as a director taught Neumann that he wanted to pare down Beckett's language to a central voice and image classically modernist in simplicity, an impulse that he used to great advantage in his later productions of Beckett's *Company* (1983) and *Worstward Ho* (1986).

Maleczech's production of *Vanishing Pictures* (1980) also used photography as a primary apparatus, though not linking the author's words to an ab-surdist reality, as Neumann had done, but demonstrating the blurriness of the photographic image, that is, how the theater is not a camera that tells a deep truth but one that often lies, powerfully and seductively. If *Mercier and Camier* harked back to the classical avant-garde, *Vanishing Pictures* joined forces with the Beats and their artistic ancestors, the bohemians, who valued a "Romantic ideal of language" before the avant-garde emerged. Originally the brainchild of singer and Re.Cher.Chez member Beverly Brown, *Vanishing Pictures* was the first full production that the studio produced, largely because Maleczech was moved to direct. Brown and Maleczech could not have been more different in their working methods and ideas about the project. As the piece's sole per-former, Brown wanted to elide her own persona as singer/actor with the spirit of Edgar Allan Poe's story "The Mystery of Marie Rogêt" (1842). Overhead pro-jections and other simple photographic techniques produced visual effects that seemed to make a series of doubles out of Brown, Poe, Baudelaire, and Mary Rogers—the woman on whose death "Marie Rogêt" was based. Maleczech was more interested in the feverish transformations that Brown's character and her environment seemed to undergo in the course of the perfor-mance. She wanted the audience to wonder why ordinary objects suddenly be-gan to behave oddly in the stage space. Directing Brown to distort her voice, Maleczech deflected attention from the supposedly rational language of Poe's narrator-detective Dupin toward the photographic effects, which seemed to multiply familiar yet unplaceable doubles.

Both *Mercier and Camier* and *Vanishing Pictures* prefigured themes and techniques used by Mabou Mines in the 1980s. At a moment when some were proclaiming the death of the avant-garde, artists such as Ruth Maleczech and Frederick Neumann were finding ways to take their avant-garde sensibilities into the new realm of solo and mediatized performance. Mabou Mines' studio Re.Cher.Chez, whose five-year history I discuss in chapter 5, encouraged young artists to "become responsible . . . and to remain passionate."[49] While it taught artistic and survival skills, it also allowed Mabou Mines to pass along the legacies of the 1960s and 1970s and created artistic relationships that have benefited the company to this day. For Mabou Mines, as for most avant-garde theater companies, the body-to-body transmission that is the foundation of the work remains an ongoing process of learning and teaching. Its members remain "bosses together," a collection of strong egos and powerful talents who are not bound in a single aesthetic but reinvent the rules, and the work, as they go along.[50]

CHAPTER ONE

"Coming Together: San Francisco, Paris, New York"

Theater groups go through growth and development much as an individual does, but few survive their adolescence. Funding is too scarce, arguments too easily fragment the company, and individual interests change. To survive, a group must be founded on professional respect for one another and demonstrate the flexibility to adapt once the initial excitement of collaborative work subsides. By 1978, eight years after its founding, the New York–based theater company Mabou Mines had reached maturity. Among the downtown theater companies and artists' collectives that had sprung up in the late 1960s and early 1970s, Mabou Mines was perhaps the best known and most firmly established. Its five founding members had begun not as neophytes but with considerable experience in acting, directing, movement, voice, writing, dramatic theory, and music composition and performance. First Ellen Stewart and then Joseph Papp had recognized their promise and given them support. In the interim, they had already weathered several crises, including a year or two with no financial support, and had found ways to not just survive but flourish. By 1978 they had a loyal audience of artists familiar with the development of their work, and now, with several productions celebrated by reviewers and audiences alike, they were attracting attention in the larger theater world.

At that point Mabou Mines' latest production, *The Shaggy Dog Animation*, was the company's most ambitious project to date, involving many collaborators as well as all company members and their younger associates. Critics were taking note of the production's performance techniques, layered narrative strategies, and heady cultural critique. *Shaggy Dog* won writer-director Lee Breuer a *Village Voice* Obie award for best play of 1978. At the time, Bonnie Marranca called Breuer's work a "theatre of images" and included in her widely distributed book of that title the foundational Mabou Mines piece *The Red Horse Animation*. Certainly Breuer was gaining his first real public visibility as a mature writer-director. Other talents in Mabou Mines, though, had matured by 1978 as well. JoAnne Akalaitis had made a very natural transition from performer to director and had garnered accolades and attention by both directing and acting in her second production, *Dressed Like an Egg*. David

Warrilow, on the other hand, by 1976 had begun to suspect that he might be leaving the company for its initial focus on personal exploration was shifting to cultural questions he did not find interesting. He had made an impression in *The Lost Ones,* a daunting adapted prose narrative, and he wanted to continue to be challenged in that way as an actor. Not drawn to directing, Warrilow had been a powerful voice for the equality of the actor in Mabou Mines, but his desire to keep the work within the group's original concept was running counter to other needs. By 1978 the members of Mabou Mines were mature artists, many with visions and ambitions of their own. To survive as a theater, the group was changing from a tightly knit collaborative to a collective or company of directors, each of whom could pursue his or her own line of work.[1] In a world that was becoming increasingly institutionalized, the members of Mabou Mines in 1978 were finding ways to remain artistic entrepreneurs. For example, as the company tackled larger productions they did not form a traditional theater hierarchy in which younger associates might be assigned specific roles defined as "assistant set designer" or "understudy." Mabou Mines continued to attract young people whose talent, curiosity, willingness to experiment, and devotion to the work trumped institutional credentials and adherence to any school of thinking on acting, design, or movement. Performance, Lee Breuer wrote in 1986, is not a profession but a "genetic program" necessary for one's personal survival and that of the culture. "Sing. Dance. Paint your faces," he advised. "Don't ask an actor why. Ask a singing bird, a prancing peacock. Ask any fish who changes colors. Applaud the *mie* [a Kabuki pose] of Tamasaburo! Applaud the posture of lions." Acting, on the other hand, "is the moment when, after performance turns around to the front, it turns back to the side. . . . And half facing you is half assing you. And that's the theatre and its trouble."[2] Like the wolf pack Breuer imagines at the origins of performance, Mabou Mines set itself apart from organized theater and acting as a credentialed profession.

First formed in 1970 with the support of the La Mama Experimental Theatre Club, founded and run by Ellen Stewart, the initial company of five— JoAnne Akalaitis, Lee Breuer, Philip Glass, Ruth Maleczech, and David Warrilow—had developed and performed small ensemble pieces attended mainly by fellow performers, writers, musicians, dancers, sculptors, and painters. Like other young artists, the members of Mabou Mines lived and worked in the only affordable spaces Manhattan had to offer—Soho and Greenwich Village warehouses and tenement buildings, which, while shabby, tended to be spacious enough to accommodate the work. The artists of Mabou Mines had their first successes performing in art galleries and museums but were noticed by New York's theatrical establishment only when their evening of adapted texts by Samuel Beckett unexpectedly became a hot ticket in 1975. By this time the company had grown, adding Frederick Neumann and Bill Raymond, with whom they had worked in Paris and San Francisco, respectively, and enlisting a substantial cadre of associates, among them artists Thom Cathcart, Nancy Graves, and Tina Girouard; dancers Mary Overlie and Terry O'Reilly; and actors Ellen McElduff, Dawn Gray, and Greg Mehrten. O'Reilly, McElduff, and Mehrten became members, as did Julie Archer and Sharon Fogarty much later. But before this period of growth Mabou Mines struggled. Ellen Stewart asked the company to leave La Mama in 1973. While this apparent setback represented, in a sense, a break with a parent who had grown frustrated with a willful teenager, it was ultimately beneficial. At first Mabou Mines' financial basis was uncertain (its only income now came from jobs as plumbers, movers, and cooks its members had taken to support themselves and one another), but the company applied for incorporation and Breuer secured a small grant. After a year or two, when the opportunity arose, the members decided with some trepidation to accept Joseph Papp's offer to associate the company with the New York Shakespeare Festival, which was housed nearby in the Public Theater. Their subsequent ten-year relationship with Papp was a highly productive hands-off arrangement that did not infringe on their independence. They brought projects to Papp's space, but, as with La Mama, they were not forced to develop work to fit a predetermined season schedule. Papp provided individual shows with rehearsal and performance space, designers with access to the Public Theater's shops, and directors with personal encouragement. Some of Mabou Mines' most successful and best-known productions—among them *Dressed Like an Egg, The Shaggy Dog Animation, A Prelude to Death in Venice, Dead End Kids,* and *Cold Harbor*—first appeared there.

A new visibility, however, did not change the type of work Mabou Mines produced. Without adopting a dominant aesthetic, Mabou Mines took audiences on a journey to deepen and alter their perceptions of reality. Breuer, for example, wanted to draw spectators in with familiar realist techniques, particularly the storytelling conventions of popular film, while juxtaposing those techniques with others adapted from epic theater, Bunraku puppet theater, comic books, or other media that play with the narrative without obscuring it. He had penned two of the company's early original pieces—*The Red Horse Animation* and *The B.Beaver Animation*—and directed the evening of Beckett shorts, but the scripts were developed in rehearsal, and it was not until he received the Obie for *The Shaggy Dog Animation* that he felt his identity as a writer had been established. He welcomed (not without irony, of course) the public acclaim and professional recognition in the downtown performance world. Breuer's vision of a choral American theater had begun to come together while he was developing *Shaggy Dog.* He was gradually realizing that he wanted to create a truly American mode of performance reflecting the multiple influences on U.S. culture. Only tangentially related to music, the choral techniques used in the Animations abjure the unified, "three-dimensional" psychological character common to realist drama for a more abstract locus, visualized as a set of cartoonish figures who interact and speak in several intertwined cultural voices. American identity becomes an echo chamber of such voices, each filtered through an unceasing feedback loop of media culture. Breuer has made his concept of a choral theater the foundation of his larger work, now entitled *La Divina Caricatura.* Since the 1980s he has brought the contributions of African, Caribbean, and Asian cultures to the forefront of his cultural epic. Hardly synonymous with the complete corpus created by Mabou Mines, the parts of the *Caricatura* performed to date have been developed both under and outside the auspices of the company. Moreover, Breuer's is only one (albeit the most visible and theoretically developed) of several artistic visions the company has fostered.

The work of other company members matured in these first years as well. While by 1978 Breuer sought to eschew the company's reputation as a collective theater with no emphasis on individual artists, JoAnne Akalaitis had embraced a new role as director and had already offered the company projects with a gendered sensibility very different from Breuer's, a striking visual palette, and connections to untapped roots in European culture. By 1978 she had been recognized with Obies for two productions, *Cascando,* adapted from a Beckett text, and *Dressed Like an Egg,* based on the writings of the French author Colette. The same year saw Maleczech and Neumann planning productions as well. Neumann was adapting *Mercier and Camier,* the first of a series of three Beckett adaptations that established Mabou Mines as a significant interpreter of the author's shorter nondramatic texts. Maleczech was mentoring associate Beverly Brown to develop *Vanishing Pictures,* the first production to come out of Maleczech and Breuer's studio for new artists, Re.Cher.Chez. By 1978 the members of Mabou Mines were already passing on what they knew. Yet they were still working on a financial shoestring. Scarcely able to rent office and performance space and pay themselves, they needed and subsequently hired a company manager and director of development to help run what had become a complex operation with several shows in simultaneous development. Mabou Mines had come a long way from the tentative experiments the founding members had first undertaken in a Paris apartment almost fifteen years earlier.

It is my purpose here to discuss Mabou Mines as a theater company designed to give its creative and nonconformist members a place to undertake work determined not by a canon, an external board of directors, or a preset season schedule but by the artists' interests and visions. Unlike a regional theater or a repertory company, the members of Mabou Mines "constitute the body which makes the basic artistic decisions" while also serving as "members of a larger Board of Directors . . . responsible for fund raising and general operating procedures," as Warren Kliewer pointed out in 1989. Artistic decisions for individual productions are handled by the member or associate who develops the project. "What this comes down to," remarks Kliewer, "is a system for protecting, on the one hand, the interests of the group as a whole, and on the other, the very important individuality of the artist-members."[3] Kliewer discusses five theaters that, each in its own way, undertook the model of the nineteenth-century actor-manager, not as a single autocrat but with all members accepting responsibility for each other and all facets of production. Collaborators could make suggestions on any aspect of the work, an arrangement possible only among partners who respect each other's artistic judgment and welcome ideas borrowed from other disciplines. Once the group's structure was in place, they found they had created a "secure little place" where no external board of directors could dictate their schedule or budgets.[4] Of course, they had to deal with one another, and, having given equal power to each member, they had to find ways to form a consensus. They did not always find it, particularly in the later 1970s. As Breuer tired of being the company's only director, others began to seek that role and develop their own projects. Younger associates were taken into the company's ranks, turning what had been a tight cluster of volatile relationships into a more open, flexible working arrangement. In some ways the company changed irrevocably. Philip Glass, while still associated with individual productions, had left in 1973 to pursue his musical interests, and David Warrilow departed in 1979. The company, however, flourished. Its structure changed to accommodate the members' desire to maintain each artist's autonomy and the company's right to self-determination as a group.

The members of Mabou Mines had come together to do work that gave them what they needed as artists whether as a group or as individuals. Having grown up largely in the postwar 1950s, a time that seemed to them (and other young people such as the Beat writers in San Francisco and the so-called absurdists in Paris) to have been cut free of earlier ethical and religious strictures, these artists, in effect, created meaning and community for themselves and their audiences. As they showed new ways of looking at the world, they also demonstrated that the avant-garde, as noted in the introduction, "rejects traditionalism in order to find again a living tradition" in which disconnected contemporary life could be grounded.[5] Regardless of whether individual members found that living tradition in a choral theater, the stripped-down work of Beckett, or collaborations with visual artists, I believe it is best exemplified by what critics Robert Coe and Don Shewey described in 1981 as the company members' "passionate commitment to their work and to each other."[6] This story of a spirit of artistic generosity and dedication to the work, and its emergence from a very specific place and time, is the story of Mabou Mines.

The group of individuals that in 1970 became Mabou Mines first began to coalesce in San Francisco and Paris in 1959–60. In fact, each founding member of Mabou Mines met the others twice for the first time. Lee Breuer and Ruth Maleczech, barely in their twenties and venturing north from Los Angeles, met Bill Raymond when they began working with the R. G. Davis Mime Troupe, which became the San Francisco Mime Troupe in 1963. Then Maleczech encountered Stanford University graduate student JoAnne Akalaitis at the office of the San Francisco Actor's Workshop, where Ron Davis had arranged for a production directed by his wife, Judy Rafael—the first abstract piece, as it turned out, in which Maleczech ever performed. While Breuer and Maleczech participated in the Actor's Workshop, Akalaitis sold orange juice in the lobby as she thought about leaving the philosophy program for acting. In the Bay Area all four encountered artists who would later play a role in the life of Mabou Mines, among them the performer Dawn Gray, dancer and choreographer Mary Overlie, artist Ann Elizabeth Horton, and composer-musicians Pauline Oliveros and Steven Reich. The next several years were full of interesting work: productions with the Mime Troupe, experiments at the San Francisco Tape Music Center, and informal performances with groups of young people who shared their interests. Because it was better established, the Actor's Workshop became an important source of work for Breuer and, to a lesser extent, Maleczech. The four had come to the Bay Area at a fruitful time for performance, one that prefigured the lively scene in downtown Manhattan ten years later. Once that scene changed and the Actor's Workshop disbanded, Akalaitis, Breuer, Maleczech, and Raymond headed in several directions.

Breuer and Maleczech later connected with Akalaitis again in Europe, where she was traveling with Glass. In Paris, which had become their home base, these young artists mixed with the émigré community, worked dubbing French films into English, and went to the theater and art museums. Paris was full of American and British writers and actors attached to one or another scene. Émigrés and expatriates still found it fairly easy to live in Western Europe, where they taught English, worked for the U.S. Army, or attached themselves to an English-language publication or organization. Breuer invited Warrilow, then editor of the English-language edition of the literary magazine *Réalités,* to work with him, Maleczech, Glass, and Akalaitis on Beckett's recently published *Play.* Neumann joined them a year or two later for *The Messingkauf Dialogues,* based on texts by Brecht. Yet this informal group was not yet a theater company. In 1968 Neumann and his wife, Honora Fergusson, moved to Italy. Glass and Akalaitis had already returned to the United States, while Breuer, Maleczech, and Warrilow continued to live and work in Europe.

The second "first meeting" occurred in 1969–70 when Breuer and Maleczech came to join Akalaitis and Glass in New York. Shortly Warrilow came, too, and the following year Neumann and Fergusson moved their family to Kingston, New Jersey, from which Neumann commuted to the city several times a week for over thirty-five years. The circle became complete when Bill Raymond, who was living in Topanga Canyon near Los Angeles, joined the company in 1974. By this time most company members were in their thirties and had families. In fact, from those first years in San Francisco and Paris, the company's founding members were already at work, developing ideas and techniques they drew on much later. By 1970, however, their attitudes and interests had entered a new phase. The company's early productions of Beckett, for example, benefited from members' involvement with earlier productions in San Francisco and Paris. Unlike other new theater companies, whose members might come straight from college or even high school, the members of Mabou Mines had some life experience and a clearer sense of what interested them and why.

The 1970s was a productive decade, "the best years of our lives" according to Neumann.[7] They began by working in the art world, sharing ideas and techniques with artists from other disciplines, and they continued by seeking recognition in the theater world, not for its own sake but to expand the possibilities for doing the work. The decade ended in a climate that in many ways was less sympathetic to their avant-garde, hard-to-categorize work. They had toured from the first, but several pieces began to go on the circuit of regional theaters, supported by funding from organizations, such as the National Endowment for the Arts, that in many cases had not existed ten years earlier. Correspondingly, the artists wanted to try their hand at ideas and production methods they had not been able to afford in their first years together.

By 1980 some members' original attitudes and desires had been clarified by their work together and the confidence it had given each of them. The company's original open-ended collaborative methods had evolved into a working arrangement I call the "company of directors," in which now mature and independent creative talents could pursue their own productions. Each director took responsibility for a project's development and could go outside the company, if necessary, to fill out the cast. Objections to a line of inquiry no longer resulted in serious company fractures, for no one was obliged to participate. As a result, the company made an enormous impact with productions as various as the poetic *Dressed Like an Egg,* which reflected on the theatrical legacies of romanticism; the philosophical love story *A Prelude to Death in Venice;* the political comedy and morality tale *Dead End Kids;* and the antiwar reflection on Ulysses S. Grant, *Cold Harbor.*

Before there were *Dead End Kids* and *Dressed Like an Egg,* however, there was *Cascando;* before *Prelude* there was *The Shaggy Dog Animation.* These pieces may not have toured, but they involved artistic choices that shaped later, better-known works. The frame of reference for these earlier productions was the downtown artists' community. Looking back to the 1970s, Akalaitis has commented:

> Mabou Mines was very much a theatre of the time. We believed that the theatre was for artists. In essence, it was an elitist, urban, educated audience who came to our work. We were not interested in theatre audiences—we were interested in *art* audiences, because our influences in the late 60's came from what was happening in the world of painting, sculpture, and performance art. Painters were performing. Performers were painting. Dancers were talking. It was a time when [artist Robert] Rauschenberg did his roller-skating piece and [dancer and filmmaker] Yvonne Rainer did *The Mind Is a Muscle.* We were intoxicated with that atmosphere. Those were the people we thought were special. When we started to perform, we performed in art galleries. . . . Mabou Mines was not political. There was no ideal about politics, or what theatre should be, could be, or how we wanted to change it. Our ideals were the ideals of excellence, and finding a performing technique that was American—one that was personal, yet very stylized and technical.

Speaking in 1996, when downtown performance had long since become in-
fused with identity politics and interculturalism and many younger companies
and artists had situated themselves in other parts of the city, Akalaitis thinks
back to the multiplicity among downtown artists that seemed rich and absorbing at the time. She characterizes as "elitist" activities that in the 1970s were
actually intended to break free of the elitism of literary theater and modern art
and the commodification of the art object. But at the same time she notes, "We
were also interested in things . . . that other companies weren't interested in—
for example, literature and collaborations with visual artists. I think we were
pioneers in those areas."[8] Mabou Mines had been deeply influenced by the
words and ideas of authors such as Kafka, Beckett, Brecht, Shakespeare, Camus, and Genet. Akalaitis herself had made use of literary texts of various
kinds: Colette's memoirs and novels, Beckett's radio play *Cascando,* and (for
Southern Exposure [1979]) the diaries of explorers Ernest Shackleton and
Robert Scott. As with its mixture of motivational acting and performance art
techniques, Mabou Mines not only devised its own pieces but adapted textual
material from classic and modern writers.

Following her undergraduate work at the University of Chicago, Akalaitis
had come to Stanford on fellowship but abandoned her studies in order to explore performance in San Francisco. At the Actor's Workshop, Herbert Blau
and Jules Irving were introducing audiences to innovative productions of
Shakespeare and the Greeks and recent European avant-garde plays now considered modern classics. In a sense, Akalaitis, Breuer, Maleczech, and Raymond
had found a literary Paris in California. They met like-minded young writers,
actors, dancers, and musicians at the Actor's Workshop, the Mime Troupe, the
San Francisco Tape Music Center, poet Laurence Ferlinghetti's City Lights
Bookstore (the publisher of Allen Ginsberg's "Howl"), and the various North
Beach hangouts that had gained fame through their association with the Beats.
They probably heard Bob Dylan and Miles Davis play in local coffee shops and
clubs. Breuer and Maleczech had not come to San Francisco with clear-cut
goals. Breuer's first taste of bohemian life there had been a brief pilgrimage in
1958 or 1959. Later in the year Breuer had returned, this time with Maleczech.
They may have had it in mind to head for Paris by way of San Francisco. The
two began by hitchhiking up the California coast, but they stopped on the way
to work small-time jobs and ended up living in San Francisco for the next five
years.

Breuer and Maleczech met at the University of California, Los Angeles
(UCLA), in 1957. Breuer's family had lived in Los Angeles for several years, but

earlier they had moved often—from Wilmington, Delaware, to Camp Lejeune in North Carolina, Long Island, Virginia, and Portland, Oregon. By the time Breuer was sixteen, the middle-class life his family aspired to had come apart. As a college student Breuer began by pursuing prelaw but quickly changed direction. He shared an apartment on the Sunset Strip, worked nights parking cars for film stars, and began to think of himself as a writer. The picture of Maleczech's background is sketchier, but a similar defining moment seems to have been her family's move from midwestern, industrial Cleveland to the desert of Arizona when she was eight years old. She later drew on the memory of this transition for *Hajj* (1983), which Breuer wrote and directed and she performed. *Hajj* intertwines a recurring theme in Breuer's work, indebtedness, with that of a pilgrimage taken into a person's history to discover the source of that life and the difficult debts owed to the past. Crossing the mountains to attend UCLA seems to have been a second important migration for Maleczech, leading her to Los Angeles and a new life. She wanted to be an actor but was not much interested in the main stage productions UCLA had to offer a theater major. Rather, she spent time at 3K7, a Quonset hut the Theatre Department had turned over to the students for their own productions, and got to know film students, who were fortunate in having equipment, money, and the freedom to pursue their own work. These were compelling opportunities in Maleczech's eyes. She was drawn to Breuer, the fascinating student-writer who decided in 1959 that he was done with school. Leaving their degrees unfinished, they left UCLA for San Francisco.

Village Voice writer Ross Wetzsteon, in his biographical article on Breuer, suggests that in setting out for Paris Breuer may have wanted to meet Albert Camus and Jean Genet, his two biggest influences, but, more important, he wanted to live their sort of avant-garde lives as he then romanticized them. If the first desire was a youthful bit of adulation, the second had a kind of fulfillment, for Breuer and Maleczech never settled in one specific location but lived a mobile, bohemian life. Europe had long been a finishing ground for American artists and writers, among them T. S. Eliot, Ezra Pound, Gertrude Stein, and Ernest Hemingway. The oppositional aesthetics of the Dadaists and surrealists survived, for example, in the writing of William Burroughs and Jack Kerouac. San Francisco, in the meantime, had supplied Breuer and Maleczech's graduate education, one oriented toward the European avant-garde, the Beat sensibility, and the cults of James Dean and Marlon Brando. Breuer and Maleczech met Ferlinghetti and other poets; they also encountered the dancer Anna (then Ann) Halprin and the founders of the Tape Music Center, composers Morton Subotnik, Ramone Sender, and Pauline Oliveros (the last of whom composed music for *Mabou Mines Lear*). Some had connections with Black Mountain College, specifically composer John Cage and choreographer Merce Cunningham. All were part of an alternative educational system that was developing across the country in the 1950s and 1960s, the project of artists and writers whose sensibilities and interests ran wild of conventional university teaching in the liberal arts. In the 1970s the "second generation" of Mabou Mines members were the students of these San Francisco artists. Member Terry O'Reilly, for example, studied dance with Barbara Dilley, who, like Mary Overlie, had trained with Anna Halprin.

In San Francisco Breuer saw himself as a writer, but gradually he was drawn into directing through this combination of literary and artistic encounters. As a UCLA student he had been introduced to the work of Samuel Beckett, Jean Genet, Albert Camus, Jean-Paul Sartre, Antonin Artaud, Jacques Giraudoux, and Jean Anouilh in a memorable course taught by Oreste F. Pucciani. Wetzsteon, writing his account of Breuer's career in a parody of Breuer's jazzy, over-the-top speaking style, recounts:

> So I write some plays at UCLA. One of 'em's even a campus cause célèbre. This woman throws her baby out the window. [This was *The Wood Complains,* the 1957 play that brought Maleczech and Breuer together, although she was cast not in the lead but in the chorus.] You know, quasi-existentialist, surrealistic, neo-Cocteau shit. It devastates everybody in LA—a lotta fun. Then I write a realistic play, then an imitation Beckett, stuff like that. I win the best playwriting award two years running. The award's presented by some big Hollywood— what was his name? Yeah, Burt Lancaster. So before I'm even 20 years old I'm a successful wild man of the theater. It sure spoils me for the world. I mean the next 15 years are no-man's land, waiting for the same sense of power and focus that flooded through me at UCLA.[9]

Writing a novel proved to be more difficult than the young Breuer had anticipated. When he and Maleczech first arrived in San Francisco, he settled down to write while Maleczech (then performing as Ruth Breuer, although it appears they actually did not marry until 1978) joined the R. G. Davis Mime Troupe, with the result that Breuer found himself alone while she rehearsed. He began to hang around the company and, through discussions with Davis, Raymond, and others, was drawn into production.[10] Breuer first came to Blau's attention in 1959, having been given a chance to direct actors affiliated with the Mime

Troupe in scenes from Brecht's *Caucasian Chalk Circle*. Like Davis, Breuer became one of several young directors who took on smaller productions at the San Francisco Actor's Workshop's second space, the Encore Theatre, from 1960 to 1964. In 1962 Breuer assistant directed a revival of Blau's successful production of *King Lear* starring Michael O'Sullivan. Although the Workshop hired many fine local actors, its funding from the Ford Foundation stipulated the hiring of "professionals" from what had been up until the early 1960s the only real concentration of actors belonging to the Actors' Equity Association in the United States: New York City. Artistic director Blau and managing director Irving often had their hands full with mixed casts of local and imported talent. Although they did train the younger, less experienced actors and directors to a certain extent, Breuer—like Raymond, Akalaitis, and Maleczech—were part of a nimbus of young people that hovered around the Workshop. Of these four, only Breuer and Maleczech were involved in Workshop productions. Maleczech had a few small parts, such as the Penitent in Genet's *The Balcony,* and she stage-managed for Blau on Brecht's *Galileo.* Breuer was hired more often and developed something of a working relationship with Blau. Breuer directed a number of ambitious projects, such as Beckett's *Happy Days* and Harold Pinter's *A Slight Ache,* followed the next year by the American premier of *The Underpants,* by Carl Sternheim, and Federico Garca Lorca's *The House of Bernarda Alba,* in which Maleczech appeared as Martirio. As his contacts and confidence grew, Breuer participated in a number of projects outside the Workshop; in 1963 or 1964 he directed a production of Genet's *The Maids* that Blau, in an interview, recalled as interesting.[11] The play featured Maleczech (as Solange), Bere Boynton, and Susan Darby, music was provided by Bill Spencer, and Judy Rafael designed the set, including a sixty-foot staircase with no railing, suspended by airplane cable.

The Workshop offered Breuer and Maleczech the opportunity to participate in the staging of plays Breuer had known only as dramatic literature. Maleczech was absorbing them both as literature and in production. They had found a particularly important model in Blau, who combined his literary and theoretical interests with dedication to production. Blau's knowledge of recent developments in the literary world informed his directing so that his younger collaborators were exposed to, directly or indirectly, ideas from such thinkers as Jan Kott, the author of *Shakespeare Our Contemporary* (1964); Eric Bentley, who had done so much already to acquaint U.S. audiences with Brecht's work; and comparatists such as Francis Fergusson, whose *The Idea of a Theatre* (1949) had influenced scholars and practitioners seeking to reinvigorate drama by reconnecting it with what were then considered its origins in ancient Greek ritual. Unknown at that time to Breuer and Maleczech, Fergusson's daughter, Honora (a future associate artist of Mabou Mines), was discovering, as they were, the European literary world. She had already found her way to Paris, where she worked with Warrilow at *Réalités*. She had grown up hearing her parents' stories (her mother was acting teacher Marion Crowne Fergusson) of the American Laboratory Theatre, where they had been assistants to directors Richard Boleslavsky and Maria Ouspenskaya. Honora also watched her parents work with student actors at Bennington College. When the family moved to Princeton University, where Fergusson père founded the comparative literature department, Honora at age sixteen apprenticed with the University Players, a talented student group that also incorporated professional actors. There she was introduced to plays by Luigi Pirandello and other moderns.[12] Just as her father's work linked theatrical experiment to its European literary and performance roots for Honora Fergusson, Blau was important to Maleczech, first for his philosophical agenda. "Herb saw the theater," she commented in an interview, "as a way of connecting to the audience's intellectual life. Or teaching the audience that it could have an intellectual life." Then, too, Blau had demonstrated that the director could be a creator, not just an interpreter: "It was very intriguing: a regular play being used to do something other than what it was written to do. . . . The plays were not overtly philosophical, but he made them be. . . . His was the first work I saw that was not interpretive of the intentions of the author."[13]

While absorbing much that San Francisco had to offer, Breuer, Maleczech, Akalaitis, and Raymond seemed to need—just as young artists do today—an environment that allowed them to cross the boundaries between literature, theater, music, art, film, and street performance. Working with Blau was instructive, but he was not a collaborative director, and Breuer and Maleczech knew from their experience with 3K7 that exciting work often emerged from a more freewheeling environment. One opportunity came out of the association between Ron Davis and the Actor's Workshop when Davis, in December 1960, initiated "The Eleventh Hour Mime Show" at the Workshop's Encore space. This program was not sponsored by the Workshop so much as housed there, free of charge, since it cost the Workshop little to allow these performances after striking the set of the Sunday evening show. Davis recounts the "shock effects" used at 11:00 each Sunday night to "dispel the coldness of the basement, the 'artistic' atmosphere and the distance between the audience and the performer." Once "warmed up," the audience might see a happening, a Beckett piece (e.g., *Act Without Words II*, in which Breuer was apparently involved), or mime, which Davis had studied extensively. Although Breuer, Maleczech, and Raymond were not primarily interested in mime, they often participated in these events, as Davis recalled later.

> At the end of each show, we allowed writer and director Lee Breuer to introduce a completely new element. One night, four of us were on stage playing football with dolls' heads and sundry props when we heard a great crashing come from the men's john just off the main seating area. The crashing continued while we marked time kicking the dolls' heads around. It got louder and louder and then, suddenly, the door of the men's room slammed open and out came Bill Raymond dressed in white longjohns with a white hood, crashing and crashing. He had four ashcan covers tied around his ankles. The abominable crash-ashcan man stepped high, crashed around on the main floor and headed for us on the stage. We had to deal with him. He won.[14]

Despite the apparent unpredictability and pure fun of these shows, Davis thought through all aspects and discussed them in detail with the performers. Just as Jerzy Grotowski, whose techniques later influenced Mabou Mines' working methods, was advocating improvisation in his training exercises for actors, Davis obviously valued this type of spontaneity, for which an actor trains but cannot specifically prepare. Breuer and, presumably, Maleczech were part of these conversations. In an interview with David Savran, Breuer remarked that he and Davis also debated theater techniques, and more recently he has given Davis credit for introducing him to the ideas of Brecht.[15] Although he later found Genet's and Grotowski's types of irony more useful than Brecht's, Breuer—like Davis and, to a lesser extent, Blau—was already trying to dissociate abstract ideas in the theater from psychological motivation of the sort advocated in Stanislavsky's influential theories. Breuer comments:

> You see the trick with Stanislavski is that basically it is so Freudian, tied to the psychology of Realism. Grotowski led us toward the possibility of working internally for abstract form. How do you motivate style? That was a question that Ronnie Davis and I debated all the way back in 1960 and that he never really solved. It was always, you motivate with realistic psychology and then you impose style.[16]

Blau's productions of Beckett, combined with the "Eleventh Hour" shows, must have raised such questions, and others like them, in a dizzying variety of ways.

Maleczech and Raymond's work with Davis held another important dimension. Maleczech counts Davis as one of her most important teachers. He showed her how a play could serve a political agenda and how politics could inform artistic choices. As a movement teacher, he offered rigorous training, something the young Maleczech needed and sought. On first arriving in San Francisco, she had worked at a small theater in North Beach, The Interplayers, in the parts of Emily in *Our Town* and the medium in *Roshomon*. Six days a week, however, she studied four hours a day with Davis at his studio in the Mission District, then rehearsed with his troupe. Everyone in his workshop contributed a small amount to the rental of the studio, an approach Maleczech borrowed in 1977–78 when she offered a workshop that led to the production of *Vanishing Pictures* and the formation of Mabou Mines' first studio for emerging artists, Re.Cher.Chez. Joining the Mime Troupe, Maleczech performed in a number of traditional commedia dell'arte productions directed by Davis. The rigor of his training was invaluable: "Putting a source of movement like that into a person's body—doing it so much that you really understood it with your body—never leaves you."[17] At the same time, Maleczech and the others were witnessing the work of Anna Halprin, who shared studio space with the Tape Music Center. Having no formal dance training, they absorbed a remarkable variety of techniques.

Although in San Francisco and Paris the future members of Mabou Mines were developing their interests in literature and collaboration with visual artists and dancers, they had not yet focused their energies on language and culture—specifically U.S. culture. They chose first to go abroad, where their mature themes and techniques developed as they began to contextualize the predominantly European influences they had acquired in California. In the summer of 1964, Breuer and Maleczech left for Europe by way of New York. The San Francisco Actor's Workshop had become a large and complicated operation, one of the first successful regional theaters, resulting in an invitation extended to Blau and Irving to run the theaters at the brand new Lincoln Center in New York. Maleczech recalls that, of the four future members of Mabou Mines, Breuer was invited to New York; he declined. Akalaitis and Raymond may have already departed earlier in 1964, Akalaitis to pursue acting classes in New York and Raymond to return with his family to the Los Angeles area, where he largely remained until rejoining Breuer and Maleczech almost ten years later. As the Vietnam War shifted into high gear, the Bay Area's experimental scene was shifting as well to a countercultural focus on street performance, flower power, and political protest and was no longer providing the experience Breuer and Maleczech felt they needed. They and the city had outgrown each other.

Breuer, for one, was apparently still trying to reach his literary mecca. If San Francisco began the graduate education of Mabou Mines' collaborators, Europe deepened it. Paris gave them a taste of being in the center of things, the excitement of a new language, not to mention the mind-expanding experience of living in an unfamiliar culture, and the first truly international artistic environment they had encountered. They had a great desire to be part of important work and the self-confidence (or perhaps a necessary arrogance) to think that they each had important contributions to make. Later Mabou Mines' identity as a collaborative theater would become visible as an ideal designed to serve the needs of these individuals, each with a personal vision and a will to power. In Europe, however, they were still young cultural adventurers traveling mostly in pairs. After arriving by freighter in January 1965, Breuer and Maleczech spent time wandering throughout Europe. Maleczech remembers that they set out for Greece, where they lived in Lindos, on the island of Rhodes, for most of a year, then hitchhiked around Turkey. In Greece they encountered Akalaitis and Glass, who on returning to Paris gave them a place to stay until they could find their own. A recent graduate of the Juilliard School's master's program, Glass was studying on a Fulbright fellowship with the formidable Nadia Boulanger. Over the next several years, the four used Paris as a home base, making trips to Berlin, New York, London, Spain, and (in the case of Akalaitis and Glass) India.

As in San Francisco, Breuer had not set out to be a director in Paris, but the urge to work on a piece was strong for all of them. The four Americans began to discuss an intriguing play that Beckett had published in English the year before. *Play* is a brief, intense, repetitive dialogue among three characters who speak from urns, only their heads visible. When the four decided to do more than discuss the piece, they focused on the work process rather than preparing a product to be performed for an audience. While they did see Breuer as a guide, there was no division of the group into set roles and no rehearsal schedule. The urgency of the work itself made it part of their lives. When Breuer invited Warrilow, whom Akalaitis had met at a theater workshop, to join them, Warrilow was astonished at the notion that the project "would *not* be [done] with a view to performing."[18] As he often recounted before his death in 1995, he had never heard of such an undertaking. He had done well in college dramatics at Reading University, landing the lead in an Anouilh play for his first role, and despite his lack of formal training had been approached twice since his arrival in Paris to perform in professional English-language productions of Beckett plays, both of which opportunities had fallen through for him. Still, *Play* was the real starting point of Warrilow's work as an actor. Like Maleczech and Akalaitis, he came from a working-class family, in his case from Stone, a small Staffordshire town in northern England. After completing a bachelor's degree in French language and literature in 1957, he moved to Paris, where he first apprenticed as an editor's assistant, then progressed to English-language editor. The work was comfortable but not engrossing; after five or six years at *Réalités,* he seemed ready in 1965 for something more demanding: "My meeting with those people who eventually formed Mabou Mines was radical to the change that took place in me. Meeting them made it almost inevitable. They shook me up so. Their way of looking at things and talking about things threw my whole structure of the universe into chaos." And he wanted more, as he noted in 1985, six years after leaving the company.

> The way that they were able to ask "Why not?" Why not the four of us work on Samuel Beckett's *Play* for four months in the evening when David is not at the office, and why not just leave it at that? We don't have to perform it . . . . I hadn't come across that kind of thinking. It was new, vital and so compelling that even though it was scary, I decided to go with it. It was the beginning of a very long, difficult, joyful and extraordinary process that is still going on.[19]

Throughout his association with Mabou Mines, Warrilow remained centered on the work's ability to unearth and lay bare aspects of each individual performer. He seemed to see performance and its risks as key to self-discovery, the buried treasure that his study of language could not completely unearth. When Mabou Mines' focus on self-discovery was supplanted by other concerns in the late 1970s, Warrilow became a freelance actor, probably best known for his solo performance of *A Piece of Monologue* (1979), which Beckett wrote at Warrilow's request.

The five avant-gardists recall the work on *Play* as a pleasurable, largely unpressured exploration. While Breuer guided the work, everyone had suggestions (Warrilow remembered) about their own characters, their look or sound. The work was its own justification. Although the five eventually performed *Play* at the American Cultural Center in 1967, they remained intoxicated with the idea of performance as a form of structured exploration, a way of life. Over the next several years, the five (as well as others such as Fred Neumann, who joined them on specific projects) would bring to the work ideas and techniques from their own experience, whether writing, acting, music, or literature. This search for new working methods and performance techniques underlay the founding of Mabou Mines in 1970 and continues to this day.

In his autobiography, Glass sheds light on how the work on *Play* was a new departure for him, coming as he did from the world of music. Glass had grown up in Baltimore and attended the University of Chicago at the age of fifteen. As a child he had played violin, then flute, and took up piano as a minor in college. His primary focus, however, was composition. In 1957 he went to New York to continue those studies at Juilliard, gaining a strong conservatory education before departing for two years in Paris from 1964 to 1966. There Nadia Boulanger took him back to the basics of a traditional European musical education and taught him rigorous compositional skills. Glass, however, was absorbing other influences that had an enormous impact on the direction his music would take. In the late 1950s, New York had offered the poetry of Allen Ginsberg and Gregory Corso, the writing of Jack Kerouac, the music of John Coltrane, and thought-provoking art by Robert Rauschenberg and Claes Oldenberg. Opera, an important form of musical theater, had been part of his education at Juilliard, but he was more interested at the time in the Living Theatre's hyperrealist productions, such as Jack Gelber's *The Connection* (1959). In Paris several years later, catalytic influences came often from this "progressive" sort of theater.

> What has always stirred me is theater that challenges one's ideas of society, one's notions of order. . . . Jean-Louis Barrault's Théâtre Odéon in Paris regularly presented new works by Beckett and Genet, and I particularly remember a stunning production of Genet's *The Screens,* directed by Roger Blin. Also, I saw the unforgettable Madeleine Renaud playing the Woman in what may have been one of the very first productions of Beckett's *Happy Days.* . . . During this period I made regular trips to London as well. We were students then and, not having much money, we often hitchhiked to London, managing somehow to pay the boat fare across the Channel, queuing all night to buy balcony seats for the National Theater, where we might see Laurence Olivier in *Othello* or perhaps Strindberg's *Dance of Death.*[20]

Most notable was Glass and Akalaitis's trip to Provence to see the Living Theatre's premier of *Frankenstein* (1964), which ran from eight in the evening to three in the morning and fascinated Glass for its extended sense of time. In *Einstein on the Beach* (1976), Glass and Robert Wilson created a similarly slowed and heightened sense of time. Such a "theatre of images" became associated with Wilson, Richard Foreman, and Lee Breuer, as well as, whether justified or not, Mabou Mines as a company. The Living Theatre, however, had another profound influence on Glass and Akalaitis and the company they would cofound. Seeking out Julian Beck and Judith Malina in Berlin while they were rehearsing *Antigone*, Glass and Akalaitis were curious to know more about the Living Theatre's work, as well as its functioning as a collective. Although Mabou Mines did not become a collective, "the Living" was one of the groups providing an exciting alternative to commercial theater for these young people, who were rethinking the foundations of performance as it cut across disciplinary lines.

Besides his memorable lessons with Boulanger and the striking influence of "progressive" theater, Glass encountered in Paris a new way of thinking about music that proved useful in other performance forms as well. Through a friend Glass was hired as assistant to the celebrated Indian sitar player Ravi Shankar, who was scoring a film by Conrad Rook. It was Glass's daunting task to write down the music as Shankar sang it, part by part, for the Western musicians who were to play it. Knowing only Western notation, Glass found it difficult to reproduce the music without allowing unwanted accents to creep in. While Western music divides time within a set framework of bars, Indian music, he found, strings "beats" together "to make up larger time values." Drummer Alla Rakha caught Glass's error.

> "All the notes are equal," he kept piping at me.
>
> The whole thing was very unnerving. I had a studio full of musicians waiting for their parts, and I had to instantaneously solve a notational problem I had never encountered before.
>
> Finally, in desperation, I dropped the bar lines altogether. And there, before my eyes, I could see what Alla Rakha had been trying to tell me. Instead of distinct groupings of eighth notes, a steady stream of rhythmic pulses stood revealed.
>
> Delighted, I exclaimed to Alla Rakha: "All the notes are equal!" He rewarded me with an ear-to-ear smile.[21]

Glass's discovery was a foundational moment for his music, including his compositions for Mabou Mines. The realignment of his thinking about time accorded with the group's approach to their open-ended work together. The notion that one could build time rather than slicing it from a predetermined "loaf" was applied to the rehearsal process as well. Although in practical terms rehearsal still led to performance, for a time Akalaitis, Breuer, Glass, Maleczech, Neumann, and Warrilow played with work practices that were, in essence, additive. The usual six- to twelve-week rehearsal period for a commercial or regional theater production did not apply. In a sense they were truly living "in performance," as they supported themselves with day jobs and met in the evenings. When they undertook *The Red Horse Animation* in 1970, it was important to present work in progress to small audiences, but by the time of the first full production the process had spanned almost a year. The members of Mabou Mines shared these alternative working methods with their downtown colleagues in music, art, and dance. Later, when they staged larger productions in theater spaces rather than art galleries, this youthful delight in extended collaboration was somewhat curtailed. Perhaps the lengthiest was the four-year development of *The Shaggy Dog Animation,* a process that some company members found unnecessarily protracted, muddying good work already accomplished. The legacy of an additive approach, however, was not entirely lost in the later 1970s, for Mabou Mines adapted to the members' financial need to take on other jobs, often in theater or film productions with more conventional rehearsal schedules. The work became, necessarily, a matter of open-ended, stop-and-start development. There are two rules now for Mabou Mines productions: all members must take their turn in developing individual projects as money becomes available; and they must support others' projects, although they are not required to participate. Extended collaboration with other artists has remained an important working principle for the company despite increasing pressures. In 2005 Maleczech commented:

> There are more claims on people's artistic lives than before. We deal with that by gathering together for a two- or three-week period—or even a month—of really intensive work on a piece. Then we all go away. . . . Then we return to it.
>
> At first I found that unsatisfying, but now I think it's good. Because when I come back, I have a different feel about the work than when I left; it's a deepening of the work that's already taken place. . . . This way is financially feasible for us, and it's a way that the most critical, objective, sometimes outrageous ideas can be brought to bear on the work that came before.[22]

One part of this legacy of additive collaboration has been the notion that the actor is an artist rather than an interpreter. At the San Francisco Actor's

Workshop, Blau had demonstrated that the director could take liberties with a play text on behalf of a worthy idea. The actor's responsibility, however, was distinct from the director's and still clearly interpretive. In moving to New York from San Francisco, Akalaitis sought to learn more about the actor's craft and role by taking acting classes with several Method-oriented teachers. From her childhood in Chicago, where her family lived in a Lithuanian Catholic neighborhood, she had had an image of actors as glamorous, special people but had not believed, until she interacted with performers, musicians, and dancers in San Francisco, that acting might be possible for her. She later recalled, "I saw that actors were people just like me, that they were as ordinary looking as I was, and what counted was that you have talent." Akalaitis was disappointed, though, at the lack of dialogue among actors and directors in her New York classes, which focused on preparing audition scenes rather than learning how to work. The late 1960s saw Akalaitis casting about for a direction. She auditioned, appeared in productions in both New York and Paris, and did summer stock. Despite an encouraging workshop with Joyce Aaron of the Open Theatre, by 1969 Akalaitis had given up on a conventional acting career.

The catalyst for this break was a 1969 workshop Akalaitis and Maleczech attended for a month in Aix-en-Provence. Akalaitis had first heard the Polish director Jerzy Grotowski lecture in New York, and she and Maleczech wanted to experience this exciting work at first hand. Neither was very interested in Grotowski's theory of Poor Theatre, in which an ensemble of actors transforms a largely empty stage space into a mystical, emotionally charged arena. The young actors were fascinated by Grotowski's work methods, which they hoped to incorporate into their own performance technique, as Akalaitis later reported.

> It was fantastic and completely changed my ideas about work. I saw a whole development of Stanislavsky that involved the body, . . . my own personal history, and . . . my value as an artist.
>
> It is very important to me that Grotowski said that an actor is as much an artist as a writer, a painter, as the playwright—that he's not an interpreter. And the high level of teaching and technique that was involved in working with him was tremendously stimulating. Richard Cieslak, too, was important. Grotowski would hand out the dogma, and Cieslak would deal with the actual physical techniques, so it was the brains and the body.[23]

Maleczech agrees, counting Grotowski as the second of the two important teachers whose rigorous bodily training has informed her work. When they gathered in New York, Akalaitis and Maleczech taught what they had learned to their friends. Here was one nonpsychological point of access, through the training of both body and voice, that Mabou Mines' collaborators could use to unearth and examine their own experience in order to reshape perception.

In Grotowski's 1969 workshop, Maleczech experienced a respect for the actor's mission that she had probably not witnessed since 1966 or 1967. Preparing a production of Brecht's *Mother Courage* with Warrilow, Neumann, and Ginger and Russ Morro (who had put up the money for the English-language production), Breuer and Maleczech went with the Morros to Berlin for ten days. As Akalaitis and Glass had done, they watched the Berliner Ensemble at work, where they saw a collaborative sharing of tasks not much different, they surmised, from Brecht's own approach to directing. While he harbored reservations about Brecht's "scientific" ideas about political theater, Breuer admired Brecht's sophistication as a writer and director and his theory of how the actor must narrate, rather than inhabit, the role. Variations on such narration have appeared throughout Mabou Mines' work. Maleczech, watching the Berliner Ensemble as an actor, noticed another of Brecht's legacies: that the face-to-face work of collaboration must be carried on in what is essentially a public forum.

> [T]he stage picture had to be so precise that they had a way of working in which several people watched the picture and would comment on it. Although there was a head director, there were several people directing at one time. There were a number of conversations going on between the directors and the actors and they were very up front. There was not a lot of taking actors aside. It was so public. It broke down what was an American Stanislavsky tradition of privacy, particularly between actor and director. And Mabou Mines jumped on that, we liked that a lot and used it a lot and still do.[24]

The work environment that interested Mabou Mines' founding members was a challenging place where ideas and techniques could be freely shared, disagreements argued passionately, and artistic choices defended. It was not for the faint of heart. But it was also a place secure in its own way, where the participants were not divided into preset roles of actor, director, writer, and so on but could learn from one another freely, knowing that the work rested on a common foundation of technique, shared ideas, imagination, intellect, and respect.

In 1969 the five who had worked on *Play* were already talking about forming a theater to be located possibly in London or New York. Juliet, the daughter of Akalaitis and Glass, had been born in 1968, and Maleczech and Breuer now also had a daughter, Clove Galilee.[25] Ready to leave Paris after five years in an increasingly uninteresting artistic scene, Maleczech was deciding that she wanted to raise her daughter in the United States.[26] In the meantime, Warrilow had made the break from *Réalités* and was auditioning for parts in London. No one was interested in his unconventional résumé other than the fact that he was seeking his first professional role at the age of thirty-five.

As the company members tell the story, their choice to settle in New York reflected a desire to create a specifically American theater and the opportunity to join a thriving artistic community. They had been immersed in a European context that in the political climate and artistic moment of the late 1960s had become inadequate for their creative needs. There seems to have been no connection between the Vietnam War and their decision to return to the United States. They were not involved in the 1968 political protests and occupations in Paris. Nor were the theater, music, and art communities in Paris experiencing the kind of fertile cross-pollination going on in New York. Not knowing what sort of theater they would create, they realized that operating in an American context now was key. While Breuer's concept of a choral American theater did not take shape until the late 1970s, he recognized that U.S. theater was still dominated by realism. Akalaitis had broken with American Method acting. Warrilow, turning away from a literary life in Paris, was about to go west and undertake a decidedly American adventure. New York was, for all of them, an exciting artistic frontier. Only Glass, who had lived there for most of the 1960s, knew the territory well. But he had shaken free of his initial immersion in the serial music of European modernists such as Alban Berg and Arnold Schoenberg. Glass's ensemble, for which he was already recruiting musicians in 1967, was playing his new additive music. He had become an artistic entrepreneur out of necessity since many musicians would not play his compositions.

Of course, they did not fully reject all their European sources. They have consistently recognized the connections between Glass's music and the earlier modernists and the debt that Breuer's vision of a choral theater owes to earlier European avant-gardists such as Jarry, Artaud, and Genet. Akalaitis's first productions as a director focused on Beckett and the popular French writer-performer Colette; in the 1980s Akalaitis added several pieces by Franz Xaver Kroetz and more recently, as a free-lance director, has gone back to plays she first saw in Europe such as Strindberg's *The Dance of Death* and Genet's *The Screens*. Nor was the Stanislavskian tradition of acting completely abandoned. The company's reluctance to embrace the Method actor's private patient-therapist relationship with a director and its turn instead to public, dialectical debate, while involving an individualistic insistence on the actor's equality with other artists, also incorporated ideas on group work drawn from Brecht, Meyerhold, and Grotowski. These alternative European influences were already becoming part of an exciting artistic scene in New York that Glass and Akalaitis were witnessing. The dancers, musicians, performers, writers, and artists associated with collectives such as the Judson Dance Theatre and Grand Union, artists' galleries such as 112 Greene Street and the Paula Cooper Gallery downtown, and Klaus Kertess's Bykert Gallery uptown, and the Open Theatre, the Performance Group, and La Mama Experimental Theatre Club were teaching each other in every performance. They brought with them at times alternative European influences such as ideas from Eric Satie by way of John Cage and Black Mountain College. While some influences seemed exclusively homegrown, such as innovations that young dancers were passing on from Merce Cunningham by way of his students, including Anna Halprin, Barbara Dilley, and Steve Paxton, other dancers, such as Alwin Nikolais, were offering a kinesthetic awareness drawn from a tradition going back to Hanya Holm, Mary Wigman, and Irmgard Bartenieff and thus to the influential German Rudolph Laban. Mabou Mines' contemporary Ping Chong brought to his choreography his parents' experience with the Peking Opera and his love of cinema, both Chinese filmmakers and German expressionists such as Fritz Lang and F. W. Murnau, with their affinity for what Freud called "the uncanny."[27] With their own eclectic backgrounds in theater, performance, music, and literature, the members of Mabou Mines had a distinct contribution to make to this international confluence of artistic traditions.

In 1969 Akalaitis wrote to Breuer and Maleczech, urging them to come back to the United States. In December they arrived, and the four celebrated the new decade by creating a theater group. With Warrilow's arrival the following spring, work began on *The Red Horse Animation.* By the spring of 1971, Mabou Mines was preparing Beckett's *Come and Go,* and Neumann, recently returned from Rome, immediately began work with Breuer and Warrilow on *The B.Beaver Animation.* New York City was the frontier that attracted them. Unlike London or Paris, or any other U.S. city, lower Manhattan offered a welcoming artistic environment at that historical moment. The new company's name said it all. It was evocative yet unidentifiable; one could not say whether it was a theater, a rock group, or a mining company. Few knew that Mabou Mines is a village on Cape Breton Island in Nova Scotia or that Breuer had favored adopting the name of another nearby town, Margaree Forks.[28] The exciting work done in downtown New York in the late 1950s and 1960s had, in a

sense, cleared away genre and disciplinary expectations. Thus, Mabou Mines'
founding members came to New York as to a new world, with the excitement
of finding an artistic space already vibrant with creativity. And, as happened
on the frontier of the American West, the sense of being able to make up one's
own life lent itself to both extraordinary individual accomplishments and the
formation of unconventional border communities that often competed with
one another but just as often displayed enormous generosity.

New York City, like the Old West, proved to be a more complicated place
than it perhaps had appeared from an eastern vantage point, in this case Europe. Making a living while doing the work, for example, was a serious concern. Given the lack of funding for avant-garde performance, Mabou Mines
had no budget of its own and no agencies to which it could apply. Such pub-
licly-funded arts support was just beginning in the United States, and regional
rather than avant-garde theaters had been the first to benefit from new private
programs such as that of the Ford Foundation. Nor was teaching a possible
way to make steady money. While those on tour conducted workshops for
hosting institutions, often art museums such as the Walker Art Center in Minneapolis, the labor and logistical difficulties involved in more permanent
teaching positions would have taken company members away from their work
together. Neumann, with a theater degree from the University of Utah and extensive acting and film dubbing experience, had no interest in teaching. At the
same time, except for temporary visiting arrangements, the academic theater
community in the early 1970s was not yet opening its doors to those who did
unconventional types of performance. Instead, everyone took day jobs. Glass
had become a plumber, and he and Akalaitis helped to found the Soho restaurant Food, where Maleczech, Breuer, and other members and associates
worked from time to time. Breuer and others moved furniture. Later Terry
O'Reilly worked in a factory. In the mid-1970s Neumann was the first in the
company to take freelance acting jobs, much as he had done in Europe.

Warrilow, in coming to New York, had taken another kind of plunge. Joining his friends in the condemned building at 336 West Twenty-third Street,
where they had set up housekeeping, he took the whitewashed room of the
musician Moondog, who had recently moved out. Akalaitis and Glass also
whitewashed another room in which the members of the newly formed theater group, along with other friends, worked six days a week on *The Red Horse
Animation*. While the surroundings were new, the work was reassuringly familiar. Warrilow recalled, "We talked a lot; I mean, a lot of ideas bandied
around and suggestions for this . . . and that, and how to develop a new narra-

tive style. Lee, I think, already had the history [of the Red Horse] in outline. So then it was a matter of daily input and daily throwing out and sometimes extreme disagreement." The larger scene impressed Warrilow as well.

The downtown art scene in New York was so new to me. It was a big time of discovery and awakening.... I had never, ever experienced in Europe the kind of sharing that existed here among the artists. They didn't hide from each other. They were not jealous of their territory or their work. They wanted to share, and they would work with each other....

[The artist Richard Serra, for whom Philip Glass was a studio assistant] invited Philip to do a drawing, to create a piece. The piece was actually made. We asked certain dancers to come to the studio and work with us and show us movement and teach us things about movement....

We saw [Yvonne Rainer] work, and one of her dancers, Barbara [Dilley], came and demonstrated some of the movement for us, how it worked, things like that.... When we were starting work on *The Red Horse Animation,* we dropped by to see [the artist] Nancy Graves.... We were talking about the piece, and she was asking questions. It was Lee that probably said, "Of course, what we really want to do is study the [Edweard] Muybridge photographs, but we can't afford the book." She immediately sat down and wrote a check for it. ... It was moving, something that touched me very deeply. I don't know if it was America; I don't know if it was that time or if they were screwed in the head, but I was very impressed.[29]

Glass has added that he often invited artists to create posters for his ensemble's performances. Soon he had an impressive collection of works by Serra, Graves, Sol LeWitt, James Rosenquist, Joel Shapiro, Brice Marden, Barry LeVa, and Keith Sonnier, the last of whom later provided the sound for Mabou Mines' *Send/Receive/Send.*

Another, very human intervention also made this "life in performance" possible. Ellen Stewart had long made a place for writers and performers to do their work at La Mama, which in 1970 was located, as it is now, at 74 East Fourth Street between First and Second Avenues. She often heard about the financial woes of these artists and responded with money (originally gleaned from her own salary as a department store fashion designer), performance space, and lots of moral support. La Mama was, in effect, a kind of maternal support system. As other Mabou Mines founding members have done, Glass gives Stewart her due.

Ellen made Off-Off Broadway a reasonable and realistic place to work. She provided a focus, first through Café La Mama, and later La Mama Etc. In the 1970s, this role was shared with Joseph Papp's Public Theater, where many of the Mabou Mines works were produced. However, it was Ellen who provided the [ensemble's] very first public support.[30]

From this perspective, Mabou Mines was, at this formative moment, an independent theater company but supported in significant ways by Stewart. Besides providing fifty dollars a week for each artist, she made available the funds to construct an acoustic floor and purchase sound equipment for *Red Horse*. Later disagreements with Stewart caused them to leave La Mama regretfully in 1973; this complete break lasted for more than twenty years. The ice seemed to thaw in the early 1990s, and Stewart allowed Ruth Maleczech to stage *Mother* at the La Mama annex in 1994.

Another support system benefited Mabou Mines from roughly 1972 to 1985. During its first fifteen years the company, like many other artists and groups, did not do much of its own administration, management, or accounting. Those tasks were done by Performing Artservices, Inc., commonly called "Artservices." Mimi Johnson, Margaret Wood, and Jane Yockel founded Artservices in 1972 "to provide professional management, producing and administrative services to a group of performing artists in dance, theater and music whose developing careers required services they could not sustain individually."[31] Their first client was John Cage, followed by Richard Foreman and his Ontological-Hysteric Theater and, notably, the Philip Glass Ensemble. Like the artists they represented, they built their work on oral agreements and strong relationships. "What has been unique about Artservices here in New York," commented Johnson, "is personal, individual commitment."[32] She recalls that the members of Mabou Mines held company meetings in Artservices' office, first at 463 West Street and then at 325 Spring Street, well into the early 1980s. Their primary contact in the first several years was the savvy and generous Yockel, who provided accounting, booking, and some tour management services, then was assisted by George Ashley, Rosemary Quinn, and intern Liza Lorwin, among others. Those who worked at Artservices knew their clients' shows and their families. In fact, Johnson's first memory of Mabou Mines was seeing their initial production, *The Red Horse Animation*.

A particularly fruitful collaboration regarding *The Red Horse Animation* came during the summer of 1970, when Mabou Mines trouped to Cape Breton Island, in Nova Scotia, to rehearse. The previous summer Akalaitis and Glass had purchased with writer Rudolph Wurlitzer a dilapidated summer camp that included a lodge, several smaller cabins, and an expanse of beach, all located near the former mining community of Mabou Mines. During their first summer in Nova Scotia, the company members, their families, and several associates explored the area for which they were named, built the acoustic floor, and began to experiment on it. Largely untouristed in those days and still less commercialized than the coast of Maine, Cape Breton now claims a substantial number of artists who appreciate its proud, private people and remote location.

What made the work on *The Red Horse Animation* unique? They were finding material in areas that other artists had rejected as uninteresting. Not everyone appreciated the mixture of motivational acting techniques and performance strategies that concentrated the audience's attention on the actor as stage object. As Breuer noted in 1975, the latter distinguished Mabou Mines' work from conventional realist theater: "We use emotional qualities in a painterly fashion that at times bears absolutely no logical or psychological relationship to a text."[33] On the other hand, they did not dismiss emotion from the stage. It was often more difficult for their artist-audiences to accept what seemed like corny emotional warmth in a time when cool abstraction, even formalism, offered what seemed a deeper, more intellectual, and thus more meaningful experience. *Red Horse* presented a highly abstracted stage picture. Yet spectators found a tightly structured narrative and discernible characters, all closely tied to Breuer's own family story. The narrative emerged more clearly when Breuer and former San Francisco associate Ann Elizabeth Horton published an illustrated version resembling the comic book adventures of a 1940s superhero. As the company's sole writer of original scripts in these early years, Breuer began by constructing texts in collaboration with the rest of the company. By the mid-1970s, however, Breuer was seeking to restore a kind of authority to his position as writer in order to sustain his vision of a piece's narrative structure throughout its development. As both writer and director, he continued to undercut emotion by layering cultural references on the material. There was, however, less input of a personal nature—that is, self exploration—from the rest of the company as a result. Restoring his own authorial voice had the additional effect of creating a particular mixture of warm and cool that has become more associated with Breuer than with the work of the company as a whole. While Maleczech as director has shared many of his techniques, Akalaitis's and Neumann's first directing ventures combined emotion and formal elements rather differently. Neumann, in particular, made more direct use of character and plot in adapting Beckett's *Mercier and Camier* for the stage. As both narrative and emotion returned to avant-garde performance in the late 1970s, Mabou Mines could be seen as both a forerunner of and a source for new developments.

Besides the three Animations, Mabou Mines produced two other lines of work in the early 1970s. Shortly after starting on *Red Horse*, they revived Beckett's *Play* and worked up *Come and Go*, presenting both in 1971. These small pieces, inexpensive to stage, drew on their earlier Beckett work and built the company's repertoire. In 1975 Breuer and Warrilow, with associate Thom Cathcart, put together for production *The Lost Ones*, another Beckett narrative, this time in a scant three weeks so the three pieces could be presented as a complete evening. Ironically, the success of this venture tied the company's reputation to Beckett more closely than its members had intended. Already in 1972, with rehearsals for *The B.Beaver Animation* under way, the company added a third line of work, termed by one writer a "collaboration series," which consisted of *Music for Voices* (1972), put together by Glass, and *Arc Welding Piece* (1972), a little-known show that had only a brief life.[34] The three lines of work were actually all part of the same collaborative approach. Like the later *Send/Receive/Send*, designed by Keith Sonnier, each piece involved one or two artists outside the company who might join rehearsals for a period or, as in the case of Tina Girouard's sculpture for *The B.Beaver Animation*, whose work the company might adapt to the needs of the piece.

Mabou Mines' commitment to artistic collaboration became perhaps its most visible contribution to the avant-garde scene. Treating the actor as an artist in his or her own right did not prevent the company from valuing the contribution of the writer if he or she was willing to be a collaborator. For many years the company has publicly declared that "Mabou Mines' focus on acting, technology, and theatrical design is directed toward the realization of language as an essential ingredient of performance."[35] How the artists realized language as an element varied from production to production. Akalaitis has advocated perhaps most strongly for the right to use a written text in unconventional ways. Not a writer herself, she borrowed Colette's words for *Dressed Like an Egg*, using period images as her starting point: "I get most of my ideas from pictures. . . . In fact, all images in the theater are visual, even the language—it's impossible to read without making pictures in your mind. The crucial thing for me is always to remain true to your images."[36] In 1976 Akalaitis had created a complete environment for Beckett's *Cascando*, as she did in 1985 for her American Repertory Theatre production of *Endgame*, in the latter case running afoul of that author's then growing tendency to enforce, through his publishers, legal ownership of his stage directions. Yet in none of these cases did she alter the characters' lines. At the other end of the spectrum, Neumann burrowed deep into Beckett's language to find clues for his staging of the narrative *Mercier and Camier,* producing images that owed much to Beckett's word choice, grammar, and etymological playfulness. Without eliding such differences in attitude toward authorship, Maleczech summarizes Mabou Mines' artistic contribution in terms of a balance between language and psychology: "The emphasis has been very heavily on language, not necessarily poetic language, sometimes documentary language . . . and the places language can take you technologically in terms of movement and vocal choices. On the other hand, . . . [Mabou Mines] engages in an awful lot of psychology for a formal theater."[37]

The fact is that Mabou Mines was not purely "formalist" in the 1970s. Rather, the company engaged a variety of forms and conventions in order to take both the artists and their audiences on a journey. In 1985 Christopher Bigsby noted that the figures of the Animations "recoil . . . from history. . . . The public world which had engaged much American theatre in the 1960s is excluded." Instead, "Breuer's works . . . propose the existence of a resistant self, under pressure but committed to the business of self-invention . . . the only synthesizing force." Bigsby connects this resistant self to romanticism: "What seems like an authoritarian form—the imposition of private images and ideas—is offered as a key to a certain freedom."[38] Breuer quoted Maleczech in making a similar point about "moving" audiences: "People asked if we were interested in moving an audience and Ruth said, Yes from one place to another. That's the best definition of what we tried to do."[39] Breuer concludes that Mabou Mines "plays the game while showing the game." Focusing always on the act of discovery, whether through irony or other means, Mabou Mines has been from its beginning a humanist theater. Bigsby, once again, makes a useful connection (although he gives little credit to the company as a whole).

Breuer's achievement in the theatre lies in the success with which his essentially simple conceits are made to express a range of subtle thought. . . . The prevailing tone is perhaps that of pathos, the posturing of the human animal being undercut precisely by the simple device of taking that animality literally. But the sympathy is real enough and, paradoxically, humanism retained its hold on the American theatre of the 1970s precisely through these inventive fables, monologues which nonetheless contrive to compress a whole range of human experiences and cultural realities into a form which eschews the conventional context for that humanism.

The forms of acting, design, and direction play their role: "The strategy seems to be to deconstruct the principal elements of theatre in order to create a pressure for reconstruction on the part of the audience."[40] As a performer Maleczech has put it this way.

> What I'm interested in is how you can translate an idea into a moment of theater—performing the performance instead of the role, which means using emotion and psychology, of course, but also formal disciplines such as music and dance, taking it all into your body and voice and sensibility. I'm looking for that mystical moment when all your preparation comes together in such a way that the performer is moved out of self into the *performance* of self—a kind of active, public meditation.[41]

An "active, public meditation" involves not just the actor but the actor's collaborators and the audience the actor faces. The public nature of what Mabou Mines does is an essential component of its humanist contribution to recent performance. Watching *Play* being performed to his music again and again, Glass began to see that the "epiphany of the piece, if I can use that word, was in a different place" each night. Catharsis, he found, was not a formula completely bound up in the play text, the stage design, or the blocking: "It's a psychological mechanism which is built into the nature of the work. . . . I finally came to the conclusion that it had to do not so much with the internal structure of the work but the relationship of the listener to the work itself." The audience actually completes the piece. While Marcel Duchamp and John Cage had introduced this idea much earlier, Glass found it striking that audiences in the 1970s began to come to the theater *with the ready knowledge* that they would play a role in the play's completion.[42] Mabou Mines helped to build that understanding.

During the summer of 1999, Mabou Mines participated in the Institute for the Arts and Civic Dialogue (IACD) at Harvard University. The artists had come to workshop Breuer's *Ecco Porco* (then the latest piece of the epic Breuer began with *The Shaggy Dog Animation*), followed by discussions with audiences of various backgrounds and attitudes. In introducing the company, institute director Anna Deavere Smith, who had once apprenticed with Re.Cher.Chez, the studio run by Mabou Mines from 1979 to 1984, seemed to echo Ionesco's view that avant-gardists "reject traditionalism in order to find again a living tradition."

> Mabou Mines would be the mainstream of experiment, if everything about them didn't defy mainstream itself. Even as we try to create a new field of art and its relationship to society, we are mindful of those who laid a groundwork, a groundwork that questioned authority from the beginning, and a groundwork that found aesthetic values where others weren't looking. And perhaps the way of working is as interesting as the work itself.[43]

What follows is an account of Mabou Mines' ways of working in the 1970s. These productions created a bridge from the company's formative years to its mature identity as a company of directors. I hope it will become apparent that they also bridged an important shift in American culture, from drama as a Eurocentric art form to theater as a broader category of public dialogue that paved the way for the many houses of performance we now inhabit.

CHAPTER TWO

Form, Force, and Flow: *The Red Horse Animation, The B. Beaver Animation,* and Other Early Pieces

By 1980 the members of Mabou Mines were engaging in a more public dialogue, evidenced by pieces such as *Dead End Kids* and the founding of Re.Cher.Chez. They had begun in 1970, though, by creating artist-centered performance for other artists. The first project Mabou undertook as a company was *The Red Horse Animation,* a distinctively American piece drawing on U.S. popular culture. At its heart lay the cinematic image of an unknown landscape where the Red Horse—a conjoining of steed and rider—escaped the regimentation of a conventional life and sought a place where he could create himself. It would appear, given the videotape records and written accounts of *Red Horse* in performance, that spectators did not see a limitless expanse but rather a small room very much like the one that had contained the work on Beckett's *Play* in Paris. Using Grotowski-inflected techniques, the performers' bodies re-created the free movement of the Red Horse, its protean image coalescing, changing, and disintegrating, only to reform itself a moment later in a new configuration. It was the essence of change and motion, with its roots not in European literature but in Hollywood film. Created to critique the romance of motion it embodied, the image of the Red Horse shivered and, as the performance ended, seemed to burn away, as though consumed by the apparatus "projecting" it. But, of course, *The Red Horse Animation* was not a film. The romance conveyed by the frame, and the disintegration of the image, instead constituted the narrative structure the performers embedded in their movements and sounds.

Red Horse was part of another frontier, that of the downtown New York artistic scene. Devised by the five artists collaborating in an empty room on West Twenty-third Street, *The Red Horse Animation* was a scene of self-creation as American, if not as familiar, as the image of the lone horseman. In 1970 New York City served as the frontier, the whitewashed room was the scene, and the characters were a group of artistic entrepreneurs. As the artists turned to U.S. popular culture for the parameters of their first original production, they put an American spin on Grotowski's and Brook's European notions of the stage as an empty space. The performance/rehearsal room was a space of potential where the actors did what the Red Horse dreamed of doing: created their own lives on their own terms, allowing their desires, rather than duty, to lead them forward.

This sketch of Mabou Mines as a new collaborative theater feeling its way forward into a working identity is the scene of self-making and unmaking that birthed first *The Red Horse Animation,* then *The B.Beaver Animation,* and finally *The Shaggy Dog Animation.* The preoccupation with the artist as subject is reminiscent of modernist works such as James Joyce's *Portrait of the Artist as a Young Man* (1916) or Thomas Mann's *Magic Mountain* (1924).[1] Writer-director Breuer, however, found much of his material in the "low culture" of popular music, comic book superheroes, and film. The Animations' making was a film in itself, with the first frame the all important scene of collaboration in the whitewashed room.

This chapter focuses on the first two Animations, both of which explore the formation of identity in the interplay of self and other. *The Red Horse Animation* depicted the shaping of a young person's romantic notions into a temporary self-mythology: "some form to hold me." *The B.Beaver Animation* became in the rehearsal process a choral narrative that worked through and organized the existence of an individual who had lost his calling and was becalmed by self-doubt. *Red Horse* and *B.Beaver* confronted myths common in American culture: the young rebel; the artist whose early fervor turns to a weary confusion and torpor; and the romantic dream of free, unfettered motion juxtaposed with the rituals and responsibilities of everyday life. How these myths shape an individual's identity was a primary focus of the first two animations. Mabou Mines expanded these ideas in *The Shaggy Dog Animation,* which was just as dense as the first two pieces but three times as long and more ambitious in scope. Whereas *Red Horse* was "a romance about motion," *Shaggy Dog* spun the American take on romantic love as a web of cultural illusions and their contributions to self-making and unmaking.

Though early, the *Red Horse* and *B.Beaver* Animations were complete, mature works. They enacted the early 1970s artist's reassessment of self in relation to contemporary American society. Developed and first performed in the context of downtown performance art, these low-budget pieces were decidedly uncommercial, reflecting instead a leisurely process of collective exploration and learning. Some critics have described this work as formalist. For example, Christopher Bigsby links the "private vision" of 1970s collaborative performance to modernism's "imposition of form on a threatening chaos": "The private myths/obsessions of [Robert] Wilson, [Richard] Foreman and [Lee] Breuer are offered to the audience as means of triggering personal moments of self-discovery through an openness to the reality of their surroundings or through momentary images which spark activity in the brain."[2] While risking solipsism, Bigsby argues, these artists effectively challenged what he calls the "unproblematic relationship between the self and its environment" found in American realist theater. Much later, in his book *La Divina Caricatura* (2002), Breuer calls himself a "counter-culture formalist," but issues of structure and form have been only one part of his, and the company's, interest in narrative. While addressing artistic creativity, a subject crucial to downtown audiences of artists and actors, *Red Horse* and *B.Beaver* also worked through cinematic metaphors to comment on larger, pervasive cultural narratives. The first two Animations were maps of the *forms* and *forces* at work in the artists' lives, particularly those that stop the creative *flow*. As from an aerial view, Mabou Mines mapped cyclical patterns of self-destruction produced by seemingly disparate cultural elements such as ego psychology or consumerism. Then, moving close up, Mabou Mines showed how the artist, trapped in human desire, struggles to break these cycles. Largely unknown when its artists were developing these pieces, Mabou Mines' reputation is closely tied to the Animations. Like the Beckett adaptations, *Red Horse* and *B.Beaver* have become signature pieces, their fame far exceeding the limited runs and small performance spaces in which they originally appeared.

"Some Form to Hold Me": *The Red Horse Animation*

The Red Horse Animation represented Mabou Mines' first identity—a new being, young and eager to find out what it was. Like much early 1970s performance art, *Red Horse* was a "piece" rather than a play; its principles of construction grew out of its central concept, in this case the "outline" of a red horse come to life. This "romance about motion" suggests adolescent fantasy. The Red Horse has no love object other than his own materialization in the world. When he has run his course, the Animation does not sentimentalize his loss of being, for his existence was a dream, the unstoppable but short-lived desiring of youth.

Red Horse was also a sophisticated examination of perception and performance. A flyer reads:

THE RED HORSE ANIMATION is a romance. Its concern is about sustaining forward motion. Structurally it is choral. The voice is narrative. Continuity is cinematic. It is performed on two planes 90° apart—a floor and a wall. The audience views from above at a 45° angle enabling the performers to transfer images from one plane to another. The horizontal becomes vertical and the vertical horizontal. Both planes appear to be in mid-air, and the audience has the illusion of its viewing angle being constantly changed, as in cinema cutting.[3]

The Red Horse Animation was performed by Akalaitis, Maleczech, and Warrilow, who with writer and director Breuer and composer Glass developed it in 1970–71 over fourteen months. Although at one point the piece ran over two hours, at completion it was a tight forty-one minutes. The action took place on two surfaces, a backdrop of rough boards in which five handholds had been cut and a polished platform of twenty wooden panels, each wired underneath to create its own distinctive acoustical effect when the actors tapped or drummed on its surface. Construction of the acoustic floor and the purchase of sound equipment were underwritten by Ellen Stewart. Like two-dimensional, animated images, the performers lay on this platform, a deliberately shallow, almost depthless stage space. Their movements created formations against the backdrop—the Red Horse galloping, cantering, trotting, with or without a rider—while their rhythmic tapping and vocalizations completed the image. They changed the horse's position or posture during blackouts to create the effect of cinematic cuts, abruptly shifting the audience's perspective. Or, using the rough board wall as a "floor," the three actors used the handholds to hang in the shape of the horse; from the audience's perspective they seemed to lie weightless on a horizontal surface that had just been perceived as vertical. At another point a black light caught the Red Horse in motion, the actors' costumes suddenly outlined in glowing red. According to a letter from Warrilow to Neumann and Fergusson, who were still in Italy, the company had considered several options for the costumes, finally settling on comfortable street clothes resewn with barely visible horizontal stripes of red thread. The clothes were treated with a white powder that showed as red under black light, producing the desired outlines. *Red Horse* stimulated a variety of associations: camera angles used by Jean-Luc Godard and Harry Smith or scenes from the films of Charlie Chaplin.

The company spent three months during the summer and fall of 1970 rehearsing Glass's music, initially at the Nova Scotia seaside camp that he,

Akalaitis, and friend Rudy Wurlitzer had bought. With the painter Power Boothe on hand to help devise a set, Glass wrote "percussive sounds . . . organized into a highly logical arithmetic system [he] later began to call 'additive process.' "[4] According to Warrilow, the actors sang not words but "interlocking syllables," each person with his or her four notes. In performance, the actors began with vocals, then added percussion; finally, the vocals were subtracted, leaving percussion only. Warrilow marked changes from one section to the next with his fist since the sections varied in length.[5] Performance of this difficult music required both precision and accuracy, which the actors achieved during the piece's run in November 1970, beginning Mabou's reputation for finely executed performance.

These movements and vocalizations were not possible without Breuer's text. In fact, in the piece's first few minutes the stage remained empty while voices recited the prelude. "DO I OWE A DEBT TO THE CINEMA?" one voice asked. The suggestion of adolescent fantasy appeared in the "story line" that was beginning to take shape.

GENGHIS KHAN CONQUERS THE WORLD SUPPLIED BY VISUAL AIDS TO ELEMENTARY EDUCATION . THE BACK ROW . THE FIRST FORM . RIGHT INDEX FINGER IN THE INKWELL . THE LEFT IN THE HOLE . IN MY POCKET . WORKING AWAY . MONGOLS LEAP THE CARPATHIANS INTO TRANSYLVANIA WAS THE SUBTITLE OF MY FIRST HARD ON .[6]

While the story line of Genghis Khan's messenger horse took shape, two other voices created the horse's physical outline and family history. Breuer had distinguished this three-track text from a traditional dramatic script by calling it "caption literature,"[7] linking it to language used in silent films and comic books. These separate tracks run parallel in the published script (1979), lending it a postmodern simultaneity. A more compelling *Red Horse,* though, had already appeared in Bonnie Marranca's 1977 anthology *Theatre of Images* in a comic book format illustrated by Ann Elizabeth Horton, a friend from the artists' days at the San Francisco Actor's Workshop.[8] Although the label "theatre of images" was widely used to discuss Breuer's (and Mabou Mines') work, they never adopted it. The comic book version of *Red Horse,* though, evoked the performance, the text counterpointing image with movement in a similarly comic way, creating a spark that "animated" the reader's imagination and brought the Red Horse to life.

Red Horse, like the other Animations, contained autobiographical elements, but Breuer, Glass, and the actors were, as John Howell put it, "only initial starting points. . . . In no sense do they play themselves; . . . individual attitudes, mannerisms and appearances, fantasies and memories . . . are refined to the point of caricature, until they acquire a dimension that relates to (but does not represent) a particular performer."[9] In this sense, *Red Horse* and *B.Beaver* were, in Breuer's phrase, "autographical," not so much represented as worked through and inscribed on the action. Later, beginning with *The Shaggy Dog Animation,* a growing number of elements from the artists' lives were worked into the material. The dog herself, Rose, borrows her name from Breuer's mother, and Rose's situation, as the sometime spouse of John, is drawn from the circumstances of Maleczech, who first performed as "Ruth Breuer" in San Francisco and married Breuer in July 1978. If it can be said that all Breuer's characters represent him, John primarily demonstrates Breuer's attachment to women and his pursuit of them. In *A Prelude to Death in Venice, Hajj, The Warrior Ant, An Epidog* (1996), *Ecco Porco* (2002) and *Pataphysics Penyeach* (2009), Breuer's borrowing from his own and other company members' lives became more open. The *Ecco Porco* character SueLee, once named Leslie, was at one time played by Leslie Mohn, the mother of Breuer's youngest son, Wah. Other figures from Breuer's life appear in various guises. There can be no doubt that while, on the one hand, company members have resented Breuer's use of their lives in his writing, on the other they have often made the best of it. Maleczech chooses to put the work first, separating out personal issues, and her example seems to have guided other members as well. Also Breuer's "borrowing" can be seen as a "happy confusion" of identities.

> Since the character or role the performance artist creates is usually predicated on an aspect of his or her own self, there exists a confusion of identities. It is a "happy confusion," as actress Ruth Maleczech of the experimental troup[e] Mabou Mines put it. The performer's real identity and the life of the created character exist at the same time, creating a sort of dual consciousness.[10]

The "confusion of identities" in *Red Horse* drew on Breuer's early life; *B.Beaver* made use of his early experience as a blocked writer. Company members' geographical and philosophical journeys from West to East are also reflected here: their years in Europe, Glass and Akalaitis's 1966–67 trip to India, and Glass's turn to non-Western styles of composition. Later portions of Breuer's omnibus work, including parts of *Shaggy Dog,* make use of Balinese, Indian, Chinese, and Japanese theater forms and techniques the company had either witnessed at first hand or learned about through the work of Brecht, Artaud, and other Western dramatists. Breuer's notion of a new American theater based on European, African Caribbean, and Asian sources had not yet coalesced, but the company's growing interest in Asian theater techniques had already emerged in *B.Beaver*. The artists' collective experience became part of the Red Horse, filtered through their collaborative process, which took suggested images and movements seemingly at random and subjected them to experiment and discussion. Thus, this Animation (and to a certain extent *B.Beaver* as well) was developed collaboratively, although the text was identified as Breuer's.

In 1976, when the members of Mabou Mines were working on *Shaggy Dog*, Breuer gave a tongue-in-cheek account of the collaborative process. It confirms company reports of their methods in the 1970s, which claim that the work was deliberately unstructured and benefited from chance occurrence and that a serious account of it tends to betray its playfulness.

> RECENTLY SOME PEOPLE HAVE ASKED US HOW WE WORK. WELL. HERE'S HOW WE DO IT. USUALLY TWO OR THREE PEOPLE ARRIVE AROUND ELEVEN THIRTY. THOSE. USUALLY. WHOSE KEYS DON'T WORK IN THE STUDIO LOCK. OR IF THEY WORK IN THE STUDIO LOCK THEY DON'T WORK IN THE FRONT DOOR. THESE ARE BAD DUPLICATE PEOPLE AND THEY GET PISSED OFF AND GO HAVE COFFEE AT THE BINI BON.

After having coffee, getting warm, and reading the newspaper:

> JOANNE RUTH AND TERRY DRIFT INTO THE BABYSITTING BUDGET. ONCE RESOLVED. CASH FLOW IS EXPEDITED BY SIGNING OVER TERRY'S WELFARE TO FRED WHO PAYS HIS UNEMPLOYMENT TO THE ORDER OF JOANNE. (WE ARE A STATE SUPPORTED THEATRE). WHO THEREUPON DISTRIBUTES BY PERSONAL CHECK.

The work has, in fact, begun. And thus the company comes to a moment when a new idea emerges.

> WE ASK OF OURSELVES SOMETHING PASSABLY ORIGINAL. PASSABLE. LESS. TO THE OTHERS OF US SITTING THERE PASSING ON IT. THAN TO OURSELVES. PASSABLE IN THE SENSE THEN THAT PASSING ON BE

PERMITTED. AND ANY. REALLY ANY. ABSOLUTELY ANY WAY WE CAN
GET TO IT IS HOW WE WORK.

AND THE QUAINT EFFECTS. RITUALS. AND PROCEDURES DESCRIBED
ABOVE. COUNT THE TIME DOWN EFFECTIVELY AND WITH MINIMAL
PRETENSE AND COMMOTION UNTIL SOMETHING HAPPENS.
SHOULD IT EVER. EVER AGAIN.[11]

But "it" did happen, and the work went on. To delete the laid-back quality of
the scene or remove the humor from Breuer's account would cause us to miss
part of the point. Deflecting attention from the notion of the art object, Breuer
redirects the reader to the nexus of relationships among the company members and associates, who in "passing on it" may pass professional judgment, decline to participate, and give each other permission to go on. The "given" of the
work process is that nothing can be taken for granted, and thus the work must
be "given anew" each day. This is not to say that by 1976 Mabou Mines had not
assembled the techniques and approaches they would continue to use and, in
fact, teach. The willingness to allow the work to be "given anew" each day, however, has remained a foundational element for the company and is one reason
why associates have characterized this way of working as thrilling, occasionally
terrifying, and often frustrating but *playful*. The last element is essential, as one
of the company's forebears, Alfred Jarry, the founder of 'Pataphysics, the "sci-
ence of imaginary solutions," knew.

In keeping with their focus on *play*, the company's earliest promotional
material for the piece encouraged spectators not to think of *Red Horse* as *a play*
in the formal sense: "It cannot be read and does not purport to make a literary
statement. As a stage piece, it tries to exist in its own terms. Stage time. Stage
space. Dramatic structure."[12] These are the terms of performance art, minimalist music, and new dance to which *Red Horse* was most closely related. As
Yvonne Rainer and Steve Paxton had done with dance at the Judson Church,
Mabou Mines took performance back to its basic elements, redefining the
process of performing. Like Edweard Muybridge's book of photographs,
which the company had consulted for its breakdown of the flow of bodily motion into visible components, *Red Horse* made spectators conscious of performance as "a romance of motion," a living, dangerous experience.

Breuer has commented that in 1970 he was already in search of a truly
American theater. *Red Horse* began this process, but its tightly controlled

choral narrative had its roots in the work of European writers and artists such as Beckett, Kafka, Robbe-Grillet, and Godard. While not understandable in either traditional theater or art terms, *Red Horse* quickly found a home in that most European institution, the art museum. In New York it played at the Guggenheim and Whitney museums, both staid uptown venues. Even Clive Barnes, who wrote a deadly *New York Times* review of *Red Horse* that suggested Mabou Mines "might have been more gainfully employed in mining," began by admitting that "more and more we can see the idea of a museum being a place where things happen rather than a place where things are preserved."[13] *Red Horse* was received most warmly in museums that had begun to embrace this concept. Although these museums and their patrons were physically and socioeconomically far from the East Village and Soho (or outside New York altogether), they played a significant role in the development of downtown performance art, usually due to the persuasive voice of a savvy curator or trustee. In the wake of happenings created by Allan Kaprow, Jim Dine, and others (including Fluxus works, Judson Theatre dance experiments, and antiwar art in the form of festivals, parades, plays, poetry readings, concerts, and demonstrations), museums could no longer isolate the art object from its creation, performance, and reception.

Nor could art be isolated from the costs of making and viewing it and spectators' desire to own it in some fashion. As Henry M. Sayre points out in *The Object of Performance,* by 1970 artists were aware of their works' commodity status in American culture. To avoid co-optation, some artists created instead what Sayre calls "objectless art," unbuyable and subversive. Often viewed as "conceptual," and thus politically ineffective or naive, this work opened the possibility of creating low-cost, highly interactive pieces that gave the artists unusual autonomy. As the art *object* dematerialized in this counterinstitutional framework, two new presences asserted themselves: work in ritual and narrative performance. Sayre treats the latter as object-events engaging a community.

> In ritual work this new object appears as a text or document or site which exists as a script or score or generating environment for ritual action. But the presentness of the object in ritual work is limited—it projects a larger or greater presence which is realized in the performance of the ritual activity itself. In narrative work this new object is a medium in which experience is worked through and organized. In this sense, narrative is, like ritual, a generating environment, but now for *cognitive* action. As opposed to ritual, the narrative object embodies presence, but only insofar as storytelling is an action in

and of itself; the score or script of a narrative is the actual event or series of events which it rehearses or "represents."[14]

While ritual and narrative work overlap at times, they should not be conflated. As the projection of a larger presence, Sayre's "ritual" work suggests an Artaudian search for a mystical or religious joining while narrative emphasizes representation, which implies an originary experience discernible cognitively but fundamentally absent from the performance. Mabou Mines' work is closer to the latter than the former. The cognitive moment asks for a quality of heightened attention from performers and spectators. As Warrilow commented to an interviewer, "Improvisation only means that which is not foreseen, that which appears at the moment. Something is always appearing at the moment. The point is how much attention do you pay to it."[15] Thus, as narrative, *Red Horse* did not offer a ritual or a repetition or rehearsal of lived events so much as the experience of a living map of a set of relationships—personal, political, cultural, aesthetic. In this sense it represented U.S. culture as a narrative existing only in performance. The art object incorporates the performance and the work that produced it, as well as the work's capacity to define and shape the artists' and spectators' lives through the story told.

New York's major art museums did not fully understand narrative and ritual performance as ways to rethink the art object when Mabou Mines performed *Red Horse* at the Guggenheim in November 1970. Sayre reports that just a year earlier an artists' demonstration (in which Mabou Mines was not involved) had failed to shut down either the Guggenheim or the Metropolitan Museum of Art on Vietnam Moratorium Day, although the activists had greater success with the Whitney. Yet the walls of the museum institution quickly became permeable to performance's infiltration. If the black tie patrons of the Guggenheim derided *Red Horse,* younger spectators responded to it warmly and with understanding.[16] If the piece was not well received at the Mickery Mokkum Theatre in Amsterdam, where, as Ellen Stewart has said, "they were not ready for the Mabou Mines," *Red Horse* toured successfully to progressive art museums and universities on the West Coast and at the invitation of curator Sue Weil made the first of the company's many visits to the Walker Art Center in Minneapolis. Other opportunities came through Stewart, whose La Mama network was already international; the Guggenheim show, the first performance done in that space, had resulted from her contacts in the art world, including Frank Loesser, a museum trustee.[17] Downtown *Red Horse* played most frequently in spaces such as the Paula Cooper Gallery,

where it had first appeared in June 1970 as a work in progress; George Barteni-
eff and Crystal Field's Theatre for the New City; and Robert Wilson's Byrd
Hoffman School of Byrds, where it appeared later with an early version of *The
B.Beaver Animation.*

A word needs to be said about the important sponsor who made this narrative performance possible. Throughout the work on *Red Horse,* Ellen Stewart provided weekly salaries for the company as well as rehearsal space at her
seven-story building at 47 Great Jones Street, which has been used by many
artists from the early years of the American Indian Dance Company to more
recent productions by Ping Chong and Pan Asian Repertory. Contributing encouragement as well as funds, Stewart clearly was the "mother" of the fledgling
Mabou Mines. Altogether she produced six early productions, including the
first two Animations; the first two Beckett pieces, *Play* and *Come and Go;* the
early version of *The Saint and the Football Player;* and *Music for Voices.* The latter piece was initiated by Glass, who provided "music in eight parts for untrained voices." In addition to the performers listed above, the participants included Kate Manheim (often seen in Richard Foreman's productions), Pamela
Fitzgerald, and Jack Thibeau, who later provided the "xerox poem" that
formed the basis for *The Saint and the Football Player.* Examining the shaping
of sound in a given space, *Music for Voices* arranged eight performers in a circle facing inward, seated on video monitors facing outward. Video cameras
were trained on the performers' faces. The audience, which formed the outer-
most circle, watched the performers' images sing in extreme, angled close-up.
The piece appeared on a bill with *Come and Go, B.Beaver,* and *Arc Welding
Piece* at the Paula Cooper Gallery in June 1972, where *Red Horse* had appeared
two years before.

Breuer directed *Arc Welding Piece* in collaboration with sculptor Jene
Highstein, who during the performance made vertical cuts in a steel cylinder
using an arc welder. Treating the sculpting as a "performance text," the performers rendered corresponding emotions by means of changes of expression
viewed through Fresnel lenses. A program note explains, "The piece is about
two forms of kinetic energy—one sculptural, the other emotional, and it is the
observer's eye that welds the two."[18] The performers included Akalaitis, Neumann, Maleczech, and Warrilow, as well as Thom Cathcart, Jeff Bingham, and
Dawn Gray. The complete twenty-five-minute version appeared with *Red
Horse* at the Mickery Mokkum Theatre in Amsterdam in December 1972.

Arc Welding Piece did not impress reviewer Arthur Sainer, who described it
as "interminable," writing, "Highstein is literally welding, lighting up the back

space, shooting sparks about, while the ensemble sits before him and faces us through funhouse glass that distorts expressions. Interesting visual phenomenae but what for? To my eyes, an elaborate doodle." He concluded about Mabou Mines, "Its ingenuity is very much in the healthy tradition of the New York art world but its narcissism is unfortunately also in the tradition of that world. Its audience is knowing, homogeneous, self-perpetuating, called together by rumor rather than necessity. The audience is aesthetically titillated but is it moved?"[19]

Trouble was brewing with Stewart. *B.Beaver* was taking several years to complete. As Mabou Mines developed other pieces, Stewart apparently felt she was not adequately acknowledged as producer. She recalls that La Mama had paid for *Red Horse*'s space at the Paula Cooper Gallery. While Mabou Mines had thanked Stewart in the program, it did not acknowledge La Mama's sponsorship; some members maintain that Mabou Mines was not a La Mama company until the fall of 1970, when the artists returned to New York and began to use the acoustic floor she had financed. In their three years as a La Mama company, Stewart apparently had differences with individual members, particularly Breuer, probably over money matters. Perhaps the company chafed under the mother's supporting hand. Whatever the reason, Stewart says only that the parting "was something that could not be avoided."[20] She and the company decline to discuss the matter. It is clear, however, that Mabou Mines left the fold regretfully. In 1979 Stewart's anger blossomed again when, in his acknowledgments in the volume *Animations,* Breuer seemed to reduce Stewart's role as producer to one of subsequent collaboration. It appears that Breuer was eager at this point to claim the Animations not just from Stewart but from his fellow collaborators. Breuer had begun to feel by the mid-1970s that he was disappearing into the company's identity as a collective. In 1980, however, he wrote a public apology to Stewart and a spirited defense of Mabou Mines, based on its own growing sponsorship of younger artists, in an article published in the downtown weekly *Other Stages.*[21] While individual accounts differ, Mabou Mines members have acknowledged repeatedly that Stewart's financial support made their early shows possible. Although Glass's piece had a limited run, Stewart always recalls the composer as the member who remembers best the company's debt to her. In *Music by Philip Glass,* he acknowledges her support warmly, as he does that of many teachers and mentors. More recently Mabou Mines has returned to La Mama. In 1994, Stewart provided the La Mama annex for the staging of *Mother* when Maleczech expressed an interest in "coming home." In recent years, Stewart has spoken warmly of the "big history" she has shared with Breuer, Maleczech, Warrilow, Glass, and other company members and notes that Mabou Mines was the first to bring the then puzzling work of Beckett to La Mama.[22]

In those early days, the work on *The Red Horse Animation* must have seemed equally puzzling. Its innovation lay not just in its recharging of the performance space but in the way it made literal the narrative language of its choral monologue by means of its staging. Mabou Mines playfully extended and reoriented familiar metaphors (such as one character's tendency to "go in circles") in order to display their tactile or mnemonic resonances (in this case, the performers' representation of the physical and psychological deadening created by a repetitive nine-to-five work routine). Like a short story or a strip of film, the Red Horse's "psychic lure [was] the drive to hold events in sequence, to traverse them, to come to an end."[23] Thus, while the actors recited the events of the Red Horse's life, they created a narrative that proceeded toward a false goal: the promise of dramatic conflict, complication, climax, falling action, and resolution. *Red Horse* in fact has no dramatic conflict or resolution; the Red Horse materializes and fantasizes a cinematic life ("story line") and, as part of that, a family life that functions as a kind of flashback or origin story. In recollecting itself as a figment of its own imagination, it disintegrates.

It will be helpful to summarize the "lifeline" of the Red Horse, which begins as a kind of tabula rasa, a consciousness with no memory. He tries on a number of identities, projecting himself into the world, but ultimately falls back into an entropic, indeterminate state. As a postabsurdist character, he is aware that he must be self-created; no identity, no preexisting truth, is available to him. Instead, the Red Horse owes a "debt to the cinema," a fantasy sparked by a classroom filmstrip about Genghis Khan. The "I" envisions himself in a montage of images depicting the khan's messengers, red horses entrusted with special missions. Each horse travels as one small part of a Siberian pony express that relays a message wrapped around an arrow "to indicate post haste." The speaker, however, is "not well-traveled"; only in running the film back can he recount the story of the Red Horse and thus form a sense of self. While Breuer carefully avoids the masculine pronoun, using instead *it, you,* or *I,* the Red Horse's narrative seems clearly a bildungsroman focused on a male subject. The bildungsroman usually addresses the growth and education of a young man as he searches for his identity. In the course of the Red Horse's "life," however, the dreamer and the dreamed become virtually indistinguishable.

The story proper begins, as one might expect, with "confusion in the middle," that is, the loss of direction experienced in midlife, when the Red Horse looks back over the romance of his youth. He sees that each horse's valiant motion is only one four-hundredth of a long chain of message carriers, a small part of a large, ultimately circular path. The Red Horse finds he is going in circles. He wonders what was

THE TRUTH OF WHAT IT WAS CONVEYING . WOULD IT NOT CRAVE A CONSTANT PIECE OF INFORMATION TO DELIVER . SAY . FOR DELIVERANCE . COULD NOT IT THEN PERCEIVE ITS GOING . AS ITS BEING . IN THE DESERT . SAY . GOBI DESERT.

Carrying messages as disparate as "VICTORY IS OURS" and "ALL IS LOST," the Red Horse's motion has no purpose. Yet he craves meaning, a message with which he can define himself. His romanticism leads him to expect that his actions ("going") will determine his character and identity ("being"). Interestingly, the Red Horse does not seem to desire a destination, a place where his message could be received. The motion is self-sufficient, but the journey, it seems, is always partial and the subject ends up hobbled, waiting for his next run. Able neither to "go" nor to "be," once again the Red Horse rewinds the reel of his life, looking for meaning in the story of his childhood. Running along a stream, he sees his reflection moving along with him. "MY REFLECTION IS MY IMAGINATION," the Red Horse decides. Remembering nothing of his origins, he invents them in the mode of the Saturday afternoon matinee, by getting "A LITTLE DRAMA INTO MY LIFE." The Red Horse's father is Daily Bread, a beast of burden who walks the threshing floor by day and stands tethered in a cow pasture by night. Daily Bread's story is a cautionary tale against the temptations of the nine-to-five life. If the worker is content to walk in predefined circles, and neither fall below nor exceed expectations, he will succeed. But Daily Bread is an overly conscientious worker betrayed by the system. When he gets the bright idea to work the threshing floor at night, he leaps the pasture fence, but "tragedy" strikes—the tether snaps his windpipe. This moment both confirms the son's rebellion and separates him from any identity offered by "the herd." The Red Horse cannot hear his father's words and "HAVING . LEARNED .. NOTHING .. ABOUT ... CIRCLES ... [STARTS] ... RUNNING."[24]

In running the film of his father's story, the Red Horse reveals the dramatic tensions in the artist's life. As John Howell notes, "The *Red Horse* is an alternately lyrical and disrupted 'romance about motion.' Tension between the horse as an emblem of primal energy and as a domesticated worker for man

cartoons the problem of realizing some framework capable of sustaining creative yet potentially destructive forces without stifling them."[25] This is seen
most clearly in the moment when the Red Horse, seeing a yellow star appear at
the tip of his father's (now silent) tongue "WHERE THE WISE WORDS
WERE . THAT SHOULD HAVE BEEN MINE . TRADITIONALLY," bites out
the tongue and runs with it.[26] He wounds his parent in the act of rebellion but
in the same moment carries away the desired, if doubtful, verbal patrimony. At
this juncture it is tempting to think of Breuer's father, who died when Breuer
was sixteen. The mute patrimony that the son, Asher Leopold Breuer, took
with him into the artist's life is that yellow star, the lost wise words, that Lee
Breuer the artist tries to re-create. But the Red Horse's story is not merely that
of a fictional individual (or of his author); together the Red Horse and Daily
Bread represent creativity and the ways in which it can be hobbled.

In the final section the Red Horse's narrative, created by the dramatic tension among his potential identities, breaks down. The Red Horse is still; he
hears voices. He realizes that he is not himself: "IT COMES TO ME THAT I
AM A REPRESENTATION . THE WAY I SUSPECT THAT I'M NOT WELL
REPRESENTED . THAT I'M NOT WELL." The Red Horse does not survive
this knowledge. The line between fiction and reality has disintegrated. There is
no resolution to the story. The Red Horse "TEARS ITSELF APART . AND
TRIES TO HOLD ITSELF TOGETHER."[27]

Having escaped the dreary routine of ordinary life, the Red Horse cannot
make an adult existence out of his "romance of motion." While experiencing
adult losses, of credibility, imagination, and then mind, the subject fails to connect with another—"I CAN'T HELP YOU . I CAN'T FIND YOU"—and thus
a self definable in middle-class psychological terms never emerges.[28] Like the
character Crow in Sam Shepard's *The Tooth of Crime* (1972), a play of the same
period, the Red Horse's fate is uncertain. Crow vanquishes and replaces the
older Hoss by mimicking powerful cultural myths that he never fully controls.
Richard Schechner, who directed the Performance Group's production of
Tooth in 1973, later developed, in concert with anthropologists such as Victor
Turner, an idea of performance as "restored behavior" or "twice-behaved behavior," which he has described as "physical, verbal, or virtual actions that are
not-for-the-first time; that are prepared or rehearsed. A person may not be
aware that she is performing a strip of restored behavior."[29] This idea is already
visible in *The Red Horse Animation*. Its reworking of familiar stories and archetypes constitutes restored behavior, configuring a subject in the way a projector "animates" the individual frames of a film.

It is probably easier to follow the *Red Horse* narrative on the page than it was to follow it during performance, for in the course of rehearsal the company teased out of Breuer's playful text a dense texture of literalized figurations. In more ways than a spectator could grasp on a single viewing, continuity was staged outside the psychological framework of the family romance. Edward Kaufman, reviewing a 1972 Los Angeles performance, points out that *Red Horse* evokes the mystery of creativity in the carefully balanced forms and structures produced onstage: "Using the technical approach of Grotowski, the Mabou Mines seek to get away from so-called 'psychological' theater—creating, instead, a non-psychological approach in which more *formal* relationships are free to exist: acting styles, movements, music, sound, speech and space."[30] While using cinematic techniques to create continuity—Kaufman lists cuts, blackouts, dissolves, overlaps, sound effects, and voice-overs—the piece mediates the actors' physical gestures through the narrative as it is spoken individually or in chorus. Rather than meshing language and gesture into a throughline, language is literalized onstage.[31] When, for example, Daily Bread's windpipe "cracks," it relates visually and aurally to performer Maleczech's snapping a red cloth as though she were "cracking a whip." The pun is further literalized as the "crack of dawn," presumably the dawning of the Red Horse's realization that he is a representation. The puns make the gesture understandable but not in psychological terms; rather, a set of related ideas is delivered in several techniques running parallel to one another. Michael Peppiatt reports that this running of stage techniques in tandem, each communicating in its own way, was one of Breuer's starting points for the piece.[32] In a sense, *Red Horse* takes performance back to its basic tenets: the empty space, the actor, the spectator. *Red Horse* onstage complicates the performance object in another way by redefining the creative ego away from the psychological and toward the narrative's mediation of elements, staging the ego's desires in the performers' coordinated movements and vocalizations. Each element—actor, language, backdrop and acoustic floor, cinematic cuts, and narrative structure—animates the cultural person(a) of the Red Horse.

The Red Horse Animation, despite its rocky early reception, carried the company forward and remained in Mabou Mines' repertoire until May 1976. At the Brooklyn Academy of Music, Warrilow suffered a leg injury during a performance, and the horse was quietly put to sleep. It had been a long run for the cast of three that never changed throughout its seven-year life span. In fact, while later productions of *Red Horse* by other artists were staged, it is not clear that anyone but the original cast could perform it successfully given its emergence from the company's founding configuration of five members, each of whom made special contributions to the work. In 1995–96 Clove Galilee restaged *Red Horse* with her father directing, Abigail Crain and herself in the two female roles, and David Neumann, son of Frederick Neumann and Honora Fergusson, in his namesake David Warrilow's part. For each performance, Jenny Rogers created a floor painting, made of brilliantly colored concrete aggregate or sand, that stained the performers' clothes, transferring the horse's image to their bodies as they gradually effaced it. Galilee modeled the rhythms, which Glass taught them, as a type of clapping seen in the Indian dance form *bharata natyam*. As a choreographer, Galilee created a much more dance-oriented *Red Horse,* while director Breuer added computer technology. This was provided for the New York City performance by collaborators from the Gertrude Stein Repertory Theatre to enhance the original notion of viewing the horse from a variety of cinematic angles. This "next-generation" version of *Red Horse,* however, remained a workshop production. Galilee has commented, "Lee wrote . . . about his father, my father's father. . . .To do something new with the piece, it would have to be about my relationship with *my* father. And probably it would be all women."[33]

The original *Red Horse* had run long enough to see a new turn in avant-garde performance when companies founded in the late 1960s and early 1970s were closing their doors and solo performance artists were beginning to crowd the downtown scene.[34] By the time of Warrilow's accident in May 1976, the company had been working on *The Shaggy Dog Animation* for more than a year. Mabou Mines had long since ceased to be a resident troupe at La Mama and was making its way as an independent company eligible to apply for grants that were becoming available from the National Endowment for the Arts, the New York State Council on the Arts, and private foundations. The struggle for independence proved to be a perennial affair for—like most other avant-garde companies—Mabou Mines has never had a stable source of income. Nor was it easy to gain recognition in the press. Traditional theater reviewers often did not know what to make of Mabou Mines if they knew of the company at all. Some company members believe, in fact, that Clive Barnes's original review of *Red Horse* postponed their "debut" until 1975, when Jack Kroll of *Newsweek* praised their adaptation of Beckett's *The Lost Ones.* Audiences on the downtown scene, however, appreciated *The Red Horse Animation* and were on hand for the next phase of the work when it appeared at the 112 Greene Street Gallery in the stuttering form of the B.Beaver.

Going against the Flow: *The B.Beaver Animation*

Mabou Mines had begun creating *Red Horse* in the whitewashed room that was the artistic frontier New York offered in 1970. When Neumann arrived from Italy in 1971, he and Breuer went immediately from the dock to Stewart's workshop space on Great Jones Street to begin work on *The B.Beaver Animation*. The B.Beaver's making was as much a public scene of shared work as it was a private scene of making and self-making. It took place in a variety of downtown spaces, perhaps the most important of them in Soho at 112 Greene Street, an industrial building that a group of artists led by Jeffrey Lew had turned into a workshop and gallery/performance space in 1970. It was a space for creating work; unstructured and rough, it could accommodate art that did not fit the atmosphere and attitudes of the pristine uptown galleries. Here a great variety of work appeared. Group shows and individual installations were presented side by side. Sculpture could move. Artists could pound holes in the floor. Anything was possible. The urgency, above all, was to do the work and see the work of others, to participate in the vital processes of *the work*. From 16 to 28 December 1972, four pieces by Tina Girouard were "activated" by performers—among them the members of Mabou Mines—who simply came in at a time of their own choosing, took off their shoes, and began to improvise. Two pieces, *Floor Space Stage* and *Wall Space Stage,* made from refuse found near Girouard's Chatham Square loft, became the set for *The B.Beaver Animation.*[35] This was the second "scene" in the making of the Animations.

If the Red Horse had been looking for "some form to hold me . . . some force to change me . . . some motion to carry me," the B.Beaver was becalmed, fixated on the loss of his creativity, "the art of damnation." Like *The Red Horse Animation, B.Beaver*'s narrative worked through and organized experience. This applied to both the spectator's experience in the theater and Breuer's as a writer. First drafted in 1968, this "stuttering rather schizoid dramatic monologue" broke Breuer's writer's block when he was trying to finish a novel.[36] Unable to produce more than three or four sentences a day, Breuer turned to a piece in which he could let language go. *Village Voice* writer Ross Wetzsteon captured Breuer's account in this fashion: "I sit down with all these Céline rhythms in my head—and all that American imagery—and I start writing *B Beaver Animation*. Fifty-six hours straight. It's a kinda short story, a dramatic monologue—three thousand words about this beaver who's afraid of the flow. Course it's really about me—all dammed up as a writer."[37] Earlier Breuer had read European authors, but in the late 1960s he began to turn his attention again to U.S. culture. The first version of *B.Beaver* marked the turn from working on Beckett and Brecht to original work, the objectless narrative performance drawn from the company's own culture and lives.

Begun in 1971 and "finished" in 1974, *B.Beaver* became one of the group's signature pieces. While they never cultivated a company aesthetic or style, the members of Mabou Mines always insisted that a project take the artists "someplace that you haven't been before," as Maleczech has put it, "so that your work can continue to grow.[38] They had returned to the United States hoping to create work that would sustain them artistically and financially. The events surrounding *B.Beaver* demonstrate how they made that work possible. They sought out first-rate collaborators, beginning with artists they had worked with before: Neumann, Raymond, and Gray. In 1971 Neumann returned from Rome at the urging of Breuer and Maleczech. Not only did he have the skills to play the B.Beaver, but also he was familiar with the piece, having read the original three-thousand-word manuscript in 1968. Breuer rewrote the text, adding elements from the beast fables of Franz Kafka. With *Red Horse* and *Play* beginning to tour in 1972, Mabou Mines added an early workshop version of *B.Beaver*. By this time Breuer had developed *Come and Go* with Maleczech, Akalaitis, and Gray, and Glass's *Music for Voices* had been broadcast on the non-commercial New York radio station WBAI.

But in 1973 Mabou Mines left La Mama, the same year that Glass severed his formal connection with the company and the Ford Foundation money ran out. The company needed rehearsal space in order to continue work on *B.Beaver*. It had grown from a two-man work in progress, with Neumann and Warrilow as the "head" and "tail" respectively, to a five-person show, with Akalaitis, Gray, and Maleczech joining the rehearsals. The makeshift set consisting of two orange crates was replaced with Girouard's unique arrangement of poles and boards, which could be manipulated like a puppet. Thom Cathcart and Steve Benneyworth had adapted the sculpture, while Terry O'Reilly created the machinery that allowed the set to collapse and moved the puppeteer's station into the light, thus turning the operator into a performer.[39] The cast played on, around, and under this loose construction, beginning what Neumann, the B.Beaver's primary incarnation, called "two and a half years on our backs and on our knees."[40]

When the company lost its connection to La Mama, Breuer managed to get a three-thousand-dollar NEA grant—Mabou's first as an independent company—to find alternate rehearsal space for the piece. The company's work continued to be interrupted by road tours of pieces already in the repertoire and by the need to lead workshops that often helped to pay the rent. Also they collaborated with the artist Keith Sonnier on *Send/Receive/Send,* performed twice in New York in November 1973. Breuer joined Akalaitis, Bingham, Cathcart, Gray, Maleczech, Neumann, and Warrilow as performers. Trios situated at two transmitter-receivers ten blocks apart exchanged messages on citizen's band (CB) radio, creating "synthesized stereo" for the audience, which was located at the first station (the performance space The Kitchen, then at 59 Wooster Street). Outside CB broadcasters could jam messages, "thus altering the timing and rhythm of the performance, and the nature of the dialogue."[41]

The work on *B.Beaver* competed for the company's attention with other ideas; then, as now, they generated more ideas than they could pursue. Breuer had begun in 1972 to explore what would become *The Saint and the Football Player.* Fortunately the casts of *B.Beaver* and *Saint* did not overlap; Breuer was able to draw on a growing cadre of young artists, many of them straight from college or high school. *Saint* employed several members and associates of the Memphis-based student group Eads Hill, including Steve Benneyworth, David Hardy, Ellen McElduff, Terry O'Reilly, and Dale Worsley, whom they had met on tour.

Terry O'Reilly, like Ellen McElduff, later became a member of Mabou Mines. By the time *B.Beaver* opened at Theatre for the New City in January 1974, O'Reilly had been working with Mabou Mines for over a year. While growing up in civil rights era Memphis, he had first encountered "working artists"—those "ordinary" workers plying their trades by day who are extraordinary performers by night—in two places. At nearby Mountain View, musicians would gather to play on the weekends; also as a college student O'Reilly had worked on construction crews, some of whose members were musicians. Both groups showed him, as Mabou Mines (and the Balinese puppeteers of *wayang kulit*) would also, that performance could be a fully realized, if not self-sustaining, way of life. A biology student at Rhodes College (then known as Southwestern at Memphis), O'Reilly audited courses led by Betsy Anthony and others in ballet, mime, tap, and the theory of acting at the Memphis Ballet Academy and Memphis State University (then the University of Memphis).

He had few opportunities, though, to pursue performance as a way of life until he worked informally with the group Eads Hill, which had been founded by students of Southwestern professor Ray Hill. Like Breuer's UCLA professor, Oreste F. Pucciani, Hill had introduced his students to recent absurdist plays. Unlike Pucciani, he also directed and participated in student productions. He played Hamm opposite Hardy's Clov, McElduff's Nell, and Worsley's Nagg in a production of *Endgame* directed by Mike Patton. Hill directed them in *Waiting for Godot* and witnessed their productions of *Happy Days* and *Krapp's Last Tape.* When Leon Russom, a former student of Hill then living in the New York apartment below that of Akalaitis and Glass, could not return to Memphis to do a workshop, he sent Breuer. The visit was successful, and the following spring Breuer returned with the company to perform *Red Horse* and have Neumann and Warrilow present the bare beginnings of *B.Beaver.* O'Reilly recognized a level of writing and commitment to excellence he had not experienced before, and Eads Hill was inspired to undertake its own work. Just as Mabou Mines was named for a small mining community in Nova Scotia, Eads was a small town where company members lived for a short time. They chose the name, said O'Reilly, in part because it could be seen from another local landmark, Pisgah, named for the mountain from which Moses saw the promised land.[42] Ellen Stewart sponsored performances of two Eads Hill shows in New York, *Unta-the* and *A Full Eight Hours,* which resulted in Hardy, McElduff, O'Reilly, and Worsley eventually moving to New York to work with Mabou Mines. O'Reilly went first, in 1972, and took up the role of puppeteer, manipulating the B.Beaver's marionette stage, with curtains rising and falling from its fourteen-foot batten. It was exhilarating to meet artists who felt, as he did, that performance, rather than traditional theater, held the most promise. He joined Barbara Dilley's dance company, later known as the Natural History of the American Dance, who, like Mabou Mines, worked with visual artists, and met musicians such as Richard Landry, Richard Peck, and Arthur Russell. O'Reilly became part of this scene, living with Dilley and another couple, Mary Overlie and Thom Cathcart, in a loft above 112 Greene Street. He went on to appear in many Mabou Mines productions, worked behind the scenes for others, and later became a member. In the 1970s the company primarily made use of O'Reilly's dance and movement skills, but in 1979 Neumann cast him in several parts for *Mercier and Camier,* and subsequently he had acting roles in *Dead End Kids, Wrong Guys,* and many other Mabou Mines shows. In the mid-1980s O'Reilly began developing his own projects, first a radio version of *The Bribe* (1988), then a stage version directed in 1993 by Maleczech in which O'Reilly performed with Black-Eyed Susan, a member of the Ridiculous Theatre. In 2001 Breuer directed Reilly's *Animal Magnetism.*

In *B.Beaver* O'Reilly encountered a central figure that foreshadowed Breuer's later characters John, the failed filmmaker of *A Prelude to Death in Venice,* and Porco, another self-traducing artist-hero. O'Reilly felt at home with

Breuer's tendency to lampoon his own attachments. In an interview he commented, "You find what your sacred cows are, and you barbecue them and eat them in front of everybody." In one version of *B.Beaver*'s written text, a voice, presumably Breuer's, offers this "take": "first beaver draft was written in france . I thought of it subtitled histoire d'une cunt . and tried to link this with beaver as in beaver shot . and to overlay the two on a rendering of calcified maleness . it always confused me . it never worked . it was too imposed . but it always stood for how not to get sucked in."[43] Breuer's most important "sacred cow" has long been the artist, a simultaneously heroic and debased figure at whom he pokes fun remorselessly. The irony of this self-attack was already embedded in *Red Horse* but took more complete forms in *B.Beaver* and *Shaggy Dog*. Breuer's positioning of the artist as alternately a debased, slavish animal or a guilt-ridden, equally abject master has often produced a many-sided parody figure that contains all the elements of Breuer's cultural critique. Interestingly, since the making of *Shaggy Dog* this figure has also allowed him to give voice to cultural stereotypes of women while claiming to be a feminist. In *B.Beaver*, however, Breuer had only begun to "write into" the combined metaphor of artist/woman. The B.Beaver is, like John and Porco, an artist, egotist, cultural commentator, and coward, but he is not yet the dog/woman/artist Rose of *Shaggy Dog*, who ultimately transcends her destructive emotional attachments. As a figure of "calcified maleness" the B.Beaver is all the things the artist should *not* be—the negative image that Breuer has often chosen to stand for a positive idea.

The B.Beaver treasures his identity as an artist, which is built on the ramifications of his exalted profession as an architect. At one time he took pleasure in his creativity; it produced the dam, at once his ship of state and a home for his wife and brood. With it the B.Beaver's imagination and dreams of greatness set sail. Now, however, the dam represents blockage and obstruction. The B.Beaver's identity has "calcified" into a self-absorbed, tail-thumping caricature, unable to learn or change. As a result, he thinks of himself as a personality who does not recognize himself in his reflections: "B.BEAVER IS A STUTTERER . HE'S A SMALL COMMUTER TRAIN OF SPLIT PERSONAL-ITIES ALL READING FOR HIS PART . OUT OF SYNC ."[44] The B.Beaver's stutter is not visible on the page except in the author's "takes" on his character's skewed consciousness. As with *Red Horse*, the text is printed in parallel columns, here divided between the "text" and the "takes." The takes form a commentary, as though the text were a subject of study, a scripture. But the commentary is sardonic, intensifying the reader's impression that the B.Beaver's self-knowledge, like his self, is founded on false premises. Still, he insists, I beaver away; therefore I am.

At the monologue's opening, the B.Beaver is both dammed and damned, faced with external threats mirroring the unpleasant but amusing truths of his divided self. He is beset by "moral anomalies," which he imagines as salmon swimming upstream like commandos set to destroy his dam-home-ship. In his inability to face reality, he further disguises them to himself as "tunafish" or "uncanny little fuckers." Narratively the B.Beaver is a subject cut to fit Freud's couch, where he takes a "pornographic position." He tries to replace reality with his stuttered re-creations of it, but his words take on a life of their own and return his repressed reality in exactly the disastrous form he fears. He lives fully in the hellish realm of illusion; he cannot distinguish self-perception from the perception others have of him. If the B.Beaver is a "slave of the subconscious," that subconscious is internalized from the culture that provides the oedipal elements of his dramatic monologue. Like the Red Horse's monologue, his words are directed inward. In this case, though, they are not the daydreams of youth but "mentation creaming all over itself in the name of rhetoric."[45]

If the B.Beaver fears his own subconscious tendencies below, he also fears the conscious struggle with the elements that lie above: a heavy blanket of snow covers the mountains, threatening to descend in spring torrents to destroy the evidence of his genius, the dam. Fear and a loss of confidence immobilize him. He has "sold out" as an artist, entranced by his own salesman's pitch—"THE WORLD'S FINEST BLEND OF CHOICE SILTS ORGANIC COMPOST EARTHY ALKALIS FRESH BROOK SHALE"—the artist blocked by his corrupted imagination. "TO HAVE DEDICATED THE WORK OF MY MATURER YEARS," he muses, "TO DAMMING ALL THAT CRAP UP TO PERFECTION."[46] "All that crap," of course, includes the self-aggrandizing attitudes that have come with his self-image as a seeker and speaker of Truth.

In this sense the B.Beaver is reminiscent of the stock commedia character Dottore, "the professor of dubious intelligence." Although there have been many variations, John H. Towsen describes the stock Dottore as a "pedant . . . who spoke in a pretentious mixture of Latin and Bolognese dialect and even dressed in a cap and gown. Rarely did he express an opinion of his own. His portentous pronouncements . . . were often excrutiatingly long, and were replete with such deep insights as 'whoever discusses a question says something or other.'"[47] Whether appearing as professor, physician, or judge, Dottore is always convinced of his own logic and self-importance. The B.Beaver's stuttering monologue could be seen as a Freudian extension of the character. Unable to resist the sound of his own voice, he addresses a plea for help in pompous

Latinate phrases: "EPISTOLUM RODANTUM AMPHIBIUM AD LIBRAR-
IUM LOCALUM." He is a creature who has lost touch with his calling, although he knows "it's calling." The natural world has become his enemy. He
notes, "I GO ASHORE . SPRING WITH A VENGEANCE . GRASS AND
FLOWERS . I WIPE MY FEET."[48] This is Cartesian man, the thinker and
builder descended from Adam who God instructed to name and thus take possession of all living things. Taken to its logical end, that possession has threat-
ened to destroy the natural world. The B.Beaver is a comic representation of
that position, the beast who has defined his very being as "going against the
flow" but whose ego produces only unusable mathematical formulas.

Although the B.Beaver is not an explicitly Jewish character, he prefigures
the ambiguous Jewishness of Breuer's Meyerhold in *Ecco Porco* and several
comics on whom that character is based, among them Mort Sahl and Lenny
Bruce. In the 1970s, though, Breuer did not make such connections explicit. Instead, he pointed to Céline and Kafka as modernist precursors, the latter offering a number of gently humorous beast fables. By the time of *Ecco Porco*,
Breuer has become interested in foregrounding Kafka's characters as Jewish, in
this case Joseph K of *The Trial* (1925), from whose death scene he borrows.

On the other hand, the B.Beaver's "loser psychology" is more broadly a dis-
tillation of the vices of modern Western life. Coarse, childish, horny, and glut-
tonous, the B.Beaver is much like Jarry's turd-shaped Ubu (from *Ubu Roi*,
1896). While waiting for a reply to his panicked plea, he "WHIPS OUT A COLT
FORTY FIVE" and daydreams about rebuilding his dam with reinforced concrete, a substance that he thinks will bring him success: "VITAL TO DEFENSE
. RESEARCH SUBSIDIZED . LOCAL BEAVER MAKES KILLING IN
BROOKSHORE REAL ESTATE." Like Ubu, he boasts and postures, but soon
his answer arrives in the mail: no help is forthcoming. The B.Beaver's loser
psychology is equally akin to Ubu's depressed contemporary, Uncle Vanya.
Aware of how late it is, both historically and personally, the B.Beaver struggles
with disappointment, hope, and fear, a struggle both mortal and comic, for the
fate to which he resigns himself is both created for him and also of his own
making. As in *Uncle Vanya* (1897), we see "A SPECIES IN EXTREMITIES . AT
ODDS WITH ITS ENVIRONMENT . A CLASSIC CASE . MUTATE . OR
FACE YOUR FATE," but in *B.Beaver* a cultural genetics has replaced the Dar-
winian fatalism of Chekhov's characters. "DOWN IN THE DNA," warns the
B.Beaver, "THEY'RE BURNING THE MIDNIGHT OIL."[49] The results, of
course, are similar. Although he does not look a hundred years ahead, as Astrov
does, the B.Beaver interrogates the future and gets as little reassurance; like

Vanya, he sees himself as betrayed and laments his lost promise as a "heavy-weight." Like Yelena, the B.Beaver is "too lazy to live" and waits to be rescued. His unrealistic plans for his brood resemble those of Chekhov's professor, whose self-absorption leads him to shape his reality according to his desires. Both characters propose to sacrifice the remains of that old enemy, nature, in order to continue a comfortable, unproductive, dishonest life not worth living.

The B.Beaver Animation demonstrates that such banal folly is still the stuff of the middle class—and the artist's life. In this case, however, Russian provincial life is replaced with a late capitalist form of American go-getterism in a time when

> A GIVEN SPECIES BLOWS ITS CREATIVE WAD . . . IT'S ALL OVER BUT THE SHOUTING . THIS DUDE IS A HEAVYWEIGHT . THE RAT WHO STANDS PAT WHILE THEY PLAY NEARER MY GOD TO THEE . AND THEN GOES DOWN . VERY RARE . HE IS ROMMEL RETREATING ACROSS AFRICA . HE IS VON STROHEIM SHOOTING GREED .

The B.Beaver's reference to director Erich von Stroheim returns us to the realm of film in which the Red Horse existed as "a romance of motion." The B.Beaver, like von Stroheim, never sees his grandiose projects fully realized. Greed (1924), which the director intended as a seven-hour adaptation of Frank Norris's naturalist novel McTeague (1899), was whittled down to two and a half hours at the order of von Stroheim's nemesis, producer Irving Thalberg. Having acquired a reputation for inflexibility and excess, von Stroheim turned from directing to a successful acting career, even playing a caricature of himself in Sunset Boulevard (1950). As the cinematic narrative of life falls apart around the B.Beaver, he also makes a transition into the final role of Bowery bum, bitter and alone. "EAT YOUR HEART OUT DIMITRI TIOMKIN," says Neumann in the B.Beaver's final "take."[50] Like a lush Tiomkin film score, the animating rhythms of his language have heightened the piece's cinematic continuity, creating the narrative illusion of the B.Beaver's "soul."

Working with "Spiritual Materialism": B.Beaver Continued

The problem is flow. don't you know . . .
    —LEE BREUER, HAJJ

Just as The B.Beaver Animation articulated themes important for both Breuer and Mabou Mines, the work process on the show from 1972 to 1979 saw the company out of its early years and into a sometimes painful period of change.[51] As the number of available associates swelled, the dimensions of Mabou Mines' shows seemed to grow as well. *B.Beaver* appeared in February 1974 as part of "A Valentine for Marcel Duchamp" at the Museum of Modern Art, but work was already beginning on what would become the epic-length *Shaggy Dog Animation.* That fall Raymond moved to New York, taking over Gray's role in *B.Beaver.* McElduff arrived a month later and succeeded Gray in *Come and Go. B.Beaver* went into another incarnation, this time as a three-man, two-woman production.

B.Beaver's staging made plain what the text suggested, that the B.Beaver does not lose his soul for in fact he does not have one. By means of "2 × 4 deconstruction,"[52] Mabou demonstrated, long before the appearance of such postmodern figures as the title character of the independent film *Being John Malkovich* (1999), the ways in which the B.Beaver is animated variously by his illusions of self. Everyone and everything onstage represented a legitimate "take" on the B.Beaver. His narrative dissolution, like that of the Red Horse, is not fully realized until "curtains!" becomes both "the end" of our animated hero and the final, literal collapse of the curtains that have made up the set.[53] The actors' takes on the B.Beaver were particularly important for the ways in which they employed gesture, facial expression, and intonation to physicalize his "breakdown." This gestural "switch imagery" gave clues to understanding Breuer's cartoon narrative but also created multiple, interlocking layers of stage business, which (as in *Red Horse*) put the narrative in the background.[54] Neumann was the B.Beaver's primary voice and image, while the four-performer chorus served as both the B.Beaver's family and the crew of his ship and also his repressed selves, extensions of his psychic trauma, and madcap images from his hallucinated environment. Reviewer Erika Munk saw them as

> bizarre aspects of various worlds that impinge on B.Beaver's: David Warrilow is a rat-faced decadent in brocade dressing gown; JoAnne Akalaitis, gravel-voiced-sexy like a '40s movie star, disconcertingly wears white-framed glasses with one lens clear, one dark; Ruth Maleczech is all garlanded false innocence; Bill Raymond, the man with the independent toes, does Viennese accents and psychotic stares.[55]

Each costume and set of behaviors was distinctive. In working through the text, the bathrobe-clad performers had added their own "bits," making the narrative a dense texture of images and allusions unfolding around the stammering Neumann. Once again Mabou Mines had tapped into performance as a self-conscious representation or rehearsal of events, denaturalizing them, as comedy has often done, to become a "generating environment" for "cognitive action."[56]

B.Beaver was an intimate but not autobiographical piece; as Neumann commented, the actors used their heads and their lives about it.[57] When Gray left, Raymond had to retool her part in order to maintain the idiom. Gray's "Cuban thing" became in a few weeks an "Indian thing," that is, an accent and costume (including an Indian loincloth or *dhoti*) added to gestures Raymond copied from a neighbor.[58] Basing her role on her high school experience as a cheerleader, Maleczech created a doll-like person who had never grown up.[59] The company was not concerned with autobiographical realism. The performers' flights of fancy were grounded in the projection of the B.Beaver's emotional reality provided by Neumann's performance. In an interview, Neumann said that he had joined Mabou Mines in order to shape a piece's rapport with the audience so that, in the careful blend of motivational, Brechtian, and Grotowskian performance techniques, the result would not overreach by being too abstract.[60] Of all the members Neumann has the most extensive background in what could be called traditional theater, particularly American realism. His performance in *B.Beaver* clearly combined an accessible psychological veracity and depth of motivation with other influences such as the gift of oneself that Grotowski asked of the actor and the epic theater actor's ability to hold his or her character at arm's length. In the 1973 performance taped at the Walker Arts Center in Minneapolis, Neumann shouted his lines in a rough, singsong litany as he seemed to grovel in front of the audience.

WOULD YOU BE SO KIND AS TO SEND ME WHAT YOU HAVE ON FRESHWATER DAMNATION . SOMETHING IN THE DO IT YOURSELF SERIES WOULD BE MOST HELPFUL . MATERIAL ESTIMATES . ANYTHING TECHNICAL ON STRESSES . BLUEPRINTS . NOT TO NEGLECT PURE THEORY . MARGINALIA . ESOTERICA . THE RELATED SCIENCES . CLAUSEWITZ ON BARRICADES . IN SHORT . THE WORKS . ON THE SUBJECT.[61]

The B.Beaver is totally debased in his plea for assistance with what should "come naturally," the protection of self and family. Neumann, appearing disheveled and soft, allowed his robe to lay limply on his bare chest, not so much playing a character as evoking the prolonged lassitude and self-doubt of the "blocked" artist. Although *B.Beaver,* like the other Animations, generally avoided a direct emotional connection between stage images and meaning, Breuer was committed to "find[ing] a way to make *acting* as sophisticated a statement as non-acting."[62] Similarly, Neumann has talked about his efforts to encourage a distinctly American vitality in *B.Beaver,* an intimate verbal energy related to the "speech from the heart" that Neumann finds in the work of Tennessee Williams.[63]

At the same time, *B.Beaver* relied on stylistic discontinuities, oppositions, and magical transformations, in fact making them a focus of the work. Neumann's performance, while emotionally grounded, was still extreme. Like the beaver chorus, Neumann switched tones and postures frequently. The stage was cluttered with the tools of B.Beaver's trade—hammer, saw, pipes, sheet metal, bucket, and drill—which metamorphosed into evocative elements of his psychic universe. The saw, for example, played as a musical instrument, also became a threatening element in Akalaitis's "trout dance": "A TROUT," the B.Beaver cries in panic. "GREAT SCOT . I SAY . MAD MEAT EATING TROUT . I BREAK THE SURFACE IN A SINGLE BOUND."[64] Earlier, while the B.Beaver waited for a reply from his local library, the sun "rose" and "set" several times, as Warrilow swung a lighted globe around his head. The globe reappeared later, in a very different guise, as the eye of the B.Beaver's "missus," into which his one tear falls. When "the missus" tries to end it all by leaping headfirst into the pool, she succeeds only in lodging herself in the muddy bottom. While this scene, like others, was narrated, not staged, Maleczech's feet, visible in the B.Beaver's bucket, evoked her comic fate.

Probably the most striking transformation was the thirty-second "tai chi sequence" during which Neumann's robe was animated Bunraku style by being held up on sticks. The actors had studied tai chi with Herman Kauz during *B.Beaver*'s development. Akalaitis has noted that her saw dance was derived from work she had done with tai chi teacher Steve Katz in Nova Scotia as well as Kauz. Standing movement often invoked the low center of gravity and slow, balanced extension of the legs and arms sought in the one-person form.[65] To animate the robe, Maleczech has said, the performers adapted ideas from the two-person "pushing hands" mode by lying on their backs and passing the sticks from one to the other, making the robe float, walk, twist, and gesture. They maintained a rhythmic constancy that made it possible to relay the sticks without visible cues, as though creating a kind of joint consciousness.[66] In the "pushing hands" sequence of "adhere, join, stick to, and follow," *joining* means

to "forget the self and follow the other," ego psychology reconceived and enacted as yin and yang.[67] In a sense, each performer became part of the process
of animation, neither effacing nor underscoring his or her individuality.

Although this sequence constituted the company's first use of puppetry, it
drew on work that Akalaitis, Breuer, Maleczech, and Raymond had been doing
for fifteen years, initially in San Francisco, Raymond's hometown. He met
Breuer and Maleczech there and, as mentioned earlier, participated in "The
Eleventh Hour" series at the Encore Theatre. With the R. G. Davis Mime
Troupe, Raymond did, among other things, Decroux's technique of isolations,
dance classes, the commedia *The Dowry* (with Carlo Mazzone-Clementi and
others), and a piece called "Ball" in which Raymond and Ron Poindexter
moved a ball between them without using their hands. In Lawrence Ferlinghetti's comic *Allegation,* directed by Breuer, Raymond donned an alligator
suit. He worked backstage at the San Francisco Actor's Workshop on serious
fare such as Beckett's *Endgame* (a play he returned to in 1980 in the role of Clov
in a production originally directed by Joseph Chaikin).[68] After appearing for
several years in Actor's Workshop productions and at the San Francisco Tape
Music Center, in 1964 Raymond moved to Los Angeles, where he lived in
Topanga Canyon, in the Santa Monica Mountains, and appeared in film and
television roles. After several years delivering milk to the artists, musicians,
flower people, and political extremists of Topanga Canyon, where he started a
weekly newspaper and broadcast local news from an abandoned trailer, he directed *Waiting for Godot* and *Play* in the early 1970s. In 1974 he went to New
York with Breuer and Maleczech and joined Mabou Mines, replacing Dawn
Gray on *B.Beaver* and *Shaggy Dog.* Raymond adapted quickly to the New York
art scene, embracing the "tough and sweet" way people thought. He played the
"screamer" in *The Lost Ones,* participated in ensemble work in Akalaitis's productions of *Dressed Like an Egg* and Beckett's radio play *Cascando,* and had a
principal role in Neumann's staging of *Mercier and Camier.* Besides stage
work, Raymond directed and/or performed in Mabou Mines radio shows such
as *Easy Daisy, The Keeper Series,* and *The Joey Schmerda Story* done in the early
1980s. These radio productions harked back to early sound work the company
had done in Paris and elsewhere. Involved in many Mabou Mines productions,
Raymond is probably best known for his work in *A Prelude to Death in Venice,*
in which he provided the voice for and manipulated the puppet representing
John, and for developing, with Dale Worsley, the antiwar "opera" *Cold Harbor,*[69] in which he played the effigy of General Ulysses S. Grant, who comes to
life and ruminates on war from his museum display case. While touring in

Cold Harbor from 1983 to 1988, Raymond directed *Flow My Tears, the Police-man Said,* adapted from the Philip K. Dick novel by Mabou Mines associate Linda Hartinian. Since leaving Mabou Mines in 1990, Raymond has continued to appear onstage, in films such as *Michael Clayton* (2007) and the television series *The Wire.* Yet he commented in 1992, "The time I've worked with Mabou Mines . . . was absolutely the best and the most creative and the most consciousness expanding."

In important ways, the work the members of Mabou Mines did on the first two Animations, as well as the early Beckett pieces, developed their choral performance skills. While working at the Tape Music Center in San Francisco, Akalaitis, Maleczech, and Raymond had done a fifteen-minute piece directed by Breuer called *Emotional Composition for Actors* (or perhaps *An Event for Actors*) with Susan Darby and possibly Bere Boynton. It involved the simultaneous cueing of emotional states among the four performers, a difficult task they were never able to re-create to their satisfaction even after Raymond was reunited with Breuer, Akalaitis, and Maleczech in the 1970s. Maleczech described the challenge this way.

> The idea was that without language we would do a series of emotional responses. It was a funny little piece because we sat in these different kinds of chairs—straight-back chair, rocking chair—in a line facing the audience. Sometimes emotional responses were supposed to be sequential, like somebody at stage left side of the line would start to laugh, smile, or whatever, and it would be picked up by the next person. . . . It took a different form in each person, so you could respond in very individual ways. . . . We knew the order, but you could respond in your own way. You didn't have to repeat the same kind of response each time. It was sort of like seeing a round. [As in *Play*] we had to start and stop on a dime. And it was mysterious when things would start. We hadn't figured out something as simple as breath cue—you had to feel out when the other people were going to start. You had to sense it.[70]

Without demanding the same kind of split-second cueing, the work on *B.Beaver* invoked a similar, syncopated inventiveness. Unlike *Play,* however, in which the spotlight's abrupt shifts from face to face compelled the actors' voices, the slide changes in *B.Beaver* did not cue the actors. It might have seemed so to the audience, which could see both the live motion and the colors and patterns projected over it. At the curtain call, both actors and slides would quickly recap the show—backward.[71]

Despite the complexity of the show's concept and the intricacy of the ensemble's interaction, *The B.Beaver Animation* was not a complicated production to tour. Once Raymond's contributions were integrated, the piece was
perfect for touring, with a simple set, limited props, and no score. In fact,
B.Beaver was designated a pilot project for a National Endowment for the Arts
touring program. Mabou Mines was required to hold public workshops wher-
ever it performed in order to gauge the need for a larger program designed to
circulate "experimental" theater around the United States. The performers'
participation in this pilot project reflected both their growing name recognition and avant-garde artists' hopes of obtaining support from the NEA and
other relatively new granting agencies. Breuer commented prophetically,
"We're really not performing for ourselves so much as for every experimental
theatre group in the United States. Because [touring] is the way they're going
to live."[72] Thus, a battery of four slide projectors was perhaps the most complicated technical element in *B.Beaver* according to L. B. Dallas. The projectors
superimposed changing "frames" of patterned color around and on the action,
evoking, as the use of color had in *Red Horse,* the flow of frames that create a
film image. Quick changes of scene and timing suggested the abrupt cuts and
simulated "camera movements" of cartoons.

Another form of discontinuity created by simple means was the actors'
physical comedy, drawn from the commedia dell'arte tradition, particularly as
it evolved into slapstick, circus clowning, vaudeville stand-up routines, and
silent-film comedy. In 1962 Raymond and Maleczech had played Pantalone
and Franchescina, respectively, in the San Francisco Mime Troupe production
of *The Dowry.*[73] Carlo Mazzone-Clementi, who had appeared as Brighella with
the touring Piccolo Teatro of Milan, stayed in San Francisco to work on commedia with the Mime Troupe and later went on to found several U.S. programs
based on his techniques. Comic oppositions of negative and positive, in which
one character or situation goes against the flow of another, are central to
Mabou Mines' work according to Maleczech.[74] Negativity taken to an extreme
is funny; in nineteenth-century circus clowning, the red-nosed clown, or *au-
guste,* would be set up as a straight man only to be knocked down by the white-
faced clown, a descendant of "first-banana" Pierrot. The dominance of the
scheming rogue was never secure. As the red-nosed stooge—"he who gets
slapped"—became the crowd favorite, he might make use of his own "slapstick" on the white-faced, elegant Pierrot and end up displacing him as trick-
ster.[75] While this type of clowning did not appear as such in *B.Beaver* (although it did later in Neumann's *Mercier and Camier*), elements were visible in

the chorus's exaggerated body stances and the extreme facial expressions, which became masks through which the actors spoke. Staging elements became "actors" participating in the narrative flow or working in opposition to it. At moments the set took on the B.Beaver's emotions. Mask and line often spoke "against" one another, leaving resolution of the opposition or discontinuity to the audience.

Shaping a "generating environment" for "cognitive action," as Sayre has called this type of work, also highlighted the company's artistic choices. Mabou Mines associate John Howell, who was involved with *The Saint and the Football Player*, was familiar with the Animations' work process. In 1974 he wrote that "the references that guide the actor are often visual images from physical arrangements."

> These may be shapes or movements that are literal (galloping horses, waddling beavers) or . . . relate to general states (joy, disaster, entropy). They may be gags or puns, (the horse dumps its load, the beaver terrified by a meat-eating trout) or derived from certain styles (Muybridge photographs, belly dancing). Initially, the choices of physical images and ordering are arbitrary: a situation is suggested and established[,] then possibilities of gesture, movement, and speech are explored. These choices are constantly transformed by director and performers alike. Their final shape, inclusion, and placement within the piece depend on a consensus of company opinion.[76]

Howell attributes the work's unity to this aesthetic "consensus," which makes the intuitively chosen shapes or movements into a set of images coordinated by the company's "open and personal approach." Performance reveals these choices to be "right" or "inadequate," leading to further choices by individual performers, who contribute not only "specific and elaborate tasks" but "an individualized, intangible output." The animation, Howell concludes, begins at that point to take on a life of its own. In focusing attention on the collaborative work that produced *B.Beaver*, Howell has captured the intertwining of group and individual and conscious and unconscious choices that characterized the company's creative process.

When it took on a life of its own, *The B.Beaver Animation* became magical. In a sense, the entire set was a puppet manipulated by a performer puppeteer who sat in full view of the audience. O'Reilly, who operated the set in some performances, describes it as "a very elaborate marionette" that demonstrated "the machinery of the working of the theater."[77] Curtains rose and fell, changed from backdrop to the sails of a ship, or waved wildly as the set itself took on the B.Beaver's emotional "load." In the midst of the B.Beaver's panic attack, the entire set sprang to life, then collapsed, thought perishing with the thinker. In the 1976 published version, the "take" on this moment reads, "the piece 'the b. beaver animation' reacts to 'the thought—perish' by dropping its load . (of two-by-fours in this case) . and flailing its curtains . if this were a comic frame 'yikes!' would be block-lettered right across it . . . nobody says it . the piece itself thinks it."[78] By displaying violent, forceful emotion across the "frame" of the puppet-set, Mabou Mines took the audience's attention away from the artist-ego, here most closely embodied by Neumann, and redirected it to the demonstration of creativity itself.

As in *Red Horse,* this dense texture of allusions to creativity was difficult for some spectators to "read" on a single viewing. In fact, as with other pieces Breuer has directed, *B.Beaver* was built as though audiences knew its story and characters. Its complex use of comic negativity—the "yikes" that leaped out of the frame—emerged from the company's focus on the work as process rather than as production. The audience could grasp and appreciate the show without understanding all the elements, while the artists knew and were sustained by the work that had produced those elements. This deflection of focus from self to the work has become even more relevant in a time of intense commercialization and commodification. Philip Glass has noted:

> When you begin to see yourself not as the center but as part of the general process, you see things from a less self-centered point of view. [The latter view] causes all the trouble: "Why isn't my name biggest on the poster? Why isn't my dressing room the biggest? Where's my limo?" If you're totally in the misery of self-absorption, there's no way you can be free to see things more objectively.[79]

A related danger for avant-gardists, notes Maleczech, is an arrogance generated not by an obsession with success but by a fetishizing of the artist's marginality.[80] B.Beaver embodied this type of "loser psychology" as well: the elitism of the artist who sees his or her creativity as self-generated, the product of a refined aesthetic sense, whether one calls it genius or the soul. The traditional avant-gardist takes a "heroic" stance in the face of overwhelming opposition, thus producing himself or herself as the other face of the mainstream artist's preoccupation with fame and acceptance. Performing *B.Beaver* was, in a sense, the humorous enactment of that arrogance, that negativity. It makes of the B.Beaver what I have called elsewhere an "abject idealist."[81]

In a 1991 article Breuer casts the avant-garde artist as a "two-handed gun" roaming the halls of government, blazing away at the agencies that emerged from President Lyndon Johnson's Great Society. Seeing the artist who takes "state support" as complicit in the evisceration of the avant-garde, Breuer turns from the image of a gunfighter gone postal to that of a domesticated dog that bites the hand that feeds it.

> An understanding of dogs is a prerequisite for the understanding of the American artistic sensibility. A dog bites the hand that feeds it. Why? Because the hand that feeds it looks like the one that whips it—and being a lazy dog, it bites the nearest hand it can get its teeth into. Why? . . . Because a dog is a domesticated animal, with the pent-up rage of the wolf that sold out and came in from the snow—a rage of self-hatred. Because the hand of the master that once saved its skin now lies upon its impotent soul.[82]

Breuer has come to believe that since the company's first NEA grant it has participated in a larger cultural agenda to domesticate the avant-garde. The agency-funded tour of *B.Beaver* was the first of many for Mabou Mines and its associates. More broadly, the regional arts alliances that grew up in the late 1970s and early 1980s joined with federal and private agencies to support the tours of Mabou Mines, Meredith Monk, Philip Glass, Ping Chong, Spalding Gray, Laurie Anderson, and many others to medium-sized U.S. cities. Only the avant-gardists willing to play the game, however, have become part of this fairly select cadre. Breuer concludes, "Buddy Holly will rise from the grave singing 'That'll Be the Day'—'the day' the Institutional Radio Choir or Moods Pan Grove get an Endowment grant."

Breuer's later, more politicized outlook on the U.S. avant-garde has its roots in the B.Beaver's loser psychology. During the work on *B.Beaver,* the company members read books by Chögyam Trungpa, which furthered their thinking on the uses of negativity. Trungpa and others have passed the ideas of Tibetan Buddhism to many artists, among them Glass, who has studied with Lama Gelek Rinpoche. Without embracing Buddhist beliefs as a company, *B.Beaver* seemed to suggest that the artist should seek a way out of individual ego and cultivate openness to influences and change. (Breuer later wrote *Sister Suzie Cinema* (1980), his "invocation to the Muse," along these lines.) Buddhism, says musician and composer Laurie Anderson, appeals to artists for its encouragement of independent thinking and questioning of authority,[83] the very terms of the B.Beaver's dilemma. He, however, cannot see beyond his ego's struggle to find himself through manipulation of—and by—the physical world. His struggle turns out to be what Trungpa calls a false heroism of the ego.[84] The harder he struggles against the flow, the deeper he sinks. Trungpa calls this state "spiritual materialism," a malady common in the United States. It never occurs to the B.Beaver that the key lies beyond the ego in replacing self-criticism with self-examination and compassion—"clarity containing fundamental warmth"—or, as noted earlier, in the "forgetting of self and following the other." But the B.Beaver has no ability to sense an other much less to learn from one. In the competitive framework of spiritual materialism, the B.Beaver has engineered his loss once again. Back to the dam, the drawing board, the multiple beaver reflections beavering away at the "stuttering schizoid monologue." No matter how many figures appear onstage, the B.Beaver is singular, locked into the cycles of desire and disappointment created by self-deception. Mabou Mines diagnosed his illness with compassionate humor.

The influence of Buddhist ideas, while certainly relevant to *B.Beaver*, emerges fully in Breuer's work only in the third Animation, *Shaggy Dog*. Here the artist Rose comes to understand that she is living in one of the six realms of existence, which Trungpa calls the "dream worlds we create for ourselves." In *Shaggy Dog* the artist struggles to escape the illusion of desire and become part of a larger concept of self developed through a friendship with a spiritual teacher. Breuer has never adopted Buddhism as a way of life, but, using its framework as an extended metaphor, he describes Rose as a "conditioned romantic" who must go through an archetypal trial in order to leave the unenlightened life and proceed to the next cultural/evolutionary step.[85] Unlike the B.Beaver, who seeks without understanding the object of his search, Rose recognizes and comments on her entrapment. No spiritual friend emerges in *Shaggy Dog;* the characters in Rose's universe, particularly John Greed, the object of her desire, are also living the "unenlightened life." *The Shaggy Dog Animation,* however, positions Rose to take the next step, which she does with the help of her rival, Leslie, in *An Epidog,* renamed SueLee in Breuer's more complete narrative version, *La Divina Caricatura: A Fiction* (2002). It should be noted, though, that Breuer has found it more difficult in recent years to separate his characters from the late capitalist world of spiritual materialism, which, like Roland Barthes's sticky *doxa,* clings to all creatures it has touched.[86] At its end, *Caricatura* circles back into appendixes, afterwords, and outtakes—all of which seem to trap Rose in the hellish realm of her life even as she passes to a supposedly better one.

Just as *The B.Beaver Animation* put into question the unthinking autoreference of spiritual materialism, company members began to find their own voices and use them more assertively in their work. On the one hand, the notion of choral narrative was becoming a way of life. On the other, Breuer complained in an interview that the collaborative creation of the performers' individual bits had ultimately undermined the piece: "Because we worked it over so much, and had so many high-powered, complicated actors who had so much wonderful stuff, ultimately the narration was overpowered."[87] The experience convinced him that he needed to have authority over his text, setting the stage for the struggles the company experienced over *The Shaggy Dog Animation*. Only in the 1979 video version, said Breuer, did *The B.Beaver Animation*'s autoreferential narrative reemerge. Produced by Breuer and Neumann with Chris Coughlin and Craig Jones under the name Young Filmmakers Video Arts, the video had music by Bob Telson, who had linked up with Breuer to write "Dyin' to Be Dancin'" for *A Prelude to Death in Venice*. This solo version narrowed the B.Beaver's identity to Neumann's single voice and form. As he spoke, the camera broke up his body into parts; without chorus or set, however, the monologue became more direct and confessional. As Neumann spoke the lines, Breuer and his collaborators used a variety of camera techniques to distance character from actor.

Breuer had continued to tinker with the script for *B.Beaver* as it was published, first in *Big Deal 4* (1976) and then in the volume *Animations* (1979). Revived at the Public Theater in 1990 as part of Mabou Mines' twenty-year celebration, *B.Beaver* was in a sense the "2 × 4 deconstruction" of the original production, a collage of nostalgia and self-parody. Neumann, who reprised his role as narrator, described this version as "a farcical kind of workout" and "kaleidoscopic," less concerned with the B.Beaver's emotional realism.[88] The original "low-tech" set, adapted by Marcia Altieri, and Gabriel Berry's motley costumes seemed to evoke a 1970s downtown atmosphere, but, recognizing perhaps that a new staging required new elements, Breuer added an orchestra (drum, electronic sax, and theremin), which performed a wild, Keystone Kops–style score by Jimmy Harry and Steve Peabody. Maleczech, Fergusson, O'Reilly, and Mehrten made up the chorus with younger associates David Neumann and Clove Galilee. O'Reilly did Akalaitis's trout dance; David Neumann did his father's leap. While the show received favorable notices for its ensemble work, it was clearly a revival worked up in several weeks. Given the general spread of postmodern and poststructuralist discourses in the 1980s, audiences were quicker to understand Breuer's "fusion of irony and lyricism, distancing and emotion, classical consciousness and pop sensibility, media allusions and archetypal imagery, spiritual yearnings and technological razzmatazz."[89]

In focusing on the first two Animations, this chapter has dealt with both the company's development and that of Lee Breuer. Breuer underwent a crisis in his artistic life during the years between directing *The Lost Ones* and receiving the 1978 Obie for Best Play for *Shaggy Dog*. In this sense, the staging of the Animations is the story of Breuer's emergence as a mature writer-director. Although he sees himself primarily as a writer, it seems clear that the potential of his writing manifests itself fully only when it is staged, when his outrageous spirals of metaphor are realized and released, in a sense, by the collaborative process. In production they are literalized, with Breuer and his fellow artists finding stage corollaries that project them forcefully to an audience. When Breuer turned to U.S. mass culture for his metaphors, particularly film and popular music, he found a way to define himself as a writer and director, embrace his culture, and yet remain distinctly avant-gardist. The *Red Horse* and *B.Beaver* Animations, prime examples of early 1970s, low-tech artistic collaboration, had led to and yet were distinctly different from *Shaggy Dog*. What followed was, in a sense, a new beginning in the company's history.

Conclusion

After the "private" scene of *Red Horse* and the "public" scene of *B.Beaver*, perhaps it is appropriate to sketch the third scene of the Animations' "making." It took place at the Public Theater, site of the work on both *The Shaggy Dog Animation* and Akalaitis's *Dressed Like an Egg*. The "interspace" of the Old Prop Shop, wedged between two floors of this former library building, was the site of scenes of gendered argument that changed Mabou Mines into a company of directors. Dedicated to one another, the group—particularly the founding members—were finding it increasingly difficult to work together. Although they have spoken little of these difficulties, it is clear that certain genies had escaped their bottles and were not about to return. Performers were finding their own visions, gaining confidence as everyone contributed to the work. Akalaitis, Breuer, Glass, Maleczech, Neumann, and Warrilow had worked together for more than ten years, a lengthy stretch for collaborators who saw themselves as self-employed. And there were growing gender-based conflicts. Much of the fighting and making up apparently focused not just on the work but on how day care was to be handled, how Maleczech and Akalaitis were managing the group's money, and who did the day-to-day tasks that kept the company running. Clearly a storm was coming in the mid-1970s, but *B.Beaver* was up and running before it broke.

At the same time, Mabou Mines was moving from gallery spaces to "legitimate" downtown theaters. While *The B.Beaver Animation* was never a "play" and had taken shape in unconventional spaces, in April 1977 it was performed at the Public Theater. In 1976 Mabou Mines had joined the mainstream theater world by beginning its association with the New York Shakespeare Festival, which the members did hesitantly, afraid of "selling out." They knew the benefits of affiliating with a producing organization—they had enjoyed that support with La Mama—but they also wanted to work for themselves and fully expected to lead the sort of touring existence Breuer had sketched out in 1974. Joe Papp, however, offered them an irresistible arrangement; while remaining independent, the company could rehearse and perform in Public Theater facilities and make use of the costume and scene shops. It was a viable "touring" arrangement, the "set" of the third and final scene in the film strip of the Animations and their making.

But before I turn (in chapter 4) to the last Animation—the first effort in what has become Breuer's all-encompassing narrative, *La Divina Caricatura*—I address the company's first broad public recognition in 1975. The evening of Samuel Beckett pieces, particularly the success of *The Lost Ones,* shaped its reputation irrevocably and happily. Not only did this production spark the arrangement with Papp, but the company's name was permanently linked with Beckett's. From time to time, neither the group nor the author was entirely sanguine about this linkage. Familiar with Beckett's work from their days in San Francisco and Paris, the company staged his smaller-scale plays and narratives when more tempting titles (such as Genet's *The Screens*) were out of financial reach. But later it took on more complex adaptations. Mabou Mines have been important interpreters of Beckett, and his work in turn has served them well. The company followed *The Lost Ones* with celebrated pieces directed by Akalaitis, Maleczech, and Neumann. In 1985, as an independent director, Akalaitis staged a controversial *Endgame.* In 1998 Maleczech was directed in *Happy Days* by Robert Woodruff. But the early productions were key; *Play, The Lost Ones,* and *Come and Go* provided excellent material for testing the company's ideas about the actor as a creator in his or her own right, equal to the writer. By empowering the actor in this fashion, the Beckett pieces set the stage for the discussions of the later 1970s in which Breuer's growing desire to retain control of his narratives ran counter to the actors' desires to build on what they had learned together. Those who were open to directing began to develop their own projects, while those who preferred to remain performers left the company sooner or later.

As the director of the three Beckett pieces that brought Mabou Mines to Papp's attention, Breuer was completing, in a sense, his love affair with absurdism and existentialism. Henceforth he would live and write in a postabsurdist, postmodern vein. Already, *Red Horse* had intimated that, as a kind of cultural effect, the figure must create itself in order to experience any kind of stable identity. Similarly, the character B.Beaver is composed of borrowed identities. Each, as the reviewer Arthur Sainer pointed out, involves "those moments when the sense of connection to one's own species begins to break down and one finds oneself tunneling into passages where the structures of other life forms become confused with one's own, where nervous systems begin to make extraordinary interchanges." It could be argued that this urge "to rearrange self, to ingest self, to make some new relationship between various layers of self and also between self and cosmos" had already begun with the absurdists.[90] In *Play, Come and Go,* and *The Lost Ones,* Mabou Mines gave a definitive account of that foundation.

Mabou Mines Lear, rehearsal of act 1, scene 1 (Atlanta, 1987). *Clockwise from bottom center:* Ruth Maleczech, Bill Raymond, Karen Kandel, Pauline Oliveros, and Ron Vawter. (Photo by Paul Ryan.)

Founding members of Mabou Mines on Cape Breton Island, Nova Scotia, (1970). *Clockwise from top:* Lee Breuer, Philip Glass, JoAnne Akalaitis, David Warrilow, and Ruth Maleczech. (Photo © Roberta Neiman.)

The Red Horse Animation set and actors. *From top:* JoAnne Akalaitis, Ruth Maleczech, and David Warrilow. (Photo by Amnon Ben Nomis, courtesy of the La Mama E.T.C. Archive.)

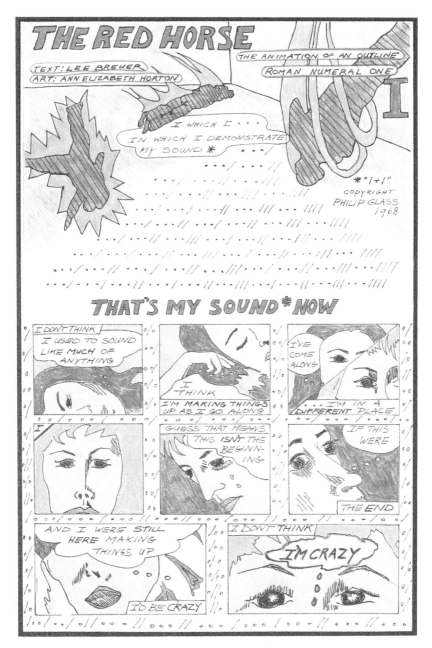

The Red Horse Animation, animated version, © Lee Breuer and Ann Elizabeth Horton, artist. "1+1" by Philip Glass © 1968 Dunvagen Music Publishers Inc. Used by permission. (From Bonnie Marranca, ed., *Theatre of Images* [New York: Drama Book Specialists, 1977].)

The B.Beaver Animation. The company works on Tina Girouard's sculpture "Floor Space Stage" at 112 Greene Street. (Photo © Tina Girouard, courtesy of The Fales Library and Special Collections, New York University, Mabou Mines Archive, Series VI, A, Box 25, Folder 1047.)

FACING PAGE: *The B.Beaver Animation. From left:* David Warrilow, Frederick Neumann, Dawn Gray, Ruth Maleczech, and JoAnne Akalaitis. (Photo by Tom Berthiaume.)

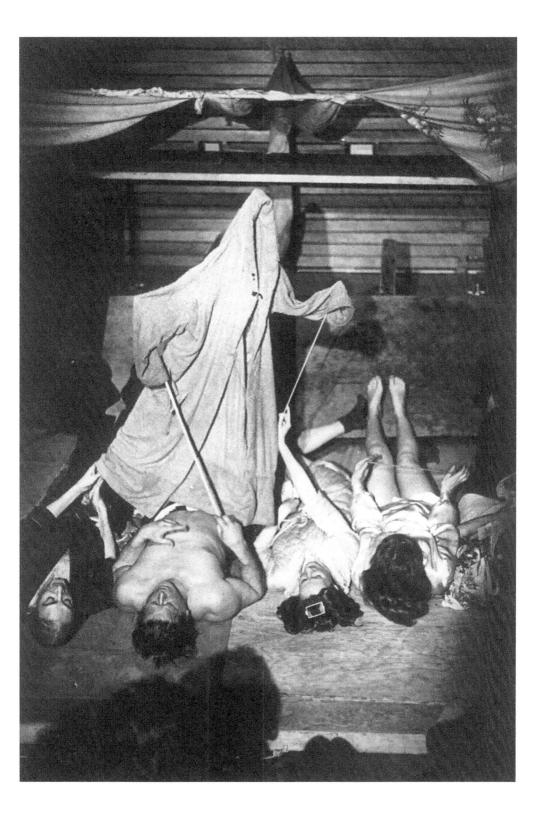

The B.Beaver Animation. JoAnne
Akalaitis. (Photo by Bill Davis.)

The B.Beaver Animation. From left:
David Warrilow, Frederick Neumann,
Dawn Gray, Ruth Maleczech, and
JoAnne Akalaitis. (Photo by Tom
Berthiaume.)

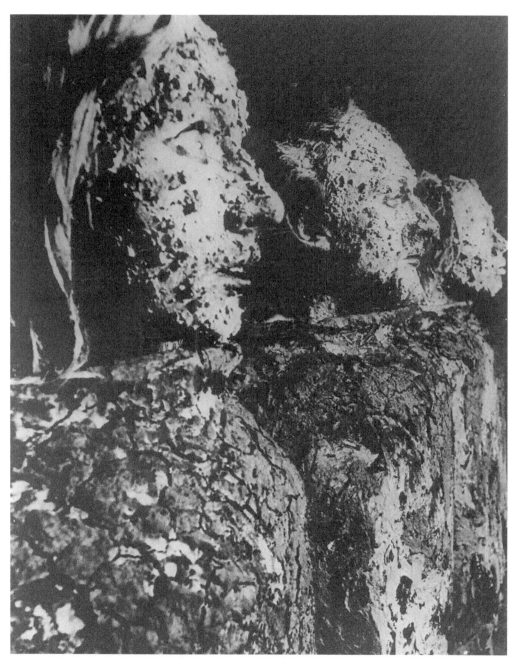

Play. From left: JoAnne Akalaitis, David Warrilow, and Ruth Maleczech. (Photo by Tony Kent.)

Come and Go. From left: Ellen McElduff, Ruth Maleczech, and JoAnne Akalaitis. (Photo by Amnon Ben Nomis, courtesy of the La Mama E.T.C. Archive.)

The Lost Ones. David Warrilow in cylinder. (Photo © Richard Landry.)

Cascando. Clockwise from left: Frederick Neumann, David Warrilow, Arthur Russell (in corner), Ellen McElduff, Bill Raymond, David Hardy (with pencil), and Thom Cathcart. (Photo by Robin Thomas.)

The Saint and the Football Player. Clove Galilee and cast members. (Photo by Peter Moore © Estate of Peter Moore/VAGA, New York, NY, courtesy of The Fales Library and Special Collections, New York University, Mabou Mines Archive, Series IV, A, Box 28, Folder 1135.)

Mabou Mines Lear. From left: Karen Kandel (Edna, as Mad Marie Laveau), Ruth Maleczech (Lear), and Greg Mehrten (The Fool). (Photo by Beatriz Schiller © 2010.)

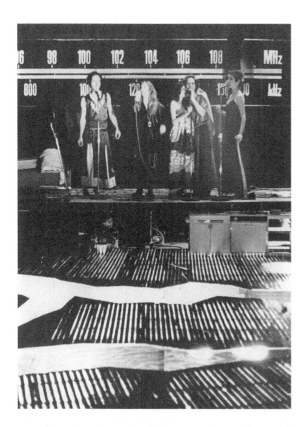

The Shaggy Dog Animation. From left:
Bill Raymond, Ruth Maleczech, Linda
Hartinian (Wolfe), Terry O'Reilly, and
JoAnne Akalaitis. (Photo © Johan Elbers,
2010.)

The Shaggy Dog Animation. From left:
Clove Galilee, Linda Hartinian (Wolfe),
and JoAnne Akalaitis (with Rose puppet).
(Photo © Johan Elbers, 2010.)

A Prelude to Death in Venice. Bill Raymond with the John puppet. (Photo © Carol Rosegg.)

Dressed Like an Egg. Clockwise from left: Ellen McElduff, David Warrilow, JoAnne Akalaitis (wearing celastic dress), and Ruth Maleczech (on floor). (Photo © Richard Landry, 1977.)

Dressed Like an Egg. From left: Ruth Maleczech, Bill Raymond, and JoAnne Akalaitis. (Photo © Richard Landry, 1977.)

Dressed Like an Egg. From left: Bill Raymond and Ellen McElduff. (Photo © Richard Landry, 1977.)

Mercier and Camier. From left: Bill Raymond and Frederick Neumann. (Photo © Bill Longcore.)

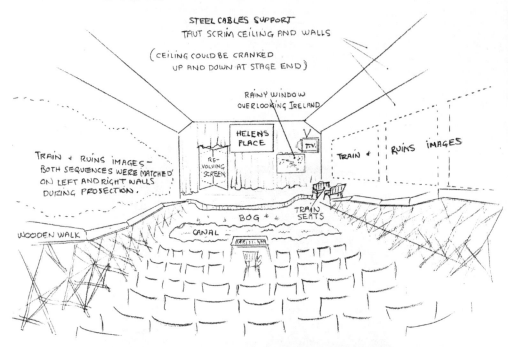

1997 SKETCH OF MERCIER + CAMIER SET (1979)
    FROM MEMORY   Bill Longcore for Iris Smith

STEEL CABLES SUPPORT
TAUT SCRIM CEILING AND WALLS

(CEILING COULD BE CRANKED
    UP AND DOWN AT STAGE END)

RAINY WINDOW
OVERLOOKING IRELAND

HELEN'S
PLACE

T.V.

TRAIN + RUINS IMAGES —
BOTH SEQUENCES WERE MATCHED
ON LEFT AND RIGHT WALLS
DURING PROJECTION.

RE-
VOLVING
SCREEN

TRAIN +   RUINS IMAGES

BOG

TRAIN
SEATS

WOODEN WALK

CANAL

Mercier and Camier. The set as
sketched from memory by Bill
Longcore. (© Bill Longcore.)

Vanishing Pictures. Beverly Brown.
(Photo © Stephanie Rudolph.)

CHAPTER THREE

Play, Come and Go, The Lost Ones:
Staging Beckett, 1965–1975

It was like being in a cage with a lion. . . . You're fully awake.
—L. B. DALLAS ON DAVID WARRILOW IN *THE LOST ONES*

Mabou Mines set out to create original pieces. The company's single most visible line of work has been Breuer's ongoing vision of life in the United States, staged in several parts, most recently *Pataphysics Penyeach* (2010). At the same time Mabou Mines has long been identified with its productions of Samuel Beckett's works.[1] In the 1970s the company performed five Beckett texts: *Play* (1971), *Come and Go* (1971), *The Lost Ones* (1975), *Cascando* (1976), and *Mercier and Camier* (1979). In more recent years, Mabou Mines has undertaken other Beckett pieces, many of them done outside the company such as the controversial 1984 production of *Endgame* directed by Akalaitis for the American Repertory Theatre. That Beckett attempted, through his representatives, to shut down that production has given the impression that he disapproved in general of Mabou Mines' productions of his plays. Some claim that in raising the performer to the level of artist the company took too many liberties with Beckett's texts. In fact, Mabou Mines have respected Beckett and sought his advice and permission for their staging ideas. He never sought to close any Mabou Mines production, and, while not always enthusiastic, he lent individual members warm support. For example, in 1979 he wrote *A Piece of Monologue* for Warrilow, who performed it after leaving the company. Beckett provided suggestions to Neumann for his productions of *Mercier and Camier*, *Company* (1983), and *Worstward Ho* (1986). These three, like *Cascando, The Lost Ones*, and Maleczech's *Imagination Dead Imagine* (1984), are prose texts Mabou Mines adapted for the stage. The early Beckett productions chronicle the members' identities and working methods as they emerged from youthful experiments in the 1960s. They used Beckett's spare language and settings, among other influences, to develop a performance discipline of their own.

Many actors find performing Beckett's plays (and adapting his prose) to be demanding, even severe; others find a kind of discipline in his strictures on the

99

actor's range of motion and speech. Discipline may seem to be a self-evident concept referencing the actor's physical and mental control and ability to reproduce words and gestures exactly. Before turning to Beckett's notion of discipline, though, it is important to point out that the members of Mabou Mines already had acquired disciplinary habits before they formed the company or presented *Play* in 1971. They were largely in their thirties—young, but not blank slates. They hankered to be their own bosses, not forced to audition continually with directors or producers who might not recognize their credentials but free to form a collaborative arrangement with each other and other artists of various backgrounds and talents. The place to do that work around 1970 was New York City. There they sought a form of artistic discipline congruent with that idea of self-determination. Although they did not embrace a single aesthetic or seek to imitate an admired director, group, or writer (such as Beckett), they had seen and done enough performance to understand that the work needed parameters. Thus, they did not seek to follow Beckett as disciples might follow a teacher. Their guide for performance discipline came from the downtown world of artists who regularly witnessed and commented on each other's work. As Breuer noted, Mabou Mines sought to combine the cool of downtown abstract art and music with the warm of motivational acting.[2] Downtown artists retained something of an avant-garde militancy in rejecting conventional middle-class values and behaviors. At the same time, Mabou Mines' notion of artistic discipline did not involve adopting any dogma.

The discipline invoked by Beckett's writing made sense to young artists working their way toward a new concept of performance. His texts encouraged discipline without requiring dogma. Akalaitis, who had studied in the 1960s with a variety of acting teachers, found the Stanislavskian director-actor relationship manipulative and unproductive and was ready for a different kind of discipline. Breuer and Maleczech had learned a great deal working with Herbert Blau in San Francisco. With R. G. Davis, Breuer had interesting discussions about Brecht. Maleczech took on a wide variety of roles, from commedia dell'arte to Genet's *The Balcony*. Rather than joining an acting studio or enrolling in a university theater program, they sought to learn outside "the college box," as Breuer has called it,[3] in ways that may seem undisciplined in the current brass-hat world of degrees, head shots, and resumés. In 1970 seeking freedom and self-determination did not mean failing to engage in disciplined practices. As Beckett knew, the writer or actor must cultivate an "inner force" in each piece in order to operate on his or her own artistic terms. Anna McMullan, speaking of his 1982 play *Catastrophe* as "an ironic portrayal of the discipline of theatrical production," finds that "it is also a defence of the play/writer/actor who . . . has access to an inner force, which, within the moral order of the play, wins out."[4] Without adopting Beckett's view of life or his aesthetic, by performing his work the members of Mabou Mines learned much about cultivating an inner force.

While faithful in presenting Beckett's words, the company did not adopt his view of the actor as interpreter. Then, as now, Mabou Mines treated the actor as an artist in his or her own right, one who uses the self as material for the work process. To trace the arc of its early development as a company is to link the use of the self as material to the cultivating of each piece's inner force. As was seen in chapter 2, the Red Horse's restless desire for a new kind of life came from all the members. They staged their first intimations of middle age in the stuttering, becalmed B.Beaver surrounded by a hooting, vamping chorus of his inner voices. *The Shaggy Dog Animation* saw them embodying their own cultural experience—the song lyrics and television personalities that shaped 1970s popular desire. In each case the character was mined from the outlines of their lived experience.

Ironically, though, the company's reputation did not yet rest on this essential trilogy. While *Red Horse* and *B.Beaver* toured to art galleries and universities around the country, it first came to the attention of the New York theater world in 1975 after staging an evening of short pieces by Beckett. Praised by Jack Kroll of *Newsweek,* the productions of *Play, Come and Go,* and *The Lost Ones* set a series of events in motion that helped the company to present *Shaggy Dog,* among other plays, at Joe Papp's New York Shakespeare Festival. Mabou Mines' reputation became linked in the public mind with Beckett.

From the first, the members of Mabou Mines were attracted to the precision and concreteness of Beckett's writing, but, as many young actors and directors have found, they had to learn to let the texts speak to them. As a student, Breuer was more interested in Genet and Camus, but when in 1962 Herbert Blau offered him the opportunity, he agreed to direct *Happy Days* at the San Francisco Actor's Workshop. *Happy Days* featured Beatrice Manley, Blau's wife and a Workshop repertory player, as Winnie. Breuer had assistant-directed for Blau and, like R. G. Davis, took on smaller productions at the Actor's Workshop's second space, the Encore Theatre, from 1960 to 1964. Pinter's *A Slight Ache* was followed the next year by the American premier of *The Underpants* by Sternheim and García Lorca's *The House of Bernarda Alba.* Outside the Workshop, he directed a production of Genet's *The Maids.* In Breuer's account, the earliest of these, *Happy Days,* was ultimately the least satisfying.[5]

During rehearsals he had disagreed with Manley, who wanted to create a thoroughly bourgeois figure. The young writer-director viewed Winnie from a more literary point of view as a ghostly existential presence and the play as a stark exploration of mankind condemned to an increasingly foreshortened existence. Breuer's approach apparently met with approval (the theater critic Paine Knickerbocker described Manley's performance as an "acting triumph"),[6] but he later realized that Manley had been right. He had misunderstood *Happy Days,* taking Winnie's apparent superficiality at face value. Moreover, he had imposed a meaning on the production rather than allowing the inner force of the piece to present itself.

By the time they began work in Paris on *Play,* Breuer was beginning to appreciate the multiple levels of Beckett's irony. The five unaffiliated artists explored the characters and then allowed psychology to fall away. The piece required three actors—a man (Warrilow as "m1") and two women (Maleczech as "w1" and Akalaitis as "w2")—to perform kneeling or standing in large urns, only their heads visible, much as Winnie is played fixed to the waist, and then the neck, in her mound. Maleczech remembers that the group approached the characters as a stereotypical Frenchman with both wife and mistress: "We worked on it exactly as you would a play or maybe like you would a movie. We worked on it in an apartment with realistic acting and Stanislavsky-style objectives and character and emotional life and everything—all staged outside the urns." Maleczech sees the play dividing into two parts, the description of the characters' lives before they entered the urns and their lives in them, subject to the inquisition of the light that shifts from face to face and compels their speech. At first the actors made no effort to speed up the lines, Maleczech recalls, but played the roles "exactly as though people were moving in and out of rooms, sitting at dressing tables, and doing their nails and so on." Maleczech's description suggests that the group, starting from the familiar parameters of psychological realism and motivational acting, worked to remove such recognizable details from the performance, much as Beckett did in writing his texts.

> Beckett's instruction is to speak as rapidly as possible throughout, which we took to heart and did. Our version of the play was nineteen minutes long, twice through and beginning the third time. That's very, very fast. . . . We wanted to be sure that the underlying meanings and life and internal workings were in place so it wouldn't be empty conceptualizing. . . . If you've done a lot of good groundwork, the residue of that work will be in the performance. And it was.[7]

In interviews Warrilow recalled the initial work on *Play* as a pleasurable, un-pressured exploration of a text through body and voice, a new, exhilarating experience for the literary editor.[8] The group took its time laying bare the characters, devising the makeup to match the appearance of the urns, and learning how to convey each character's compressed passion without moving either the unseen body or the visible head.

Although it is easy for a reader to grasp the tone of strained comedy in the love triangle, the immobility of those three touching urns belies the intimacy of the three characters' lives. To the audience their melodrama seems distant and foolish. The sense of the characters' individuality is obscured by each actor's lumpy, grayish makeup and hidden body, "the neck held fast in the urn's mouth."[9] That is not to say, however, that the words actually spoken do not have a delicate and important role to play in the spectacle. Taken purely as a written text, the characters' lines, not surprisingly, are full of recriminations and one-sided recollections. Each head recounts events, producing clichéd scenes of confrontation that alternate between pairs of characters, although all voices are represented in the speaker's "narration." "'I smell her off you,' she kept saying," comments m1. The wife's words take on an ironic edge in the husband's voice; like the encapsulated bodies of the actors, the characters' melodrama is contained.

While the specifics of the dialogue never come into focus, the immediacy of the characters' suffering and the claustrophobic banality of their romantic triangle seem inescapable in the spectacle of the bodies trapped and displayed as objects before the audience. Bonnie Marranca wrote after seeing the play in 1975 at Theatre for the New City:

> Lee Breuer . . . has captured the Beckettian landscape of lost souls in stunning *mise-en-scènes*. Front spotlights that first surface on the three horizontally aligned urns (designed by Jene Highstein) suggest the Byzantine icons of medieval art. The cascading flow of words that pour out of the mouths of husband, wife, and mistress in sequential monologues are interwoven and repeated endlessly, orchestrated by an inquisitory spotlight. The eternal triangle is doomed to repeat the banality of their soap-opera drama that only Beckett could give philosophical significance to by dividing it into two parts: the emptiness of the past and the now of recognition.[10]

After they had presented *Play* in 1967 at the American Cultural Center (then on the rue de Dragon), they set aside the piece and went on to other interests, among them a staging of *Mother Courage*. When Akalaitis and Glass and then Breuer and Maleczech returned to the United States, where Warrilow soon joined them, they took up *Play* again in 1971 in a very different environment. They had become a theater company affiliated with the La Mama Experimental Theatre Club, where they were the first to stage Beckett.[11] With Ellen Stewart's help, the members of Mabou Mines became part of a community of artists who had turned Soho and the East Village into a bohemia of unsupervised, unstructured artistic experimentation. In their first production, *The Red Horse Animation,* they subversively explored the human experience—specifically, their own. For *The B.Beaver Animation,* they improvised on Tina Girouard's sculpture at the 112 Greene Street Gallery. They saw work done in various unstructured spaces. In this minimalist and conceptualist performance context, Beckett's insistence on the discipline of word and body began to make a different kind of sense to them. In artistic terms, they were cultivating a discipline of their own. They combined motivational acting with presentational techniques. The unique juxtaposition of representation and abstraction seemed, as critic Gary Houston noted, "to make the audience *concentrate,* as if its vision were framed by a lens, not on people as speakers but on objects in the space, be they people or things."[12] In other words, they subjected the audience to a kind of discipline. This approach fit well with the discipline required of the actors in *Play.*

The artists returned to *Play* less out of an interest in rethinkng the piece than in expanding their repertoire. With the performers, composer, and director together again, they could have staged the 1967 version without difficulty. The experiences of the past four years, though, brought new dimensions to the Beckett work. For example, in Europe Breuer and Maleczech had seen the Berliner Ensemble in rehearsal. Akalaitis and Glass had talked with Julian Beck and Judith Malina after watching the Living's production of *Frankenstein.* Perhaps most important, Maleczech and Akalaitis had participated in a two-week workshop with Jerzy Grotowski and Richard Cieslak in 1969. As a result, Beckett's bottled-up *comédie* lost its French context for Mabou Mines, and when they began to rehearse the company members did not repeat their Stanislavskian exercises.

Instead, psychology was replaced with Grotowskian techniques that extended Stanislavsky, mixing warm and cool in the animation of the characters. The company members did not consciously employ Grotowskian techniques, but in the two years since the workshop they had made their way into the work process as Maleczech and Akalaitis taught what they had learned to the others. Maleczech notes that they were careful to separate Grotowski's technique from his aesthetic, which they did not adopt.

> Lee and I did go . . . to Poland and saw what the aesthetic was really—kind of angst-ridden, Second World War—no postmodernism, virtually no art-world content to it at all. It was largely biblically based. . . . But the core was that you could extend Stanislavsky beyond a kind of American movie-acting level of performance—realism, or naturalism even. You could push the boundaries of that into other areas, areas that could include great extensions of motion and physicality. That was what was important about Grotowski [for us].[13]

Akalaitis and Maleczech had discovered in Grotowski's discipline, rather than in his dogma, a way to explore and create through bodily movement. He had extended Stanislavsky for them so that they found compressed in the urns not "a version of behavior, a version of realism," with its focus on the recognizable patterns and tiny details of daily life, but the larger human story. Maleczech recalls having to restrain herself from pressing forward in the urn as she spoke in order to rechannel the realist, Stanislavskian impulse into her voice and the impossible speed of the words. The actors projected an "affective athleticism," a concept used by Antonin Artaud and found in Grotowski's work as well. Artaud had described forces channeled through the actor's body and released in part through the voice, which could be used as a musical instrument or transmitter of sound images. In *Play* this athleticism communicated the actor's energy entirely through the breath channeled through the unseen torso. For this reason, I believe, Beckett's stage directions instruct the actors to kneel or stand, rather than sit, in the urns. The actor's physical discomfort contributes directly to the play's impression of anxious, fragmented subjectivity.[14]

Akalaitis, in a 1976 interview, identified Grotowski as the teacher who had encouraged her to think of herself differently as an actor: "It is very important to me that Grotowski said that an actor is as much an artist as a writer, a painter, as the playwright—that he's not an interpreter."[15] She noted that as a result she did not work to please the director or the audience but "for the piece." With regard to how she approached character through physical action and task, Akalaitis described a breaking down of the Enlightenment distinction between self and world that seemed to owe as much to the company's work with Beckett's texts as to Grotowski's techniques.

I notice in rehearsal that there is an idea . . . executed physically. I do not mean
in terms of movement, but in terms of changing your body. And when you
change your body, you change your face, . . . your voice . . . I go beyond myself
one more level, and keep looking at myself, and try to get a picture of someone,
and then try to fill in the picture *through myself*. It's like you project something,
like a slide on a wall and try to fit yourself into it. . . . You put yourself in a physical posture, and it changes your voice—and it begins to change the way you feel.

A literal example of this technique occurred in Mabou Mines' production of
Beckett's "dramaticule" *Come and Go,* first developed in 1971. Once again
Breuer directed Maleczech and Akalaitis. The third character, however, was
played first by Dawn Gray, whom they had met in San Francisco, and later by
Ellen McElduff, who began working with the company in 1974. Maleczech describes a process by which the actor linked the words to images from the actor's
past, while the audience viewed the actors literally as images framed in a mirror. The actors performed behind the audience at a spot from which their image would be visible in the mirror. It was as though the audience was "spying
through a telescope, or down Alice's rabbit hole, at a shimmering trio clustered
on a park bench."[16] Just as *Play* used a spotlight (run by Breuer) to compel
speech from each figure, *Come and Go* constrained and distanced the movement of the three figures by framing them in the rectangle formed by the mirror, as though they were "birds on a branch."[17] To each character is attributed
a secret, which one companion shares with the other while the character is offstage. When she rejoins her friends, the sequence repeats twice, the roles
changing each time. Thus, physically and narratively the piece comprises a series of interlocking circles. In the final moments, the three figures join their
hands in an elaborate pattern. "I can feel the rings," says one, but, as Beckett
notes in his stage directions, "No rings apparent."[18] As in *Play,* any differences
that might suggest individual, realist characters fade in the more formal counterpoint of the movement, colors, and voices. As McElduff comments:

[The costumes] were long, Victorian-style coats. Mine was purple, Ruth's was
a kind of burnt-orangey red—these were very dull colors—and JoAnne's was
kind of a yellow-green color, kind of a gold. We all had small hats [with] feath-
ers [and] veils, just the kind that cover your eyes. . . . It was all very small and
faded in a way. . . . One actress would lean towards the actress sitting immediately next to her and whisper in her ear and then go back. . . . When the whispering started, when one would lean over to the other, it was kind of a little

quick movement, a birdlike movement. . . . Unless you were whispering to
someone, your hands were folded in your lap, except at the very end of the play
. . . [when] we were all touching hands. It was, I think, a beautiful image.[19]

Maleczech notes that, while the actors did not excavate their characters as they
had done in 1965 with *Play,* she recalls the use of "secrets," a Stanislavsky exer-
cise, to inform the "tiny responses" the characters have to one another as the
tension and awkwardness grows among them. In order to project themselves
into the frame of the mirror, the actors used images from their own experience
to shape body and voice.[20] Moreover, because the actors were positioned behind the audience, they had to project their voices backward, in a sense
through the backs of their heads, so the audience did not sense their presence
and break their concentration on the framed images before them. For McElduff, the visual focus in the mirror was complemented by the aural icon of the
actors' voices. Breuer wanted a crying sound to emerge from the whispered
lines, just "lips with a sibilant sound behind it." In the silences, he added a coo-
ing that, in response to a cue light, the actors made in the top of their throats—
a quick, delicate, almost inaudible pulsing that evoked the sound of birds or
crying and then, at the removal of the light, faded into silence once again.

Similarly, *Play* provided several frames into which the actors projected
themselves and their experience. Chief among them was the inquisitorial light
that compelled the characters' confessions. With the constraints imposed by
the three urns and Beckett's stage directions regarding spatial relations and the
actors' posture, the precise movements of the spotlight reinforced the discipline of Grotowski's techniques. Thus, while Grotowski freed Mabou Mines
from authorial intent, apparently in direct collision with Beckett's expectation
of adherence to textual "author-ity," in the work process the two disciplines
meshed well. Mabou Mines had made no changes in Beckett's text. The New
York production may have hewed more closely to Beckett's direction not to allow the characters' emotions to spill over into a growing intensity in the words
and lighting. Intonations and expressions remained even and precise, as Beckett had specified.

The company also removed several musical phrases written by Glass in
1965 that were to appear at random moments in the piece. At that time, the
music had been a new departure for the young composer, who found that
writing for the theater produced what he has called "my most innovative work,
. . . often to be worked out and developed later in my concert music." Glass recalls his composition for *Play* as

music based on two lines, each played by soprano saxophone, having only two notes so that each line represented an alternating, pulsing interval. When combined, these two intervals (. . .written in two different repeating rhythms) formed a shifting pattern of sounds that stayed within the four pitches of the two intervals. The result was a very static piece that was still full of rhythmic variety. The piece gave birth to whole series I wrote at this time, including a concert work for JoAnne Akalaitis and Ruth Maleczech (in which they declaimed a soufflé recipe over my music), and culminating in a string quartet I wrote in 1966.[21]

Such work built on Glass's studies with Nadia Boulanger and on challenges encountered, such as transcribing Ravi Shankar's music, to form his "new musical language." The score for *Play* was an important beginning for Glass (and Mabou Mines, for many of whose productions Glass has composed). Breuer recalls:

[Philip] produced four or five . . . saxophone phrases that were rather abstract . . . on a tape. [Y]ou wouldn't know precisely where they would come in. They were like another voice. . . . a contextual voice. . . . So there was this variable that when an actor was speaking with this music behind him, they would have an emotional quality that would be different from another time. It was like a little air in the piece.[22]

For Maleczech the music added little to her experience of the piece. "It was like an element that went through the play, like the wind or the rain. That's the way I related to it. I was never able to take it into account rhythmically, for example. . . . So I treated it as though it were a natural element."[23] Although Maleczech regrets not being able to take advantage of the music, it appears that the randomness of the phrases tended to work against the willful rhythm set up by the light. In New York, Breuer counted out musical beats for Beckett's punctuation: one count for a comma, two for a semicolon, three for a period, four for an ellipsis. Mabou Mines recognized that the artist's acquired sense of discipline is the necessary guide. As actor Brenda Bynum—not a Mabou Mines member —has said, "The rules give you the freedom."[24]

Mabou Mines acquired another form of discipline from the Berliner Ensemble, which they had observed in the late 1960s. Mabou Mines' rehearsals were and are more public and dialogic, indeed more raucous, than those of Grotowski's Theatre Laboratory. It was crucial for the artists to develop the work under the gaze of their colleagues—each other. Projecting an image, an other, which the actor then attempts to become, suggests the painful search for wholeness that Anna McMullan in her 1993 book finds in the characters of Beckett's later plays. In Mabou Mines' work, however, the actor's anxiety about that projected image is modified by the bruising pleasures of trying on its behaviors in the course of the work, done not in isolation but in concert with the rest of the company. Just as Beckett found writing to be an activity both painful and essential, one with which he could not go on and yet did go on, so the work process for Mabou Mines was the essential impossible activity, allowing the actors to take on externalized images, postures, and utterances.

The most complete expression of this form of discipline occurred in Mabou Mines' 1975 evening of Beckett, which brought together for the first time its productions of *Play* and *Come and Go* with a new piece, *The Lost Ones*. Neither Maleczech nor Akalaitis was available to create new work. Maleczech had recently had her and Breuer's second child, Lute Ramblin. Zachary Glass—Akalaitis and Glass's second child—was born in 1975. Both women performed, however, in *Play* and *Come and Go*. The evening drew the reviewers' praise and good houses, even in its first run in March. Joe Papp and his wife, Gail Merrifield Papp, who ran the New York Shakespeare Festival's Play Development Department and knew something of the company's work, read Jack Kroll's review in *Newsweek,* in which he called Mabou Mines a "valiant group," the program "remarkable," and *The Lost Ones* "one of the most original and magical of all Beckett productions."[25] The Papps attended the evening of Beckett shorts when it was restaged in October 1975 at Theatre for the New City, then located at 113 Jane Street in the West Village. Founders George Bartenieff and Crystal Field were interested in Mabou Mines' work and had offered them performance space. Without taking on companies as resident artists, as Stewart did at La Mama, Bartenieff and Field produced the work of many artists in this way. The company split the modest ticket price (a $2.50 donation) with them and provided its own set, lighting and sound technicians, and costumes. Breuer recalls that *The Lost Ones* cost only eighty dollars to stage. Although he already had the concept for the large foam cylinder that the actors and audience would occupy, he and designer Thom Cathcart had to improvise a cylindrical space with heavy curtains to achieve a total blackout.[26] Since *The Lost Ones* took place within the smaller cylindrical space, which held fifty people, the show had to be repeated each night. Between the two performances, both audiences watched *Play* and *Come and Go* in an adjacent space. Joe and Gail Papp found *Play* "extraordinary, exceptional" and Warrilow in

The Lost Ones "magnificent," a "commanding, interesting, unusual presence."[27] When Papp invited the company members to reprise their Beckett pieces at the New York Shakespeare Festival early in 1976, they took a step toward a more visible place in the theater world. They had made it through a difficult transition since leaving La Mama. Finding space and funding would continue to be difficult, but on a show-by-show basis they began to open pieces developed elsewhere, and rehearse new ones, at the Public. While several company members expressed anxiety about linking themselves to a "commercial" producer whose success with *A Chorus Line* had impelled him to move it to Broadway in July 1975, their relationship with Papp turned out to be fruitful and lasted eight years. His financial success allowed Papp to support, among other companies, Mabou Mines.

It is interesting to consider in terms of authorship and authority both "Mabou Mines Performs Beckett," which brought the company to Papp's attention, and the relationship the company developed with him. The New York Shakespeare Festival supported many authors and directors by staging their original plays, just as Stewart did at La Mama. Yet Papp never exercised a producing authority over the company; he appreciated the artists' talent and desire for self-determination, and he recognized their need for material and aesthetic support. Gail Papp recalls:

> [Mabou Mines] were an extraordinary artistic company, the likes of which he didn't know anywhere else. They were unique . . . he sensed that immediately . . . even more as he talked to them. . . . There was no question in his mind that they had a need for space then. He was actually loath to commit space because it meant he had to adjust his season—what *he* wanted to do. . . . The presence of another group that was autonomous . . . ordinarily that was a proposition he'd find absolutely unattractive. . . . But Mabou Mines were a huge, wonderful exception because of their high artistic, unusual nature—the talent involved.

Papp saw himself not as a father figure but as a problem solver, a producer who (at least in regard to Mabou Mines) did not interfere in the development of the work but provided support, space, and the occasional loan. While he initially perceived Breuer as the group's spokesperson and "main creative force," according to Gail Papp he quickly realized that everyone was multitalented. *Cascando, Dressed Like an Egg,* and *Dead End Kids* all came to the Public Theater despite Akalaitis's reservations about this "benign dictator." While she was drawn to Papp's charisma and appreciated his support, perhaps his deeper connection with her, and with Mabou Mines more generally, lay in a mutual desire to be enterprising about art and to work for oneself. Like Breuer, Papp saw himself as a working-class entrepreneur who had to deal with powerful institutions to get what he needed. Like Akalaitis, he was the child of immigrants. Just as he had learned that producing theater "was not only about giving culture to the people. It was about *listening to* the people . . . and putting them on stage,"[28] Akalaitis by 1980 was looking to direct plays for audiences beyond the downtown artists' community. Admittedly, Papp's insistence on identifying the New York Shakespeare Festival as *his* theater was not Mabou Mines' approach to running a collaborative company. Yet Papp recognized their commonalities. When he later selected Akalaitis to lead the New York Shakespeare Festival (she served as artistic director from Papp's death in October 1991 to March 1993), she agreed in part because "I felt I shared part of Joe's aesthetic agenda and political ideas."[29] Among other Mabou productions staged at the Public during the company's eight-year tenure were *The Shaggy Dog Animation, A Prelude to Death in Venice, Mercier and Camier, Wrong Guys* (1980), *Company, Hajj, Through the Leaves,* and *Cold Harbor.* They used a variety of spaces in the renovated former New York Public Library building, among them the Little Theater, in which *The Lost Ones* appeared, and the Old Prop Shop, a performance space that Mabou Mines helped to create. Breuer, Akalaitis, and Neumann worked on non-Mabou productions at the Public Theater during the years Papp sponsored Mabou Mines, and Breuer (assisted by Maleczech) directed an extravagant production of *The Tempest* (1981) at the Delacorte Theatre in Central Park that Gail Papp cites as only one of the many risks Papp took as producer and never regretted.

The production of *Play* that Papp first saw in 1975 had changed very little from its 1971 premier. *Come and Go,* on the other hand, had lost Dawn Gray, who left the company, probably in 1974, to join a Sufi commune on Thirteenth Street, where she changed her name to Chalisa. Although Gray has made no public comment, several people have suggested that she may have felt bruised by the rough and tumble of mutual critique that goes on in Mabou Mines rehearsals. Just as Akalaitis found it difficult to stand up to Papp when he made sexist remarks to women, Gray was not able to use the company's "negativity" as a tool.[30] Ellen McElduff took over the role of Ru in fall 1974, first appearing at the New York Theatre Ensemble in December. Earlier that year, McElduff and David Hardy, who were married at that time, had moved to New York from Memphis, and *Come and Go* represented her first work with Mabou Mines. She had seen the company perform while she was still a student of Ray

Hill at Rhodes College, then called Southwestern at Memphis. McElduff recalled in an interview that Mabou Mines introduced the members of Eads Hill
to Ellen Stewart, who supported them financially as a branch of La Mama in
Memphis.[31] Younger and less experienced than Maleczech and Akalaitis, McElduff was a bit intimidated, particularly since she was joining an existing production rather than helping to develop a new piece. That experience would
come the following year with *Cascando,* Akalaitis's first project as director. At
Maleczech's urging, McElduff had attended a Grotowksi workshop in
Philadelphia (probably in 1972) when she and other members of Eads Hill first
came to New York to perform their original piece *Unta-the,* but she did not
fully understand Grotowski's techniques at that time. The company welcomed
McElduff, though, and in 1974 she quickly became part of the free-ranging discussion and experiment of rehearsals. For the next five or six years, McElduff
worked exclusively with Mabou Mines. After several additional years of sporadic work with the company during which she lived primarily in Louisiana,
she joined it in 1985. McElduff has performed in many Mabou Mines productions, among them *Dressed Like an Egg, Dead End Kids,* the radio shows *The
Keeper Series* (1980), *Flow My Tears, the Policeman Said* (1985), and *Mabou
Mines Lear,* and outside the company both onstage (e.g., in *Southern Exposure*
[1979], for which she won an Obie) and in film (e.g., in *Working Girls* [1986]
and *JFK* [1991]). While many company members began to develop their own
projects as a means of retaining parity in the company, she preferred to remain
an actress. She credits her involvement with Mabou Mines, including the exciting early work on *Come and Go* and *Cascando,* with providing stimulating
acting challenges, not to mention a supportive artistic community.

In the celebrated 1975 evening of *Play, Come and Go,* and *The Lost Ones,* the
company's discipline of word and body was on full display. As McMullan
claims for Beckett's later plays in general, "the performer's body is . . . at the in-
tersection of resistance and subjection of the will to authority and control
which Beckett both parodies and enacts."[32] As quoted earlier, the actor culti-
vates an "inner force" through the ironic portrayal of discipline itself. The key
to that force, though, is the actor's willing "subjection to . . . political or actan-
tial power," in this case that of the playwright, Beckett. Warrilow's performance
in *The Lost Ones* illustrates this point. Breuer and Warrilow had adapted the
text in three weeks from the story Beckett published in 1970. In Cathcart's
cramped cylindrical playing space, which evoked the confining dimensions in
which the Lost Ones live, Warrilow performed only inches from the spectators.
The actor's own concentration and disciplined awareness of the body seemed

to contribute directly to the spectator's engagement. Ruby Cohn describes the experience.

> Shoeless, the spectators enter a dark foam-rubber cylindrical space in which tiers of foam-padded steps are built from floor to ceiling. An ugly sulfurous glow emanates from the sides of the steps, but spotlights follow Warrilow around the cylindrical playing area. Electronic music by composer Philip Glass approximates the text's "faint stridulence as of insects." Cutting Beckett's text by a third, Warrilow graduates from a dry and seedy academic clinically observing a small cylinder to a naked human essence who draws an equation between the tiny celluloid dolls and ourselves, but his involvement deviates, mesmerizing us to its changes. In various dull lights . . . he recites Beckett's text, his voice a resonant stringed instrument. After about half the playing time, but quite late in Beckett's text, as the temperature rises in *our* fetid cylinder, Warrilow removes his clothes to enact the several torments of the cylinder's inhabitants.[33]

Early in the show, as Warrilow narrated, he unpacked the "dolls" from a narrow case tied with ribbons and placed them one at a time in the circle of light on the floor, first tiny ladders and then human figures. While viewers could see that his words and actions were related, neither his eloquent dispassion nor his later bursts of frenzy and frustration seemed to represent a specific character. In an interview, Warrilow admitted that he had avoided creating a narrator who seemed omnipotent or invulnerable, which would run counter to the author's compassion for "the lost ones." Instead, by means of Grotowskian image work, Warrilow and Breuer effected, by subtle shifts in the narrator's stance from observer to actor, a public exploration of Warrilow's private self without doing so explicitly and yet in full consonance with the text.[34] Even at moments when the narrator seemed to mime the characters' blind groping or cries of despair, the production created an emotional implication for the audience without resorting to pantomime. For example, after describing the searchers, who scale the ladders looking for "a way out," Warrilow gave the audience "a first aperçu" of the group Beckett calls sedentary searchers. A searcher could produce, if stepped on, "such an outburst of fury as to throw the entire cylinder into a ferment."[35] In the midst of Warrilow's sentence, without pause or warning, he stepped hard on the foot of an actor in the front row, usually Raymond, who then shrieked with an inhuman intensity. The scream seemed "formal," as though a door had opened to admit it and then abruptly closed, shutting it

out. A few lines later Warrilow would step on the foot of a second plant, sometimes McElduff, who remained silent and motionless.[36] In the cylinder's
confined environment, Raymond's scream, and perhaps McElduff's silence as
well, seemed to overwhelm the senses and, like Warrilow's words, became the
experience rather than representing it.

There was a third actor planted in the audience. In a scene near the production's end, as the lights faded to black and Glass's music came up, the audience heard Warrilow say, "There does none the less exist a north in the guise of
one of the vanquished."[37] Beckett describes her thus:

> She squats against the wall with her head between her knees and her legs in her
> arms. The left hand clasps the right shinbone and the right the left forearm.
> The red hair tarnished by the light hangs to the ground. It hides the face and
> whole front of the body down to the crutch. The left foot is crossed on the
> right. She is the north. She rather than some other among the vanquished be-
> cause of her greater fixity. To one bent for once on taking his bearings she may
> be of help.

Linda Hartinian (then Wolfe) played "the woman vanquished." In the taped
performance, the camera switches from Warrilow to her seated nude figure,
her hands on her knees, her head down. Then, with feet together, knees somewhat apart, her hands, fingers still interlaced, come up over her head and hold
back her hair to show her face. Her knees spread in a slow, controlled movement to reveal her torso. Again slowly, she closes her legs as lights fade to black.
While she conveyed the abjection and vulnerability of the vanquished, Hartinian focused her attention not on the character's feelings but on "numbers,"
timing the movement perfectly. Having recently left the University of North-
ridge, where she was a psychology major, to join Raymond in New York, she
had little theater experience, but she had supported herself in college as a go-
go dancer, and, as with other Mabou Mines associates, that seemingly irrele-
vant experience proved useful. She had no acting assumptions to unlearn. Her
"clean" attitude toward the character's "greater fixity" put the focus on exter-
nals.[38] In the hands of another playwright, such a female figure could have
seemed a conventional muse for Warrilow's narrator. In *The Lost Ones*,
though, the audience sat, like the vanquished, in a featureless environment
that had no "true north." In the next blackout, Hartinian disappeared and that
reference point along with her.

The actors' bodies, in their beauty and vulnerability, became a screen on which Beckett's words were "projected." A few minutes before Hartinian appeared, Warrilow's narrator had already stripped off his clothing. Warrilow at first had resisted Breuer's suggestion that he perform the latter scenes nude, but he agreed to try it and found the nudity entirely appropriate. "It completed the circle of identification between the humans and these little figures," he commented later.[39] The key to diminishing his sense of vulnerability was simply trying it. Later he suggested that this was one moment in a longer process of learning to drop unhelpful oppositional notions of actor versus audience, nude versus clothed body. Also, over the six years during which he performed *The Lost Ones*, he overcame the assumption that one had to be a dancer to dance, a musician to make music. He began, as he said, "to use the body as a way of creating symbol and cipher and of depicting energy in action and in space." Similarly, he said, "when I was performing *The Lost Ones* . . . an understanding came to me that I *was* a musician, if only because I used and modulated my voice."[40]

It appears that Warrilow focused from the first on the demands of the text, letting it inform his choices rather than excavating the psychology of the Lost Ones. He did not engage in the "forfeiting" of character that he and his fellow actors had undertaken in their first rehearsals for *Play*. Speaking of actress Hildegard Schmahl, who had similarly researched the characters of May and her mother for a German production of *Footfalls*, Jonathan Kalb comments that she only "succeeded [in the role] by means of a radical self-denial."[41] Under Beckett's direction, Schmahl focused instead on the externalities of the role. This orientation allows a clear and unsentimental image to develop for both the actor and audience: "An artificial immovability develops; a tauter articulation takes over the soft, agreeable modulation. A concentrated creation of art does indeed emerge, a cold, stiff encapsulated being; the 'being for itself' of the figure comes across."[42] The clarity of this stage image makes it possible to see how the parts of Beckett's play relate to one another. Just as Schmahl's concentration was enhanced, the onlooker (in this case Walter Asmus) found himself fully engaged in the action. The actor's own disciplined awareness of the body seems to contribute directly to the spectator's interest in spite of the fact that actor and spectator may be concentrating on somewhat different aspects of the action. Kalb praises Warrilow as one such "inadvertent interpreter" of Beckett.

> Warrilow *does* think about text, but does not use those thoughts consciously to motivate his performance. He internalizes them, makes them a part of his gen-

eral attitude toward the play; one might say that he translates them, in a way, into musical terms, becoming a kind of informed instrument. . . . It's as if actors were required to undergo a two-step process in which the second step cancels the first: analyze the text as a conventional play, and then push that knowledge to the back of your mind in order to concentrate on the verbal music. But [Warrilow does] not need to work at forfeiting character because he never consciously adopt[s] recognizable personalities to fit decided-upon ideas about text.[43]

What made *The Lost Ones* so memorable that spectators still mention it thirty years later? As with his later Beckett roles, Warrilow did not assume his character's essence before he began; rather, he stayed on the surface of the role, focusing on its external qualities and projecting himself into a moving if unsentimental image. Beckett's narrative suggests that such a whole being does not exist within the walls of the cylinder. It is merely "the ideal preying on one and all."[44] There was probably a moment in this experience, as there was in the production of *Play*, when the audience's gaze subjected Warrilow's body to an unendurable form of discipline—unendurable, in this case, not for Warrilow but for the audience. Their complex, difficult position of surveillance undermined the authority of their position as watching subjects and thus the distinction between themselves and the objectified actor. In this way, Mabou Mines found the inner force of *The Lost Ones*, which put the human subject, as McMullan puts it, "on trial." It is not surprising that a long silence often followed the performance, as spectators struggled to deal with the piece's powerful rearrangement of their understanding.

Conclusion: Discipline and Author-ity

There are those who might say that in several Mabou Mines productions of Beckett's texts the artists showed little discipline in one regard—respecting the writer's legal authority over the disposition of his words. Their staging of *The Lost Ones* was admittedly much more than the reading they had originally sought the rights to perform. Publisher Samuel French had provided permissions to stage *Play* and *Come and Go*, but *The Lost Ones* was not a play. When approached, Jean and George Reavey offered to contact Beckett, whom they knew, to obtain the necessary permission. By the time they returned with the favorable reply, the situation had changed, as Breuer noted in a 25 August 1975 letter to the author: "Your answer . . . 'o.k. straight reading' was communicated to us at the end of our third week of rehearsal—in the course of which we had discovered a method of presentation that excited us tremendously but was not precisely the 'straight' reading that you designated would be in order."[45] Mabou Mines proceeded with the production, then took it on tour in April and May. Sometime between March and June, the author learned of the production and reportedly wrote to Jean Reavey, "Your friends did a sort of 'crooked' straight reading."[46] Through Performing Artservices the company paid royalties to Grove Press for performances already given and suspended plans to perform the play again until they heard from the author. In October the company paid additional royalties for the second run.

Breuer felt that he and Mabou Mines were done a great disservice by Deirdre Bair's account of this episode in her biography of Beckett. As she does with descriptions of other unorthodox productions of his plays, Bair emphasizes the negative in describing *The Lost Ones*, noting only that the "straight reading" had become a "dramatic monologue" in a "cocoonlike set" in which Warrilow and a young woman appeared nude at certain points. Bair claims that Beckett did not interfere with the production, out of friendship for the Reaveys, but soon after "sent a covering letter to [Barney Rosset, his publisher], stating simply that he would not interfere with productions of his plays on aesthetic grounds even if he had the right to do so, because once started, there would be no end." He would, however, retain complete control of productions when he was involved in them.[47] As Breuer maintains, Bair's juxtaposition of Mabou Mines' production and Beckett's letter to Rosset makes the situation seem much worse than it apparently was in Beckett's eyes.

It appears that the report of Beckett's reaction constrained Mabou Mines from showing *The Lost Ones* again in June 1975 at Theatre for the New City, as planned. In August Breuer wrote his letter in an effort to clear the air with Beckett before attempting to revive the evening of Beckett pieces in October. Beckett apparently did not reply. Still, he did not try to prevent Mabou Mines from continuing to show *The Lost Ones;* in fact, in Berlin, during a 1976 European tour that Beckett approved, he saw the sets for this production and *Cascando* and met the company members, minus Breuer, who was in Amsterdam.

Beckett's relations with Mabou Mines remained warm. He gave Neumann permission in 1977 to stage *Mercier and Camier* and later *Company* and *Worstward Ho*. All of these are nondramatic texts requiring considerable adaptation for staging. Warrilow, for whom Beckett wrote *A Piece of Monologue*, performed *The Lost Ones* until 1981. On 30 April 1978 he responded "okay with me" to Warrilow's request for permission to do a television film of

The Lost Ones for PBS and signed off with "Warm greetings to you all."[48] When Mabou Mines presented the stage version in 1979 for Beckett's seventy-fifth birthday celebration at the Théâtre nationale populaire—a celebration that Beckett did not attend, having a policy never to see productions of his plays—the show was well received and favorably reviewed. Warrilow was careful to explain to the French press the play's development, mentioning Beckett's comment, made to the company in Berlin, that while his theater pieces usually germinated from an aural idea, *The Lost Ones* had begun with a visual image. Mabou Mines, said Warrilow, treated such a narrative as entirely real, transforming it into a staged abstraction by means of voice, gestures, and spatial arrangements.[49]

In 1986, after corresponding with Beckett off and on for five years about her production of *Imagination Dead Imagine*, developed with his permission, in collaboration with scientists at the Massachusetts Institute of Technology, Maleczech wrote to Beckett for permission (which she received) to return the production to MIT and then tour it to the University of Iowa. In closing, Maleczech wrote:

> A second generation of theater artists has begun to try to realize your work. My daughter [Clove Galilee] is the young woman in the hologram—you did get the photo, didn't you? And my son [Lute Ramblin Breuer] just completed work on a radio play of *All That Fall* with David Warrilow and Billie Whitelaw.
>
> On this, your 80th birthday, the theater artists of Mabou Mines join others around the world in wishing you well and thanking you for your generosity in allowing some of us to feel our way through your language in our own ways. I'm sure that must have, at times, been a painful and unrewarding experience for you. However, for those of us who have tried, it has led to another world of artistic expression.[50]

The members of Mabou Mines found ways to do their work that sometimes pushed the edge of convention and decorum. While respecting Beckett as author, they also approached the work as theater artists in their own right. They sought to cultivate the inner force of the actor by using artistic discipline to counter conventional notions of authority, just as Beckett's texts do. Although the company was only half a decade old in 1975, its members' long years of work together, in some cases since the late 1950s, had begun to bear remarkable fruit. Breuer's youthful, rather academic notion of *Happy Days*, followed by a work process on *Play* that began with French sexual comedy and ended by forfeiting character, had profited by the development of the company's own sense of artistic purpose and discipline with the Animations. In 1975, why did Mabou Mines' evening of Beckett make such an impression? As suggested earlier, discipline, when embraced, produces readiness. Mabou Mines had begun to present mature work, brilliantly conceived and executed, a clear example of the artists' readiness to use themselves fully as material for performance.

CHAPTER FOUR

"See yourself as a heavyweight":
Cascando, The Saint and the Football Player, The Shaggy Dog Animation, Dressed Like an Egg

In a 2007 cover story for *American Theatre*, Randy Gener characterizes Mabou Mines' history as a "love story" in which Maleczech, while a director in her own right, has more often served as Breuer's primary actor and muse. While acknowledging other members, Gener ends his article quoting Breuer: "Ruth was the love of my life. She is certainly the love of my life as an artist."[1] Given Breuer's complicated professional and personal lives, he asserts in a surprisingly nonironic way Maleczech's centrality in his life and work. Perhaps that "love story" helped to keep Mabou Mines together even after several members left in 1990 and, heavily in debt, the company experienced several particularly dire years. In treating Mabou Mines as "the avant-garde of coupledom," though, Gener overlooks other couples that were central to the company's longevity and plays into Breuer's tendency to place himself at the center of company relationships. Linked to this problem is Gener's assertion that Mabou Mines became a company of directors only after 1990. In fact, this shift in the company's working methods and character had begun as early as the mid-1970s when Akalaitis, Maleczech, and Neumann developed their own preoccupations and styles. At the same time, the group continued to self-identify as a company of equals and increasingly was being pegged as a collective in the press. As a writer, Breuer began to feel as though he were disappearing in the talk of collective creation. After staging *The Saint and the Football Player* (1975), he turned to writing a series of works that, as it has turned out, has provided him with a means of making his "myth."[2] In the meantime, Akalaitis tested her hand at directing with Beckett's *Cascando* and then gained a new visibility with a much larger, more complex show based on the writings of Colette. *Dressed Like an Egg* premiered while Breuer's *Shaggy Dog Animation* was still in rehearsal. Akalaitis became the second director in Mabou Mines, with a sensibility and vocabulary of her own. While Breuer was beginning his master narrative, which carries the weight of memory, Akalaitis began by adopting a deliberate forgetfulness. Rather than Breuer's gender parodies, she multiplied gendered positions. This juxtaposing of narrative and collage, memory and forgetfulness, gendered stereotype and gender ambiguity, enriched the work of Mabou Mines.

I weave several recurring elements through my discussion of these four plays. The company's collaborations with artists such as Nancy Graves, Ree Morton, Alison Yerxa, and Mary Overlie exemplify the "nonhierarchical" work that analyzed artistic forms and reinterpreted them. From 1974 to 1977 choreographer Overlie was developing a "toolbox" that came to be known as the six View Points. In this period Mabou Mines also consolidated working principles, even as members' relations to one another shifted. Some couples split up; others formed. Some of the artists' children began to participate in the work. Company members' shared professional interests sometimes foundered on gender conflicts. With the women's movement as backdrop, I trace through discussions of individual plays how Breuer and Akalaitis chose to represent gendered difference in their productions. The contradictions of being both free and fettered, experiencing the terrors and opportunities of commitment, come to the surface in both the plays and the collaboration that produced them.

Cascando and The Saint and the Football Player, 1974–1976

As work progressed on The B.Beaver Animation, Akalaitis became more interested in research and rehearsal than in performance. As an actor she was "an extraordinary presence and a wonderful comedienne," according to Hartinian, who attended many B.Beaver performances,[3] but Akalaitis was finding it difficult to stay focused during the Animations' increasingly lengthy development process, and performance itself was losing its appeal.

> I always knew that I was not at heart a performer because I didn't have the interest to continue the work when the rehearsal was finished. I was only interested in rehearsal. . . . Performers make it new every night, they make it deep every night. . . . I was going to the theater and feeling depressed before the performance because . . . I had to repeat it.[4]

At the same time Akalaitis expressed a new confidence and willingness to expose who she was.[5] In 1975 she received permission to adapt Beckett's radio play *Cascando* for the stage. Moving from performer to director was not, at first, a major shift for Akalaitis, who, like all Mabou Mines members, was accustomed to group development of a new work. She found that she loved directing—it fit her "bossy" and "controlling" personality, she later joked—but instead of controlling the actors she worked collaboratively, valuing her fellow artists' input.[6]

Cascando: The Production

Akalaitis began work on *Cascando* with a visual notion but no plotting, says McElduff.[7] After several years of choral work, Akalaitis was ready to reconsider "traditional" theater and motivational acting: "I just wanted to create a piece in which actors could work on characterization."[8] She found, though, that *Cascando* did not lend itself easily to a study of psychology or motivation. The production exhibited the same mixture of warm and cool, dramatic acting and sculptural performance, that had marked Mabou Mines' earlier pieces. Akalaitis used the company's ironic layering of performance techniques that had given earlier works such as *The B.Beaver Animation* an intriguing complexity and humor.[9]

 Cascando did hint at techniques and approaches Akalaitis would develop for later productions such as *Dressed Like an Egg* and *Dead End Kids.* Roger Copland described her first show as "an extraordinary tapestry of tiny activities" reminiscent of Warrilow manipulating *The Lost Ones*' tiny figures in their miniature environment. Rather than amplifying a central textual image, though, Akalaitis's production supplemented the image with "a collage of lapidary delicacy and complexity."[10] *Cascando* involved not two or three performers but seven: Neumann, Raymond, and Warrilow and associates Thom Cathcart, David Hardy, Ellen McElduff, and Arthur Russell. Akalaitis created the visual image of several people around a table in the cluttered corner of a room. That room might have been on the deserted winter coast of Nova Scotia where "people [are] trapped in their own world, because the outside world is so formidable and so uninviting."[11] During rehearsals in fall 1975, the actors learned the "gnarly" Nova Scotia accent from a recording Akalaitis provided. Working on Mabou Mines' usual minimal budget, she brought props from the converted camp on the west coast of Cape Breton Island where the company had rehearsed *The Red Horse Animation.* This private geography informed the work but was not meant to be available to audiences.[12] Erika Munk commented that the set seemed borne down by the weight of the past.

Four men and a woman are around a table, another in a corner, another in a rocking chair. All have an underground, sub-prole air. The room is an incredible junk pile of ugly old objects, photos, a used tire, a souvenir polar bear, a dirty tortoise shell, a goldfish in a bowl, rusty kitchen ware. Not cute like Greenwich Avenue nostalgia shops but dirty, depressing; nobody's bothered to throw anything out of their lives.[13]

Akalaitis had departed from the spare production style of *Play, Come and Go,* and *The Lost Ones.* Seeing the *Cascando* set in Berlin in 1976, Beckett observed somewhat cryptically, "Well, you certainly have adapted it." Akalaitis felt he did not like it but out of politeness said nothing. Beckett gave the company permission to continue its tour of *Cascando,* clearing the Swiss rights by jotting on a paper napkin "OK for Mabou Mines to do *Cascando* in Switzerland. Sam Beckett."[14]

Akalaitis adapted the play by changing the medium but not the script. While some lines were heard over a radio, she replaced the original broadcast's music by Marcel Mihalovici with a score written by Glass. Nor did Akalaitis personalize the play's three elements—Music, Voice, and Opener. Cellist Arthur Russell, dressed like the rest of the cast in heavy jacket and cap, sat and played in the upstage right corner of the set. The cast spoke both in unison and individually as Voice, their lines prompted or cut off by Neumann in the role of Opener. Seated in a rocking chair, Opener was heavier, more earthbound, than the ascetic narrator of *The Lost Ones,* but like Warrilow he was extrapolated from the text, where the figure of "Woburn" is more motif than character. Woburn's bulky figure seems to be gravitating as well—falling, then lying face down in the muck of his struggle between the hills and the sea. In the meantime, Voice struggles to finish a life or a story akin to Woburn's unfinished journey, a final effort to fulfill all those stories that have come before.

Here the resemblance to *The Lost Ones* ended and another—to *Dressed Like an Egg*—began. Rather than underscoring the despairing struggle to create, Akalaitis's production was "a dense, visual, and sometimes quite funny hour." Again Munk's account seems the best informed of the New York reviews.

The woman [McElduff], who is the central presence of the collective Voice, is pregnant, wide-eyed, a little vacant, and smug. . . . She takes out some cards. There is no sound except the creaking of [Neumann's] rocking chair and a sort of occasional asthmatic wheeze. She shuffles and deals; they play some game I couldn't grasp but made me laugh. This works into building card houses. Careful placements, held breath, collapses, reconstructions. Breathtaking concentration on this useless endeavor. The rhythm of the rocker seems to control the tension and movement. They are passing time, making art, failing, continuing: a metaphor for the entire text.

While McElduff's was the most specific feminine voice in the piece, feminine imagery and activity pervaded of the production of *Cascando*.

> Later each Voice starts an activity: knitting, soap carving, fixing an intricate bit of machinery, doing a coloring book. One has painted watercolors of lighthouses, cliffs, dunes, all by the sea. This isn't busy overproduction: Each actor shows how Woburn's stumbling venture toward the infinite is related—positively and negatively—to all our busywork. An egg appears from [Warrilow's] knitting; they're giving birth to the story.[15]

In retrospect, Raymond sensed "an underlying feminist politics" in *Cascando* that linked it to the more consciously political *Dressed Like an Egg*.[16] There Akalaitis expanded a technique she tried in *Cascando* by visually enlarging Woburn's reported journey. Colette's lines were fully amenable to the director's playful expansions and variations on an artist's self-reflection. There the delicacy of memory provided a virtual sense of the past as always present yet not graspable. In *Cascando*, Akalaitis translated the story, which unfolded over time, into a space at once mysteriously hermetic and effusively associational. She used spatial volume as a corollary to the radio play's voices and music.

This kind of approach is objectionable to Beckett scholar Enoch Brater, who claims that "this radio play authorizes no such thing as physical embodiment."[17] Admittedly, the cluttered space of Akalaitis's production hardly suggests Beckett's juxtaposition of internal voices. The stage space as a kind of human cranium appeared most clearly in Neumann's production of *Company*, where large, inwardly tilted satellite dishes focused attention on the internal voices of Neumann's character. Yet in their work on *Cascando* with choreographer Mary Overlie, Mabou Mines seemed to have "summoned [the past] as pure mood," much as the radio play does in Brater's view. Ruby Cohn defines *cascando* as a "slowing down of tempo, diminishing of volume." Writing about the text, she says, "[T]he imagination has had to live *through* the world in order to retire into what it hopes to find as itself. There has to be a melody before cascando."[18]

Cascando: The Work Process

Like earlier Mabou Mines productions of Beckett, *Cascando* combined motivational and performative acting techniques, narrative and association. Akalaitis noted:

> [Dancer and choreographer Yvonne] Rainer was a very big influence. From her performances I learned that a series of events was not necessarily tied together through narrative, nor was it necessarily subjective. There was a connection which was very plastic and had to do with space and the subconscious—an accrued association in the events.[19]

Finding these connections was not easy, particularly for the younger performers. McElduff had puzzled over the company's work on gesture and sound, elements seemingly unconnected to one another or to definable characters and plot. Without answering her questions directly, Akalaitis and Warrilow assured her she would "find it." In fact, at a certain point in *Cascando* rehearsals the "weird, offbeat gesture" that Akalaitis instructed McElduff to make suddenly made sense to her, and she "made it her own."[20] Akalaitis collaborated with her performers as equals, drawing on the right image or gesture produced and using it where needed. A more thorough exploration of character would come later, in the company's research for *Dressed Like an Egg*. *Cascando*'s cast combined members (though not Breuer or Maleczech) and associates, some of whom were not actors. Sculptor Thom Cathcart, after designing the set for *The Lost Ones,* had become Mabou Mines' most important, though not its sole, technical person. (After he left, the company took on its first "official" full-time technical director, Robin Thomas, in 1977.) David Hardy, who saw himself as a writer, had minimal lines in *Cascando* and a non-speaking role in *Saint* and did not perform again.[21]

For *Cascando*'s choreography Akalaitis turned to Mary Overlie, a member of Barbara Dilley's dance company and the director of her own company from 1975 to 1985. Overlie was familiar with Mabou Mines from her work the previous summer on *The Saint and the Football Player*. She lived with Cathcart in a loft space over the gallery at 112 Greene Street with another couple, Terry O'Reilly and Cynthia Hedstrom, a future company manager. Like several Mabou members, Overlie worked nearby at the restaurant Food. O'Reilly, who also danced with Dilley's company, designed and rigged lights for *Cascando* and installed magical effects. He recalls the play's final moments in terms of its very hot white light, which had the effect of

> flattening the set and [taking] all of the color out. . . . Mary took the spatial change from three dimensional color to one dimension—I won't say black and white, but washed out—as a cue as to how to make the dance. Everyone was flattened against the back wall. The time and place suddenly lost its realism. The dance itself was very abstract and moved at the speed of tai chi, very slow. It seemed to be about trying to find an exit. . . . Very beautiful. No one had done anything like it.[22]

Overlie recalls that her premise for *Cascando* was "to physically invoke [the play's] fractured reality." The structure she created for the actors' (and characters') physical reality "would basically eat itself and disappear. . . . The psychological atmosphere in this play is so delicate and unusual that any stage directions using mundane or pedestrian reality would anchor the audience too much . . . making the actors fight to establish this delicacy by words alone."[23] Early in the process she had hit on an idea that seemed to propel the work forward: "I had the actors make up and memorize a physical script that was made up of movements which had no logic from one move to the next and no connection to the language of the script. As I recall, the actors were delighted because they could suddenly . . . work the script effortlessly." Taking Beckett's objective in *Cascando* to be "a resounding rejection of hierarchy at every turn and therefore a destination that points to a totally non-hierarchical experience for the audience," Overlie created a "sub script" of movement for the actors that would try to support this idea. She avoided emphasizing individual staging elements that fit Beckett's text (such as blocking, spatial orientation, timing of gesture, and kinesthetic action appropriate to emotional logic), instead fracturing them. Movements were set, one by one, so the performers would see only their own personal relationship to these tools. The resulting action on stage, says Overlie,

> is simply a set of choices made in relationship to and partnership with the tools . . . used to communicate with the audience in live theater. The written script was hung onto this movement script, clearing the way for the words and scenario to float and mingle with the physical life of the actors, in this thrilling independence, able to inform and fulfill each other.

As Mabou Mines began to develop the final scene of *Cascando*, O'Reilly's two-dimensional lighting was added. Overlie was surprised: "What happened was strange. The lighting seemed to take an absolute editorial knife, picking up only one in twenty gestures. These gestures then became emblems of the play. The actors started to work with that information, using the highlighted gestures and props as additional characters. Something like a sub script developed, which carried back into the actions which were taken in the beginning." Both Overlie's and O'Reilly's comments suggest an experience of heightened perception caused by a sudden deceleration—a *cascando*. Thought exceeds stimulus, images jump out, and one experiences a sense of vertigo.

The technique Overlie hit on, of creating a physical reality that anchors the actor as independent of the scenario, clearing the way to work with more options and facility with the script, became a principal means of applying her "toolbox" of six View Points to theater. Overlie has continued to develop her ideas in her teaching at New York University's Experimental Theatre Wing (founding teacher, 1977–87; director, 1989–91; currently associate teacher), and also in her work done elsewhere in the U.S. and Europe. Director Anne Bogart has acknowledged her teacher as one source from whom she has "stolen" ideas, among which the term *Viewpoints*, spelled as a single word, has become probably the best known.[24]

Cascando demonstrated Akalaitis's debt as a director to early 1970s performance modes poised between dance and theater. Although her directing technique quickly developed, she continued to produce work that connected space and the subconscious by means of "an accrued association in the events." Valuing performance's immediacy, Akalaitis did not film *Cascando* or *Dressed Like an Egg*, as Breuer had done with the first two Animations and *The Lost Ones*. She has continued to be less interested in preservation of past productions than in current work, a deliberate forgetfulness. As a result her earlier work is less well known. Breuer, Maleczech, and Neumann, on the other hand, more interested in narrative and its shaping, have taken an active role in telling Mabou Mines' history. *Cascando*, which won an Obie for Akalaitis in 1976, came at what Breuer calls the company's "moment of budding."[25] As Akalaitis began to rival his visibility as a director, Breuer sought to regain his identity as a writer. Akalaitis has not challenged this view. But rather than suggesting a radical shift in the mid-1970s, she has spoken of continuities in Mabou Mines' work. In 1988, she noted, "What we have in common is a belief in a style of acting that is technically complicated; one that is able through the actor's body and voice, to make various comments on the text. Not intellectual comments, but comments that take the text through a journey."[26] *Cascando* resembles *The Lost Ones* in taking text "through a journey"; it looks ahead not just to *Dressed Like an Egg* but to productions Akalaitis has done both with and outside the company.

The Saint and the Football Player: The Production

It appears that Akalaitis never favored a long development period for a show. *Cascando* took approximately six to eight months to develop because, like Breuer's *The Saint and the Football Player,* it had to compete for the company's time with tours of *The Lost Ones* and *The B.Beaver Animation.*[27] By the time *Cascando* toured to Europe in fall 1976, Akalaitis had already begun work on *Dressed Like an Egg.* She did not tinker with her first show but left *Cascando* for the actors to renew each night. The point, for Akalaitis, was to do the work and then leave it behind.

Work on Breuer's *The Saint and the Football Player,* by contrast, had begun in 1972, with the piece continuing to change after its 1973 presentations at New York University's Loeb Student Center, the Paula Cooper Gallery, and the Dance Gallery. Still a resident company at La Mama, Mabou Mines was developing *B.Beaver* while also performing *Music for Voices* for the last time in February and staging *Send/Receive/Send* in November. Leaving La Mama late in 1973, the company focused on presenting workshop productions of *B.Beaver,* often in tandem with *Red Horse.* In February 1976, however, after gaining attention with *The Lost Ones,* and with *Cascando* in rehearsal, Mabou Mines premiered a much expanded *Saint* during a monthlong residency at the Pratt Institute in Brooklyn. The opportunity to work again on *Saint* had come the previous summer when Richard Schechner and Mercedes Gregory's organization, A Bunch of Experimental Theatres, arranged a residency for its member companies at the American Dance Festival at Connecticut College. The second residency produced an even more elaborate *Saint,* including not just the eleven players (outfitted in unnumbered white uniforms bought by Ellen Stewart in 1973) but an announcer, a singer, and referees, cheerleaders and baton twirlers, a high school band, a halftime dance of forklifts, and a snowstorm of confetti. Breuer did not expect to stage it again. The Bunch managed, however, to arrange a European tour in fall 1976 through the International Theatre Institute, which designated theatrical exchanges celebrating the American bicentennial. The International Telephone and Telegraph Corporation (ITT) sent *Saint* (with seventeen actors) to Hamburg, Belgrade, Zagreb, Amsterdam, and Düsseldorf. This tour ran concurrently with appearances of *Cascando* and *The Lost Ones* in Berlin and Geneva, a piggyback tour Breuer arranged and then ran while hopping from one venue to the other.

The burgeoning of *The Saint and the Football Player* from a "sports-art performance" small enough to be presented at the Walker Arts Center in June 1973 to a pageant requiring the cavernous expanse of the Pratt Institute's Activities Resource Center indicated Breuer's growing desire to break out of the constricted spaces and high-art aesthetics of Mabou Mines' gallery work. Reviewer Arthur Sainer commented sympathetically, "Something about bigness is getting to [Breuer] . . . and something about Pop America is getting to him [as well]."[28] Indeed, Breuer's twin interests in pop culture and oversized productions seemed to lengthen the development and rehearsal periods for *Saint* and *Shaggy Dog* as he worked popular idioms from film, music, and sports into the mix. To Bonnie Marranca he commented, "You know what I'm doing—I think I'm doing *8-1/2*—a big Fellini movie—50,000 people running in different directions."[29] The turn to pop culture had another intent: expanding Mabou Mines' audience without losing the work's ironic layering of voices. "Breuer refunctions popular iconography to produce a more intelligent and socially relevant work than most found in 'political' theater," Marranca claimed. This "art with popular imagery" was intended to appeal to a general audience as well as to the downtown art crowd.

Saint, appearing for single performances at infrequent intervals, was a challenge for some spectators, but others enjoyed its playful formalism. The pretext for *Saint* had been Breuer's desire to "translate a poem into an image series" using the rigorous physical geometry of football plays to generate "vertical yardage," which John Howell called "a spiritual attitude, a kind of ecstasy."[30] "Xerox Poem" by Jack Thibeau juxtaposed grainy photocopied images of a female saint and a touchdown, thus creating a "very serious gag" that suggested, among other things, the "I-saw-God-when-I-scored syndrome." Thibeau had wanted to isolate a visual image before it became consciously verbal and literary. Football was a potent cultural icon whose political and social implications could be invoked implicitly, as Thibeau noted tongue in cheek to *Sports Illustrated:* "The mere sight of football uniforms re-creates a whole level of consciousness."[31] After watching an early incarnation of *Saint* in Minneapolis, reviewer Mike Steele agreed.

The minute the 11-man team in full uniform trotted out on the Walker Audi-
torium floor, the crowd cheered. . . . The team lined up and began going
through chants. "On one," "hut two" and so on. Instead of random chants,
however, the words are a carefully orchestrated poetic music by Philip Glass,
using the language of football with the rhythms of football. . . . The ball is
snapped in slow motion and from there the players go through a series of
typically athletic moves, from the slow motion beauty of hand-offs and
passes to the brutal force of the play—and the players really crack heads,
causing an extra kinesthetic response in audience members who have also
played the game. Women referees wander through, keeping things under
control with whistles, signals and gun blasts. At one point, a referee unrolls a
dotted line sweeping from the passer to the receiver. Circular neon lights flash
on at each end of the pass. The passer throws, the receiver catches, every
cliché of football is conjured.[32]

Glass's calling music quickly established the serial patterns of the piece, while
the "plays," done in television-style slow motion, abstracted the game and
commented on it.

Performed exclusively indoors, the early version of *Saint* was, in Breuer's
words, a "total put-on of macho." Hardy noted that this "pageant," a "fantasy
piece for boys," had drawn several cast members to their first Mabou Mines
show: "Everybody loved the idea of using football in this way and banging each
other around."[33] Among those who answered the call were Hardy, O'Reilly, and
Steve Benneyworth, all of Eads Hill; John Howell, who agreed to participate if
he could play quarterback;[34] author Thibeau; L. B. Dallas; John Pynchon
Holms; and Greg Mehrten. The company encountered very different physical
challenges when, working with Connecticut College students at the American
Dance Festival, Breuer added Overlie's halftime choreography, a contact improvisation with a fleet of vehicles coordinated by Holms. For the first time,
Saint was performed outdoors using car headlights for illumination and ra-
dios for sound.

Mehrten joined the American Dance Festival production at Connecticut
College immediately after graduating with a degree in theater arts and directing from the University of California, Santa Cruz, where he had taken a workshop with Breuer. At the festival he took workshops with Richard Foreman,
Charles Ludlam, the Performance Group, André Gregory, Twyla Tharp, and
Trisha Brown, but he was drawn to Breuer's ideas and the company's way of
working. Very quickly, Mehrten became exclusively involved with Mabou

Mines. He assisted directors, helped run the office, collaborated on shows, and, like other young associates devoted to the company, did not worry too much about the lack of money. "I worked on all the shows for six years," he recalled. "I was totally Mr. Mabou, it wasn't possible for me to do anything else, so [in 1981] I told everyone I wanted to become a member."[35] Often Mehrten lent his distinctive voice—"a great comic voice," notes Don Shewey, "the weary whine of a blasé Bloomingdale's habitué." Just as voice and language are central yet often overlooked in Mabou Mines' work, so Mehrten contributed centrally, often in unseen ways, to the success of shows in the late 1970s and 1980s. He performed in *The Shaggy Dog Animation, A Prelude to Death in Venice, Dead End Kids,* and *Wrong Guys* before becoming a member, then appeared in *Cold Harbor* (as well as designing costumes and tableaux), *Flow My Tears, The Policeman Said,* and the radio show *The Joey Schmerda Story* (1984). As a younger member, Mehrten had no opportunity to direct a company-sponsored show until 1984, when he staged his own script, *Pretty Boy,* based on Wedekind's Lulu plays, and followed it by writing and performing in *It's a Man's World* (1985), directed by David Schweitzer. As an openly gay man who had difficulty finding financial support for his projects, Mehrten told Shewey in 1984 that Mabou Mines was making it possible for him to do his own work.[36] Maleczech had given him a great role ("the evil bisexual homicidal maniac Eddie Sesqui") in *Wrong Guys,* in which six male actors played a range of male sexualities against the conventions of film noir. In *Mabou Mines Lear,* Mehrten's last show as a company member, Breuer cast him in the important role of the fool. Mehrten literally towered in a drag queen's high heels, evening gown, and feather boa over Maleczech's gender-reversed Lear. In playing a "distorted mirror" of her gendered power, Mehrten embodied the production's rich and complex account of gender as construction. That account had begun in Mabou Mines' male-female gender struggles of the mid-1970s, arguments in which Mehrten had little part, but the company's increasingly complex and subtle treatment of gender reflected the emergence of gay culture in general and, most immediately, Mehrten's sensibilities and interests. That influence began with *Saint,* where he played the announcer and head cheerleader, parts Breuer created for him.

Saint was Overlie's first collaboration with Mabou Mines, initiated after company members saw a concert of her solo performances at Saint Mark's Church in 1974 or 1975. While difficult at first, the work turned out so well that the halftime show seemed to rival the game itself. The idea to employ contact improvisation apparently came from O'Reilly, who had been working with dancer and choreographer Steve Paxton. O'Reilly recalls that they improvised a move called the drip, "where you land on someone and you drip like wax down them." Conceiving that the drip could be done on a car, O'Reilly noted that "the shape, the fenders, the hoods . . . presented the same kind of surfaces that the dancer presents to her partner in contact."[37] Overlie's version of this story does not mention O'Reilly but otherwise agrees with it:

> I asked Lee if I could use the cars in the choreography of the half time [show]. Lee liked the idea right away and . . . I started to research twenty dancers doing contact improvisation with the cars. Basically I came to use the cars and the people as separate visual elements, overlaying them to create a whole. I remember the dancers in a straight line down the field, the cars coming in toward them at a right angle from either side. The cars stopped next to each other in a zipper formation, obscuring the . . . one or two dancers between each car. The cars peeled out toward the edge of the field they were facing and the dancers were gone (hiding inside the cars). The cars drove into a circular pattern and as they circled the field, the dancers rolled out onto the ground. That was the drip.[38]

While Overlie and Breuer continued to appreciate each other's work, they did not collaborate again. Overlie attributes this to the combination of high pressure and movie-type "glamor" in Breuer's working style, which seemed to run counter to her own "bare trust and love of mechanics." Yet the resulting halftime show was, she said, "huge, mysterious and sometimes startlingly beautiful."

Curiosity about the seldom seen production had grown with the company's reputation, so much so that in 1976 the *New York Times, Village Voice,* and *Soho Weekly News* ran articles on the expanded production's anticipated premier. Arthur Sainer seemed to have been transported by the piece's conception, recommending that parents take their children for the piece's "sheer circus immensity."[39] He judged it "a lovely blast of an idea" that transported football into a ritual of "unending foreplay" and "stoned-out serial actions." Despite technical problems, *Saint* worked a kind of magic on many participants and viewers. Henry Hewes described the American Dance Festival performance as "a skillful parody [that] leaves its audience strangely disquieted about the almost religious commitment that both football watcher and football player seem to need in order to make the sport worth all the attention and effort."[40] Breuer had deepened his original formalist conception—"see[ing] how much energy a piece could hold and retain form"—with a more immediate sense of cultural events.[41] Primed by the Watergate scandal, President Richard Nixon's resignation, the fall of South Vietnam, and the cultural posturing surrounding the American bicentennial, Breuer spoke of *Saint* as "metatheater that grabs the collective unconscious of America at its roots." Football is about conquering territory, Breuer told Bonnie Marranca; it shows the link between the Puritan ethic and American imperialism. If the performers experienced euphoria when putting on their uniforms, they also demonstrated to audiences that football had become a state religion. "God isn't dead," quipped Breuer. "He's at the Super Bowl."[42]

Some performers felt, however, that *Saint* had become overcomplicated. By 1976 Hardy had left to tour with *Cascando* and *The B.Beaver Animation,* which he helped run. He had enjoyed his work on *Saint* but felt that Breuer directed pieces that were best in mid-development, when "it's still spare enough."[43] When *Shaggy Dog*'s development began to run even longer than *B.Beaver*'s and grew more intensely conflicted, Hardy left the show. *Shaggy Dog* was a turning point for the company. Warrilow dropped out because the show had a California sensibility to which he could not relate and he felt he had nothing to contribute.[44] *Shaggy Dog,* however, was a beginning for Breuer—a validation of his work as both writer and director. It was the last show in which he directed Akalaitis. Mabou Mines began to become a company of directors in order to accommodate the strong egos of mature artists ready to take on their own, often larger and more complex projects. The key to this transition lay in the separating spheres of Breuer and Akalaitis.

The Shaggy Dog Animation: The Production

From Breuer's perspective, *The Shaggy Dog Animation* was his second validation as a writer. The first had come in the mid-1950s, when his student plays stirred interest at UCLA.[45] In the late 1960s he had finished a novel and written an early version of *B.Beaver,* but not until *Shaggy Dog* received an Obie for Best Play of 1978 did Breuer feel visible as a writer. The *Animations* were subsequently published in 1979 in a handsome hardback volume introduced by Bonnie Marranca, who had included Ann Elizabeth Horton's "comic book" version of *Red Horse* in her 1976 anthology *The Theatre of Images.*

Since the hoopla surrounding *The Lost Ones* had died down, Breuer had felt himself in a "no-man's land" characterized by a public interest in Mabou Mines as a collective of artists who apparently devised their pieces, and their lives, together. Both financial pressures and a sense of personal anxiety impelled him to strike out in new directions such as teaching at the Yale University School of Drama in 1977 and directing plays outside the company such as *Lulu* (1980) at the American Repertory Theatre and *The Tempest* (1981) for the New York Shakespeare Festival. A measure of Breuer's anxiety had to do with gender issues that were filtering into the company members' lives and work process. For these reasons, *Shaggy Dog* marks an important step in Breuer's preoccupation with a kind of cultural behaviorism in his work.

At the time Breuer was writing *Shaggy Dog,* he had only a vague sense of the shape *La Divina Caricatura* would take. At first the larger narrative had no name. By the mid-1980s he had begun to speak of *Realms,* an epic tracing a soul through six modes of existence, the earthly realm being represented in *Shaggy Dog* and *Prelude.*[46] By the early 1990s Breuer's six-part "performance poem" had become *Animation* (or *Animations*), a three-part work that focuses on a triangle of characters whose lives are traced through the six realms. The triangle consists of characters that first appeared in *Shaggy Dog:* John, a washed-up 1960s filmmaker; Rose, a dog who loves John and aspires to be a film editor; and Leslie, an actress and Rose's human rival. In 1996 Breuer completed Rose's story in *An Epidog.* In the third part, *Ecco Porco,* the primary subject, after living as a dog and an ant, returns as a pig based loosely on the persona of the B.Beaver.

Shaggy Dog, with its gender parody, outlined the trajectory of the master narrative by introducing "the wages of attachment."[47] This quasi-Buddhist phrase refers to emotional connections by means of which human beings locate and define themselves. Breuer's character John, an aging experimental filmmaker, finds in his dog, Rose, a "partner in security" in front of whom he can do anything. John has internalized the dog's view of him as "master of the dog, . . . master of his art, . . . master of life." When Rose runs away, John becomes a void, caught in the hell of his borrowed identity. At the same time, Rose is a fragmented subject trying to make sense of her comically romantic view of the world. To that end audiences hear her reading the "Dear John" letter by means of which she attempts to exorcise her own attachment. Rose has internalized American culture's bifurcated sense of itself: an ego composed of a veneer of romanticism concealing a "hard-boiled business ethic." As Rose goes about her day in her Soho loft, she struggles to cope with the culture's voices as they come to her through film, radio, and other media. Thus, *Shaggy Dog* operates on two levels—indeed, it was originally conceived as two plays—a sound track that carries the memory-narrative of John and Rose's romance and a highly ironized, disjunctive image track that attempts to rid itself of the narrative.

Although Rose does become a film editor, radio lies at the heart of *Shaggy Dog*. Perhaps for this reason the play opens with the image of a radio dial.

> The house lights go out; the entire rear wall lights up. It represents the tuning band of a radio—a 23-foot long radio band [designed and built by Alison Yerxa]. In front of it eight [*sic*] people are standing with their backs to the audience . . . dressed in tight jeans with loose-hanging multicolored blouses; some are in long robes. In front of each person is a microphone. The red pointer on the radio band moves noisily, passing several stations. It stops and a child's voice (Clove Galilee) is heard. She recites in soft modulation a Dear-John letter from Rose, the dog, to her owner John. Then the other actors join in, and gradually the monolog, spoken alternately by several voices, describes Rose's entrance into John's life.[48]

Shaggy Dog was divided into three parts dominated by types of popular music—rock, Latin and country and western, and jazz—which carry their own mythologies of love. As Marranca notes, "Music so dominates contemporary notions of romance that people identify experience with the musical theme it suggests to them." *Shaggy Dog*, Breuer said, functioned as the "echo chamber" necessary to give the words "I love you" context and meaning.[49] But the meaning is elusive; just as all the actors were miked, the narrative was filtered through clichés. In the sound track, Rose comments:

> YOU STARTED TO CRY . AND COVER ME WITH KISSES . I PRIED YOUR HAND AWAY AND LICKED YOU ON THE FOREHEAD . GOODBYE . DEAR . I SAID . AND SANK INTO THE NIGHT LIKE A PIECE OF BACON IN A BOWL OF SPLIT PEA SOUP . I LOVE YOU ROSE . YOU CRIED . INTO THE WAVE OF SPLIT PEA NIGHT THAT COVERED ME . I LOVE YOU JOHN . I CALLED.

At the same time, voices on the image track are saying: "ROSE . LOOK AT THE SPACE YOU'VE CLEARED . CAN YOUR NEW LIFE COME AND LIVE WITH YOU . IS THERE ROOM . IS THERE TIME . ALL THAT OLD JAZZ ." The actors spoke in an American version of *Sprechstimme*. They had listened to recordings, taking verbal tonalities or phrasings indicative of specific singers, and then left the recordings behind. The result was a type of choral speaking by means of which Rose is abstracted. The words address not John or the audience so much as the culture that has "created" them. As in other

Mabou Mines productions, a staging element—a light, a musical phrase, an image distorted through a Fresnel lens—would take over the moment and speak.[50] Never before, though, had Mabou Mines electronically filtered virtually all the sound in a production.

> The actors' voices weave in and out. Lines are delivered by one or two voices while words, at times, are repeated by several so that a choral pattern evolves. At times the sound amplification and distortion take over—words and meaning are lost, moods accentuated. Several times the lights as well as the sound control are shut off; an actor turns, faces the audience, flicks a lighter that illuminates his/her face and says a few words in a direct, natural voice. Then, after a split-second blackout, the previous image returns. Related sound effects are interspersed; the sound of water being poured in a dog's bowl, the sound of a whistle, fingersnapping, panting and howling.[51]

The distortion of voices (doubling, altering pitch, fading either in and out or up and down the scale) emerged from an Eventide harmonizer/synthesizer controlled by Robin Thomas, while Mehrten and Jessie Nelson provided radio-style sound effects produced mechanically but also filtered electronically. The electronic filtering was Breuer's first full-blown move toward that notion of choral theater to which later pieces of *Caricatura* such as *The Warrior Ant* and *An Epidog* have contributed.

"Choral theatre is alive and well inside of popular lyricism," Breuer remarked in 1978.[52] In everyday speech, slang, popular music, and Hollywood film Breuer found metaphors that touched the changing nerve system of American culture with its growing sensitivity to cultural difference. Choral theater is founded on oppositions—"sparks jumping a gap"—to create a new perception. These oppositions are not just verbal, but also visual, "visual puns on verbal ideas." One such pun was the "axe" with which Rose struck the set at the end of part I. The solidity of Rose's life dissolved as her apartment separated into seven pieces that scattered in all directions, a few moving directly toward the audience. "The metaphor of Rose's *Vogue* type of decoration, of *interior* decoration, is the decoration of one's mind in the light of romanticism and the attempt at splitting it," Breuer commented. "The split is done with a sword and so we use an axe as a joke because axe of course alludes to guitar, and one says 'one's axe,' one's thing, one's weapon." As a result of this technique, audiences tended to recall the overall effect or individual moments rather than losing themselves in the story. The juxtaposition of image and sound track was visible in the set, a two-thirds-scale Soho loft furnished with working appliances and running water. Each room corresponded to an aspect of Rose's ego.

> Each of these has its imagery, its own color, its own symbolic shape. The bedroom is greed, the bathroom is pride, the kitchen hate or aggression, the cutting-room jealousy and the living-room, the center, is stupidity. The idea is that the four wings of the mandala all stem from ignorance, and stupidity is interpreted simply as inability to see the truth.

In negotiating the gaps between oppositions, audiences focused on their own cultural assumptions. Rather than parody, Breuer called this "play[ing] the game while showing the game," a variation on Brecht's *Verfremdungseffekt.*

Elsewhere I have written about *Shaggy Dog* as an extended metaphor of the avant-garde in the mid-1970s, when artists began to receive the mixed blessing of federal and private grant monies.[53] Breuer sees Rose, the dog, both as the artist subject to the whims of middlebrow grant-distributing cultural institutions and as the "female" part of himself, which likes to "eat shit." Rose's self-hatred causes her to bite the master's philanthropic hand. As the story of "an unenlightened life," *Shaggy Dog* "writes into the metaphor" of the avant-garde artist as dog. In Southern California slang, says Breuer, a "dog" is a woman with no mind of her own, someone who adopts the views of her man. Breuer develops the metaphor so fully that it appropriates other elements in the text, namely, Breuer's effort to alleviate the anxiety of his "sweaty grapple with the self."

> My only writing teacher, ever, at San Francisco State, was named Herb Willner and the only thing I remember him telling me is, "write into the metaphor." I really believe that. I don't think I've ever followed any other advice about writing. The key is the moment I can formulate the metaphor, when it reverberates. A dog. A dog as the precise metaphor for the male-female sociopolitical entity in terms of feminism today. A dog and a master. A leash. A chain. That kind of a thing. I really feel I'm writing a parable.[54]

Breuer's intent to "write into the metaphor" is unabashedly totalizing. He appropriates material from the lives of family and friends, and from other cultures, in order to drive into the heart of the metaphor and articulate all its meanings. Rather than being autobiographical, Breuer creates an "autograph," "a way of making my myth," a form of writing that appropriates elements from his own and company members' lives but reshapes them, using metaphor, to fit into *La Divina Caricatura*. For example, Breuer described the events of *Shaggy Dog* as a "prototypical love affair circa 1957–1977," "twenty years of emotional programming" that paralleled the span of his relationship with Ruth Maleczech. As an expanding company with several families whose children were old enough to participate in the work, Mabou Mines was facing new personal and financial pressures. Still, it would be a mistake to identify the events of *Shaggy Dog* too closely with the lives of Breuer, Maleczech, or Leslie Mohn, the namesake of Rose's rival, Leslie.[55] Breuer's insistence on peopling *Caricatura* with characters resembling those to whom he is attached, personally and professionally, constitutes "social archetype," not family history. As an "autograph," *Shaggy Dog* allowed Breuer to speak from another point of view, in this case his take on a woman artist's perspective, though not necessarily that of Maleczech, Mohn, or Maude Mitchell, his current partner and the actress with whom he developed *Mabou Mines Dollhouse* (2003).

For Breuer, the theatrical literalizing of metaphor gives language an opportunity to reshape reality through parody. Such a reshaping does occur in the staging of his work. Breuer's intent to "write into the metaphor," however, can overwhelm other elements in his language. In spinning out the chain of relations, Breuer's language seems to foster a kind of inward spiral, narrowing the inventiveness of his fictional universe. As Peggy Phelan notes, metaphor "works to secure a vertical hierarchy of value and is reproductive; it works by erasing dissimilarity and negating difference; it turns two into one."[56] Breuer's later intercultural works—for example, *The Warrior Ant* and *The MahabharANTa* (1992)—are particularly susceptible to metaphor's tendency to erase cultural differences even as he tries to articulate them.

As a production that deals with the formation of Rose's feminist consciousness and identity amid the siren songs of American popular culture, *Shaggy Dog* was the prelude to Breuer's "chronicle of the gender wars."[57] In fact, he staged John's part of the story separately as *A Prelude to Death in Venice*. Breuer was ahead of other directors in realizing that men needed to reexamine gender roles too. Yet, given the self-referential quality of his metaphors, Breuer may have been less interested in the feminine than in how female characteristics participate in forming masculinity. Comparing *Shaggy Dog* to Maleczech's *Vanishing Pictures* and Akalaitis's *Dressed Like an Egg* heightens the contrast. In the latter, distinct gender lines faded as male and female figures, straight and gay, took on each other's identities in a series of intriguingly framed orientalist poses. But Breuer has generally shunned gender ambiguity in favor of gender stereotype.

Emily Apter points out that stereotype can pose a threat other than that of intimidation or repression; while an individual may face the latter, a more interesting type threatens gender orthodoxy itself by "pretending an identity into existence."[58] Breuer sees his use of cliché in this light, as stereotype that turns on the culture that created it and torments its "master" through parody. Rose and John, dog and master, could be read as incarnations, for example, of Rita Hayworth and Glenn Ford in the 1946 film *Gilda,* where such a parody takes place. Gilda, trapped in the image of the fallen woman, consciously performs it for Ford, the lover who has spurned her. She constitutes a "colonized subject" in Apter's terms; in Breuer's she would be a character suffering "the wages of attachment." Gilda chooses from the menu of gendered stereotypes she is offered. Apter seeks to recoup stereotype for late-twentieth-century postcolonial circumstances "as the bad object of colonial mimicry [allowed] to return as a good object of subjectification, shattering politically fixed colonial subjects into a multitude of refractive, potentially emancipatory subject positions." While Hayworth cannot escape stereotype in *Gilda,* her husband-director Orson Welles fragmented her image literally in the famous hall of mirrors scene in *The Lady from Shanghai* (1948). Similarly, Breuer attempts to emancipate stereotype in *The Warrior Ant,* with gender playing backup to his primary intercultural themes. As with the *Verfremdungseffekt,* the first step, shattering the stereotype, is easier than the second, reviving it as a set of viable options. In *Shaggy Dog,* Breuer attempted only the first step, producing a multitude of refractory selves that Sylvère Lotringer characterized as ecstatic rather than emancipatory. Rose has no proper body but is represented across the body of the production as "a collection of disjointed quotations that . . . are never allowed to cohere."[59]

Still, *Shaggy Dog* was the first work to join Breuer's metaphoric narrative style to the directing techniques of his later intercultural projects. He was beginning to use what Homi Bhabha calls "metonymic logic" in his staging. That is, Breuer presented a subject "graspable only in the passage between telling/told, between 'here' and 'somewhere else.'"[60] Three or four actors manipulated the puppet Rose while projecting the disassociated voices of sound and image tracks.

On the rear raised platform at the left, a bed is set; lying down on it is a doll dressed . . . in blue jeans and blouse. Three actors and one actress crouch around the bed, while two other actresses are at each pillar. They all carry microphones. . . . The actors move [the puppet] around—either as a rod-and-stick puppet or strapped to the waist of someone, her arms attached to the arms of the actor. (In the latter position, either of the two bound together can be seen as extensions of the same persona; the actor, too, is being "manipulated"—through their connection to the sound system.) Onto this puppet the monologs are projected. At times the lines seem voiced through her; at other times the actor appears to be making a kind of aside conversation with the puppet, totally neglecting the presence of the audience.[61]

This dispersion of subjects reflects Japanese Bunraku storytelling, which is divided among puppeteer, narrator, and musician. Breuer had first seen Bunraku with Maleczech and Warrilow while living in Paris.[62] But Bunraku artists seek to surmount the disassociations created by this division in order to form the impression of a seamless narrative. If Rose's story had been played as written, with its insistent metaphors, this traditional Japanese theatrical convention might not have countered them with a metonymic logic. But Mabou Mines, under Breuer's direction, played the metaphors against one another and the commentary of the image track. Also, in rehearsal Breuer took a fairly straightforward connection between radio song lyrics and the characters' emotional states and abstracted it. The visceral, alienated, rock-and-roll sensibility of their story was the medium in which the fragmented thoughts of John and Rose floated. After seeing *Shaggy Dog*, Gerald Rabkin wrote:

In confronting the piece you must first of all resist the impulse to impose conventional order and meaning. The shaggy dog reference is accurate: the thematic "punchline" is anticlimactic. What Lee Breuer, who conceived the piece, and Mabou Mines have done is to create a work with a musical rather than a conventionally dramatic structure. This is not a play. Characters are consciously ambiguous and undefined. Language is not causal and sequential. The piece weaves fragments of sound and image which derive from recurrent motifs into a disturbing, amusing, moving elaboration on the disassociated sensibility of our age, an age whose "center does not hold." We are bombarded continually by images magnified, reduced, manipulated by our one supreme skill—technology. Mabou Mines dissects, enlarges, reduces, reassembles, *animates* these images into new configurations. In so doing it seeks to reduce their power over us and the power of those who manipulate and exploit them.[63]

While *Shaggy Dog* demystified American culture, it did not liberate Rose from the sound track of romantic conventions. Breuer considers *Shaggy Dog* a feminist work that defused sexist stereotypes and presented Rose as the victor in her struggle with the culture. She, unlike John, achieves enough insight to build herself a new life. But, as the following discussion of the piece's development will show, some members consider *Shaggy Dog* a monument to Breuer's anxiety over the disappearance of traditional gendered behaviors. As Breuer remarked, "[T]he liberation movement that for me hit closest to the bone was feminism. You're dealing with attitudes that may be even deeper than racism, and any male has got to feel ambivalent about it. The position of power was sweet, and that's why we held on to it for so long."[64]

The Shaggy Dog Animation engages both kinds of stereotypes, the productive and the regressive. As such, it is a crucial production in Breuer's development of a metonymic performance logic for his master narrative. *Sister Suzie Cinema* also juxtaposes visual and aural elements and is preoccupied with music and film as the alienated forms that best express a "difference within" American culture. As Breuer expanded on his metonymic logic in *The Gospel at Colonus* and *The Warrior Ant,* he seems to have discovered that locating and claiming the stereotypes is the first step to an intercultural "double scene" of the sort Bhabha has described. Metonymic strategies need constant renewal in order to counteract metaphor's appropriative tendencies. In other words, Breuer's shift from a focus on the isolated male subjectivity to a "feminist" focus on the community of "self and other" was—and is—an on-going struggle to allow "difference within."

The Shaggy Dog Animation: The Work Process

At this point the story of *The Shaggy Dog Animation* as Breuer's "autograph" opens up to the struggle within Mabou Mines to define its way of working and its future. Several members and associates agree that in the mid- to late 1970s they were struggling with questions of self and other—how to accommodate those who wanted to direct; distribute funds among shows; pay a growing group of associates and staff; and, most important, deal with members' increasingly diverse cultural and aesthetic sensibilities. In the three-year development of *Shaggy Dog,* these conflicts came to the fore in part because the piece examined gender and power in its focus on the "wages of attachment."

Work had begun on *Shaggy Dog* in early 1975, with Breuer writing first the opening and closing sections, then (as the company rehearsed *Dressed Like an Egg*) the second, middle section. Mabou Mines began rehearsing *Shaggy Dog* at Wonderhorse on East Fourth Street, later a rehearsal space for the New York Theatre Workshop. The company worked on *Shaggy Dog* at the American Dance Festival for several successive summers and presented it as a work in progress at the Open Space Theatre (in Soho) and the Paula Cooper Gallery. Most rehearsals, however, took place in the Old Prop Shop, an unused, between-levels space at the Public Theater, which also provided "surplus materials [including three aluminum beams from Andrei Serban's production of *Agamemnon*] and access to construction facilities."[65] The show previewed twice at the Public, then opened in March 1978.

The set's development influenced the relationship among puppets, performers, and those who created the multiple vocal effects. In part I, the action began on the higher, upstage platform in front of the radio dial but soon focused on the lower platform, an area twenty-five feet square that formed Rose's loft apartment. Fractured into pieces at the end of part I, it was re-formed for part II, but the hyperreal apartment was never again complete. Pieces were moved off so that the action could focus on selected areas such as the upper platform where dual telephones flanked John and his puppeteer, Raymond, in part III. The lower platform was based on a concept by the sculptor Gordon Matta-Clark, best known for *Splittings: Four Corners,* the suburban New Jersey home he sawed in half and tilted to reveal the space inside. The set evolved from plywood construction to an elaborate Plexiglass design. In a detailed 1978 article, Susan Spector emphasized that a series of group decisions had changed the play to take advantage of new design possibilities.

> The construction of the floor for Rose's loft illustrates how Mabou Mines evolves its playing space through a series of group decisions. As originally conceived, the floor had to support only Rose and her household equipment, it had to enclose 150-watt floodlights for one special lighting effect, and it had to split into irregular sections on cue. . . .
>
> When Mabou Mines moved to the Public Theater a more complex idea for Rose's floor came out of discussions involving the whole company. The floor, it was decided, would break into seven jagged segments, and the entire structure would be fitted together to look like a Plexiglass lightbox with transparent top and sides, [a design that proved to be] too fragile and too costly.
>
> After further discussion, the company carpenter made the seven segments using Plexiglass only for the top surface. Heavy plywood sides and 2″ × 3″

transverse joists added enough strength so the floor pieces could slide, roll, or tilt when the floor came apart.

During the construction of this floor, the company decided to make Rose's loft "super-real." Since they were adding quality kitchenware, stainless steel fixtures, neatly mitered sheetmetal details, and ceramic tiling to give Rose a fashionable SoHo living space, the hardwood flooring used in the best loft conversions was called for. . . . [C]onventional flooring would have again eliminated the light from below. Their solution was to use 1/4″ × 2″ pine strips laid over the Plexiglass with 1/4″ spaces left between adjacent strips. This allowed light to pass upward easily and yet looked like solid flooring when it was lit from above.

After this step was completed, the company saw that Rose's floor could bear substantial weight. The director and actors started blocking movement onto it, and the staging developed in new ways. Now, not only Rose but the actors as well could move around on the floor of her loft.

Among those who worked on the floor, Alison Yerxa and John Pynchon Holms built the first version, while Don and Rebecca Christensen designed the second, with credit for construction going to Holms and Jerry Mayer. Yerxa commented in an interview that official credit for design on *Shaggy Dog,* as on other shows directed by Breuer, did not always reflect the way in which a designer's concept might be adapted or supplemented by those of later contributors.[66] While Breuer himself objected to characterizations of Mabou Mines' work as collective, multiplying collaborators apparently caused similar frustration for those who wanted control over the execution of their concepts.

Julie Archer, who in 1976 arrived in New York from Minneapolis, was asked to devise a horizontal curtain. The curtain, made to look like a bank of clouds, disguised the lower platform during the opening scene, then would whisk back and up to reveal Rose's loft. After her first attempt was destroyed when someone walked across her quilt of inflated white trash bags, she devised a sturdier assembly of cotton attached to clear plastic sheeting, with a batten allowing the curtain to fold back on itself as pulleys raised it up to travel offstage. This was not her first set piece for Mabou Mines. Although her primary job for the company had been babysitting the members' children, Maleczech had persuaded Akalaitis, then rehearsing *Dressed Like an Egg,* to let Archer make a lighter-weight replacement for the disintegrating mock-up of Colette's dog, Toby-chien.[67] Archer went on to design sets, lights, projections, or puppets for several Mabou Mines productions, including *Wrong Guys, Hajj, An Epidog,*

Belén—A Book of Hours (1999), *Ecco Porco, Cara Lucia* (2003), *Red Beads* (2005), and *Song for New York: What Women Do While Men Sit Knitting* (2007). While she stayed on the company's margins for years, Archer's involvement intensified when she and Liza Lorwin, producer of *The Gospel at Colonus,* developed *Peter and Wendy* (1996). Maleczech persuaded Archer to become a company member in 2002.

From the beginning Archer and other Mabou associates were concerned with creativity rather than job titles, and the company did not ask for formal credentials. Everyone was pressed into service to devise solutions for the many challenges of *Shaggy Dog.* As with Toby-chien, which had been made for twenty-five dollars, the artists often had little or no budget and limited time. Sometimes it came down to finding the person who did not already have several assignments and was willing to tackle a problem. These young people were eager to work with the company and gladly put in the hours, successful completion of tasks leading in some cases to larger assignments on other shows. Archer has commented, "When Lee and I work together . . . at its best, he'll give me a scenario—not a literal one—and then he leaves me alone. It can be a series of adjectives, a seed. Then I'm off. He draws from so many sources. He scatters that out, and I go in. It's so rich and prolific."[68] Linda Hartinian both performed in *Shaggy Dog* and constructed the two puppets, but, equally important, some of the show's character came from her "hit" in rehearsal on a "'50s pop romantic tonality."[69] On the other hand, Robin Thomas recalls working on *Shaggy Dog* and *Dressed Like an Egg* as Mabou Mines' first "official" technical director, anticipating the more traditionally defined roles to come in the 1980s.[70]

Construction of a weight-bearing stage had allowed for the development of Bunraku-style puppetry involving three to four actors. If *Shaggy Dog* changed direction to accommodate new staging possibilities, it was also shaped by the unique contributions of its cast members. Breuer wanted to "take [out] all of the acting,"[71] leaving a more distanced performance style. Each performer seemed to find his or her answer. As well as removing the acting, Breuer imposed, according to Neumann, a "raw sensibility,"[72] which Warrilow apparently rejected. Others wanted to explore this rawness. Among those, Maleczech produced a searing reading of Rose's final lines that has remained among spectators' most vivid memories of the production. When Breuer rewrote passages from part III as *A Prelude to Death in Venice,* he credited Maleczech with its single most creative idea: playing the action against the triptych of windows previously hidden behind curtains in the Old Prop Shop so that Raymond, the puppet John, and the two telephone booths were silhouetted against the buildings facing the Public Theater on Lafayette Street. This arrangement occasionally called for Raymond to improvise additional wiseguy lines for John, directing them through the open window to passersby who yelled at him from below.

Raymond was comfortable with *Shaggy Dog*'s California sensibility. He felt in synch with Breuer and devised several bits for his performance, ideas that transformed others' parts as well. In part II he modeled his performance on a particularly sleazy television preacher, prompting Breuer to rewrite the lines to accommodate a country and western motif. Wearing tuxedos with no ties, Raymond and O'Reilly spoke-sang their lines rapidly: "BUNNY . SONNY . LET ME TELL YOU SOMETHING FUNNY . WE'RE LOCKED IN SYMBIOSIS HONEY . I'M YOUR HOT DOG . YOU'RE MY YUMMY . AND THAT'S WHAT I LIKE ABOUT THE SOUTH." Hartinian, a relative newcomer to acting, also shared Breuer's California sensibility, having also grown up in the San Fernando Valley. As in *The Lost Ones*, she counted in her head to distance herself from the action. She found it easy to deal with the work as process but had difficulty, as they all did, keeping up with Breuer's changes. He altered specific script elements, such as taking out all the prepositions or pronouns in their lines, to put the performers at odds with their parts. In some cases he reassigned bits to other performers, sometimes causing hurt feelings but keeping the cast at a distance from both the story and the audience.

Although Neumann appreciated Breuer's search for new techniques, he found the vocabulary of *Shaggy Dog* too specific to the downtown performance world and tried to compensate for that and the "glassy-eyed" performing by finding readier cultural connections in vocal impersonations of television chef James Beard and actor Telly Savalas, best known for his 1970s series *Kojak.* Apparently Neumann and Akalaitis cared least for the piece and to a certain extent went their own ways in performance, but this may not have been as radical a difference as it sounds. Neumann notes that Breuer "had to make do with a lot of acting" in his own performance. As in other pieces, Neumann used feeling as a palette of elemental "representation" colors that, combined with other actors' more "presentational" effects, created the warm and cool results for which Mabou Mines was known. *Shaggy Dog*, in many ways, continued this work for Neumann. Akalaitis also connected her work in *Shaggy Dog* to earlier shows, describing her performance process as beginning with an idea or image, which, when executed by the body, changed her voice and her feeling for what she was doing.

In *The Shaggy Dog*, the process was: start with . . . "mature female warmth and sexuality; vocal, work with the voice." There was very little physical stuff; I was just working vocally with the microphone. So I started with what I thought was sincere female sexiness. Then someone said, "Oh, that's like Billie Holiday"— which I had never thought of. Then I hooked on to Billie Holiday specifically. I listened to her records, started trying to imitate her vocally, and then tried to abstract it, hooked on to something like Billie Holiday, then made a commitment, because I really liked the way she sounds. One day . . . there was an idea that we would say the line, and between the lines would make some sort of physical punctuation. So I worked with that—and with the microphone and the microphone cord. . . . I said, "You came for me," and I would go "Shachoo! Shachoo!" [punctuating this with a sharp hip thrust to the side].

Afterwards Ruth said, "That's great, JoAnne, that's S&M [sadomasochism]." It had nothing to do with S&M for me; it had to do with the physical punctuation of a vocal phrase. Then I . . . studied S&M a little bit. So *not* through my choices, but through something that happened to me in rehearsal, and by the observation and help of the people, I got into two things that never would have occurred to me.[73]

Akalaitis calls this "a typical example of how Mabou Mines works," but as rehearsals for *Shaggy Dog* continued she began to question the show's accessibility, suggesting at one point that they cut part II altogether. Hartinian suggests that Akalaitis's fatigue with the ongoing rehearsal process and the show's seemingly unmanageable length began to speak through her performance as a humorous reading against the line. Puppetry had been added fairly late, with a brief demonstration of Bunraku techniques given by Pittsburgh puppeteer Margot Lovelace. Both Akalaitis and Raymond, otherwise untrained in Bunraku, were expected to manipulate their puppets—Rose and John, respectively—single-handedly through fairly complex actions. Often Rose, manipulated with clear Plexiglas rods, required at least three puppeteers, the first taking the left arm and the head while the second manipulated the other arm and the torso and the third the legs. After attempting to work John in this manner, Raymond grew impatient with the technical difficulties created by the small space and suspended the puppet from a rope tied around his neck. Handling the puppet alone at these moments, Raymond eliminated the need to manipulate the arm-rods, instead having the sleeves of John's costume slit so that Raymond's hands would appear as the puppet's. This elegant solution complicated the action in amusing ways, as John addressed Raymond from time to time. In part II, in which Rose makes cream puffs in her kitchen, Akalaitis also decided to hang Rose from a rope tied around her neck, leaving her hands free while the puppet swung comically to and fro, "like a cape or a dead body."[74] By adding her misgivings about *Shaggy Dog* to her performance, Akalaitis created another layer of meaning in her manipulation of Rose. Her hostility toward *Shaggy Dog* as Breuer's "glorifi[cation of] women's sexual slavery"[75] contributed comically to Rose's lingering frustration with and attachment to John.

Length, form, and accessibility were the issues over which the company's larger struggle of "self and other" took place. Breuer welcomed the cast members' contributions in many cases, but he wanted to stay in control of *Shaggy Dog*, feeling he had ceded too much of *B.Beaver* to ideas from the company. His continual script changes seemed to parallel his emphasis as director on distilling the soundtrack's musical essence. When cast members asked him to take out forty minutes, although those cuts would have reduced their own roles, Breuer seemed to agree, Mehrten said, and then returned with forty minutes of *additional* material. Company members responded to such changes in a variety of ways. On the one hand, the writer was "sort of sacrosanct" for Mabou Mines according to Mehrten.[76] The cast might question changes or argue for cuts, but the writer's wishes were carried out. On the other hand, for Akalaitis making changes, particularly during the run, had to do with the amount of control a director exerts on a process that he or she refuses to leave.[77] Akalaitis commented broadly, "I'm not sure that anything is better because it's rehearsed for three years; in fact, I think, the opposite." Akalaitis felt they were becoming trapped in problems and processes familiar from other productions. Relations among the company members were being addressed in *Shaggy Dog* at neurotic length, producing a "gulag" atmosphere even as cast members were growing artistically and producing performances much more sophisticated than those of *B.Beaver*. It might have been better, Akalaitis said, for the artists to blow up at one another occasionally. Interestingly, Breuer sees this period as the time in which Akalaitis came to prominence due to the timeliness of her feminist approach and the similarity of her visual "minimalism" to the directing style of Robert Wilson.[78] In other words, Akalaitis had begun, like Rose, to "see [herself] as a heavyweight." She, according to Breuer, "got the power" for the next several years, garnering most of the public attention, while Breuer (like John) struggled to escape "the wages of attachment."

This is, though, only one take on events. As Mabou Mines began to accept younger artists as members, several founding members initiated their own projects. Akalaitis saw these changes as ways to keep the work fresh. Breuer was looking for himself in the expanding autographic universe of *La Divina Caricatura*. Personal and cultural memory was Breuer's storehouse of metaphors, but it proved in *Shaggy Dog* a heavy weight for the company. Just as Rose never seems to escape her attachment to John, or "the insatiable thirst for the infinite,"[79] Breuer remained—for a time—within the expanded universe of himself.

Dressed Like an Egg: The Feminine Juxta-posed

While Breuer was writing and directing an autographical master narrative articulating the weight of memory and attachment, Akalaitis was exploring forgetfulness. She approached her second directing project as a way to commit herself to the lived moment as she had experienced it as an actor. She was also recommitting herself to a connected relation with her fellow artists. Just as Breuer was feeling lost in the talk of collaboration, Akalaitis drew on her and her fellow artists' experience to put the show together layer by layer. How does this process involve forgetfulness? Far from deploring "the wages of attachment," *Dressed Like an Egg* celebrates the free and yet unfree life of emotional commitment. Akalaitis wanted to explore romance as an inheritance of romanticism—attitudes, images, narratives, forms—that still shaped life, history, and memory in the late twentieth century. Her primary source was the French author Sidonie-Gabrielle Colette (1873–1954), who had made romance in all its forms her subject. Fully aware of the trap posed by romantic love, Colette habitually allowed herself to forget and step into the trap again. On the other hand, this "lucid woman" relied on her work to constitute another, necessary type of experience—a focus on the moment of writing—drawing on and reconfiguring her memories.[80] Colette avoided large intellectual frameworks. Delighting in the way her literary characters took on minds and lives of their own and despairing over the "humiliating fate of an author who is unsure, before writing, of what he will write," Colette described herself as "free, forgetful, and willing to answer for my forgetfulness."[81] Akalaitis, similarly, has learned to use the past while relinquishing control of it, an approach first visible in *Dressed Like an Egg*. She often claims that she can't remember the details of the work done in the 1970s and 1980s. Her attachment, now as then, is to present work in the moment.

How did *Dressed Like an Egg* (called *Colette* by the company) explore her romanticism? How did it make living moments out of her life story? First, it used Colette's own words. Akalaitis's published script is subtitled "taken from the writings of Colette."[82] She was drawn to the author's exquisite rendering of a woman's experience and, while contributing a few passages of her own, drew most of the script from Colette. Second, Akalaitis wanted to draw elements from an accessible type of theater, the music hall tradition, where motivation and feeling played a stronger role and in which Colette herself appeared. Finally, Colette's work offered Akalaitis an opportunity to explore with the company a timely political and personal subject, gender roles, specifically the sensibility of a woman who had not called herself a feminist but whose work was experiencing a new popularity. *Dressed Like an Egg* was timely, Akalaitis explained in 1978, because

> there is a process of self-definition going on among women. We're past the first, political impulses, the equal-pay, child-care, jobs part of it. Now there's a heading back to mothering and a discovery of what is feminine. . . . What made [Colette] special was her commitment to [a very romantic conception of love]. Her point of view may not have been liberated, but she was tricky. It's a really brilliant expression of consciousness. . . . I wanted to investigate romanticism, make a theatrical statement about the romantic form. Not sentimental or corny, but romantic.[83]

Colette's attitudes about romance and romantic role-playing fit Akalaitis's purposes as she found her own directorial point of view. For her, as for Colette, there was no firm distinction between the popular forms of romantic feeling, whether soap opera, novels, or theatrical melodrama, and the behaviors that mirrored those forms. As Akalaitis knew, the formulas of nineteenth-century romanticism continue to flourish.

Colette was born in Burgundy and moved to Paris at age twenty. After ten years of marriage to Henry "Willy" Gauthier-Villars, under whose name they published her *Claudine* novels, Colette began to develop other friendships. Linked romantically with both men and women, she lived what many considered an exotic, even scandalous life, crossing genders as often as her characters did. As a writer, she was celebrated for both her subject and her style, with its loving attention to the details of moment and place. Erika Munk describes Colette's romanticism as "self-aware, gently debunking inflated emotion and rhetorical poses, but truly committed so that the easy solutions of cynicism were avoided."[84]

Dressed Like an Egg's narrative structure followed Colette's life beginning with her mother, Sido, from whom the young girl learned a "compelling, fierce, and secret rapport . . . with the earth and everything that gushes from its breast."[85] Spectators unfamiliar with Colette could perceive a series of scenes drawing on symbols of romantic love. The audience faced a proscenium space divided by several layers of curtains. At the front, a maroon half curtain, adapted from the Indian dance theater Kathikali and from Brecht's epic theater, moved across the stage, leaving a gap that framed the action. Occasionally the audience could see feet and legs beneath the half curtain or action extending above it. A silver lamé curtain hung upstage left, while in front of a flowered curtain, stage right, a smaller "window shade" was raised and lowered. Bands of colored light in Colette's favorite shades—amber, white, pink, blue—cut across the rectangular spaces created by the curtains. Colored footlights masked by seashells cast a music hall glow upward on the actors' faces.[86] *Dressed Like an Egg* was an "homage to the theatre," Akalaitis wrote in the published script. It "focuse[d] on the movement of light and curtains and the high emotional content that these have in the theatre."

Dressed Like an Egg opened at the Public Theater in May 1977. Glass provided music, Overlie worked with the cast on dance movement, and Robin Thomas designed the lighting with refinements by Beverly Emmons. In the published script, Akalaitis acknowledges the "extensive creative input" of everyone involved, including costume designers Dru-Ann Chukram, Ann Farrington, and Sally Rosen, as well as Thomas, Rebecca Christensen, David Hardy, and Dale Worsley. O'Reilly contributed to the curtain designs. The five actors involved were Warrilow, Raymond, Maleczech, McElduff, and Akalaitis (acting in and directing a show for the first and last time). Visually each woman evoked Colette at a certain age, while Raymond and Warrilow took on aspects of Colette's three husbands and her music hall colleague Georges Wague. Also visible were Colette's fictional characters, whom she (like Breuer) had based on herself, her friends, and her family. All the actors spoke Colette's lines and thus were not so much characters as manifestations of her personality, her prose, and her time and place. The play ended with the writer on her deathbed, seeking "the last flashes of astonishment" from the world outside her window. Most material came from events in her life and writings around the time of World War I. Rather than a clear narrative of these years, *Dressed Like an Egg* was layered with the writer's (and the company's) reconsiderations. Thus the linear progression of Colette's "story" was less apparent than Akalaitis may have intended. From scenes of seduction and marriage to "the cage" of married life, in depicting the care of children or the free fall caused by a lover's abandonment, the production alternated between a heightened slowness and sudden flurries of action. Movement, sound, acting, and scenography crossed boundaries, with the actors becoming at times part of the scenery while set pieces became part of the action. In short, Colette's narratives became forgetful once again.

Key to these effects was an ambiguity created by multiplying gendered subject positions, a technique Akalaitis used again in *Dead End Kids* and *Through the Leaves*. In an early scene that exemplified this ambiguity, Maleczech and McElduff danced toward one another, only their legs and feet visible under the maroon half curtain. A pink stripe of light filled the gap between the edges of the curtain as the women, the heels of their shoes lit from within, "dance[d] slowly towards each other, flurries of movement, hesitations, tapping, quick brushes." The women appeared again, this time fully visible, carrying hand mirrors in which they examined themselves ("or maybe each other," Akalaitis comments) as they backed toward one another. Both were wearing turn of the century lingerie suggesting young girls emerging from the attachments of childhood into the dance of romantic love. The half curtain framed the two dancers by shifting stage left as they moved, thus keeping them in the pink stripe of light. Colette's lines, however, were spoken not by the women but by Warrilow as he paced in front of the silver lamé curtain. The entire scene, in fact, was framed in a series of prosceniums created by curtains that moved laterally, rose, fell, or unfolded to animate the mood of the moment. Perhaps the most vivid effect appeared when, behind the curtain, Akalaitis lifted McElduff, causing her legs to disappear from view. They were replaced by the legs and feet of a man and woman, the woman's represented by Raymond's hands in women's shoes. The delights of "The Dance" resulted in part from the intriguing ambiguity of the gendered images and voices. The scene's final image, the immense shadow of a seated, snoring bride projected on the window shade, seemed to express impatience with received wisdom about a woman's life.

MAN 1 [Warrilow]: She's much prettier when she's sad.
Well, tell her sad and sentimental stories.
She looks rather like Beatrice Cenci of the Barberini Palace.
With her red carnation, she looks more like a dove stabbed to the heart.
Can't you think of something better than to compare her to a wounded bird and a decapitated woman?

Immediately the window shade rose. Warrilow walked to the sleeping bride (McElduff) and after measuring the light with a meter snapped an Instamatic photo of her. The shade dropped to the floor, and in its place rose an enlarged copy of the photo he had just taken: McElduff in bridal veil and gown gazing at her idealized mirror image.

Akalaitis's fragmenting and reordering of the images of love and marriage reproduce for the audience the fragmenting and reordering of gendered behavior associated with the *belle époque* when Colette was a young wife and writer. Colette had several identities that overlapped. She passed as a respectable woman while at times the ambiguity of her sexual identities provided a pass to various shadow worlds, among them the music halls and the literary salon of Natalie Clifford Barney. Colette noted that in her circles "masculine and feminine beauty ranked equal, . . . you used the same appreciative words for the marvelous legs and narrow hips of a handsome gymnast as for the shapeliness of a female acrobat or dancer."[87] This crossing of boundaries was essential in *Dressed Like an Egg* to the actors' trading of characteristics. Akalaitis allowed the writer's multiple identities to mingle in the ambiguity of her male and female, and straight and gay, stage representations. As Munk notes:

> Explanations are unnecessary; the ignorant spectator has a wealth of meaning and overtones available in this sensuous, funny, lovely investigation of the romantic spirit. . . .
>
> The boudoirs, the lacy lingerie, the eternal gazing in mirrors, the dated "shocking" homosexuals in kimonos and lesbians in tuxedos, are never mocked but presented for our sympathetic consideration. Colette was extraordinary in her freedom and her acceptance of unfreedom: she knew as much about independence and about love, its opposite, as anyone. Three actresses embody her different aspects: Akalaitis is the child, the writer, the observer; Ruth Maleczech is the wife, the older woman in love; Ellen McElduff is the beauty on the trapeze, the performer, the vagabond. William Raymond, bearded and suited, is threatening while a bit comic as the husband, and also— not in that character—moves us with a painful narrative of waiting. As for David Warrilow, he has turned French, looks like Barrault overtaken by posing, and graces every move and word.[88]

Rather than letting the metaphors of *Dressed Like an Egg* write themselves, spinning off in a universe of their own, Akalaitis grounded the images created in the play in an alternate rhetoric, one that anticipated more recent warnings against gender stereotypes. This rhetoric, according to Apter, "leaves only a ghostly and sometimes ghastly trace of the stereotype behind in the wake of its performances."[89] Akalaitis had figured the shifting and multiple rhetorical positions of gender as poses. *Dressed Like an Egg* found in the poses of Colette's circle a plurality of strategies—"acting, outing, being, doing, passing, and meaning," as Apter says.

Colette directed her readers' attention to the passage of time and the rich complexity of the moment, a move that Akalaitis reproduced with an emphasis on being and doing. A good example appeared in "The Bath," in which "a file of people partially hidden by the half curtain, one by one, extend arms into the frame and pour steaming water from a variety of containers into the bathtub."[90] Filling the bath took about three minutes, an eternity to some spectators, but one designed to foster an all-inclusive absorption. Xerxes Mehta found debts to Robert Wilson and Richard Foreman in "the planes of action, the stretching of time, the shuttered areas of focus, the mix of acting objects and objectified actors, the stately progression of vast and mysteriously evocative tableaux."[91] Akalaitis acknowledged the similarities elsewhere but also claimed that the play's extensions of time emerged more immediately from the quality of concentration she noticed in her son when he was learning to tie his shoelaces.[92] It also came from the "living in the moment" that Akalaitis and other Mabou Mines actors sought when they performed. The clearest expression of this absorption appeared in a scene devoted to the care Colette's mother gave her during a serious illness. As Akalaitis lowered a shaking McElduff into the steaming bath, she said (in Sido's words), "Yes, you were my golden sun. I used to tell you that when you came into a room where I was, it grew lighter." Avoiding sentimentality with an immediate blackout, the scene's tone changed with the "sound of water splashing." With light restored, Raymond appeared and continued, in the Burgundian "Colette voice," used by all the actors, "But you know, this child has been most precious to me, yes she has. She has told me such delicious stories of her boarding school."[93] Two, perhaps three, sets of mother and daughter were elided here: Sido and the child Colette; Colette and her daughter, nicknamed "Bel-Gazou"; and perhaps Akalaitis and her own daughter. Nor can we overlook the voice of Willy, Colette's first husband and collaborator on her *Claudine* stories. Multiple voices spoke through Raymond, interrogating gender distinctions without collapsing them into androgyny.

As with romantic love, the issue is commitment. "Women *are* more emotional and more attached than men," Akalaitis commented to Terry Curtis Fox. "[Colette] said not only was it *all right* to have that commitment, it was *neces-*

sary."[94] Akalaitis's turn to commitment, like Breuer's focus on "the wages of attachment," examines what binds us, often painfully, to other people. Breuer claims that he abandoned the emotional tangle of Mabou Mines in the mid-1970s by fleeing to California, regressing into a "second childhood," and then reemerging feeling creatively recharged.[95] At the same time, Akalaitis was saying that parenting provided her with important ideas and techniques for *Dressed Like an Egg*. Absorption in the moment, which when juxtaposed with other moments creates "an accrued association in the events,"[96] involved focusing not on the captive but the shackle, the point of connection, the bond that is half real and half imagined, the fruitful dilemma of being free and fettered. Like Colette, she usefully turned her feelings into art. The scene "The Cage," for example, explored "the relationship between the lived moment and the *shape* of a particular mode of the imagination." In the late 1970s Colette's mode of imagination filled "a felt and present vacuum," commented Mehta, for "to extract spirit from dead matter (our stock Romantic baggage) the *process* of fragmentation and reintegration must be made visible in the work, must, in fact, become the work."[97] The actors spoke Colette's lines on the sense of loss experienced in the pleasures of love and the imagination's impulse to envision abandonment and regret at moments of great happiness. Key to the creation of "The Cage" was a photograph Akalaitis found of the young Colette "leaning against parallel bars in her gym with such a poignant and lost and courageous look, that it really touched a lot in me."[98] The image inspired Ree Morton to create a freestanding celastic dress, which is worn like a pose by each actress in turn.[99] At one moment Warrilow lavished caresses on the dress rather than the woman wearing it. Audiences were delighted when Akalaitis slipped her hand out of its extended sleeve and left it on stage. Like the trace of a stereotype, it embodied the shackle.

The shape of Akalaitis's imagination, with which she measured the lived moment of commitment, had to do, as it did for Colette, with the pose of forgetfulness she adopted as director. Delighting in the way her literary characters seemed to take on minds and lives of their own, Colette also despaired over the "humiliating fate of an author who is unsure, before writing, of what he will write."[100] Akalaitis, similarly, came to the project with a commitment to discover Colette in the process.

Dressed Like an Egg: Theatricality and the Work Process

Akalaitis had begun work on *Dressed Like an Egg* with a short development period and a highly plotted, rather conventional play in mind, but as she worked with the company the show became less plot driven and rehearsals stretched over the course of a year. As in other Mabou Mines shows, the traditions that informed the piece emerged in self-conscious forms, with several layers of implicit commentary. *Dressed Like an Egg* had the popular energy of vaudeville, pantomime, and melodrama or of 1970s counterparts such as television soap operas. B.-St. John Schofield, who became a company member after doing technical work on the show's tours to Europe and Australia, points out:

> It's a vulgar piece of theater in that it revels . . . in twentieth-century interpretation of nineteenth-century theatrical performance, with all these draperies, the little entr'actes. . . . It's archaeological biography because it took really popular theatrical forms in terms of staging . . . and exposed them to a reconstructed Mabou Minesesque narrative . . . narrative being the strongest concept in the company.[101]

Probably the best example was "The Pantomime," a comic entr'acte played by Raymond and McElduff. It was drawn from two pantomimes that had helped establish Colette's popular appeal as a music hall performer and her notoriety as a demimondaine. The scenario owes most to the popular *La chair* (1907), whose romantic story, setting, and themes were familiar:

> In a smuggler's cabin on the Austro-Hungarian border, the beautiful Yulka [Colette] lives with the fierce smuggler Hokartz [Wague]. . . . The latter discovers that Yulka is unfaithful to him with a handsome young officer [usually played by Wague's wife, Christine Kerf]. In a burst of jealousy, Hokartz tries to stab Yulka, but instead his dagger tears her dress, and Hokartz, overwhelmed by her beauty, kills himself.[102]

Raymond and McElduff acted out an exaggerated version laden with orientalized tones. Moving sideways in a narrow corridor paralleling the footlights, Raymond, in a painted leotard trimmed with fur "à la Nijinsky," leaped dramatically to McElduff, dressed to suggest an Egyptian princess, much as Colette had been in *Rêve d'Egypt* (1907). An observing workman announced, "Let loose a breast!" whereupon Raymond ripped down half of McElduff's bodice. Brushed away, he approached again with a knife and with a wide menacing sweep—stabbed himself in the neck. As he sank behind a ground row of pyramids, she smiled at the audience.

In developing *Dressed Like an Egg,* Mabou Mines had discussed, among other things, what a "romantic gesture" might be. Embedded in "The Pantomime" were several gestures that had intrigued the male audiences of *La chair,* a piece they usually chatted through until the moment when Colette's costume fell away. She had made a name for herself by performing "naked," that is, without tights. In a postcard depicting the final scene, Colette stands, eyes discreetly lowered, her famously bare arms and legs revealed to the camera. But she also proudly displays her breasts, causing Wague to draw back in awe and terror, like Menelaus at the first sight of Helen's body. As the man dies from exposure to the femme fatale, Colette's face is serene, madonnalike, a "natural" site of contradictions. Colette puzzled over this romantic belief in women's natural identity. Early in her marriage she had already adopted the bobbed hair of the cross-gendered "vagabond." In the first stages of her affair with the Marquise de Morny, Colette dressed occasionally, as "Missy" did habitually, in men's clothing. Public response to individuals exhibiting both delicacy and virility carried a heavy charge of anxiety. In "The Pantomime" Mabou Mines highlighted this uncertainty in a "goofy" rendition of the outraged lover, with Raymond lampooning his character's passion.[103]

How did the company arrive at such reconstructions? When, according to Akalaitis, some of her original script ideas did not work, "the piece really benefited from the collaboration."[104] They discussed the piece's structure, the choice of written materials, and the themes of romance and theatricality. Often the actors offered passages from Colette's writings they wanted to explore. Tish Dace reports, "JoAnne remembers Bill Raymond as the principal idea man. 'His application was constant. He'd actually jump up in rehearsal and try something with the lights, and it was his idea—a real stroke of genius—to mask the footlights as seashells.'" In order to perform on the trapeze, McElduff studied acrobatics with Nina Corsavina and continued to work with her for several years afterward. Artist Nancy Graves constructed a moving frieze, a narrow, hundred-foot motorized painting of stars designed to move across the top of the proscenium at a foot per minute. Unable to regularize the frieze's movement during the first run in the Public Theater's Old Prop Shop, Akalaitis reluctantly dropped it.[105]

Another collaborator was Mary Overlie. Having worked together before, Overlie and Akalaitis communicated easily. One might carry out an idea the other had suggested. Overlie found it difficult to isolate her own contribution: "I think, in the end, I had a hand in the timing, in facilitating the acting, in the design of the scenes and the atmosphere, but specifics were never certain, it was always JoAnne directing. I was like a book on a table that she would sometimes wander over and read."[106] As in later productions, Akalaitis began the work by giving her collaborators a brief "recipe" of what she had in mind. For *Dressed Like an Egg,* says Overlie, the recipe was something like "I am thinking about the actors speaking the script with their feet, lots of silence, an egg which is a character and must be choreographed along with the actors." Mystified, Overlie went away to work out ideas. After two weeks she returned with little more than a thought: "Eggs can dance." Combining this with the image of a lowered curtain (perhaps developed in Overlie's absence), "things fell into place. . . . I worked with the actors, rehearsing them into making characters with their feet." Raymond played with the notion of feet as characters, bending over behind the lowered curtain and putting his hands in women's shoes, creating in the gap between curtain and floor the gender-bending "dance" of legs and feet. Thus, Overlie, Akalaitis, and the company spun out ideas, playfully elaborating on each other's contributions.

Dressed Like an Egg "quoted" those who habitually put events in quotes. There was Colette, of course, but also Cocteau, Pirandello, Genet, and Brecht in his ideas on estrangement and the probing beams of light of Beckett's later plays. Rather than Beckett's emphasis on authority and control, though, Akalaitis's beams seemed to allude to Colette's ironic, theatrical expression of her own pain, as in the scene "The Novel." For Mehta the beams of light used in this scene both interrogated and revealed:

> A luxurious bedroom, semidarkness, all five performers present: Akalaitis at her writer's table, open book in hand; Ruth Maleczech and David Warrilow, the aging, possessed, but silent, principals; the young Ellen McElduff on the floor, watching; and, astonishingly, Bill Raymond on the canopied bed, passionately delivering almost the entire narration, dialogue and all. A pencil-thin beam of light from the wings roams over the scene, illuminating, directing, questioning, and, I suspect not coincidentally, reminding us of those tormenting and inquisitorial beams that energize the late Beckett shorts this company does so well. . . . Raymond: "I sprang to my feet. The violence of my movement overturned my chair and I said furiously. . . ." But Maleczech rises slowly and moves to the mirror on the wall, where the beam catches her drawn face. A romantic cliché both loved and, through internal refraction, proved. "He was pacing up and down the bedroom." But Warrilow silently smashes his fist on the table, the beam catches the gesture, and a cup and saucer slowly, in dreamtime, *float* to the floor.[107]

Mehta concludes that this scene "casts its beam on the source of all desire, the passionate mind" in its double act of concealment and revelation. The reader senses Colette's deepest feeling when she poses. Mehta quotes the actors quoting Colette: "Are you imagining, as you read me, that I'm portraying myself? Have patience: this is merely my model." Akalaitis's distancing devices increased the spectators' sympathy for those who are free and fettered by revealing the binary of gendered experience as the painful limit that teaches *how* we are bound to the objects desired. In the ambiguously gendered images of "Opium," the production highlighted that limit. Mehta again:

> Two homosexuals in gorgeous blue and cream kimonos walk up and down in the white light "stripe." They wind music boxes, delicately caress themselves, and speak in high, soft voices of tea, biscuits, opium. They are not mocked, but rather regarded tenderly, and with regret, for "How difficult it is for respectable people to believe in innocence."

Akalaitis remarked, "The white stripe of light and the curtain movement and the persistent vertical path of the two men [Warrilow and Raymond] seem . . . at the same time pure and decadent."[108] By making visual a binary notion of emotional commitment, Akalaitis was able to make new and palpable Colette's rethinking of gender.

Unlike *The Shaggy Dog Animation,* which was too large to tour, *Dressed Like an Egg* traveled to Europe in 1978 and Australia in 1980.[109] Akalaitis found herself being sought out by the press as a company spokesperson, a role Breuer (not on the tour) had more often filled. She spoke of her desire to seek a wider audience and to "keep trying something new."[110] She seemed to relish her visibility and Mabou Mines' opportunity for change and growth. The innovations of *Dressed Like an Egg* carried over to later work, most vividly *Through the Leaves.* There Akalaitis "posed" stereotypes to the audience as though posing questions—stereotypes that, once again, reveal a tremor within their orthodoxy.

Gender and the Future of the Company

I have suggested that collaboration on *Dressed Like an Egg* had a less hierarchical character, and was less conflicted, than that of *The Shaggy Dog Animation.* It would be a mistake, though, to draw too sharp a contrast. The members of Mabou Mines and their associates had worked out of a common encyclopedia of ideas and techniques in development since the 1950s. Despite differences in emphasis, *Dressed Like an Egg* and *Shaggy Dog* were "nonhierarchical" in Overlie's sense of the term.

> Our common interest was the disassembling of the voices of theatre and dance and the endless possibilities that were emerging for reassembly . . . everything was taken to be as sacred as everything else. . . . Grotowski still believed that emotion and story were the primary objectives of theatre. Cunningham still used a traditional approach to the body. We did not. There was an essential break being made, and we all arrived in our own worlds of investigation. Those worlds were connected by the breakdown and reinterpretation of tools and message.[111]

Most of those involved in the productions of the 1970s work recall them as the most inventive and consciousness expanding of their careers. They uncovered ideas and approaches that would be used in later work. *Shaggy Dog* has become, like *Dressed Like an Egg*, an important example of the company's working methods.

Accordingly, I want to end this chapter not seeing Breuer and Akalaitis in opposition but considering how in making this work they changed the local culture they shared: Mabou Mines as a collaborative theater. Akalaitis and Breuer brought about the "company of directors" by leaving the original concept of Mabou Mines behind—Breuer in the mid 1970s, Akalaitis a few years later. The leaderless collective, with its involvement of the entire company in each show, never returned. Remaining was an interest in evoking the lived moment and a growing body of techniques to create it. Akalaitis's focus on the life of Colette in *Dressed Like an Egg* seems to resemble Breuer's creation of an "autograph" in *The Shaggy Dog Animation*. In his use of his own life, however, Breuer's approach is closer to that of Colette herself, that is, her distinctly autobiographical writings. It is ironic that variations on this "woman's art," grounded in a speaking subject's testimony, should be Breuer's preoccupation while Akalaitis borrowed Colette's voice to locate the rich texture of her life and times. Not herself a writer and uninterested in staging a master narrative, Akalaitis used metaphor as only one tool among many, looking to create at the same time striking metonymies of a more connected emotional life.

This was an important period for Akalaitis; within three or four years she developed several other shows, including *Southern Exposure* (1979)—not a Mabou Mines production at the time—and *Dead End Kids* (1980) and tried her hand at filmmaking. She, along with other members, benefited when the company began to do its own grant writing. By the early 1980s staff members such as Marion Godfrey were raising funds at a level the company had never seen before. Still, funding never met the company's needs. Akalaitis wanted to bring in younger people and expand the core group of members because Mabou Mines had become, in her opinion, something of a dysfunctional family. "It's got to change, it's got to be fluid," she commented.[112] For her, community means that members are empowered to speak and their voices have an effect. Clearly, for a time Akalaitis felt empowered and eager to speak outside the company as well as within it. Her new prominence helped to foreground public discussion of the "collective" nature of Mabou Mines. Ironically, reviewers such as Tish Dace picked up on the radical nature of the collaboration concept and wrote about it, with the result that just as the company became more diverse the members found themselves falsely idealized. As working artists and parents, they had managed to forge an artistic democracy, but being coproducers of each other's work often put their personal needs in conflict.

In fact, Mabou Mines remained a group of strong-willed individuals. The work exploring multiple gender positions and questioning binary ways of thinking and being could not eliminate gendered conflicts within the company. Breuer and Akalaitis were operating within the group's reality principle, that is, the financial circumstances setting the parameters for the struggle to get the work done. The company's piecemeal transformation into a type of coalition I call the "company of directors," while an elegant solution in many ways, did not finally meet Akalaitis's needs. Like Neumann, Breuer, and others, she began to take on freelance jobs, a move that reinforced her interest in reinterpreting well-known plays. When she finally left Mabou Mines in 1990, her work life had been elsewhere for some time. Akalaitis's desire for the company to keep it "fluid" had not taken the form she had in mind. While younger members were taken in, few developed their own shows until the mid-1980s. Some, like Schofield, had already left the company at that point. Money continued to be a problem with so many members competing to develop their own shows. Younger artists often did not want to join the competition or were reluctant to spend long periods in rehearsal.[113] As a result, after making the film *Dead End Kids* (1986) Akalaitis did not direct a Mabou Mines production until the reprise of *Through the Leaves* in 1990. Instead she was guest directing at various theaters, finding in her work with other actors and designers (and the occasional Mabou Mines member or associate) the fluidity and type of commitment she had found in her work with Mabou Mines.

Breuer, in a sense, "left" in the mid-1970s before *Shaggy Dog* was finished.

He had always generated more ideas for projects than he had time to complete. Now he sought ways to stage pieces both outside and inside the company. He was on the track of a consuming idea of an American choral theater. Thus, with obvious differences, both he and Akalaitis were beginning to seek a more public art, one with wider support and larger audiences. This was true for many performers, directors, and choreographers emerging from the downtown art world. Breaking away from their avant-garde stance, these artists expanded their work with institutions while trying to maintain their working methods. In fact, Mabou Mines' work successfully reached new audiences, broadening the company's focus and reputation. Throughout the 1980s *A Prelude to Death in Venice* and *Cold Harbor* toured to regional theaters they had never visited before with funding arranged through a variety of arts advocacy organizations.

Fundamentally, though, Breuer still bills himself in terms of the avant-gardist, that is, one who sees himself in opposition to the mainstream. Commenting that *Shaggy Dog* was his best work to date, he declared, "I'd rather lose the audience and keep the piece."[114] In 1991, with his work having appeared at the Brooklyn Academy of Music, the Spoleto Festival, and the Kennedy Center, Breuer called himself a "two-handed gun." As such he accepts funding from arts organizations in order to underwrite work that turns around and bites the hand that has fed it.[115]

Akalaitis began to value a more public art at the time of *Dressed Like an Egg* and also gave up the countercultural rhetoric. "The avant-garde has become accessible," she commented in 1978. "The more popular, the better, I think. Theater is a public art, and I'm committed to that."[116] It is clear, though, that she, too, has not entirely crossed over to the mainstream. Her stagings of Shakespeare, Büchner, Euripides, Behn, Williams, Beckett, and Kroetz often spark controversy. Joe Papp apparently felt that Akalaitis had the right combination of talents when he appointed her artistic director of the New York Shakespeare Festival in 1991. Yet her dismissal in 1993 showed that she was perceived as a director who brings to whatever she does an avant-garde and thus "difficult" sensibility.

The final chapter takes up the company's development at the end of the 1970s in work produced by two new directors, Ruth Maleczech and Frederick Neumann. How could Mabou Mines accommodate the work of *four* directors? How would the demands of touring established work and developing new work be reconciled? Would the company abandon the world of the art gallery altogether? Did the work change to accommodate new audiences? Warrilow believed that Mabou could "reconcile esthetic considerations with the needs of an audience," albeit not in the ways it had in the early Animations.[117] Mabou Mines was trying to "see itself as a heavyweight," trying to transfer itself to a plane of professional existence where ideas could be funded, and thus realized, rather than having to settle so often for half effects, or opposite effects, as it had for earlier shows.[118] Thus, there were several, sometimes conflicting agendas at work in the late 1970s. Akalaitis's desire to keep the company growing and "fluid" both fostered new work involving younger members and caused her to shape projects that took a larger share of the company's budget. While Breuer sought to stage more ambitious works that would articulate his vision of an American classicism, he also created smaller works with selected members of the company. He began to initiate projects elsewhere and then bring them to the company as Mabou Mines productions, a move that both enhanced and drained the company's resources. As the next chapter will demonstrate, however, other members had already set out to develop their own work as well, which presented additional challenges and rewards. Like Rose in *Shaggy Dog,* each new director had begun to see him- or herself as a heavyweight—the contender, wannabe, magic maker, alchemist, con artist, and boss. But to do that is also to become "teachers of the faith."[119] For the first time, Maleczech, Raymond, and Breuer began to consider founding a new organization, one that would foster the work of younger talents, a move that resulted in the development of Re.Cher.Chez, the company's first studio for emerging artists. Re.Cher.Chez marks the period when Mabou Mines itself became a heavyweight—a company of directors.

CHAPTER FIVE

A Company of Directors: *Vanishing Pictures, Mercier and Camier,* Re.Cher.Chez

The members of Mabou Mines agree that the company's first ten years were an extraordinary period, in Neumann's words "the best years of our lives." The swapping of ideas and roles had made them artistic equals, with "everyone using their brains to make pieces."[1] After the success of *Dressed Like an Egg* and *The Shaggy Dog Animation,* both of which won Obie awards, projects began to multiply. Neumann visualized a large-cast production of another Beckett prose work. In 1978–79, while he was developing *Mercier and Camier,* Breuer, Maleczech, and Raymond had begun Re.Cher.Chez, a studio for the performing arts where, under the guidance of experienced collaborators, emerging artists could continue their education in avant-garde performance or seasoned artists could expand their skills. Founded in September 1979, Re.Cher.Chez began staging work in progress and by May 1980 had organized its first Mayfest, a series of completed shows. Maleczech saw the premier of *Vanishing Pictures,* originally a Re.Cher.Chez project, in February 1980. *Vanishing Pictures* and *Mercier and Camier* were, in a sense, the final productions of the company's first decade and the first productions of its second.

This chapter focuses on the ways in which *Vanishing Pictures* and *Mercier and Camier* helped lay the groundwork for the 1980s by introducing two new directors. They bear witness to the company's continuing interest in the work as a "journey of experience" that brought together the visual arts with a "romantic ideal of language" surviving from the earliest work it had done in the 1950s.[2] Through the lens of Beat, existentialist, and absurdist writing and experience, the members of Mabou Mines were and are connected to the legacies of the classical avant-garde (the surrealists, Artaud, Lautréamont, and others) and earlier moderns—the bohemians and flâneurs (Charles Baudelaire, Paul Verlaine)—who preceded the European avant-garde, reaching back even to late romantic writers such as E. T. A. Hoffman and Edgar Allan Poe. While looking forward to later performance, Mabou Mines' work in the late 1970s also solidified these connections to heavyweights who had long ago sought to refresh perception and "make it new."

This chapter also points to Mabou Mines' future as a company of directors. Up to the early 1980s, its members had created, with the crucial help of Stewart, Papp, and Performing Artservices, a way to do the work. Money was never plentiful, and financial and personal crises did occur, but up to the late 1970s the company was able to rehearse more or less continuously with most or all of its members involved. Choices made at the company's founding also played a role. For Akalaitis the key to creating this "secure little place" had been the fact that every member served on the board of directors and, when money was available, received the same pay.

> The structure [in the first five years] was really brilliant in that everyone got paid the same amount no matter what you did, no matter whether you worked, and that was an amazing equalizer. Everyone being on the board of directors is a great idea. It came out of a bunch of people whose egos were too big to submit to any other ego. It was like a bunch of mud wrestlers: let's draw a truce here! We're all equal! A bunch of very tough people who were not necessarily idealistic about this socialist structure but who said, "Hey! I want to be my own boss. You can't be my boss. Let's be bosses together."

The artists of Mabou Mines have never abandoned this idea, although both external and internal pressures began to alter the form that "being bosses together" took. In 1978 the "secure little place" was secure no longer. As discussed in earlier chapters, both Warrilow and Breuer were considering ways to leave the company (although Breuer has never officially left). Casting began to go outside the company and its associates, and members began to take acting or directing jobs elsewhere. Breuer and Akalaitis, making themselves available as freelance directors, began to use the company as a home base while Maleczech and Mehrten worked exclusively on company projects and tended to day-to-day business. Neumann, O'Reilly, and Raymond found ways to combine outside work with a continuing presence in the company. But in the late 1970s the members found it more difficult to agree on which projects should be funded and how the work should be scheduled and performed. As a result, a necessary compromise developed—perhaps less consciously than by a process of trial and error—that allowed the work to continue while changing the company's structure; that compromise I call "the company of directors." As downtown theater companies either folded or adapted to the new circumstances of the

1980s, under which survival demanded a higher level of promotion and networking, Mabou Mines became less a countercultural collective of artistic equals than a group of "bosses" in a different sense—that of directors who also appeared in each other's work.

For Neumann, directing seemed a logical progression for both himself and other members.[3] Late in the 1980s, members often identified themselves in interviews, programs, and grant proposals as coartistic directors. Being a boss meant identifying oneself as a director with a personal vision and an oeuvre, although the latter was a perception often imposed from the outside. Being bosses together reflected the uneasy combination of individualism and group support that Mabou Mines had borrowed from the Beats. The voice and vision of a single artist, hurling himself or herself at the "harsh wall of America," also resulted from a community of fellows who found that, as Henry James had noted much earlier, "every man works better when he has companions working in the same line, and yielding the stimulus of suggestion, comparison, emulation."[4]

Mercier and Camier: *The Theater Is a Camera*

Frederick Neumann's journey of experience with Mabou Mines is tied most closely to Samuel Beckett, whose work he first encountered in 1953. Neumann did not appear in a Beckett production until Akalaitis staged *Cascando* in 1975, but he had seen *En attendant Godot* (*Waiting for Godot*) in its initial Paris production at the Théâtre de Babylone, and his years as an actor living in postwar Paris exposed him to plays by Beckett and his contemporaries.[5] Neumann's travels in Europe had preceded those of Mabou Mines' founding members by fifteen years. He had spent a few years studying acting at the University of Utah, then returned in 1947 to Europe, where he lived until 1971. Seeing Paul Robeson and Orson Welles work on their productions had thrilled him as a student in Utah, encouraging him to take theater seriously, but he did not pursue it actively at first. Hitchhiking around Europe, taking occasional teaching jobs or other work, Neumann took shelter in theaters and opera houses when he could afford a ticket but not a hotel. He experienced in the process a wide variety of performance. He had first come to Europe when William Burroughs did, but he was much less attuned to the Beats than to European writers and artists. Later, having settled in Paris and studied for three years at the Sorbonne and a private school, he began to work with French national radio and then became involved with film and television. This work brought Neumann into contact with American and British writers and actors who had formed groups to stage plays in English. There he met director John Berry, who introduced many émigré actors to the work of the Actor's Studio. Neumann acted frequently at the Paris Theatre Workshop run by Gordon Heath and Lee Payant. He met the future members of Mabou Mines through the film dubbing they all did, first Akalaitis in 1964, then the others at the Workshop. He also met his future wife, the actress Honora Fergusson, in Paris, where they worked on various productions. Coincidentally she had already met Warrilow at the offices of the journal *Réalités*. In 1966, Neumann collaborated with Breuer, Maleczech, and Warrilow on a production of Brecht's *Messingkauf Dialogues* that was apparently stopped by Helene Weigel to accord with the terms of Brecht's will. According to Neumann, a portion of the piece appeared in 1967 or 1968 with Weigel's permission in a production called *Theories*, directed by Breuer at the Edinburgh Festival, that also incorporated material from Artaud, Stanislavsky, and Delsarte.[6] Neumann and Fergusson also worked with Breuer, Maleczech, and Warrilow on a staging of *Mother Courage*. In 1967, however, the couple moved with their two young sons, David and Chris, to Rome, where they lived and did film work until 1971. By the time Fred joined Mabou Mines in New York, the Neumanns had an enormous variety of performance experience in live theater, film, radio, and television. Neumann was perhaps the first member to take on outside acting jobs to help pay the bills, jobs that have ranged from Shakespeare in the Park to O'Neill on Broadway, regional theater, and small parts in major studio films. At the same time Neumann preferred to make edgier, avant-garde work, often using and then playing against techniques of motivational acting.

Mercier and Camier was the first of three texts that Beckett gave Neumann permission, one by one, to adapt for the stage. Beckett's willingness and encouragement demonstrated his regard for Neumann, with whom he met in Paris at least twice. Creating these three productions was, in Neumann's estimation, "a terrific school" from which he extracted Beckett's principle "the simpler the better."[7] He applied this maxim quite successfully to his subsequent adaptations of *Company* (1983) and *Worstward Ho* (1986). From the first Neumann paid close attention to Beckett's language, finding within it the visual concepts that he extrapolated into production designs. In this regard Neumann privileges metaphor over other language elements, much as Breuer does. For the novel *Mercier and Camier* Neumann wove the physical parameters of Beckett's universe into a complex, encompassing environment, not in Richard Schechner's sense of the term but in Artaud's sense of spectacle. The audience would experience the "thing-in-itself," pared away from its representations. In a

sense Neumann began from the surrealist position that the artist should bur-
row underneath or supplant conscious meaning with preconscious experience,
treating language as a substance rather than a medium. Thus, articulating
meaning was less important than correspondences among production design,
acting style, structure, music, and language. Here Neumann's approach differs
from Breuer's self-consciously poststructuralist ironies. Assuming gender
rather than examining it, eliding specific places and times, *Mercier and Camier*
became a kind of "universal" experience of Beckett's world, full of gaps, elisions,
and jumps. Neumann's determination to stage Beckett's text as fully as possible
reintroduced a traditional relationship of production as interpretation of a
written text. Thus *Mercier and Camier* had three contexts: the historical avant-
garde's search for immediacy, contemporaneous Mabou Mines work that
treated that search ironically, and a literary tradition in which the writer serves
as the authoritative source of meaning and representation.

Neumann's first choice for production was actually Beckett's early novel
More Pricks Than Kicks (1934). After the success of *Cascando* and *The Lost Ones*
and the company's meeting with Beckett in Berlin, his permission may have
seemed a certainty, but in response to Neumann's October 1977 letter of inquiry, sent via Grove Press, Beckett refused to grant it. The refusal may have resulted in part from a misunderstanding over the type of production Mabou
Mines intended or from a confusion of titles at the press; in his letter Neumann had discussed the proposed production in the context of the company's
Animations, about which Beckett apparently knew little. Despite Neumann's
efforts to clear up the misunderstanding, Beckett remained adamant, writing,
"Please leave the poor little thing alone." In mid-December Neumann wrote
again, this time regarding *Mercier and Camier*. Beckett's typically succinct permission ("OK—*Mercier & Camier*") arrived promptly.[8]

Beckett wrote *Mercier and Camier* in French in 1946, a year before *Waiting
for Godot*, but it was not published in full until 1970, with the American edition
of the English translation appearing five years later. This "road trip by rogues"[9]
takes the reader through a variety of Irish locales detailed in a way not found
in Beckett's later work, particularly his plays. Beckett may have felt the text had
not been sufficiently pared down to "reveal this thing-in-itself, the metaphysical, essential, recurrent form."[10] Certainly the work's almost realistic detail increased the challenge of staging it.

Neumann sees his stagings of Beckett's texts as "chamber pieces" similar to
his later plays.[11] In this regard Neumann's productions resemble *Play, Come
and Go,* and *The Lost Ones,* directed by Breuer, or Maleczech's *Imagination*

Dead Imagine, each of which concentrated the spectator's attention in a confined space using film-inspired framing techniques suggested by the text. In Neumann's words:

> We have asserted many a time that we have a different approach to things, and I suppose it was certainly a reaction to the competition that was coming from films. Maybe it was more unconscious than deliberate that we found ourselves creating small pieces, intimate pieces, that could be watched "close-up" by a small group of people. . . . Beckett suited us, and suited me, quite perfectly because one person might be able to deliver an entire text, by himself, inventing or performing the different persons.

The use of a single voice accorded with Beckett's advice, "the simpler the better." Mabou Mines had reproduced the texts' filmic quality visually in *Play's* single directorial spotlight, the mirror in which the three figures were viewed in *Come and Go,* and the enclosed environment of *The Lost Ones.* Like Warrilow in that production or Ruth Nelson in *Imagination Dead Imagine,* Neumann narrated *Company* and *Worstward Ho.*

But *Mercier and Camier* was staged on a larger, more opulent scale. Neumann wanted both a cinematic intimacy and a rich, complex live production mediated like *Shaggy Dog* by filmic montage and soundtrack. In an early scenario, Neumann outlined a production involving eleven characters and a live chorus of thirty to forty voices that would produce "sculptural" crowd effects and rhythmic punctuation for the action. As in *Shaggy Dog,* sound and visual effects were to become actors standing in for audience participation in the event: "The voices might be an expression of an urge the audience wishes to utter or, tauntingly, to cut through certain moods of silence . . . a constant play of alternatives, as the scenes of the novel are a constant play with the expected line of the narrative."[12] While Neumann's original concept proved too expensive to stage, he did have a cast of eight, one of whom (O'Reilly) played five separate roles. The character Watt, in recordings made by Warrilow, narrated from a video screen and a series of projections. To create the aural effects Neumann asked Glass to write music, which became in effect a score. From the first Neumann planned to use photographic projections (less expensive than film), which would be superimposed on and complement the live action. These effects could be comic.[13] *Mercier and Camier* was for Neumann, like *Shaggy Dog,* imbued with a distancing irony relevant to both the post–World War I time of the text and the state of the arts in the late 1970s: "In Beckett's early stuff there was much more humor, apparent humor or immediate humor, that works the effects of the irony of our split nature: . . . To be such *grandees* for the arts and [yet] such petty, bickering, miserable, cruel creatures."

After an initial delay, a work-in-progress production appeared in October 1978 at the Performing Garage as part of New York University's Beckett Festival along with *Not I, Come and Go,* and *Fizzles 1, 4 and 7.* Neumann had developed *Mercier and Camier* while working hard to raise funds, as company members had to do for their projects. Neumann revised the script and premiered *Mercier and Camier* at the Public Theater on 25 October 1979. Whereas earlier rehearsals took place in the usual way, at spaces scattered from East Third Street to Westbeth, the company was able to finish rehearsing and perform in LuEsther Hall.

It appears that Neumann had the concept firmly in mind and a well-developed script before beginning rehearsals. He worked on the adaptation at his and Honora Fergusson's home in Kingston, New Jersey. Commuting almost daily, Neumann has been fully involved in the company's work while less involved in its day-to-day operations. Fergusson had not yet had the opportunity to work with Mabou Mines,[14] but now she took on the role of Helen in *Mercier and Camier* and participated in the design and construction of the costumes. Their sons David, age fourteen in 1979, and Chris, twelve, also had brief roles. Later Fergusson collaborated more intensively with Neumann on *Company,* helping to adapt the text, taking a small role, and codirecting. She also appeared in *Worstward Ho* and other Mabou Mines shows such as *Flow My Tears, the Policeman Said* (New York University production, 1988), and the revival of *The B.Beaver Animation* (1990). Now an associate artist, Fergusson has appeared in *Mabou Mines Lear, Ecco Porco,* and *Mabou Mines Dollhouse.* With Neumann as director, she had developed and performed in her own project, the "image drama" *Starcock* (1985). The production featured projections of paintings by Apple Vail, the daughter of English Dadaist Lawrence Vail and writer Kay Boyle. Like *Mercier and Camier, Starcock* brought forward personal history and artistic influences from the European cultural scene. Fergusson and Neumann had known Vail's family, including Peggy Guggenheim, Lawrence Vail's first wife, in Paris. Apple Vail, who by 1985 was living in Florida, wrote the narrative and collaborated with Fergusson and Neumann on the production.

Neumann imagined *Mercier and Camier* as "a diaphanous dialogue," that is, a dialogue between characters who imagine the world as a kind of interior landscape,

a layered timeless world . . . of country, town and interiors. It is clear[,] though
one aspect of this world is more brightly perceived than the others, we are for-
ever present in all of its aspects and move with ease from one to the other as
though we were lighting up one corner of the mind more than an other, a mere
shift of the imagination.[15]

This is Mercier and Camier's "gossamer world of fiction," the "cocoon" of a
good book that engrosses.[16] It is also the stifling, complacent world that the
young Beckett tried to escape when he left Ireland, a world made permeable
and discontinuous through layers of memory. In Beckett's text a narrating
voice, self-contained yet recriminatory, comments reflectively on Mercier and
Camier's travels. In Neumann's adaptation several characters shared the permeable screen of memory by dividing the narrator's text among them. The
characters now spoke their own lines and as many of the narrator's asides as
Neumann could reasonably include in the script. Mercier and Camier filtered
the audience's perception of events, an idea made palpable in sequences where
their silhouettes, projected onto a scrim that surrounded the audience, argued
silently. The scrim was crucial, for it could be translucent, transparent, or
opaque as the moment demanded—a cocoon-environment, silver screen, and
lens all in one.

Mercier and Camier's road trip seems to serve no useful purpose, but "they
give each other response . . . so they can function in the world," reflected Neumann.[17] Even a lack of response is a signifier out of which the other makes
meaning. "I wouldn't know the difference unless you were there," says
Camier—or Mercier. The lapses in their friendship, their occasional separa-
tions (which begin and end the narrative) reinforce their sense of being together. They share a scepticism about metaphysical questions, nervousness
and superstition when darkness falls on the countryside, and a surprising ability to express themselves, often in biblical terms. Introduced to one another on
the street by Watt (who as the fleshless narrator of the play knows full well that
they are acquainted), they are hurried along to a pub where Watt plans to buy
them drinks. "A pity Dumas the Elder cannot see us!" remarks Watt. "Or one of
the Evangelists," replies Camier. "A different class Mercier and Camier for all
your faults," Watt rejoinders ironically.[18] They are the "grandees" who see
themselves set apart from the complacent, unenlightened herd, but in a moment they become the "petty, bickering, miserable cruel creatures" who beat a
policeman to death for no apparent reason.

Yet the two are not indistinguishable one from the other; in fact, Neumann sought to underline their differences as straight man or red-faced clown (Mercier) and first banana or white-faced clown (Camier). This was not always so. Originally Neumann had cast himself as Camier and as Mercier Frederic Kimball, an actor and writer whose dry wit and facility with language he admired. Kimball was larger in frame, voice, and presence, as Beckett had written Mercier to be. He would play the "disillusioned intellectual" to Neumann's earthier, less pessimistic character.[19] But ultimately Neumann decided that he and Kimball were too physically similar. For his part, Kimball had grown disenchanted with the project and withdrew. Neumann improved on this false start by casting Raymond as Camier and himself as Mercier, restoring the characters' physical distinctions in a way consonant with their personalities. Thinking, as Beckett often did, in etymological terms, Neumann identified Mercier as the one who sells thread and Camier as the one who "delivers." The two should resonate as sidekicks, each needing the other but neither dominant.

After the work-in-progress presentation, Neumann continued to adapt Beckett's material, having already elided several scenes and rearranged the order of events to make the piece more playable. He reasoned that the cinematic narrative lent itself to a montage whose flow was more important than the linear sequence of events. In 1980 Beckett confirmed this decision by reassuring Neumann that his text was a "picaresque piece of writing" and he did not object to a rearrangement of scenes.[20] Neumann introduced elements outside the time period "of bicycles, and early motor cars" to reinforce the sense of experiencing a disjointed overlapping of memories. Glass, Neumann's composer for this show, has asserted that Beckett was engaged in his texts in an extreme fragmentation of narrative similar to William Burroughs's and Brion Gysin's experiments with cutout poetry.[21]

While Neumann took pains to create disjunctures, he also sought to restore an apparent seamlessness to his rearrangement of scenes. "Everything," he said, "was supposed to be in flow."[22] Thus, between scenes there were no blackouts, like a stream of consciousness novel or film presented from a single character's point of view. Similarly, the theater space, within its scrim cocoon, tapered down intimately at the front, suggesting the focus of three-point perspective, at which the audience could see a folded backdrop of a Dublin street visible through a window. The apparent contradiction between disjuncture and flow in the production's concept may have caused some confusion for spectators. Janice Paran felt that the rearrangement of scenes created gaps in the story and that the live actors, like the "mesmerizing" narration, remained unintegrated with the ongoing visual effects.[23] But the concept of incorporating flow within disjuncture was sound. As William Harris wrote:

> [Neumann has] tried to mirror the refracted, somewhat translucent images of the book by creating a set which surrounds the audience: a giant scrim shell, or theater within a theater. Although the lines of this shell are sharp, it conveys a flexible softness. Images appear in front of it, on it and through it.
>
> . . . Neumann's intent is to establish peripheral perception, much the way characters and events are perceived in the book through the eyes of Mercier and Camier. Characters are introduced quite suddenly and then disappear with the same illogical rapidity. Thoughts interrupt other thoughts. Beckett was playing with the conventions of the well-made novel. [Neumann remarks that Beckett is] "constantly poking fun at how long-winded the book is. Or he arbitrarily decides to wander through another quarter of the mind. It's arbitrary, but it's apt."[24]

It remains to be seen, of course, if assigning much of the narrator's voice-over to the characters themselves allowed the audience to retain this metafictional humor. What kind of "journey of experience" did Neumann's "diaphanous dialogue" produce? An alternate experience, he hoped, that would reconfigure the senses.

"Heavily designed"

From the first, the production design for *Mercier and Camier* was the chief locomotive of the concept. As on other shows, the company discussed the work; in fact, O'Reilly maintains that company members had been discussing Beckett's text as early as 1975.[25] Neumann invited several members and associates to create aspects of the set. L. B. Dallas, who in July 1978 signed on as Mabou Mines' full-time stage and sound designer and technical director, designed the scrim and its supporting cable structure, as well as proscenium pieces that created individual acting areas. Dallas had first participated in a Mabou Mines show, after leaving the University of Florida in 1969 and moving to New York to study art, as a performer in *Saint and the Football Player*. He ran *The Lost Ones* and *B.Beaver* and staged-managed *Shaggy Dog* but thereafter mostly designed sound. His many designs included *Company* and *Cold Harbor*. With Linda Hartinian and Alison Yerxa, he won a Maharam Citation for Design on *A Prelude to Death in Venice* in 1980. While Dallas was never interested in developing his own projects and worked outside the company as well as in it, he became a member in 1979. In November 1990 he left the company to study structural engineering.[26]

The walls of the Public Theater's LuEsther Hall, a proscenium space flanked by pillars, were completely dressed in scrim material, including a scrim ceiling that could be raised or lowered a few feet at the front. Action took place both in front of and behind a flat in the middle of which a specially constructed doorway and window were set. As rain dripped in the black doorway, it also washed down intermittently between the window's two panes. Raymond had designed the window's circular pumping system, while Hartinian had created the nine-foot cityscape seen through the window's rain effect. At stage left Dallas evoked an Irish pub with two wooden benches facing one another and a television above, on which Watt was seen and heard.[27] At stage right a revolving door designed by photographer Bill Longcore was set in the scrim-covered flat. Overlapping the front of the stage and extending closer to the audience, which was seated on floor cushions or chairs on risers, Neumann had the flat stage covered with sawdust to create the "bog" in which Mercier and Camier would occasionally loll. It was one of Sabrina Hamilton's jobs to wet down the sawdust with tea, making it appropriately brown and "shitty."[28] In front of the bog a narrow trough of water (the "canal") extended across the stage. The close proximity allowed scenes to transform quickly from one imagined location to another.

The action extended, however, to less accessible areas, incorporating the rest of LuEsther Hall. Sculptor and dancer Suzanne Harris designed the "road-ruins-horizon," a pair of stick-built walkways that flanked the audience seats, rising with the rake of the seating so that Neumann and Raymond could speak to one another above the audience's heads as the characters made their way to the back of the space. On the scrim walls above the walkways, projections appeared extending the full length of the audience. Neumann intended to take the audience along on Mercier and Camier's journey to the extent that in act 2, when the pub benches are transformed into train seats, the wall projections became a surreal landscape outside the train car. As the "landscape" moved slowly by, this "Southward Bound Express" seemed to take the audience straight into the "black hole" of the empty doorway at center stage. It was, in fact, a local bound for hell, as the noseless, legless character Madden (O'Reilly) remarks: "Not alighting? . . . You're right, only the damned alight here."[29] Spectators were to be drawn "close up" into Mercier and Camier's experience. Madden, Neumann notes, reflected their reduced lives: "The second act is a choral piece about a man who's been through a lot. [Madden] has lost his nose to spite his face. . . . But it also strikes me as some kind of image of what Europe was like when Beckett finished this novel at the end of World War II. Life was, if not noseless, then eyeless and earless and hairless.[30] Probably the best examples of this reduction are the single bicycle, umbrella, and sack that Mercier and Camier must share. Neumann added a single raincoat, made by Fergusson, which both actors occupied as though Siamese twins. Mercier and Camier do not accept their reduced existence. For them the prostitute Helen is "of Troy, Florence, Paris, Dublin, etc." As Helen, Fergusson was ensconced in a second-story bower, a sheltering pleasure palace to which the men often retreat. Awash in lurid red and yellow lighting, Neumann, Raymond, and Fergusson engaged in a mime of "fingering and fondling" brought close by a skillful use of lighting and projections on the scrim drapery that fronted the second-story space. The audience simultaneously saw the live actors *through* the projected close-ups; a kind of wide-angle seaminess filtered through images airbrushed by the characters' romanticism. Occasionally the projected images were superimposed one on the other, as when "in a slow dissolve, Fred's huge upside-down face, mouth open in ecstasy/agony, receives a cracker from a lady's fancy hand."[31] Such images were the production's most potent "close-ups."

In fact, the entire set was a camera. Neumann had recruited Longcore, for whom he (as well as the Breuers) had worked as a photographic model. Since 1970 or 1971 Longcore had lived in an Avenue A apartment across the roof from the apartment of Breuer, Maleczech, and their children. Longcore had discovered "ways to advance from simply making photographs 'of' things and places, toward new kinds of more or less abstract photographs that were sometimes able to coax thoughts, or feelings, or impressions to the surface of the viewer's imagination."[32] He drew on this work to capture the dreamscape of Mercier and Camier, their random wanderings, and the permeable universe they inhabit in an abstract montage projected onto two areas of the set, as well as the side walls. One image smoothly dissolved or faded into another. Human or animal shapes sometimes appeared in nonrepresentational landscapes. Longcore "keystoned" the images, elongating them by turning the slide projectors to one side so that the image hit the scrim at an acute angle. The images "were vignetted in that strange shape so that they would become a soft-edged thing . . . thirty [to] fifty feet long." The coloring and shapes were decidedly nonrealistic, although urban and rural landscapes appeared as well. A hammer might appear against a starscape; stone walls dividing fields might extend to the horizon. All were designed to visualize references in the script.

Longcore also worked with Dallas and Neumann on the characters' appearances in silhouette, as though created by a magic lantern or shadow puppetry. He did several shoots with the actors, created black and white transparencies, and then made slides, softening the edges of the characters' outlines and hand washing the images with color. Using back projection, these silhouettes would appear on the four scrim panels of the revolving door, first seeming to approach, then to move away. A "leisurely sequence of . . . images illustrating the Storyteller's rundown [Warrilow's voiceover] of doings on St. Ruth's Square introduce[d] Mercier and Camier in stark black and white silhouette photos."[33] The silhouettes showed them meeting, arguing, and "setting off," growing smaller in the distance until their images disappeared. Later the silhouettes duplicated and enhanced the two live actors onstage, the multiple images of each character juxtaposed in the manner of a film montage. Perhaps the most impressive effect occurred in the opening scene.

> Accompanied by Philip Glass' delicate electronic score, a sound like the tinkling of tiny prisms, the scrim panels began to revolve. Shadowy images were projected onto the panels: a bottle on a tray, then the outstretched arm that held it, presently the figure of a man, a waiter. The projections became larger, the shadows seemed to draw nearer, and all the while the moving panels multiplied and elongated each image as it made its circle. Again and again the silhouette of the waiter glided by. Suddenly the panels reflected the real shadow of the same figure, not a projected one, and a real waiter emerged from the revolve, tray in hand. And because he was on roller skates, his movement simply continued the fluid arc of his shadowy predecessor; he glided across the floor to the bar, as effortless as a dream. This sweep of movement, sound, and image, exquisitely executed, carried the audience like a wave; it was theatrical imagining of the first order.[34]

The set's permeability was the production's best expression of Beckett's universe, where black holes can swallow light and matter, a man might walk and talk yet be missing body parts, or an umbrella thrown into the air might not reappear.

Crucial to the projections' success was the purchase of several dissolve units that allowed the pairs of projectors to fade out one image as another emerged. Longcore set up a reel-to-reel tape to control the changing of the slides with inaudible signals. Automating the complicated sequences allowed Chas Cowing (who mixed the sound) to run it without assistance.[35] Unfortunately it also had the effect of controlling the tempo, a factor with serious consequences for both the actors and musician Harvey Spevak. The production design began to drive the play.

"Making it new"

Although the needs of the design were demanding, Neumann sought in rehearsal to put the actors at the center of the show. After the work-in-progress presentation, *Mercier and Camier*'s rehearsals went into hiatus as Breuer began developing *A Prelude to Death in Venice*, which featured Raymond.[36] Neumann seems to be of two minds about Breuer's activities during these years. While he believes that *Prelude* took Raymond away from work on *Mercier and Camier*, he has also suggested that Breuer was making an effort in the later 1970s to do outside productions in order to give other members more space in which to develop their work. Certainly several directors were seeking the time and attention of the same company members, resulting in frequent discussions and votes at the weekly meetings.

The actors were glad for the opportunities. O'Reilly was eager to perform and ultimately played five roles: the gliding waiter, a nonspeaking role that benefited from his dance experience; a passerby wearing a sandwich board; and three speaking parts—two law officers and Madden. As Madden, O'Reilly wore a wooden mask designed by Lisa Wujonivich. Raymond and Neumann shared Madden's monologue in the train sequence, "turn[ing] it into a rhythmic roundelay that echoes the rattling of the railroad."[37] As in Beckett's text, Madden's account of his violent life produces no moral conclusion. Just as Beckett's narrator withholds comment, saying "nothing is known for sure," the production seems to have emphasized the texture of Madden's language rather than its content. As the gliding waiter, O'Reilly made himself weightless, his effort undetectable as he entered and turned on the television to reveal Watt's face. The waiter was the instrument of Watt, this "god yapping away on tv,"[38] replacing Beckett's several bourgeois proprietors determined to keep respectable establishments. Foreigners in their own country, Mercier and Camier never know exactly where they stand. Yet O'Reilly's gliding waiter also seemed a welcoming figure, a dream of acceptance drawn from Neumann's memory of his own years abroad: "In Spain you clap your hands and somebody appears, all dressed up in black tie, and serves you up these things while you watch the world go by on the sidewalk, and you feel that you are visiting some strange, wonderful paradise."

Warrilow's Watt—his last role in a Mabou Mines production—was a veritable god of narration, joining Beckett's narrator with the text's overhearty, meddlesome, brooding Watt. Early in the work Neumann realized that Warrilow would not be performing live, so he planned the "storyteller/Watt" as the voice of an "Irish/English man of 40 to 50 years of age."[39] Unlike the gentle, passive main character of the earlier *Watt* (written in 1942–44, published in 1953), Watt in Beckett's *Mercier and Camier* "is changed almost beyond recognition . . . loud and violent. In the course of a quiet conversation with Mercier and Camier in a pub, he quite unexpectedly seizes Camier's stick, breaks the pint glass of a complete stranger with it, and shouts 'Fuck life!' "[40] Neumann's storyteller/Watt is a necessarily voluble and moody deus ex machina. His outburst seems to follow from his earlier renunciation of his narrator's duties, when he refuses (or becomes unable) to decide the order of events much less the characters' motivations: "The whole question of priority, so luminous hitherto, is from now on obscure."[41] Neumann joined the narrator's self-repudiation with Watt's self-destructive outburst, leading inevitably to the character's removal from the action. It appears that the storyteller/Watt extinguishes himself, first growing drunk and furious, then lapsing into a stuporous sleep. Finally the waiter turns off the image of Watt's drunken face.

Combining Watt and the narrator into a single character meant rearranging scenes and possibly losing the continuity that Beckett's narrator, despite his renunciation, provides. This same sort of single or solo voice later gave *Company* and *Worstward Ho* their narrative coherence. Yet the concept of the beautiful, bodiless voice suits the narrator of *Mercier and Camier* well. Eric Levy believes that Beckett's narrator "has no self beyond the characters he invents" and that the need for self defines him.[42] By retaining Watt's vocal violence and jettisoning his body, Neumann made his narrator's absence "the most convincing presence in the play," as reviewer James Leverett noted.[43]

Reviewers agreed that Warrilow's reading of Beckett's language also made Watt's appearances memorable. In an otherwise harsh review, Leverett admitted that Warrilow "compels us with the poetry by creating an intimate reality of character and action behind it." While mistaking the storyteller/Watt for "an omniscient observer," Mel Gussow noted that "the sight and the sound of Mr. Warrilow snap the play to attention. With his ashen face and oracular voice, he is a figure with a magnetic attraction for Beckett."[44] Gussow goes on to argue that the show would have benefited from Warrilow's live presence. Having Watt onstage, however, would not have restored the narrator's "intervening consciousness"[45] and might have interfered with Neumann's intent as director.

He sought to focus the production on the cinematic articulation of the central couple, i.e., the shared picaresque imagination of Mercier and Camier. As Levy points out, the narrator attempts to fix his own sense of self through theirs. Levy sees the couple as Beckett's alternative to a collapsed Descartian subject.

> Beckett looks beneath the rubble of collapsed conventions for the last safeguard and testament of subjectivity and finds it "quite simply in the saving of a rela-tion, a separation, *a couple,* however impoverished the components: the I with its possibilities of acting and receiving, the rest in its docility as the given." . . . The couple's function is to protect subjectivity by assuring its relation to a world by which it is bounded, any world, even that of its own torment or solitude.[46]

As an early work, *Mercier and Camier* does not offer the detailed articulation of the paired characters in *Endgame* or even *Waiting for Godot*. Yet Neumann seems to have relied on the relation to convey the production concept; through the two characters' shared imagination the audience took its jour-ney of experience.

The bond between Mercier and Camier surfaced in the lazzis that accom-panied the dialogue. The first of these appeared, according to Paran, early in the show: "They entered through the center door, side by side, each with his outside arm through the sleeve of the oversize raincoat they shared, Mercier holding an umbrella over them, Camier with a satchel over his shoulder, Fred-erick Neumann's beefy Mercier already the perfect foil for Bill Raymond's sprightly Camier."[47] Getting in and out of the raincoat proved to be a lazzi in itself, with each actor using a hand to cinch or unbuckle the belt. The lazzis seemed to derive from the white clown/red clown distinction, with Neumann as the more serious and physical and Raymond as the lackadaisical partner, the butt of every joke. The roles were sometimes reversed, with Camier unexpect-edly upstaging the straight man. Or they played in unison, such as a five-minute sequence in which they simply laughed with no apparent cause. The laughter was "contagious," recalled Raymond, moving from one to the other and back again like a "virus" that "communicated" the characters' relation out to the audience.[48] The lazzis did not clarify the characters' psychology for the audience so much as bring out the comedy of their absurd relation.

These techniques were apparently not sufficient to realize the bond be-tween Mercier and Camier. Activity remained activity, commented Paran, "an apology for the dialog instead of an extension of it."[49] It appears that insufficient rehearsal time prevented the actors from bringing the elements of the comic relation together. The actors struggled to balance warm and cool, narrative continuity and disjunction. Raymond in particular felt the lack of time.

> I need to rehearse enough so that . . . everything is second nature and I don't have to depend on memorized texts. It's simply there, so that I'm actually saying something and intending a new thing every time I say it. . . . I call it a "sub-essay." . . . [In *Mercier and Camier*] there were not a lot of new discoveries being made while we were performing—which is my favorite. That's when you get closest to . . . an event.[50]

Raymond's "event" seems to be what Maleczech has described as "taking the audience on a journey," which is dangerous for both actor and spectator. As discussed in chapter 3, this is Mabou Mines' corollary to the reader's experience of Beckett's exacting language: giving oneself up to a discipline in which one finds the freedom to play. In rehearsals for earlier Beckett productions, the physical execution of the text eventually projected the actor into the idea itself. The work process paralleled Beckett's writing process, painful but necessary. *Mercier and Camier*'s work process seems to have been truncated.

Neumann had been right to visualize a central trope around which the action could revolve. Perhaps he had too complex a central image, or too many images, so that none could be brought into close-up. As a result, Beckett's text needed "a more economical representation," as Neumann has acknowledged.[51] A leaner *Mercier and Camier* might have allowed photography to become the central trope, streamlining action and language to the high contrast and abstraction of the projections. Longcore would have liked to do more of the "close-up" dissolves to enhance the actors' inventiveness: "Since actors such as these . . . invent myriad refined actions and expressions as a matter of course in their work, I wish I could have been able to use my work to magnify more of this, as well as to provide atmosphere, scenery, mood and so forth. Some of which we did do."[52]

Being faithful to Beckett's language was imperative for Neumann. In earlier Beckett productions members of Mabou Mines had used their own lives as primary material, through which they read the texts, and for some company members this attitude continued.[53] Being faithful to Beckett's words seemed to imply, for director Neumann at least, a need to reduce their indeterminacy and elicit recognizable characters. From the beginning Neumann and Raymond had been more interested in motivational acting than were Warrilow,

Maleczech, and Akalaitis. These three, like Beckett actors Jack McGowran and Billie Whitelaw, sought to internalize Beckett's words without needing to form character, making the words a type of music that they as instruments played. Neumann and Raymond chose not to forfeit their characters' "recognizable personalities [consciously adopted] to fit decided-upon ideas about text."[54]

Most reviewers treated Neumann's production of *Mercier and Camier* as a work in progress. They may have given it less credit than it deserved, particularly for the casting, the devising of imaginative staging solutions to difficult narrative shifts, and the incorporation of cinematic "flow" within disjunction, as in Beckett's text. Beckett scholar Ruby Cohn felt the critics had been too hard on the production because few were sufficiently familiar with the text to follow the action.[55] Neumann was not daunted by the lukewarm reception. In 1980 he met with Beckett to discuss *Mercier and Camier* and in subsequent meetings received Beckett's approval to "go on" and adapt *Company* and *Worstward Ho* for the stage. In a sense *Mercier and Camier* looked ahead to Mabou Mines' productions of the 1980s. It put together, perhaps for the first time, dissolved photographic projections and video, combinations of still images and filmic continuity. Alone of Neumann's three Beckett productions, *Mercier and Camier* shared with *The Shaggy Dog Animation* a filtering of the actor's visual presence. But *Mercier and Camier* remains in many ways unique. It did not amplify and distort spoken language, as was done in *Shaggy Dog*. As an ingeniously low-tech, but large-scale production, Neumann's first Beckett adaptation taught him both what he wanted to do and what was not viable for his later work.

Cohn sees *Mercier and Camier* as Neumann's attempt to hold Mabou Mines together with a project written by the author who had provided the words for its first recognized productions. This production was intended, perhaps, to restore the company's early, close-knit sense of collaboration.[56] It seems more likely, though, that Neumann, like Akalaitis, Breuer, and Maleczech, sought to shape work distinctly his own. As an actor who draws on the author's text to shape his performance, Neumann has found his strength as a director in molding all production elements to the author's language, specifically to a through-line he finds in the text. In transliterating that language into stage symbols, chief among which is the body and voice of the actor, Neumann has contributed a classical modernist interpretation of Beckett to the company's body of work. Honing his approach with his productions of *Company* and *Worstward Ho*, Neumann has interpreted Beckett as the solo voice narrating its "journey of experience" not as an aesthetic of resistance and accommodation, as Breuer and Warrilow created in *The Lost Ones,* but as an exploration of aesthetics to answer the absurdity of that experience. Neumann found in *Mercier and Camier* a voice split among characters. It was a "noseless" voice, thin and reduced, more evocative of Europe in the late 1940s than the United States in the 1970s.

Bringing this production into the future was its attempt to link high-art intentions to an apparatus of mass culture, namely, photography. In this sense, Neumann shared a fascination for "the actual, the contemporaneous, the photographic" with Maleczech, who (as we will see) used photography in her first production to link the nineteenth century with the twentieth. *Mercier and Camier* spoke to audiences in an artistic language whose elements precede the absurdists and the Beats by almost a hundred years, when the first bohemians strolled onto the streets of Paris, London, and New York. Maleczech linked the birth of photography with its fascinating processes and both of these with two writers whose work paralleled the development of photography: the French poet Charles Baudelaire; and his chosen American ancestor, Edgar Allan Poe. In this case photography did not visualize an author's account of an absurd reality but rather blurred the distinction between reality and fiction. Using the voice as a primary instrument, *Vanishing Pictures* reminded audiences that the correspondence between written word and object is not one to one. The intervening, ironized sign complicates that relation, a sign represented variously in *Vanishing Pictures* as the vocalized word, the photograph, and Poe's French biographer, Baudelaire.

Vanishing Pictures

In 1980 Ruth Maleczech directed *Vanishing Pictures,* a piece written and performed by Beverly Brown and based on the tales of the American poet and journalist Edgar Allan Poe. Poe was a bohemian both in the popular sense (he lived unconventionally and died alcoholic and abject) and in T. J. Clark's sense of the mid-nineteenth-century French bohemian's self-conscious role-playing. As a precursor of the avant-gardist, the bohemian

> caricatured the claims of bourgeois society. He took the slogans at face-value; if the city was a playground he would play; if individual freedom was sacrosanct then he would celebrate the cult twenty-four hours a day; *laissez-faire*

meant what it said. The Bohemian was the dandy stood on his head: where the dandy was the bourgeois playing at being an aristocrat (hence his pathos), the Bohemian was the bourgeois playing at being a bourgeois.[57]

As Beverly Brown researched Poe's life and tales, she became interested in his playful, paranoid narrators, solo voices at odds with conventional morality. Brown was particularly interested in "The Mystery of Marie Rogêt," based in his tale on the actual murder of a New York woman, Mary Rogers. Poe projected a solution to the murder that proved false. Brown identified with Poe's journalistic embarrassment over being caught sensationalizing the event and his struggle to rewrite the story's conclusion. Like Baudelaire, she admired the beauty of Poe's prose and had a similarly obsessive and uncanny feeling that when she read Poe she was reading about herself.[58] Ultimately the script for *Vanishing Pictures* consisted of material drawn from Poe's stories, Baudelaire's letters and poems, and French art songs sung by Brown. The production would be a "journey of experience" based on an aesthetic of the individual subject gone paranoid, outlaw, or mad. Poe, Baudelaire, Marie Rogêt/Mary Rogers, and Beverly Brown were to be joined in a single speaking voice. In this sense *Vanishing Pictures* reached back to an earlier, humanist "romantic ideal of language" from Poe's time, before the avant-garde had emerged from the bohemian. The production also reached back in making photography, and its early history, integral to its nineteenth-century narrator. To understand the show's two related but distinct ideals of language—pure versus ironized icon—it is necessary to understand the interaction of two very different artists working together in the studio setting of Re.Cher.Chez.

"A classic guild": Re.Cher.Chez.

By 1980 Richard Schechner was declaring the end of humanism and Bonnie Marranca was lamenting the avant-garde's inability to embrace any sort of literary tradition that could pass the work down to younger artists. Theater groups were disappearing, and yet younger artists continued to migrate to New York in search of places in which to experiment. Noting that actors, directors, and designers often had nowhere to continue exploring avant-garde performance techniques, Maleczech, Breuer, and Raymond founded Re.Cher.Chez as "a studio for avant-garde studies in the performing arts." Lasting five years, from 1979 to 1984, Re.Cher.Chez was part of an oral tradition of working. As a laboratory for performance ideas, it made crucial connections for both emerging artists such as Beverly Brown, John Pynchon Holms, Dan Hurlin, Jerry Mayer, Anna Deavere Smith, and Kate Stafford and better established performers such as actress Beatrice Roth and musician and performance artist Laurie Anderson. Pieces developed at Re.Cher.Chez went on to full productions at Theatre for the New City, P.S. 122, the Performing Garage, Kiva, Inroads, and Franklin Furnace.

Re.Cher.Chez was unique in a number of ways. Artists of widely differing backgrounds were accepted. The studio was a place not to learn the basics but to continue working and training, just as film actors often returned to the Actor's Studio to refresh or expand their skills.[59] Participant Bethany Haye commended Re.Cher.Chez for being, unlike Lee Strasberg's studio, a cooperative effort that did not "promote a specific style or dictate a single aesthetic." The artists determined the extent of their involvement and, to accomplish their work, were provided with "rehearsal space, a forum for critique, exchange of ideas and especially access to mentors." Breuer predicted:

> If all goes well with this idea of a studio and if it grows healthily, it can be for the experimental wing of the field what in its best years the Actor's Studio was for the mainstream. A laboratory where talents can mature. Protected. By not so much as a professional school as by a classic guilt [guild] with its masters, journeymen and apprentices to the craft.[60]

In a sense, Re.Cher.Chez was designed to keep alive the 1970s grassroots approach to performance in which training was broad, informal, and eclectic. Maleczech and Breuer sought to integrate directing with design and acting, as they did in their work with Mabou Mines. At the same time, the idea of a guild bridged the early 1970s tradition of experimentation and the growing career orientation of many 1980s artists, particularly performance artists. As Hamilton has pointed out, many younger actors and directors have been trained too narrowly in their specialties for this kind of work:

> They are not going to be capable of making the kind of work Mabou Mines teaches you to make. . . . Who is it for? Who does it serve? . . . [The members of Mabou Mines] think about the audience, which is why it hasn't gone off into that performance art limb. . . . There's a humanistic core to the work and an intellectual integrity to it. [Technology] is always in the service of something else.[61]

The studio's influence is visible in work by Anna Deavere Smith, Jerry Mayer and John Pynchon Holms, and member Greg Mehrten, whose *Jungle Fever* began at Re.Cher.Chez and went on to P.S. 122. Re.Cher.Chez employed a very old-fashioned method of oral teaching, Maleczech explained.

> In colloquial French, [Re.Cher.Chez] means "a bit old-fashioned," which may seem strange for an avant-garde studio. . . . But because very little documentation has been developed in experimental theater over the past 20 years, we are based on an oral teaching tradition that really is somewhat old-fashioned these days.[62]

Acting and directing are traditionally oral traditions, with the transmission of techniques depending on individual memory and sporadic publication. Because avant-gardists in the 1960s and 1970s rejected the idea of preserving the work, valuing instead the "authenticity" of experiencing it, they were not invested in this already fragile tradition. Nor, as Marranca points out, did artists have the traditional support of literary critics and scholars who had often provided a kind of continuity for modernists such as Brecht or Piscator in established but venturesome European theaters.[63] While Marranca had seen Breuer's Animations into print in 1979, a literary establishment comparable to those of 1920s Europe simply did not exist. Re.Cher.Chez's founders wanted to provide connections to earlier work by example and by providing participants with the resources and safety to try new ideas on their own.

Insight into Re.Cher.Chez's work process comes from Haye, who joined the studio after taking workshops in 1976 from Maleczech and Breuer at Denver's Theatre Lab West. (Raymond apparently dropped out of the studio shortly after it was founded.) The series consisted of ten days of five hours each, with extra sessions added for solo work. Although Re.Cher.Chez did not adopt this schedule, its working methods were based on the same principles of exploration and answered questions the workshop had raised.

> [Breuer and Maleczech] were tireless; we were kineticized, mobilized, startled, frustrated and amazed as the devastatingly simple exercises progressed from one session to the next. A personal idiosyncrasy, a quirky energy leak would be discovered, isolated, exaggerated, played with, stylized and eventually folded into the treatment of some text. We used byproducts of our conscious behavior we had never noticed or had always fought against and by the end of the workshop had conned complete little performance pieces out of ourselves. A dynamic rapport developed between us and the instructors.[64]

Later residencies were done at Princeton University, the Minneapolis Play-wrights' Center, and the Washington (DC) Project for the Arts, each conducted by a single Mabou Mines member and two studio artists. Arranged through a network of approximately twenty-five academic and professional advisers, res-idencies were offered either in three- to four-week formats or for shorter peri-ods in which workshops were combined with performances of Re.Cher.Chez's work.[65]

Studio artists, most of whom were already located in New York, enjoyed a more relaxed and extended version of this rapport. Re.Cher.Chez was designed not just to elicit production concepts but to bring those pieces to a stage of de-velopment not possible in a workshop. Located in the basement of 94 Saint Mark's Place, Re.Cher.Chez was open year-round as a rehearsal space and from September to May as a forum for comment and suggestions from the artistic directors and studio members. Maleczech and Breuer did weekly critiques, usually at Friday evening meetings, and the following Monday evening the artists would present fifteen-minute pieces of the work. These "Piecemeal Mondays" later moved to the first weekend of each month. Finished work ap-peared twice a year, most importantly at the annual Mayfest, a monthlong fes-tival of full-length productions. Yet, with no specific course to complete or any requirement to finish work within a defined period, studio members tended to stay or, once a piece was finished, return to do new work.

According to Breuer, the project that served as a model for Re.Cher.Chez was *The Taud Show,* developed in 1978 by Jerry Mayer and John Pynchon Holms.[66] Holms had assisted Breuer and Overlie on the halftime show for *The Saint and the Football Player;* later he and Mayer approached Mabou Mines for advice on a show based on the work of Antonin Artaud. Breuer suggested changes to Mayer's script, and he, Maleczech, and Raymond attended several rehearsals to advise director Holms on shaping the production. They found the help invaluable: "Mabou Mines then offered its loft at no charge for our first performances (we initiated the MONDAY NIGHT PERFORMANCE SE-RIES) and helped make us a connection with The Public Theatre which re-sulted in a 14-week run in the Old Prop Shop Theatre."[67] For this work, per-former Mayer earned an Obie award.

Re.Cher.Chez transmitted Mabou's working principles to many artists, making its influence pervasive. Perhaps, in a sense, company members were emulating Ellen Stewart, who had provided them a protective space and the means to work at a crucial time in their development, and Joe Papp, who dur-ing Re.Cher.Chez's existence was supporting Mabou Mines productions and thus the mentoring of these younger colleagues as well. As Mabou Mines found in turn, sponsors sometimes go unacknowledged. In his article "The Funding Game," Breuer thanked an angry Stewart, distressed over his lack of public acknowledgment for her support, but his language was colored with ambivalence and guilt.[68] (In fact, his phrase "classic guild" is printed as the pun "classic guilt.") While acknowledging that all of Mabou Mines' early projects were in fact La Mama projects, the company then having no separate public identity, he hints that Stewart was reluctant to grant the company independence. On the other hand, he compares her anger to his own at being unacknowledged by Mayer and Holms with regard to *The Taud Show.* They made amends later, for in the same grant proposal in which they offered the specific praise quoted earlier they noted Re.Cher.Chez's broader contribution to the development of new work. Breuer made his own move at reconciliation in "The Funding Game," noting everyone's need for credit in order to glean support from granting agencies and corporate sponsors, which "want to see the work getting out. The people getting in. The credits getting it on with other credits that are getting it on with fiscal realities. . . . Perhaps we can summon a deeper compassion for all us players of this sad compulsive game. There's no way not to be trapped by your own imperatives."

A wide variety of work appeared under the aegis of Re.Cher.Chez. The artistic directors' sensibilities were not necessarily reflected in the work. They were not creating clones of themselves but a community within which the work could be seen and critiqued. The directors' job was to bring their critical acumen to the process.[69] Then, at Mayfest, the work met a broader audience. The first Mayfest schedule suggests a combination of finished and in-progress work: short pieces by David R. Schanker, including a monologue called "Watertower" spoken by Suzanne Buchko and a film "documentary" on suicide; book-in-hand readings from Doris Lessing; a narrative tale based on American Indian legends; solo dance; a film montage; and electronic sound experiments. None ran longer than fifteen minutes.

"The effects of fever"

From Re.Cher.Chez's first season came the Mabou Mines production of *Vanishing Pictures.* A press release describes it as a one-act, fifty-five-minute "'piecette,' a type of French salon theater popular in the late eighteenth and early nineteenth centuries."[70] The roots of *Vanishing Pictures* went deep into postromantic literary traditions, but the show's ironic style of presentation had

more in common with the Animations, Beckett's later plays, and autobiographical solo performance, which was becoming popular in the late 1970s. Beverly
Brown had sung originally in conventional opera, but she came to *Vanishing
Pictures* with experience in avant-garde musical theater as well. In 1976–77, she
sang several roles in Charles Ludlam's version of Richard Wagner's *Der Ring des
Niebelungen,* and she developed solo programs of French art songs.[71] Brown
also had knowledge of theater. For many years she worked for the theater
scholar and poet Stefan Brecht, who in late 1978 recommended to Brown that
she take a course from Maleczech. Class members devised a play from a literary
subject, either an author or a work, a process familiar to Maleczech from
Mabou Mines' adaptations of Beckett and Colette. Maleczech accepted Brown
into the class after interviewing her. As the course progressed, the dozen students shared ideas on their projects. Getting a positive response to lines she read
from Poe's stories, Brown participated in the class's presentation of its work to
an audience of friends.[72] As part of Re.Cher.Chez, Brown continued to develop
Vanishing Pictures and gave additional work-in-progress performances.
Re.Cher.Chez was exactly what Brown needed. Already an accomplished vocal
performer, Brown now had an opportunity to broaden her abilities and produce a truly interdisciplinary adaptation of her source material.

   Watching Brown's piece develop apparently enticed Maleczech into directing a full production.[73] In 1975 Maleczech had directed McElduff in a restaging
of a production of *Not I* begun in Memphis with Ray Hill. Maleczech, however,
thinks of *Vanishing Pictures* as her first production as a director. In 1979 she
was already involved in *Dead End Kids,* in which she played Marie Curie and
other characters, and was contributing ideas to *A Prelude to Death in Venice*
and *Mercier and Camier.* Like Neumann, she seemed ready to undertake her
own project, although directing did not really change her collaborative way of
working. Maleczech was attracted to the organic performance connection that
Brown had found among Poe, Baudelaire, and songs by Debussy, Ravel, and
Satie. Once they had decided on a full production, Brown and Maleczech began staging that connection through photography and prose, that is, both visually and aurally. Although as a Re.Cher.Chez project *Vanishing Pictures* was
not yet affiliated with Mabou Mines, the juxtaposition of light and sound was
akin to *The Shaggy Dog Animation* and *Dressed Like an Egg.*

   In early fall 1979, with the show's concept barely realized, Maleczech met
with Brown regularly at her apartment to discuss the production and the direction Brown's reading was taking.[74] While Brown was fascinated with Poe's
life and aesthetics, Maleczech was attracted to the juxtaposition of visual and

aural poetry, the way in which the songs seemed to "rise from the stage." Maleczech wanted strange, unsettling transformations of the sort suggested in Poe's prose and to be fulfilled by Brown's interaction with the set. As Terry Curtis Fox wrote of the production:

> Like the novels of Sax Rohmer, the stories of Edgar Allan Poe induce the effects of fever: things appear slight, disjointed; perspective is just askew enough to merge hallucination and shadow. Any attempt to reproduce this experience on stage confronts an apparent contradiction: the concrete physicality of the theatre goes against the very nature of the work. Yet this state is precisely what Ruth Maleczech has evoked in her production of Beverly Brown's *Vanishing Pictures*.[75]

Rather than seeing a conflict between "concrete physicality" and the "fevered" life of the imagination, Maleczech saw the two intersect as the show transformed a constricted, two-dimensional world into three dimensions. She wanted the audience to wonder: why did this object behave in that way? Brown, on the other hand, was asking: what makes Poe's use of language beautiful? What makes it funny? Why does this narrator seem so familiar? And later: who is this talking?[76]

Despite these differences, Maleczech and Brown agreed from the start that *Vanishing Pictures* should involve photography.[77] As a two-dimensional medium that opens the imagination to three (or four) dimensions, photography creates a reality for the viewer. Brown noted that Poe and Baudelaire had witnessed photography's early development and that the two poets' photographic portraits had long been significant cultural icons. In that, from the first, photography had been used to document crime scenes and other real-life events, as well as for artistic purposes, Brown found the camera lens "kind of merciless in a way." She connected photography's production of the uncanny with the oddly clinical narrative voices of Poe's detective fiction. Both produced doubles, common in late romantic fiction, which suggested in the 1970s a fascinating return to the archaic origins of "human nature," just as Jung's theories of the collective unconscious and Freud's notion of the uncanny offered ways to understand that nature's darker but beautiful and hence seductive side. One of Brown's sources quotes Baudelaire on art's uncanny ability to transform the world: "So much has been said about [Monet's] *pastiches* of Goya that he is now trying to see some. . . . Do you doubt that such astonishing parallels can occur in nature? Well then, I am accused of imitating Edgar Poe! Do you know why I have studied Poe so patiently? Because he resembles *me!*"[78] Baude-laire's desire to be Poe's original shows the two sides of photography: its ability to reveal the human subject while putting him or her into question. Just as crime photography, particularly the mug shot, seems to promise absolute identification of the body and thus of human individuality, photography in *Vanishing Pictures* seems to promise a way back to Mary Rogers or to Poe. Brown sought that way back. In fact, as we will see, the photograph produces an unknown subject, a fevered composite rather than an authentic original. Director Maleczech, having just explored similar composites in *Shaggy Dog* and *Dressed Like an Egg,* had less faith in such originals and, while acknowl-edging photography as a medium of icons, seemed more interested in its ca-pacity to dissolve the authentic subject into its prerecorded copies. As in *Mercier and Camier,* photography was the affordable apparatus of mass cul-ture that in this case put the effects of Poe's fevered subjectivity on the stage.

"Very grassroots"

If *Mercier and Camier* had a limited budget, *Vanishing Pictures* began with no funding at all. Brown recalls that the students contributed to the rent at 94 Saint Mark's Place until the first grant money for Re.Cher.Chez came in. Maleczech presumably applied the studio's limited operating funds to the pro-duction, but for the most part she paid for the production herself, taking out $3,500 in loans.[79] In the meantime, the production had become "a project of Mabou Mines," the first outside production to receive such a designation.

The show's primary expenses involved photographic images integrated into the design (and also developed onstage, although this was not costly). Un-like *Mercier and Camier,* which involved a professional photographer, Maleczech and several young Mabou Mines associates designed *Vanishing Pic-tures'* photographic effects and pop-up set. The work was "very grassroots," says Stephanie Rudolph, with everyone trying their hand at tasks for the first time.[80] Rudolph became acquainted with *Vanishing Pictures* through Linda Justice, who did the initial work on photographic projections before leaving the project. Rudolph was a photography student at the School of Visual Arts but thought of herself as a painter; she did realistic paintings from slides. Julie Archer, in the meantime, had been living that year in California, where on a visit Maleczech invited her to design the set. She, Rudolph, and Maleczech re-call the work as highly satisfying; the team re-formed the following year to do *Wrong Guys.*

Having never designed before, Archer suddenly found herself involved with three productions, *Vanishing Pictures, A Prelude to Death in Venice,* and *Sister Suzie Cinema,* the latter two of which she lit. As on *Shaggy Dog,* set design for *Vanishing Pictures* was collaborative and informal, with everyone offering suggestions. Both Archer and Rudolph credit Maleczech, however, with contributing many ideas, particularly on lighting, and being the production design's "train engine."[81] The artists needed to create "the effects of fever" cheaply and imaginatively. Archer's set concept involved images appearing from nothing then disappearing. Early in her travels around the set, Brown would pull open a door, from which unfolded a nineteenth-century desk or secretary. As Brown opened each drawer, "two-dimensional slivers" would pop up to become a working table lamp, a quill pen, and a liquor bottle. The secretary's lid folded down to form a usable writing surface under which Brown could crawl in her character's later moments of insanity. Archer constructed the pop-up pieces using foam core and Rudolph's hand-tinted black-and-white photos of wood grain and furniture detail. The artists also covered the "room's" perimeter with Rudolph's photographs of wood molding. When lit, the hand-tinted photos created a self-reflexive photographic illusion of nineteenth-century craftsmanship. Archer continued to work on pop-up techniques, realizing her ideas most fully in her and Liza Lorwin's *Peter and Wendy,* directed by Breuer.

Light as technique and theme was really the most important set element. Rudolph used Kodaliths to make large, inexpensive black-and-white transparencies. Within areas of the wall "molding," Kodalith light boxes were mounted unobtrusively. As Brown recounted the narrator's imagined scene of the attack on Marie Rogêt, the light boxes came on one by one in the darkness above Brown's head, as though magically representing the narrator's mental images. The artists also used Kodalith in the show's opening sequence in combination with an overhead projector. Beginning in total darkness, a thin, vertical red line of light picked out Brown's figure, her antique white gown torn at the shoulder. She held a dish of developing liquid in which an exposed Kodalith print floated. The sequence was timed precisely so that by the time Brown finished her opening narration she had deposited the bowl on the overhead projector and the image became visible to the audience. The image was a close-up of Brown's face seen in the circle of the bowl's rim. The projector's red safety light added an eerie effect that was compounded when Archer superimposed on the Kodalith images of first Poe and then Baudelaire so that the three faces seemed to merge into a new photographic subject whose mouth appeared to move. It was, Brown has said, a face belonging to "everybody and nobody."[82] As in Poe's stories, the stranger was a double, familiar yet unplaceable. In this way *Vanishing Pictures* was "about" the photographic process and the historical role photographic portraiture has played in shaping the human subject as a collection of lifelike characteristics performed. In a sense lighting became an actor expressing the narrator's pervasive anxiety and repressed psychic ambivalence, just as Brown's face became part of the mise-en-scène. Under Maleczech's direction the distinction between outer and inner, self and other, appearance and feeling, material world and soul became a Moëbius strip of beautiful, eerie continuities.

For Brown this effect resembled a Jungian image of the collective unconscious; invoking the uncanny was her way of universalizing the work. Similar moves were being made in the 1970s by academics who saw Poe and other writers as artists drawing on the collective unconscious, in the process asserting that Poe speaks to all of us because he reaches a structural level below or beyond individual difference. In more recent years it has been noted that such intellectual moves tended to read authors as universal in order to confirm boundaries of national character and gender identity. Thus, the suggestion in *Vanishing Pictures* that Poe, Baudelaire, and Brown could be "combined" to form a gestalt personality may have been in part a rather conservative artistic move—one reasserting this universalist perspective—in a progressive time of feminist consciousness-raising and nascent ethnic awareness.

"The solo paranoid voice"

While the production design was apparently worked out fairly quickly, between late fall 1979 and January 1980 Brown's role seemed to develop more slowly. Poe's rather static tale was not the most obvious choice for staging. His detective, Dupin, solves the mystery at home by analyzing newspaper accounts of the murder. In fact, Poe's emphasis on the complexities of narrative voice made the details of the murder itself almost superfluous to the production. Unlike Arthur Conan Doyle's more formulaic "realist" subjects, Sherlock Holmes and Dr. Watson, Poe's detective Dupin and his unnamed narrator have more in common with the interstitial personalities that appear in texts by Borges and Beckett (or Hoffmann and Hawthorne), where voices narrating and narrated seem to blend or exchange positions in the absence of quotation marks. In a series of narrative frames Dupin quotes several lengthy newspaper accounts. Poe's narrator comments on these events and the conclusions Dupin draws. Then, too, Poe adds opening editorial footnotes to claim that his original account, though lacking details, had presented "not only the general conclusion, but absolutely all the chief hypothetical details by which that conclusion was attained."[83] The "general conclusion," of course, had been in error. The real Mary Rogers apparently died after a botched abortion, her body dropped in the Hudson River. But Poe was not interested in Mary Rogers. He had announced in his original motto, drawn from Novalis's *Moralische Ansichten* (published 1802), that his was an "ideal series of events" paralleling the Rogers murder. Poe's editorial voice expands on this idea: "Thus all agreement founded upon the fiction is applicable to the truth: and the investigation of the truth was the object." Poe's identity as a credentialed journalist was compromised when the published account of Mary Rogers's true fate contradicted his story's conclusion. Poe's revision now sought to reassert those credentials.

Brown was deeply interested in Poe's predicament. Fully aware that Poe's revision continued to blur the distinction between truth and fiction, she sought to use a single character as narrator, a figure whose gender, background, identity, and fate were ambiguous. Brown's interest originally had been piqued by Poe's quirky French and his use of obviously phony Paris addresses, a trail of clues of the sort Freud often used to link creative writing to repressed psychic phenomena. The romantic interest in the uncanny had already produced dual tales and characters, emanations of that submerged ambivalence. Brown was particularly drawn to Poe's "William Wilson," a tale about a man stalked by a figure bearing his own face and name. Wilson tells his own story, taking that name in order to conceal his real identity. But that identity is never revealed. One "Wilson" dies by the other's hand—the double dies as well—and yet Wilson's voice remains "in circulation" to tell the story. *Vanishing Pictures* created a similarly ambiguous figure bearing the Freudian characteristics of such doubles.

Brown preferred to see her role as sexually ambiguous, a manifestation of characters, narrators, and authors in equal measure. Despite the taciturn quality of Poe's prose, she did not find any of these doubles cool and analytical, but rather fully engaged, obsessed, and paranoid. Here Brown's performance seems related to the picaresque narrators of other Mabou Mines pieces, such as *Shaggy Dog*, or the characters of William Burroughs or Thomas Pynchon. Brown whispered, sang, and narrated, always going back to the focus of Poe's obsession. Yet onstage her appearance and voice were distinctly feminine. While speaking Poe's lines, she seemed to represent Marie Rogêt, who, like "William Wilson," speaks from beyond the grave. Taking Brown's character as feminine, Rudolph saw the role as "an innocent walking through a disturbing set of memories." Similarly, Maleczech has described her as "an obsessed, roving, violated Victorian woman."[84] The songs that seemed to emanate from the stage were actually written for a soprano voice. Thus, a body gendered female, singing songs gendered female, narrated and behaved in an obsessive manner gendered male.

For Brown the figure was "universal." In this respect Brown shared Poe's aesthetics more than she shared those of her fellow collaborators. Maleczech and Brown agree that the songs did not counterpoint the action but related more to the mood of the mise-en-scène.[85] For Brown they created "a French note or comment" that distanced her character from the events "like adding music to a movie." She had seen the 1942 film made of "The Mystery of Marie Rogêt" by Universal Studios; the voices of camp actress Maria Montez and other actors could be heard in audioclips played near the production's end. Brown, however, did not want to use the songs as an estranging effect. Maleczech, on the other hand, did not want Brown to sing full voice but rather to "mutter" the lyrics.[86] Rather than have Amiram Rigai, Brown's accompanist, perform live, Maleczech had Brown follow a recorded version put through a harmonizer, much as Mabou Mines had done in lip-synching the music for *Shaggy Dog*. Maleczech seems to have intended this artificial-seeming voice to be something like Burroughs's "talking cure" for the culture's addiction to the referential image. Burroughs's work in the 1970s sought to outline the "shadow" that falls between the eye and the object it views by identifying that shadow as the prerecorded word. Uninterested in restoring a direct relation between eye and object, as Artaud had tried to do with the theater of cruelty, Burroughs used language against itself—re-recording it, as Tony Tanner suggests, and playing it back against itself.[87] Similarly, Maleczech wanted to dissociate voice from narration. Brown apparently objected to this approach. She had trouble finding the cues and was distressed to be perceived to be lip-synching rather than singing. Maleczech's approach, however, received support in Fox's report of the production's final moments, when the audience read Mary Rogers's fate from an actual newspaper account projected on the back wall. Both Brown's singing style and Satie's humor broke the pathos of the revelation.

> Maleczech reveals the facts of the case by transforming the screen which has been the piece's backdrop: Suddenly a panel is revealed with a newspaper account of the solution to the crime. Brown then appears and sings a ditty by Erik Satie with mixed French and American lyrics: the song is at once an

affirmation of the cross-cultural and cross-sexual fascination which has been *Vanishing Pictures*'s leitmotif and a fairly chilling reminder that only hard-edged humor can break the sentimentalist's love of death.[88]

Maleczech's first production resembled other Mabou Mines productions in developing a metaphor-concept using ironized vocalizations and making virtuoso performance demands on Brown. As with McElduff's early work on *Come and Go* and *Cascando,* Brown was left to find a way to render Maleczech's directions. Maleczech would not demonstrate what she wanted, says Brown: "She would never put her body in the light so I could see what they saw. Somehow that went against her grain."[89] In fact, it went against Mabou Mines' grain. Generally Maleczech assumed that in rehearsal the performers would work to the point where they "found something," all the while depending on their knowledge of one another to get through any difficulties. *Vanishing Pictures'* team, however, had not worked together before. Brown was not intimately involved in the set's design and construction or the devising of effects, and she related to the tech crew primarily through Maleczech. Moreover, Brown was distracted by her role's technical demands for complex sequences or transformational effects while she sang or narrated. Coming from opera, where the performer does everything to protect her voice, Brown wanted to "relax" into her performance. Relaxing ran counter to Mabou Mines' avant-garde idea of making the experience new each night. Brown tried to refrain from protesting Maleczech's nightly notes and her cutting and adding lines. "She had a lot to do in the show," comments Rudolph. "I think she felt pushed around about it. She felt it was her piece."[90] Maleczech describes their collaboration as "tempestuous" but gives Brown credit for being game.[91] On the whole Brown received warm praise for her singing and criticism for her acting.[92] Fox adds, "One would never have expected so delicate and musical a work from as tough and earthy an actress as Maleczech. At the same time, Brown's theatrical inexperience has encouraged Maleczech to graft her own highly idiosyncratic mannerisms onto the singer's performance."[93] Brown herself was satisfied only when, during the final run at the Performing Garage, she worked out a new ending that underscored the mystery of Poe's narrative voices. Breuer, filling in for Maleczech (who was on tour in Australia with *Dressed Like an Egg*), agreed to the changes.

Vanishing Pictures was generally well received as Maleczech's directorial debut and Re.Cher.Chez's promising first full production. Although some reviewers wanted the piece to have a stronger concept, to "let the audience know what its own relationship to the material is,"[94] evidence suggests that the production design was evocative and stimulating. It garnered an Obie for Maleczech and Archer, who were listed respectively in the program for conception/direction and set design. Unfortunately the contributions of Brown, the show's originator and sole performer, were seldom acknowledged. Just as Poe had made Mary Rogers a "narrative absence," the public seemed to overlook Brown. Moreover, because it looked away from gender issues, the production seems to have had no feminist resonance at all. Its aesthetics were firmly planted in another frame of reference, that of the historical avant-garde. Even Akalaitis's phrase, "the romantic ideal of language," has no specific gender connotations. Instead it harks back to Artaud's call for no more masterpieces. *Vanishing Pictures*'s recognizably ironized counterpoint between vocal and visual staging elements placed it within that 1970s search for an exit from "the fouling entanglements of language." As Burroughs had written in *The Ticket That Exploded* (1967), "The Not There Kid was 'not there.' Empty turnstile marks the spot—So disinterest yourself in my words. Disinterest yourself in anybody's words."[95]

Conclusion: "Theater *futur*"

In his review of Re.Cher.Chez's second Mayfest, former Mabou Mines associate John Howell noted that the studio represented both *"deja vu* and theater *futur.*"

> In 1971, Mabou Mines meant a collaborative way of working, singleminded experimentation, poverty-row invention and works-in-progress at make-do spaces for small but devoted audiences. Based on the evidence of Mayfest, Re.Cher.Chez seems a good bet to carry on this difficult yet productive tradition for a 1981 generation of theater artists. After only two years, and with virtually no resources other than the energy and skill of its mentors and members, its studio program already gives the lie to those Jeremiahs who see experimental theater as a sterile landscape of aging stars who leave no legacies. My advice to all such burnt-out alarmists: find Re.Cher.Chez.[96]

Howell notes the ways in which the artists continue the Mabou Mines "tradition" of artistic experimentation. Fernando Doty's *TERM: OIL* received praise for grounding itself in the sort of performance poem for which Mabou Mines had become known: "dense, narrative text, a rhetorically distanced delivery of lines, a detailed choreography of physical action, inventive use of props and space and mucho hi-tech media." Most coherent and forceful, he found, were two productions that anticipated emerging issues of race, gender, class, and age in the 1980s: Bonnie Greer and Josette Bailey's adaptation of *Incidents in the Life of a Slave Girl* and Retirees' Theater Workshop in *Things Happen But They Change*, directed by Chris Kraus and Ruth Maleczech. Both productions, and their audiences, were interracial. Breuer and Maleczech were connecting with a growing interest in solo performance art, particularly work by women and artists of color who were finding their voices in this accessible, affordable medium. Julie Archer later worked with Breuer and Maleczech on the latter's one-woman performance of *Hajj* (although it was not strictly a solo performance; their son, Lute Ramblin Breuer, appeared in the show on video.) Anna Deavere Smith has been celebrated for solo performances of multiple roles in her extended project "On the Road: A Search for American Character." Both *Fires in the Mirror* (1992) and *Twilight: Los Angeles, 1992* (1993) have brought the countenances and words of a wide variety of Americans to the stage. Smith has even introduced a subtle avant-gardist sensibility to her work on creating civic dialogue and also in television series such as *The West Wing* (2000–06) and, most recently, *Nurse Jackie* (2009–), in which she plays hospital administrator "Gloria Akalitus."

Howell's defense of Re.Cher.Chez seems to respond to a lively discussion then going on in Bonnie Marranca and Gautam Dasgupta's *Performing Arts Journal* (now called *PAJ: A Journal of Performance and Art*) about whether the avant-garde, and humanism more generally, was in decline. In 1982 Richard Schechner answered again in the affirmative and listed six causes: (1) "the emergence of 'performance texts' as distinct from 'dramatic texts'"; (2) "the failure to develop adequate ways of transmitting performance knowledge from one generation of theatre workers to another" (echoing Marranca's concern about the lack of a supporting literary establishment); (3) "dissolution of [performance] groups and the concomitant rise of solo performing"; (4) "lack of money coupled with the ways money must be raised and accounted for through applications and reports"; (5) both "stupid journalism" and "serious journals that have not provided enough of a forum" to support experimental work; and (6) "an end to activism in the society-at-large."[97] Schechner found solo performance particularly destructive to what he called thirty years of "body-to-body training." Those groups that had survived stayed together out of financial exigency, "like bad marriages." While praising Mabou Mines, Schechner criticized the work of many emerging artists, including

Re.Cher.Chez's productions, writing, "These imitations lack the discipline of a mastered and/or rejected technique."

Several artists countered Schechner's perspective, at least one pointing out that his account might have been colored by the dissolution of his own Performance Group. Matthew Maguire, cofounder of Creation, noted the mainstreaming of avant-garde performance and the fact that solo artists were using both traditional narrative structures and the newest media techniques they could afford. Rather than lamenting the loss of the avant-garde's oppositional stance, Maguire seemed to anticipate its place within a culturally saturated environment where, he hoped, the avant-garde would serve as society's consciousness.[98] Setting aside theoretical discussions altogether, Maleczech reminded readers that rather than looking back or ahead it is important to "become responsible . . . and to remain passionate." The work must die because it is "born to die," but in its creation Mabou Mines and Re.Cher.Chez have "nurtured and furthered the art of the theatre in . . . extraordinary ways." Re.Cher.Chez artists' future, she went on, is bound to her history with Mabou Mines, "whose creativity gives me the room for my future, for my personal unknown."[99] Re.Cher.Chez fostered a *two-way* creativity between and within generations while continuing Mabou Mines' founding principle of "being bosses together."

Several Re.Cher.Chez productions became affiliated with Mabou Mines. Besides *Vanishing Pictures, The Comfort Cage,* a radio play by Dale Worsley, became a Mabou Mines production after appearing in December 1980 at the first Piecemeal Monday of Re.Cher.Chez's second season. Directed by Raymond and engineered by Dallas, this play kicked off "The Keeper Series," which featured McElduff, O'Reilly, Warrilow, and Raymond. Also in the second season Doris Chase's film *Lies,* written by Breuer, performed by Maleczech, and with music by Bob Telson, was shown at a Piecemeal Monday. A "doo-wop opera" Breuer was developing with Ben Halley Jr. led to *The Gospel at Colonus,* an independent production, with Liza Lorwin, who had become Re.Cher.Chez's executive director (and staff) in 1981, serving as producer.[100] As a creative site Re.Cher.Chez advanced the work of Breuer, Maleczech, and other company members while they taught artistic and survival skills to less experienced artists. It allowed mentors to pass along their knowledge of "the collective sixties and the conceptual seventies."[101]

Although they had birthed Re.Cher.Chez, the members of Mabou Mines were still developing their own survival skills in an always changing economic climate. In 1985, the year after Re.Cher.Chez disbanded, they left Performing

Artservices and began handling their own bookkeeping and promotions. Their informal residency at the New York Shakespeare Festival was ending. At the same time, institutional funders—primarily the NEA's InterArts Program, the New York State Council on the Arts, and the Peg Sandvoort Foundation—were becoming more reluctant to underwrite Re.Cher.Chez. They saw it as a school that needed to produce quantifiable numbers of official graduates and to charge tuition, which Maleczech refused to do. In short, Re.Cher.Chez came to an end because it ran out of money and because Maleczech, who had taken on an increasing share of the administration and mentoring, was tired.

Since Re.Cher.Chez disbanded, the company has continued to nurture emerging artists. In the 1980s the company took on several new members, and the nimbus of associates and staff grew as well. For example, Joe Stackell, who contributed ideas to *Vanishing Pictures,* also worked on *Sister Suzie Cinema, Cold Harbor, Hajj, Belén: A Book of Hours, Ecco Porco,* and other shows. In 2002 he became company manager and then general manager. A second example is Karen Kandel, who first met Breuer and Maleczech around 1986 when they cast her in *Mabou Mines Lear.* Starting in 1975 she had performed in several pieces by composer and director Elizabeth Swados and in 1985 a Gertrude Stein play directed by Anne Bogart. The work on *Lear* rekindled Kandel's love of performance. She liked Breuer's way of coming back to a show repeatedly and also his encouragement to improvise and find the extreme, grotesque side of her character, Edna (Edgar). Like many associated with Mabou Mines, Kandel was not trained to act, design, or direct (she had studied literature at Queens College), and her openness to collaboration made her a good fit for the company. She appeared in *Jungle of Cities* (1991) and *Ecco Porco* and wrote the poem celebrating the borough of Queens for *Song for New York: What Women Do While Men Sit Knitting.* Her reputation as a collaborative artist with exceptional performance skills was confirmed by her work in *Peter and Wendy,* in which she serves as narrator and, while interacting with various Bunraku, shadow, and other puppets on a pop-up set, voices all the characters as well. Along with Honora Fergusson, Clove Galilee, and David Neumann, Kandel is a Mabou Mines associate artist.[102]

David Neumann was too young in the late 1970s to have been a member of Re.Cher.Chez, but after appearing in *Mercier and Camier* he has collaborated with Mabou Mines on several productions while developing work independently or with other companies. He has been a member of Doug Varone and Dancers and a founding member of the Doug Elkins Dance Company. Like Clove Galilee and other performers who are adult children of avant-garde artists, he has both sought to develop his own performance identity and helped to pass along his parents' valuable legacies. While collaborating with established avant-gardists such as Mabou Mines, Laurie Anderson, Peter Sellars, and Mikhail Baryshnikov, David Neumann develops work with other emerging artists such as puppeteer and director Amy Trompetter and choreographer Stacy Dawson. As artistic director of "advanced beginner group," he helps younger artists find work and develop their skills. And, like his grandfather, the influential scholar Francis Fergusson, David Neumann also shares his knowledge in a university setting—in his case, by teaching improvisation and movement for performance at Sarah Lawrence College.

In addition to fostering individual talents, the company members never gave up on running a studio. In 1991 they founded Mabou Mines *Suite,* a continuing program of annual residencies that provides rehearsal space, a limited budget, administrative and technical assistance, and mentoring by the company's current members. Mabou Mines *Suite* looks to the future, as its name suggests; mailers always include the dictionary definitions of *suite,* including "a set of matched pieces," "a following," and (perhaps most important) "to be continued."[103] Like Re.Cher.Chez, *Suite* has fostered both established artists (e.g., composer Carter Burwell) and emerging artists (such as playwright Ricardo A. Bracho and puppeteer Jane Catherine Shaw). More closely affiliated with Mabou Mines, *Suite* offers artists the company's performing space, ToRoNaDa, adjacent to its office in the P.S. 122 Community Center.[104] As always, Mabou Mines focuses on how to perpetuate the work.

EPILOGUE

The Work Continues

Among the many lively communities that developed in the late 1960s and the 1970s on the downtown arts scene, only one theater organization was designed solely to protect the others. A Bunch of Experimental Theatres was a loose confederation of theater and dance companies that included Mabou Mines, Cutting Edge, Meredith Monk's House, the Manhattan Project, the Ontological-Hysteric Theater, Stuart Sherman, the Ridiculous Theatre, Section 10, and the Performance Group. In their 1977 manifesto Richard Schechner, founder of the Performance Group, and Richard Foreman, who still runs the Ontological-Hysteric Theater, characterize the Bunch as part of a century-long tradition of art theater devoted to personal vision. Maintaining that "even group work is a version of individual vision," they sought a passionate spectator who would follow the development of the work.[1] But the question remained: how to develop whole audiences of such passionate spectators who would also support it?

The Bunch lasted only four years, from late 1973 to early 1978, but it offered ideas to downtown artists who had to find new ways to survive in the 1980s. Organized by the artists themselves and led by Schechner and Mercedes "Chiquita" Gregory, it assisted companies with practical tasks: booking events and residencies, sharing resources, and finding grants and other financial support. Mabou Mines participated in a Bunch festival held in 1977, organized in part by Breuer, and residencies in Connecticut, New York, and Washington, DC. The Bunch made a difference for several years but relied on the labor of already busy member artists who struggled to support themselves, do their work, and help one another. As Schechner and Gregory began to create networks with universities and use more aggressive marketing techniques, the artists' support for the Bunch wavered. Still, the organization constituted an effort to keep the artists in control of their own work as theaters headed into what the manifesto accurately warned would be "harsher times." Many groups, such as Schechner's Performance Group and André Gregory's Manhattan Project, did not survive into the 1980s. Mabou Mines survived in part by recognizing that doing work for audiences of fellow artists was not enough either artistically or financially. In some places outside of New York City—the Walker

Art Center in Minneapolis and a few university campuses such as Rhodes College (then Southwestern at Memphis)—spectators' knowledge of Mabou Mines was more continuous, but to sustain the work the company also had to look beyond these institutions. It began to tour more frequently to festivals, regional theaters, and performing arts centers, with the result that new audiences began to be aware of Mabou Mines.

While the challenges grew in the 1980s, the company grew as well and developed some of its best-known work. *Cold Harbor* and *A Prelude to Death in Venice*, just two examples, toured the country and abroad as well. The development of regional organizations to support touring was one factor; the assistance of Performing Artservices, the Bunch, and the staff at the New York Shakespeare Festival was another; and the hiring of skilled development directors and company managers was a third. It remained necessary for the artists to support one another. Many continued to work day jobs, but increasingly they took opportunities to work on shows with other artists and organizations. Mabou Mines members and associates, and their productions, were gaining wider recognition and winning many awards. The company was considered by many to be the preeminent avant-garde theater company in the United States.

Akalaitis had felt since the late 1970s that the founding members of Mabou Mines had outgrown one another in a natural way and should collaborate with other artists.[2] One way to do that was to join forces with artists who had their own companies or at least had no need to affiliate with Mabou Mines. Many successful collaborations of that sort have come about. Bringing younger artists into the company was another way to expand the circle of collaborators. They have enriched the company's pool of talent and contributed successful projects, such as Julie Archer and Liza Lorwin's stage adaptation of the novel *Peter and Wendy*, which they asked Breuer to direct. Encouraging younger members and associates to develop their own projects helped them also to develop more mature artistic identities. As Sabrina Hamilton put it, "There was a pressure [felt by younger members] to make your own work almost as a way of becoming a grownup or fully fledged company member, especially in the light of probably having come in as Lee's person or JoAnne's person."[3] In some cases, problems developed. By the early to mid-1980s not only was the first generation of members competing for funding and company time, but so were another half dozen younger members whose ideas did not always find opportunities for production. Associate Stephanie Rudolph, for example, stopped collaborating with the company because she needed time and a more stable income with which to develop her own work.[4] Some who left have continued to collaborate on specific shows.

One situation the company avoided in the 1980s was being taken over by burgeoning administrative staffs, as the English company Joint Stock was, for example, when its founding members went on to other pursuits. Mabou Mines has continued to be an artist-run, artist-managed theater. Many former company managers and development directors, among them Stephen Nunns and Joanna Adler, were and are directors and actors as well.

In the 1980s Mabou Mines stopped calling its work "experimental," recognizing that the word, outside the context of the downtown avant-garde, suggested that its members were not sure of themselves or what they wanted to create. They spent more time communicating the work on grant applications or in promotional interviews. After 1985 they began to keep their own books and met new challenges in finding space and coordinating multiple projects in development and on tour. They both struggled and prospered. They had become entrepreneurs of personal vision and also personal and group survival.

In the early 1990s Mabou Mines almost disappeared. It had just spent several years developing and staging *Lear,* which had created a hundred-thousand-dollar debt. At a 1990 meeting it was suggested that the members dissolve Mabou Mines and move on. Instead they distilled the group down to four members—Breuer, Maleczech, Neumann, and O'Reilly—while Akalaitis, Raymond, Mehrten, Dallas, and McElduff left, each for his or her own reasons. Yet all of the current and former members I interviewed spoke of their work with Mabou Mines as invaluable. And the work went on, albeit on a thinner shoestring. By 1995, with the debt paid off, it was clear that Mabou Mines was able once again to stage more ambitious shows. It has rebuilt with a slightly larger core of co-artistic directors. Julie Archer eventually moved back to New York and became a member in 2002. Playwright, actor, and director Sharon Fogarty had already joined in 1999 after first appearing in tours of *Cold Harbor* and *Mabou Mines Lear,* serving as artistic director of the Daedalus Theatre Company in New York City and producing most Mabou Mines productions since 1994. She premiered her first Mabou Mines show, *Cara Lucia,* in 2003.

I began this book with Liza Lorwin's comment that "the process is the romance." The romance continues. Breuer staged *Porco Morto,* the next piece in his epic choral narrative, in 2009, just as the film version of *Mabou Mines Dollhouse* was released on DVD. *Dollhouse* and *Peter and Wendy* continue to tour internationally. O'Reilly is working on a joint production of *Brer Rabbit in the*

Land of the Monkey King with the Hong Kong–based Ming Ri Institute for Arts Education and the Guangxi Puppet Art Troupe of China. Neumann is working on scenes from *Endgame* in which he would play Hamm to son David Neumann's Clov. Maleczech and Archer, among other activities, tour with Fogarty's production of *Cara Lucia,* now called *Lucia's Chapters of Coming Forth by Day.* Fogarty opened *Finn* in 2010, the year of the company's fortieth anniversary. In *American Theatre* Randy Gener wonders at the company's longevity and points to the continuing "love story" among its members—collaborators still passionate about the work.[5]

Mabou Mines' avant-garde "search for a living tradition" connects it, oddly enough, to another tradition, that of humanism. In Akalaitis's view, Mabou Mines continued in the 1980s to cling to an almost "classical" identity in its "concern with literature and the poetics of literature, the mystery of language." She locates the company's aesthetic in the individual's "journey of experience," the performance narrative created jointly by the writer, actor, and spectator. Far from dismissing language from this journey, Akalaitis concludes, "Indeed, language is . . . the center and beginning and end of all theater."[6] Both Mabou Mines' productions and Akalaitis herself continue to explore and critique the "romantic ideal of language." That critique emerged through Poe, Baudelaire, Lautréamont, Kafka, and Colette, among others, but most immediately from post–World War II writers who questioned the referential authority of language. In Breuer's work, autographical film metaphors, not autobiography, operate as a persistence of vision. More generally, the playful triangulation involved in Mabou Mines' productions both rejects and ironizes the humanist self, that is, Man. Just as the word *love* can be heard only in an echo chamber, a belief in personal vision and human progress has to be approached through "tacking," situated in a process of becoming, not a definable end.[7]

Community, collaboration, and company are three related concepts that have tacked their way through this narrative. In the 1960s such concepts carried the idealism of the civil rights and women's movements, which sought to create collective power in order to return it to the people. The muting of those ideals turned some artists to a localized sense of hands-on counterculturalism and produced, among other phenomena, the group theaters of the 1970s. They have continued the long history of humanism even as they have helped to transform it.

What forms did humanism take in the context of the 1970s? The age of reason, according to Tony Davies, had produced two types of humanism: "humanity as the hero of liberty," as embodied in the French and American revolutions; and the German philosophical notion of seeking understanding (not freedom) as the "key to human fulfillment and emancipation."[8] But imperialism shared humanism's belief in reason and individualism and revealed the flaws in its noble aspirations. By the late nineteenth century, Man, as seen by Friedrich Nietzsche, oscillated between a "desire for fulfillment and the consciousness of failure." After the death of God, remarks Davies, "there is nothing to do but start from scratch with what remains: a rebellious bundle of bodily and psychic needs, a deep urge to survive and transcend, a treacherous and indispensable language." This task the avant-garde undertook in the twentieth century. It is no accident that Lee Breuer's *Ecco Porco* harks back to Nietzsche, nor that for Mabou Mines "Man" is not just "*porco*" but "*morto.*" Breuer extends the humanist master narrative as a postmodern parody. Abandoning its claim to freedom, the 1970s avant-garde has worked from what Davies, after Emanuel Lévinas, calls a "humanism of the irreducible other": "Humanity is neither an essence nor an end, but a continuous and precarious process. . . . Our humanity is on loan from others, to precisely the extent that we acknowledge it in them." Already in Mabou Mines' earliest production, *The Red Horse Animation,* a protean image constructed of three moving bodies and a choral voice was "groping towards language and consciousness."

In the 1970s Mabou Mines groped toward a gendered consciousness. In struggling with the dilemmas of work and personal life in a small, mixed company of strong personalities, the members of Mabou Mines created through performance, as I have said, a more complete human identity for each other. The dilemmas are not resolved; the identities will never be complete. But on the cusp of the millennium, the artists were still building on what they had learned from that "sweaty grapple with the self."[9] In her 1999 production of *Belén: A Book of Hours,* Ruth Maleczech sought to translate for the stage the experience of women seldom seen by reaching across the divides of cultural, national, and religious difference. As a collaboration among artists from Mexico, Argentina, and the United States, *Belén* revived the voices of woman incarcerated in the "refuge" of the Recogimiento de Belén during its inconceivable 250-year history in Mexico City. The women housed in this prisonlike building were wives, widows, mothers, prostitutes, and women who had tried to live unconventional lives. Maleczech's history with Mabou Mines allowed her to create a working context in which actor and director strove together for a "performance of self, a kind of active, public meditation," through which some parts of the lost lives of the women of Belén were recovered.[10]

Many of Mabou Mines' stories remain to be told, and I hope to tell some of them. While occasionally looking ahead, this book ends in 1980 at a historical moment when many audiences were just becoming aware of Mabou Mines. I have attempted to bring to light the company's original romance with the work process and to document the undocumentable—the early work that was designed in so many ways to live in its development and to "die" onstage while its creators "devour life."[11]

Mabou Mines Chronology, 1957–1980

Abbreviations

ABET = A Bunch of Experimental Theatres
AWP = Arc Welding Piece
BBA = The B.Beaver Animation
C&G = Come and Go
DEK = Dead End Kids
DLE = Dressed Like an Egg
LO = The Lost Ones
M&C = Mercier and Camier
MV = Music for Voices
PDV = A Prelude to Death in Venice
RHA = The Red Horse Animation
RT = "retrospective time line" (created by Ellen Levy) for the company's twentieth-anniversary exhibit "Mabou Mines: The First Twenty Years," curated by Tom Finkelpearl (with assistance from Mabou Mines archivist Joanna Adler) at the Grey Art Gallery, New York University, January 1991 (personal copy). Some dates in the retrospective time line differ from my own.
SDA = The Shaggy Dog Animation
SE = Southern Exposure
SFP = The Saint and the Football Player
S/R/S = Send/Receive/Send
VP = Vanishing Pictures
WG = Wrong Guys

The following chronology is a work in progress based on archival documents, interviews, press materials, and previous chronologies, all of which incorporate partial and conflicting information. It is a guide to the company's productions, work-in-progress presentations, and tours, as well as significant arrivals and departures of company members and associates. While, despite my efforts to check for accuracy, it may still contain inaccuracies and omissions, it should demonstrate the complexity of developing and running multiple shows, which became Mabou Mines' life "on tour." All locations are in New York City unless otherwise noted.

1957

"Lee Breuer and Ruth Maleczech meet at UCLA" (RT). After studying French language and literature at Reading University, David Warrilow moves to Paris. Frederick Neumann has been living in Europe since 1947. Philip Glass finishes studying at the University of Chicago and moves to New York to attend Juilliard.

1958

Honora Fergusson arrives in Paris and begins working for *Réalités*, where she meets David Warrilow.

1959–64

Breuer and Maleczech work in San Francisco with the San Francisco Actor's Workshop and the R. G. Davis (later the San Francisco) Mime Troupe. They meet Bill Raymond, JoAnne Akalaitis, Dawn Gray, Ann Elizabeth Horton, and others.

1959

Breuer directs Raymond and Maleczech in an R. G. Davis Mime Troupe production of *The Caucasian Chalk Circle* and is noticed by Herbert Blau. In 1959–60 Dawn (later Chalisa) Gray performs with the Mime Troupe.

1960

Akalaitis and Raymond work occasionally at the Tape Music Center, run by Pauline Oliveros, Ramone Sender, and Morton Subotnick.

In December, Maleczech (under the name Ruth Breuer) and Raymond perform in *The 11th Hour Mime Show*, which runs until January 1962. Breuer does sound for *Event I*.

1961–63

Probably in 1961 Breuer directs *Emotional Composition for Actors* with Raymond, Maleczech, Akalaitis, and Bere Boynton in San Francisco. In 1962 he directs *Happy Days* for the San Francisco Actor's Workshop. He assistant-directs Blau's revival of *King Lear*. He also directs *A Slight Ache*. He teaches a Scene Study class at the R. G. Davis Studio. Maleczech and Raymond perform in *The Dowry* for the San Francisco Mime Troupe. In 1963 Breuer directs and Maleczech performs in *The Underpants* and *The House of Bernarda Alba* for the Actor's Workshop. He directs a non-

Workshop production of *The Maids*. Breuer and Akalaitis see the Living Theatre's *The Brig*. For the Mime Troupe, Maleczech performs in *Event II* and does set and costume construction on *The Root*.

In Paris, Warrilow meets Samuel Beckett. Probably in 1962 Neumann and Fergusson meet in France.

1964

Akalaitis moves to New York and meets Philip Glass. They depart for Paris, where Glass studies with Nadia Boulanger on a Fulbright fellowship (1964–66). They see the Living Theatre's production of *Frankenstein* in Provence.

In the summer Breuer and Maleczech leave California for New York, seeing much of the United States on the way. They stay briefly in New York, then travel to Europe by freighter. In the meantime, Raymond moves to Topanga Canyon near Los Angeles, where he lives from 1964 to 1974.

Fergusson and Neumann work on a production of *In White America* in Paris.

1965

In January, Breuer and Maleczech arrive in Greece, where they live for a year on the island of Rhodes. They hitchhike around Turkey. "On a trip to Greece, Akalaitis and Glass encounter Breuer and Maleczech who then move back to Paris with them. Later that year, the four of them, plus literary-editor-turned-actor David Warrilow, start work on Beckett's *Play* which they presented at The American Cultural Center in Paris in 1967" (RT). Glass composes music to which Akalaitis and Maleczech recite a soufflé recipe (*Music for Small Ensemble and Two Actresses*).

1966

In the fall Akalaitis and Glass leave Paris for India, where they stay until March 1967. In 1966 or 1967 Breuer and Maleczech visit Berlin for three weeks and see the Berliner Ensemble at work, while Warrilow goes to Poland and sees Grotowski at work.

1967

Play is performed at the American Cultural Center in Paris. Akalaitis and Glass return to New York City, where Akalaitis takes acting classes and Glass founds the Philip Glass Ensemble.

Neumann, Warrilow, and Maleczech work with Breuer (director) on *Mother Courage*.

Late in the year Fergusson and Neumann move to Rome, where they live until early 1971. While in Rome, Neumann works at various dubbing, directing, and acting jobs.

1968–69

"Neumann, whom Akalaitis had met at a film dubbing audition in 1964, collaborates on a production [*Theories,* based on *The Messingkauf Diaries*] with Breuer, Maleczech, and Warrilow which they present at the Edinburgh Festival" (RT). Neumann and Fergusson move to Italy.

Probably in 1969 Breuer writes the first version of *BBA* (short story); he also begins a novel called *The Run* and a film (probably unfinished). Maleczech and Breuer consider a move to England from France. Warrilow returns to try acting in London for six months before moving to New York. In April 1969 Maleczech and Akalaitis attend Grotowski's Theater Laboratory workshop in Aix-en-Provence. In December, at Akalaitis's urging, Breuer and Maleczech move to New York, where they live temporarily with Akalaitis and Glass on West Twenty-third Street. Later Breuer and Maleczech live on Saint Mark's Place and East Sixth Street.

1970

Warrilow arrives in New York early in the year. Mabou Mines is founded by Akalaitis, Breuer, Glass, Maleczech, and Warrilow. With support from Ellen Stewart's La Mama Experimental Theatre Club, a portion of *RHA* is presented at the Paula Cooper Gallery.

Raymond directs a nonMabou Mines production of *Play* in Topanga Canyon with Linda Hartinian (then Wolfe) in the cast.

The members of Mabou Mines spend the summer at property recently bought by Akalaitis, Glass, and Rudy Wurlitzer on Cape Breton Island, Nova Scotia. The acoustic floor is built. In the fall Stewart begins paying group members salaries. *RHA* premiers November 18–21 at the Guggenheim Museum.

1971

Neumann and Fergusson return to the United States and settle in Kingston, New Jersey. Neumann joins Mabou Mines, and rehearsals for *BBA* begin. In April *Play* is reworked and performed privately for members of the Yale University faculty, New Haven, Connecticut. In May *Come and Go* is performed at the Brooklyn Bridge Festival.

In June *Play* opens at La Mama. *C&G* is performed at La Mama.

In March, Breuer teaches a workshop at Rhodes College (then called Southwestern at Memphis) and meets David Hardy, Terry O'Reilly, Ellen McElduff, Dale Worsley, and Steve Bennyworth. In the fall *RHA* and *BBA* are staged at Southwestern, where McElduff and O'Reilly, among others, see Mabou Mines' work for the first time. In addition *RHA* and *BBA* tour to Minneapolis; the West Coast, including Pasadena (October); and Vancouver (November). While in California, Breuer and Maleczech ask Raymond to come to New York, but he declines.

1972

In the spring Eads Hill performs *A Full Eight Hours* and *Unta-the* in New York City. McElduff attends a workshop with a Grotowski group in Philadelphia.

Music for Voices is broadcast on WBAI. Early in the year *RHA* and *Play* tour to the University of Oregon, the University Art Museum in Berkeley, UCLA, Pomona College, and the University of California, Davis. In April a revised and expanded *RHA* premiers at the Whitney Museum, where *C&G* also is performed. In June *MV* and *AWP* appear as works in progress at the Paula Cooper Gallery. In the fall work begins on *SFP*. In December *RHA, MV,* and *AWP* appear at the Mickery Mokkum Theatre in Amsterdam, the Netherlands.

1973

"Ellen Stewart's Ford [Foundation] money runs out in 1973. She asks Mabou Mines to stay on, hoping they will start developing work more quickly. If the company stays, it will be unable to apply for independent funding. Reluctantly they leave La Mama and receive their first grant from the NEA. [Performing] Artservices, a cooperative arts' management service, takes an interest in Mabou Mines and adds the group to its distinguished list of clients such as John Cage, Philip Glass, Richard Foreman. It's a relief; JoAnne and Ruth have been running the limited money 'badly' " (Robert Coe and Don Shewey, "Q: Is Mabou Mines Plural or Singular? A: Both," *Soho Weekly News,* 29 April 1981).

Glass travels to India to arrange for a Mabou Mines tour. The company receives an invitation but cannot finance the tour. Glass officially leaves Mabou Mines to pursue his own work but continues to collaborate with company members. In February *MV* has its final performance at The Kitchen.

L. B. Dallas begins his association with company on *SFP.* In April workshop productions of *SFP* are performed at the Loeb Student Center, New York University; the Paula Cooper Gallery; and the Dance Gallery.

O'Reilly arrives in New York and begins work on *BBA*. In June *SFP* and *BBA* appear at the Walker Art Center in Minneapolis.

In November *Send/Receive/Send* appears at The Kitchen. Richard Schechner and Mercedes Gregory form ABET. Mabou Mines joins, probably in 1974.

1974

"Village Voice OBIE Award for General Excellence to Mabou Mines" (RT). Mabou Mines incorporates the Mabou Mines Development Foundation, Inc.

In January *BBA* opens at Theatre for the New City and in February appears as part of "A Valentine for Marcel Duchamp" at the Museum of Modern Art. A full-length *SFP* with halftime show is performed at the Pratt Institute, New York City. In the summer ABET companies participate in the American Dance Festival at Connecticut College. Mabou Mines artists work on and perform *SFP*.

McElduff and Hardy move to New York City from Memphis. Raymond arrives in New York in September to become a member of Mabou Mines. In early November Raymond invites Linda Hartinian to join him. She later appears in *LO*.

In December *C&G* and *BBA* appear at the New York Theater Ensemble. McElduff has replaced Gray in *C&G*, while Raymond takes her place in *BBA*. Gray moves to a Sufi commune on Thirteenth Street. Probably in late 1974, Mabou Mines receives a three-thousand-dollar grant from the NEA, which allows it to find alternative rehearsal space for *BBA*.

Work begins on *SDA*.

1975

Akalaitis and Maleczech help to found a day care center in the P.S. 122 basement.

From 6 to 23 March, *Play, C&G,* and *LO* are presented as "Mabou Mines Performs Beckett" at Theatre for the New City. In April, the Kroll review appears in *Newsweek*. On 24 April, Jane Yockel of Performing Artservices, on behalf of Mabou Mines, writes to Grove Press to seek Beckett's permission for the "dramatic reading" of *LO*. Beckett agrees but later objects to the "crooked straight reading." On 25 August, Breuer writes to Beckett. From 16 October to 9 November, *LO, Play,* and *C&G* reopen at Theater for the New City. After Joseph Papp and Gail Merrifield Papp attend a performance, Mabou Mines begins a long-term association with the New York Shakespeare Festival (1976–84).

In April, *LO* and *BBA* tour to Ohio Wesleyan University; the Museum of Contemporary Art, Chicago; and the Space Above the Biograph Theater at Northwestern University, Evanston, Illinois. In early May, *BBA* and *LO* appear at the Walker Arts Center, Minneapolis; and the Loeb Drama Center, Cambridge, Massachusetts.

In the summer Robin Thomas travels from Minneapolis to join a workshop on *SFP* at the American Dance Festival at Connecticut College. Mabou Mines participates with other ABET members (Manhattan Project, Meredith Monk's House, Ontological-Hysteric Theater, Performance Group, Ridiculous Theatre, and Section 10). Mabou Mines performs an outdoor version of *SFP*. After graduating from college, Greg Mehrten attends the workshop and begins working with Mabou Mines.

1976

"Village Voice OBIE Awards for performance to David Warrilow in *The Lost Ones*; for direction: JoAnne Akalaitis for *Cascando*; for music: Philip Glass for his work with Mabou Mines. 'A Comic of *The Red Horse Animation*' published privately" (RT). Julie Archer moves to New York.

In 1976–77 a workshop of *DLE* is conducted at the Old Prop Shop, Public Theater. Breuer writes part I and probably a portion of part III of *SDA* during Mabou Mines' work on *DLE*. In January the first work-in-progress of the *SDA* prologue appears at the Paula Cooper Gallery.

In February *SFP* reopens at the Pratt Institute. Mabou Mines artists are in residence for a month, working with members of the Theatre Department. Thomas returns and does technical work. In March *LO* reopens in the Little Theater, Public Theater. On 8 March, Beckett gives permission for a European tour of *LO*.

In April *Cascando* opens at Richard Foreman's loft in New York City, and *RHA* appears at the Brooklyn Academy of Music. Warrilow breaks his leg during the final performance on 7 May.

In the summer Mabou Mines returns to the American Dance Festival. In August *BBA* tours to the Festival de Nancy in France. The script of *BBA* is published in *Big Deal 4*.

In the fall there are two simultaneous tours. *LO* and *Cascando* appear at the Berlin Festival in September. There the company (except for Breuer) meets Beckett, who sees the *Cascando* set. *Cascando* also tours to Switzerland. Breuer manages both this tour and *SFP*, which appears at the Deutsches Schauspielhaus (Hamburg), at the Theater of Nations Festival (Belgrade), in Zagreb, at the Mickery Mokkum Theatre (Amsterdam), and at the Internationaler Kunstmarkt in Düsseldorf. In November *Cascando* reopens at the Little Theater, Public Theater.

Probably in 1976, Warrilow leaves the cast of *SDA*.

1977

"Village Voice OBIE Award for Distinguished Production to *Dressed Like an Egg*, Maharam Citation for Design to JoAnne Akalaitis for *Dressed Like an Egg*. *The Red Horse Animation* by Lee Breuer published in *Theatre of Images* by Drama Book Specialists. Villager Theatre Award to *Dressed Like an Egg*" (RT).

Alanna Heiss, who runs the P.S. 1 Museum in Queens, offers Mabou Mines space on Dwayne Street, then Leonard Street. Mabou Mines works and performs in the building's clock tower.

In February and March *Cascando* appears at Public Theater and tours to the Syracuse (New York) Civic Center. In April, *BBA* appears at the Little Theater, Public Theater.

Thomas works full time as technical director, primarily on *DLE*. On 5 May, *DLE* opens at LuEsther Hall, Public Theater.

In late June *SDA* previews at Theater for the New City and in August is performed as a work in progress at the American Dance Festival (Mabou Mines' third year at the festival). In the fall Breuer organizes "The Bunch Festival 1977," which includes previews of *SDA* at the Public Theater.

On 4 October Neumann writes to Beckett for permission to stage *More Pricks than Kicks*. Beckett refuses through Grove Press.

1978

"Village Voice OBIE Award for Best Play to Lee Breuer for *The Shaggy Dog Animation*. Villager Theatre Award to *The Shaggy Dog Animation*, Soho News Award for Best Ensemble: *The Shaggy Dog Animation*" (RT). Early in the year ABET disbands. Breuer and Maleczech marry. Archer returns briefly to Minneapolis.

Neumann receives Beckett's permission to stage *M&C*. Sabrina Hamilton signs on as assistant stage manager.

In January Breuer completes the script of the full-length *SDA*. In February *SDA* has previews, probably at the Old Prop Shop, Public Theater, where it premiers in March. In late April it reopens at the Public Theater and runs through early June.

Periodically *BBA* and *LO* tour throughout the year. In February and March they appear at Skidmore College (Saratoga Springs, New York) and with *DLE* at the Walker Arts Center, Minneapolis. In the spring B.-St. John Schofield arranges for Mabou Mines to perform *BBA* at The 99 Cent Floating Theatre Festival (Pittsburgh).

On 23 April Warrilow writes to Beckett for company permission to film *LO* for PBS with Suzanne Weil as producer. The affirmative response is dated 30 April.

In June *DLE* appears at the New Theatre Festival (Baltimore). Schofield joins the crew and continues with the tour to Europe in the fall. While Thomas works at the Delacorte Theater (New York Shakespeare Festival), in July Dallas signs on as a full time stage and sound designer and technical director. In December Thomas leaves the company to work full time at the Shakespeare Festival.

From 20 October to 4 November work-in-progress versions of *M&C* and *Not I* are presented with *C&G* and *Fizzles 1, 4 and 7* (probably not a Mabou Mines production) at the Performing Garage as part of New York University's Beckett Festival.

In November and December *DLE* tours to the Théâtre Gérard Philippe, St. Denis (Paris), the Mickery Mokkum Theatre (Amsterdam), and the Schouwburg Theater (Rotterdam).

1979

"Village Voice OBIE Special Citation to JoAnne Akalaitis, David Warrilow, and Ellen McElduff for *Southern Exposure*. Los Angeles Dramalogue Critics' Award to Lee Breuer (Direction) and David Warrilow (Performance) for *The Lost Ones*. *Animations* by Lee Breuer published by PAJ Publications" (RT). Archer moves to California.

In January *LO* is performed at the Théâtre Nationale Populaire (Lyon) for Beckett's seventy-fifth birthday celebration.

In February Akalaitis's nonMabou Mines production *SE* previews at the Performing Garage, where it premiers in March and runs to 8 April. It also tours to Baltimore, where it appears at the New Theatre Festival.

In April a *PDV* reading is held at Franklin Furnace. Also *SDA* appears at the Long Wharf Theatre, New Haven, Connecticut, and *PDV* is performed at the Mark Taper Forum, Los Angeles. In June and July *PDV* is performed as a work-in-progress at the Old Prop Shop, Public Theater.

In May Warrilow officially leaves Mabou Mines, while Dallas and Schofield become members.

In the summer Thomas works with Akalaitis on a film, then he and Sally Rosen move to California. She returns in 1980 to do costumes for *DEK*.

Maleczech and Breuer create Re.Cher.Chez. On 1 December Re.Cher.Chez presents Piecemeal Monday #1, an evening of performances by various artists, including a tape by Beverly Brown and *The Comfort Cage,* part of "The Keeper" series.

In October *M&C* premiers at LuEsther Hall, Public Theater.

In November *PDV* is performed at the Mickery Mokkum Theatre, Amsterdam. A work-in-progress script of *PDV* is published as part of the series *Plays in Process* (New York: Theatre Communications Group, 1979).

In late 1979 Archer returns to New York to work on *VP* and *SSC*.

In December Breuer's production of *Lulu* featuring Neumann premieres at the American Repertory Theatre in Cambridge, Massachusetts.

1980

"Village Voice OBIE Awards to Julie Archer and Ruth Maleczech for their design of *Vanishing Pictures,* Bill Raymond for his performance in *A Prelude to Death in Venice,* and Lee Breuer for his script and direction of *A Prelude to Death in Venice.* San Francisco Critics' Circle Award for Best Touring Production to *A Prelude to Death in Venice.* Maharam Citation for Design to L. B. Dallas, Linda Hartinian and Alison Yerxa for *A Prelude to Death in Venice.* National Federation of Community Broadcasters Radio Programming Award to Mabou Mines for *Easy Daisy*" (RT). Staff member Marion Godfrey becomes Mabou Mines' first company manager.

"The Keeper," a series of four radio plays (*The Comfort Cage, Easy Daisy, Laughing Stock,* and *Tiger Heaven*), written by Worsley, is produced by Mabou Mines and distributed by National Public Radio, Pacifica, and the Australian Broadcasting Company.

In late January *VP* opens at Theater for the New City; in March it reopens at the Performing Garage.

In March *DLE* tours to Australia, specifically the Adelaide Festival and Sydney Opera House and Tasmania (Launceston and Hobart). The Tasmanian tour is sponsored by the Tasmanian Theatre Company. Raymond joins the cast in Australia from Paris, where he has performed Clov in Joe Chaikin's *Endgame* at the American Center in Paris. Neumann understudies the part of Nagg.

Probably in late spring, a scene from *DEK* is performed at a benefit at Town Hall.

In May, *PDV* opens at the Old Prop Shop, Public Theater. It tours extensively, sometimes with *SSC,* which opens in June at the Old Prop Shop, to San Francisco, Los Angeles, Brussels, Paris, Milan, and elsewhere.

Re.Cher.Chez hosts its first Mayfest, a month of public performances. In the summer workshop performances of *WG* are presented at the Old Prop Shop. From 26 June to 3 July a nonMabou Mines production of *RHA* directed by Bennett Theisse appears at the Randolph Street Gallery.

In November *DEK* premiers at the Public Theater.

Notes

Acknowledgments

1. The epigraph by Liza Lorwin is quoted in Lynn Yeager, "Community Theater," *Village Voice,* 27 May 1997, 82.

2. *The Red Horse Animation* first appeared in *The Theatre of Images,* edited by Bonnie Marranca (New York: Drama Book Specialists, 1977). Text and photos were published in Lee Breuer, *Animations: A Trilogy for Mabou Mines,* edited by Bonnie Marranca and Gautam Dasgupta (New York: Performing Arts Journal Publications, 1979).

3. Under the name Iris Smith, "Mabou Mines' *Lear:* A Narrative of Collective Authorship," *Theatre Journal* 45, no. 3 (1993): 279–301; "The 'Intercultural' Work of Lee Breuer," *Theatre Topics* 7, no. 1 (1997): 37–58; review of *Lear, Journal of Dramatic Theory and Criticism* 5, no. 2 (1991): 197–201; and review of *Happy Days, Theatre Journal* 51, no. 1 (1999): 86–88. Under the name Iris Smith Fischer, "Wild Dogs: Lee Breuer's New Book of Fiction Runs with the Pack of Literary Avant-Gardists," *American Theatre,* November 2002, 71–73; "The Discipline of Word and Body: Mabou Mines Stage Beckett, 1965–1975," in *Text and Presentation 2006,* edited by Stratos E. Constantinidis (Jefferson, NC: McFarland, 2007), 43–57. The last title, an earlier version of chapter 3, appeared in Italian translation as "La disciplina di parola e corpo: I Mabou Mines mettono in scena Beckett, 1965–1975," in *Beckett and Puppet: Studi e scene tra Samuel Beckett e il tetro di figura,* edited by Fernando Marchiori (Pisa: Titivillus, 2007), 182–201. A brief discussion of Ruth Maleczech's *Song for New York* opens "C. S. Peirce and the Habit of Theatre," in *Changing the Subject: Marvin Carlson and Theatre Studies, 1959–2009,* edited by Joseph Roach (Ann Arbor: University of Michigan Press, 2009), 118–48.

Introduction

1. Margo Jefferson, "Fun-House Proportions Turn Dominance Upside Down," *New York Times,* 24 November 2003, B3. Despite the appearance of *fun-house* in the article's title, Jefferson does not use the word or concept herself.

2. Lee Breuer, "The Actor Evolves," *Soho Weekly News,* 7 July 1977, 42.

3. "Looking for a Miracle" (featurette), *Mabou Mines Dollhouse,* dir. Lee Breuer, Pour Voir, 2008, DVD.

4. I have not been able to locate the exact source for the metaphorical contrast of warm and cool that I have used here and elsewhere. The idea if not the imagery appears in Gary Houston, "They Mix Acting and Performing," *Chicago Sun-Times,* 27 April 1975.

Houston's article is based on an interview with Lee Breuer, who may have originated the phrasing.

5. Mabou Mines. "The Work," www.maboumines.org/work.html, accessed 21 June 2000. The Web site no longer carries this page.

6. James M. Harding and Cindy Rosenthal, eds., *Restaging the Sixties: Radical Theaters and Their Legacies* (Ann Arbor: University of Michigan Press, 2006), 308.

7. Dale Worsley, interview by the author, 15 June 1994.

8. Una Chaudhuri identifies three types of interculturalism. The first, an effect of global mass communication, "flatten[s] cultural differences into a homogeneous mediocrity" (Una Chauduri, "The Future of the Hyphen: Interculturalism, Textuality, and the Difference Within," in *Interculturalism and Performance: Writings from PAJ*, edited by Bonnie Marranca and Gautam Dasgupta [New York: Performing Arts Journal Publications, 1991], 192–93). The second, exemplified in Chaudhuri's opinion by Peter Brook's *The Mahabharata,* colludes unwittingly with cultural imperialism, "in which the West helps itself to the forms and images of others without taking the full measure of the cultural fabric from which these are torn" (193). The third, less a definition than a set of interrelated propositions, sketches a vision of theater as a self-conscious practice of "modeled *differentiality*" (193) by means of which social and ethnic stereotypes are breached, that is, "simultaneously evoked and undermined" (204).

9. Mark S. Weinberg, *Challenging the Hierarchy: Collective Theatre in the United States* (Westport, CT: Greenwood Press, 1992), 22.

10. Harding and Rosenthal, *Restaging the Sixties,* 9.

11. Richard Goldstein, "The Souls of Art Folks," *Village Voice,* 4 June 1979, 49.

12. Harding and Rosenthal, *Restaging the Sixties,* 12.

13. While Mabou Mines was beginning to shake off its reputation as a collective, journalists, having discovered the company in the mid- to late 1970s, were celebrating it for just that feature. For example, see Tish Dace, "Mabou Mines: Collaborative Creation," *Soho Weekly News,* 18 May 1978, 22–23, 35; and Robert Coe and Don Shewey, "Q: Is Mabou Mines Plural or Singular? A: Both," *Soho Weekly News,* 29 April 1981, 9–12. Coe and Shewey wrote (ten years after the company was founded), "Behind the ongoing story of Mabou Mines is the dream of the ideal artistic collective." Despite their authors' use of the term *collective,* though, both articles contributed positively to the company's reputation.

14. Quoted in Carol Martin, "After Paradise: The Open Theatre's *The Serpent, Terminal,* and *The Mutation Show,*" in *Restaging the Sixties: Radical Theaters and Their Legacies,* edited by James M. Harding and Cindy Rosenthal (Ann Arbor: University of Michigan Press, 2006), 98.

15. Breuer is quoted in Gabrielle Cody, "Behavior as Culture: An Interview with Lee Breuer," in *Interculturalism and Performance: Writings from PAJ,* edited by Bonnie Marranca and Gautam Dasgupta (New York: Performing Arts Journal Publications, 1991), 209.

16. Arnold Aronson, *American Avant-Garde Theatre: A History* (London: Routledge, 2000), 205–7.

17. Ibid., 205.

18. Richard Schechner, "The Decline and Fall of the (American) Avant-Garde," *Performing Arts Journal* 5, no. 2 (1981): 48–63; 5, no. 3 (1981): 9–19.

19. Quoted in James M. Harding, "An Interview with Richard Schechner," in *Contours of the Theatrical Avant-Garde: Performance and Textuality,* edited by James M. Harding (Ann Arbor: University of Michigan Press, 2000), 213, 207, 211–12.

20. Louise Steinman, *The Knowing Body: Elements of Contemporary Performance and Dance* (Boston and London: Shambhala, 1986), x.

21. Ann Charters, ed., *The Portable Beat Reader* (New York: Penguin, 1992), xxvii.

22. Spalding Gray, writer and actor, *Swimming to Cambodia,* dir. Jonathan Demme, Evergreen Entertainment, film 1987, video 1996.

23. Ruth Maleczech, "Am I Dying While I'm Devouring Life?" *Performing Arts Journal* 6, no. 1 (1981): 45.

24. JoAnne Akalaitis, "JoAnne Akalaitis: We Are the Ones," interview by Anne Cattaneo and David Diamond, *Journal for Stage Directors and Choreographers* 10, no. 1 (1996): 12.

25. Quoted in Alex Witchel, "On Stage, and Off: A Public Forum," *New York Times,* 22 March 1993.

26. Frank Rich, "Opening a Window at a Theater Gone Stale," *New York Times,* 21 March 1993, AL2, 32.

27. Quoted in Porter Anderson, "Teasers and Tormentors: Jettisoning JoAnne," *Village Voice,* 23 March 1993, 94.

28. Richard Schechner and Richard Foreman, "A Bunch Manifesto," unpublished manuscript, probably July 1977, Richard Schechner Papers and *The Drama Review* Collection, 1943–2007, Department of Rare Books and Special Collections, Princeton University Library.

29. The epigraph is from Bonnie Marranca, "The Aging Playwright and the American Theater," *Village Voice,* 16 June 1992, 94.

30. Associated Press, "New York Playwright Wins $355,000 Fellowship," *Kansas City Star,* 17 June 1997, A4.

31. Lee Breuer, "The Two-Handed Gun: Reflections on Power, Culture, Lambs, Hyenas, and Government Support for the Arts," *Village Voice,* 20 August 1991, 89.

32. Comparing capitalist language to the "jargons" of Marxism, psychoanalysis, and Christianity, Barthes says, "The (thereby much higher) pressure of capitalist language is not paranoid, systematic, argumentative, articulated [as are these others]: it is an implacable stickiness, a *doxa,* a kind of unconscious: in short, the essence of ideology." Roland Barthes, *The Pleasure of the Text,* translated by Richard Miller (New York: Hill and Wang, 1975), 29.

33. Pierre Bourdieu, "The Field of Cultural Production," in *The Field of Cultural Production: Essays on Art and Literature,* edited by Randal Johnson (New York: Columbia University Press, 1993), 29–73.

34. Roland Barthes, "From Work to Text," in *Image-Music-Text,* translated by Stephen Heath (New York: Noonday Press, 1977), 155–64.

35. Susan Letzler Cole, *Directors in Rehearsal: A Hidden World* (New York: Routledge, 1992), 208.

36. Lee Breuer, interview by the author, 25 January 1996.

37. Quoted in Cody, "Behavior as Culture," 214.

38. Breuer, "The Two-Handed Gun," 90.

39. James M. Harding and Cindy Rosenthal, "Introduction," in *Restaging the Sixties: Radical Theaters and Their Legacies,* edited by James M. Harding and Cindy Rosenthal (Ann Arbor: University of Michigan Press, 2006), 16.

40. Sally Banes, *Greenwich Village, 1963: Avant-Garde Performance and the Effervescent Body* (Durham, NC: Duke University Press, 1993), 51, 144, 145.

41. Breuer, "The Actor Evolves," 42.

42. Arthur J. Sabatini, "From Dog to Ant: The Evolution of Lee Breuer's Animations," *PAJ: A Journal of Performance and Art* 26, no. 2 (2004): 57.

43. Charles C. Mann, "Doo Wop Opera and Greek Gospel Tragedies," *Mother Jones,* April 1987, 31.

44. This brief account is indebted to Marvin Carlson, "Semiotics and Its Heritage," in *Critical Theory and Performance,* edited by Janelle G. Reinelt and Joseph R. Roach, rev. ed. (Ann Arbor: University of Michigan Press, 2007), 22. For a more detailed discussion of feminist theater scholars' use of semiotics, see pages 20–23.

45. Julia A. Walker, "The Text/Performance Split across the Analytic/Continental Divide," in *Staging Philosophy: Intersections of Theater, Performance, and Philosophy,* edited by David Krasner and David Z. Saltz (Ann Arbor: University of Michigan Press, 2006), 38.

46. The late Ron Vawter, a longtime member of the Wooster Group, also appeared in several Mabou Mines productions, among them *Mabou Mines Lear* (1990).

47. Northrop Frye, *Archetypes of Criticism: Four Essays* (Princeton: Princeton University Press, 1957), 34.

48. Roland Barthes, *Critical Essays,* translated by Richard Howard (Evanston: Northwestern University Press, 1972), 257, quoted in Henry M. Sayre, *The Object of Performance: The American Avant-Garde since 1970* (Chicago and London: University of Chicago Press, 1989), 253. In this compelling chapter Sayre finds commonalities between Mabou Mines' work and the thinking of Roland Barthes.

49. Maleczech, "Am I Dying," 45.

50. A thoughtful, if somewhat one-sided, alternative view of the company is presented by Deborah Saivetz, whose monograph on JoAnne Akalaitis in rehearsal is based in part on the author's involvement in two non-Mabou productions that Akalaitis directed in the early 1990s. In discussing Akalaitis's earlier work with Mabou Mines, Saivetz acknowledges that the company denies having any single aesthetic, but she detects "certain over-arching aesthetic ideas, and ideals, [including] the notion that performance is physical, that the physical triggers the emotional, that the actor is a generative as well as interpretive artist, that performance is an expression of the self and of personal history, that making theater is a collaborative endeavor, and that the formal aspects of theater such as structure, architecture, composition, space, objects, music, and light convey emotional values." Deborah Saivetz, *An Event in Space: JoAnne Akalaitis in Rehearsal* (Hanover, NH: Smith and Kraus, 2000), 44.

Chapter 1

1. The terms *collective* and *collaborative* (or *collaboration*) are often used inter-changeably. I follow Mabou Mines' tendency to avoid the word *collective* inasmuch as it refers more accurately to companies like the Living Theatre, which have both organized the work to provide equal access to all members and in some cases led a communal life. In *Challenging the Hierarchy: Collective Theatre in the United States* (Westport, CT: Greenwood Press, 1992), Mark S. Weinberg notes that 1960s collectives had 1930s prece-dents such as the Workers Laboratory Theatre and the Living Newspapers (part of the Federal Theatre Project) where socialist organizational principles were entwined with a notion of enfranchisement for the common citizen. American collectives in the 1960s advocated "participatory democracy" (13) in which every member had equal access to power without sacrificing individuality—a "confederation of differences" (14). Such "people's theatres" also set out to be models for social change, while others engaged au-diences in new, subversive behaviors (18–19). Collective performance enfranchises the audience as well, often encouraging some form of participation, which then (it is hoped) transforms the individual and, perhaps by inspiration, leads to a broader social enfranchisement. Thus, Weinberg casts theater collectives as "task groups" of "theatre workers" with a shared set of values and identity (9).

Part of Weinberg's description fits Mabou Mines, but his vocabulary remains in-debted to 1930s socialism, tending to impose a sense of structural rigidity on the groups rather than finding their internal sense of discipline—that is, how the work often de-termines the group's identity—and a correspondingly vague idealism about how the work influences both artists and audiences. As avant-gardists, the members of Mabou Mines thought of themselves in terms of art and its place in society. Their vocabulary owes more to the Beats and absurdists than to Erwin Piscator, Judith Malina's mentor, or the Bauhaus. Even with regard to the company's first ten years, the term *collaboration* better describes the members' professional relations with one another and their work with artists from various disciplines. All theater is by nature collaborative; here the term refers more specifically to working relations that allowed the artists to avoid predefined roles (actor, director, designer, and so on) and instead participate in and comment on the work more flexibly. *Collective* only becomes useful in relation to Mabou Mines' work after 1978 or 1979, when I occasionally employ it to refer to the loosening of the company's strictures on members engaging in outside work. While in the 1970s com-pany members tended not to seek such work as individual actors, directors, or design-ers, by 1980 the pattern of everyone being involved in all company productions had broken, and the group began to turn from working on one production at a time to hav-ing several in various stages of development. Adapting in this fashion, Mabou Mines furthered its own survival as a company by allowing individuals to enhance both their artistic development and the minimal incomes the company could provide them (and only when they were working on a show). Thus, since 1980 the company has been a kind of producing collective or, as Alexis Greene terms it, "a collective of co-artistic directors with no single artistic leader" ("Mabou Mines Turns Twenty," *Theater Week,* 29 January

1990, 13). My preferred phrase is simply "a company of directors." All original members (except Warrilow), as well as several subsequent members, have become directors who develop their own projects both inside and outside the company. The arc of each member's work history invokes one strand of the company's intertwining history of collaboration.

2. Lee Breuer, "The Theatre and Its Trouble—An Essay," in *Sister Suzie Cinema: The Collected Poems and Performances, 1976–1978* (New York: Theatre Communications Group, 1987), 52 (published earlier as "The Theatre and Its Trouble," *American Theatre,* November 1986, 38). Tomisaburo Wakayama (1929–92) was trained as a Kabuki actor and judo instructor, and became a martial arts star of numerous Japanese cult films. He was perhaps best known for his television role as Ogami Itto, the Lone Wolf.

3. Warren Kliewer, "Artists in Charge: The Revival of the Actor-Manager," *Back Stage,* 14 July 1989.

4. JoAnne Akalaitis, interview by the author, 17 August 1993.

5. Eugene Ionesco, quoted in Louise Steinman, *The Knowing Body: Elements of Contemporary Performance and Dance* (Boston and London: Shambhala, 1986), ii.

6. Robert Coe and Don Shewey, "Q: Is Mabou Mines Plural or Singular? A: Both," *Soho Weekly News,* 29 April 1981, 9.

7. Frederick Neumann, interview by the author, 6 November 1997.

8. JoAnne Akalaitis, "Conversation with JoAnne Akalaitis: We Are the Ones," interview by Anne Cattaneo and David Diamond, *Journal for Stage Directors and Choreographers* 10, no. 1 (1996): 9–10.

9. Ross Wetzsteon, "Wild Man of the American Theater: Lee Breuer Turns His Life and Off-Broadway Upside Down," *Village Voice,* 19 May 1987, 19, 20. Wetzsteon's article provided material on several earlier points as well.

10. Lee Breuer, interview by the author, 20 November 1993.

11. Herbert Blau, interview by the author, 10 December 1993.

12. Honora Fergusson, interview by the author, 2 June 1994.

13. Ruth Maleczech, interview by the author, 30 October 2001.

14. R. G. Davis, *The San Francisco Mime Troupe: The First Ten Years* (Palo Alto, CA: Ramparts Press, 1975), 18, 21.

15. Lee Breuer, interview by the author, 14 December 1993.

16. Lee Breuer, "Lee Breuer," interview by David Savran, in *In Their Own Words: Contemporary American Playwrights* (New York: Theatre Communications Group, 1988), 9.

17. Ruth Maleczech interview by the author, 30 October 2001.

18. David Warrilow, interview by the author, 1 June 1993.

19. Quoted in Laurie Lassiter, "David Warrilow: Creating Symbol and Cypher," *The Drama Review: TDR* 29, no. 4 (1985): 3.

20. Philip Glass, *Music by Philip Glass,* edited by Robert T. Jones (New York: Harper and Row, 1987), 4–5.

21. Ibid., 18.

22. Ruth Maleczech, "Song for New York: An Interview with Ruth Maleczech," interview by Wendy Weckwerth, *Theater* 35, no. 3 (2005): 56–57.

23. JoAnne Akalaitis, "JoAnne Akalaitis," interview by Sally R. Sommer, *The Drama Review: TDR* 20, no. 3 (1976): 6.

24. Ruth Maleczech, "Two Women: Creating Their Own Worlds—An Interview with the Wooster Group's Elizabeth Lecompte and Mabou Mines' Ruth Maleczech," interview by Wanda Phipps, *High Performance,* spring 1990, 34.

25. Maleczech had named her Clove 333 Galilee, but French authorities refused to include the numbers in the official birth records. Galilee embraced performance as a child and continued to appear in Mabou Mines productions such as *Dead End Kids, Imagination Dead Imagine,* and *Mabou Mines Lear.* She directed a reconstruction of *The Red Horse Animation* (1995), developed in the company's studio for emerging artists, Mabou Mines *Suite.* Since 2001 she has been a company associate artist, taking major roles in *Animal Magnetism* (2000) and *Red Beads* (2005). As an independent experimental theater artist and choreographer, she has developed several projects, among them *Trick Saddle* (2003) and *Wickets* (2007–2009) with Jenny Rogers.

26. Ruth Maleczech, interview by the author, 3 May 1993.

27. Steinman, *The Knowing Body,* 78, 54.

28. Lee Breuer, "Lee Breuer," interview by Michael Goldberg, *Bomb,* summer 1996, 25. The meaning of Mabou Mines remains mysterious. Located in a region crisscrossed with First Nation, French Acadian, English, and Scottish cultures, the town's name is usually rendered as "shining waters." Mi'kmaq Indians called the place "Madawak," made from two words (*mauii* or "put or come together" and *bouik* or "flowing like a river"). Bridge Museum, Mabou, Cape Breton Island, Nova Scotia, 8 August 2003. A former coal-mining town, Mabou Mines does indeed sit at the mouth of the Mabou River, which flows into Mabou Harbor and thus the Northumberland Strait.

29. David Warrilow, interview by the author, 1 June 1993.

30. Glass, *Music,* 8, 23.

31. "Performing Artservices, Inc." www.artservices.org/artservices.html. Accessed 24 July 2010.

32. Mimi Johnson and Rosemary Quinn, interview by the author, 13 October 1995. The following material, in the text and below, is from this interview.

Mabou Mines was always involved in certain aspects of tour management. According to Johnson, Mabou Mines members almost always made personal contacts with venues to initiate bookings. In the late 1970s the NEA encouraged artists to begin handling their own management and bookkeeping in order to contain costs and broaden the spectrum of artists who could be supported. Artservices tended to choose artists with avant-garde sensibilities. At the same time, because Artservices managed many clients, among them composer Robert Ashley, the Viola Farber Dance Company, choreographer Molissa Fenley, and Grand Union (including Trisha Brown, Barbara Dilley, Douglas Dunn, David Gordon, Nancy Lewis, Steve Paxton, and Yvonne Rainer), they were not able to do in-depth fundraising for each artist or group. As public and private grant funding became more available, Mabou Mines hired individuals, such as Marion Godfrey, its first development director, and took on interns to work on applications and other development tasks at the Artservices office. By the early 1980s the company had as many as five projects in various stages of development at one time. As they gained confidence in handling their own business affairs, Mabou Mines "graduated," as Rosemary Quinn puts it, and left Artservices altogether, amicably, by 1985. Quinn, while still doing part-time bookkeeping for the company, performed as the Curator in *Cold Harbor* and Heather Hart in *Flow My Tears, the Policeman Said* (1985). She has since developed a project in the Mabou Mines *Suite* program.

33. Gary Houston, "They Mix Acting and Performing," *Chicago Sun-Times,* 27 April 1975.

34. H. Merton Goldman, "Where Conceptual and Performance Art Meet: Mabou Mines Creates Multidimensional Theatre," *Theatre Crafts* 12, no. 3 (March–April 1978): 20.

35. Mabou Mines, "Mabou Mines," publicity handout, probably 1990 (personal copy).

36. Quoted in "Mabou Mines," *New York,* 23 February 1981, 30.

37. Maleczech, "Two Women," 35.

38. C. W. E. Bigsby, "Lee Breuer," in *A Critical Introduction to Twentieth-Century American Drama,* vol. 3 (Cambridge: Cambridge University Press, 1985), 214, 212–13.

39. Lee Breuer, "Lee Breuer of Mabou Mines: Media Rex," interview by Sylvère Lotringer, *Semiotexte* 3, no. 2 (1978): 53–54.

40. Bigsby, *Critical Introduction,* 3, 212, 216.

41. "Mabou Mines," 30.

42. Philip Glass, "Interview with Philip Glass," interview by Nicholas Zurbrugg, *Review of Contemporary Fiction* 7, no. 2 (summer 1987): 104.

43. Cited as "Anna Deavere Smith (introducing *Ecco Porco* at the IACD, Harvard University)." Mabou Mines, company fund-raising letter, November 1999 (personal copy).

Chapter 2

1. Arthur Sabatini makes a convincing case for Mann's influence on Breuer's writing in "From Dog to Ant: The Evolution of Lee Breuer's Animations," *PAJ: A Journal of Performance and Art,* 26, no. 2 (2004): 52–60.

2. C. W. E. Bigsby, "Lee Breuer," in *A Critical Introduction to Twentieth-Century American Drama,* vol. 3 (Cambridge: Cambridge University Press, 1985), 213, 214.

3. Flyer, "*The Red Horse Animation* and *The B-Beaver Animation,*" n.d., viewed at the Mabou Mines archive, Mabou Mines office, New York City.

4. Philip Glass, *Music by Philip Glass,* edited by Robert T. Jones (New York: Harper and Row, 1987), 8. Power Boothe is credited in Breuer's volume *Animations: A Trilogy for Mabou Mines* (edited by Bonnie Marranca and Gautam Dasgupta [New York: Performing Arts Journal Publications, 1979]) with creating the nine-foot-high wall, while

Richard Hayton and Tom Reid are given credit for building the acoustic floor. Boothe seems to have come up with the idea for the floor.

5. David Warrilow, personal letter to Frederick Neumann and Honora Fergusson, n.d. (probably written sometime between 19 and 25 November 1970), personal papers of Frederick Neumann.

6. Breuer, *Animations,* 35.

7. John Howell, "Some Form to Hold Me," *Art-Rite* no. 5 (spring 1974): 14.

8. Bonnie Marranca, ed., *The Theatre of Images* (New York: Drama Book Specialists, 1977). In association with the Johns Hopkins University Press, Performing Arts Journal Publications reissued this volume in 1996 with an afterword by Marranca and a black-and-white printing of the comic *The Red Horse Animation.*

9. Howell, "Some Form to Hold Me," 15.

10. Quoted in Louise Steinman, *The Knowing Body: Elements of Contemporary Performance and Dance* (Boston and London: Shambhala, 1986), 29.

11. Lee Breuer, "How We Work," *Performing Arts Journal* 1, no. 1 (1976): 29, 30, 31.

12. Program, "*The Red Horse Animation,*" 18–21 November 1970, Guggenheim Museum, viewed at the company archive, Mabou Mines office, New York City.

13. Clive Barnes, "Stage: Trio of 'Red Horse Animation,'" *New York Times,* 20 November 1970, 32.

14. Henry M. Sayre, *The Object of Performance: The American Avant-Garde since 1970* (Chicago and London: University of Chicago Press, 1989), 17.

15. David Warrilow, quoted in Laurie Lassiter, "David Warrilow: Creating Symbol and Cypher," *The Drama Review: TDR* 29, no. 4 (1985): 9.

16. Warrilow, letter to Neumann and Fergusson.

17. Ellen Stewart, interview by the author, 4 November 1992.

18. Mabou Mines, *Arc Welding Piece* program notes, viewed at the company archive, Mabou Mines office, New York City.

19. Arthur Sainer, "Hot Weather Avant Garde," *Village Voice,* 8 June 1972, 56.

20. Ellen Stewart, interview by the author, 15 May 2002.

21. Lee Breuer, "The Funding Game," *Other Stages,* 20 March 1980, 10.

22. Ellen Stewart, interview by the author, 15 May 2002.

23. Dudley Andrew, *Concepts in Film Theory* (Oxford: Oxford University Press, 1984), 16.

24. Breuer, *Animations,* 41, 41, 42, 43, 48.

25. Howell, "Some Form to Hold Me," 15.

26. Breuer, *Animations,* 47.

27. Ibid., 51, 51.

28. Ibid., 52.

29. Richard Schechner, *Performance Studies: An Introduction,* 2nd ed. (New York and London: Routledge, 2006), 29.

30. Edward Kaufman, "Out of La Mama by Le Living," *The Staff* (Los Angeles), 11 February 1972, 18.

31. Noël Carroll, "Mabou Mines, The Performing Garage," *Artforum,* May 1974, 78.

32. Michael Peppiatt, "Mabou Mines," *Financial Times,* 4 January 1973.

33. Clove Galilee, interview by the author, 13 August 1997.

34. The piece's touring history, after its premier at the Guggenheim Museum, includes an expanded version (performed with *Come and Go*) at the Whitney Museum. Then, with an early version of *B.Beaver, Red Horse* went to the West Coast, Minneapolis, Memphis, and Vancouver in 1971; with *Play* to Oregon and California; and to Amsterdam. In 1974, after *B.Beaver* opened, the company revived *Red Horse* to play in tandem with it, first at the Byrd Hoffman School of Byrds and then at the Performing Garage.

35. Robyn Brentano and Mark Savitt, eds., *112 Workshop/112 Greene Street: History, Artists and Artworks* (New York: New York University Press, 1981), 41.

36. Flyer, "*The Red Horse Animation* and *The B.Beaver Animation,*" n.d., viewed at the company archive, Mabou Mines office, New York City.

37. Ross Wetzsteon, "Wild Man of the American Theater: Lee Breuer Turns His Life and Off-Broadway Upside Down," *Village Voice,* 19 May 1987, 26.

38. Ruth Maleczech, interview by the author, 28 October 1994.

39. Terry O'Reilly, e-mail message to the author, 3 January 2010.

40. Frederick Neumann, interview by the author, 26 June 1991.

41. Keith Sonnier, "Keith Sonnier: *Send/Receive/Send,* November 29–30," *Avalanche* no. 8 (summer–fall 1973): n.p.

42. Terry O'Reilly, interview by the author, 26 January 1996.

43. Lee Breuer, *The B.Beaver Animation, Big Deal* 4 (fall 1976): 8.

44. Breuer, *Animations,* 59. Unless otherwise noted, quotations are taken from this version.

45. Breuer, *The B.Beaver Animation,* 4.

46. Breuer, *Animations,* 59, 63.

47. John H. Towsen, *Clowns* (New York: Hawthorn Books, 1976), 64.

48. Breuer, *Animations,* 60, 63.

49. Ibid., 66, 66, 67, 67.

50. Ibid., 66–67, 70.

51. The epigraph is from Lee Breuer, *Hajj: The Performance,* in *Wordplays 3: An Anthology of New American Drama* (New York: Performing Arts Journal Publications, 1984), 134.

52. Mabou Mines, "Mabou Mines' *The B.Beaver Animation*" (program), 1990, New York Shakespeare Festival. Public Theater, New York City (personal copy).

53. Erika Munk, "Art of Damnation," *Village Voice,* 11 April 1977, 81.

54. "Switch imagery" is from Carroll, "Mabou Mines," 78.

55. Munk, "Art of Damnation," 81.

56. Sayre, *The Object of Performance,* 17.

57. Frederick Neumann, interview by the author, 26 June 1991.

58. Bill Raymond and Linda Hartinian, interview by the author, 9 August 1996.

59. Ruth Maleczech, interview by the author, 22 October 1996.

60. Martin Lucas, *Mabou Mines: The First Twenty Years,* videotape created for the

twentieth anniversary retrospective exhibition of the same name, curated by Tom Finkelpearl at the Grey Art Gallery, New York University, 2–13 January 1991.

61. Mabou Mines, *The B.Beaver Animation,* videotape of excerpts from performance at the Walker Arts Center, Minneapolis, June 1973.

62. Robb Baker, "Mabou Mines: Animating Art," *Soho Weekly News,* 12 December 1974, n.p.

63. Frederick Neumann, interview by the author, 26 June 1991.

64. Breuer, *Animations,* 65.

65. JoAnne Akailaitis, interview by the author, 5 January 1997.

66. Ruth Maleczech, interview by the author, 22 October 1996.

67. T. T. Liang, *T'ai Chi Ch'uan for Health and Self-Defense: Philosophy and Practice,* edited by Paul B. Gallagher, rev. ed. (New York: Vintage, 1977), 92.

68. Bill Raymond, interview by the author, 20 November 1997; Bill Raymond and Linda Hartinian, interview by the author, 9 August 1996. Unless otherwise noted, the following material on Raymond's activities is also drawn from these interviews.

69. Bill Raymond, interview by the author, 4 November 1992. The following quote is drawn from this interview.

70. Ruth Maleczech, interview by the author, 30 October 2001.

71. L. B. Dallas, interview by the author, 14 September 1993.

72. Quoted in Jonathan Abarbanel, "The Mabou Crew, Mining a New Vein in Theater," *Panorama* (*Chicago Daily News*), 19–20 April 1975, n.p.

73. The Mime Troupe changed its name in 1963. For a highly personal account of this production, see R. G. Davis, *The San Francisco Mime Troupe: The First Ten* Years (Palo Alto, CA: Ramparts Press, 1975), 31–36.

74. Ruth Maleczech, interview by the author, 22 October 1996.

75. John H. Towsen, *Clowns* (New York: Hawthorn Books, 1976).

76. Howell, "Some Form to Hold Me," 15. The following quotations are also from this article.

77. Terry O'Reilly, interview by the author, 21 June 1993.

78. Breuer, *The B.Beaver Animation,* 6.

79. Dimitri Ehrlich, "Pop Musicians Look to the East, Again," *New York Times,* 28 May 1995, H25, 31.

80. Ruth Maleczech, interview by the author, 22 October 1996.

81. Iris Smith Fischer, "'Abject Idealism' as Ungrieved Loss in Recent U.S. Avant-Garde Performance," paper presented at the annual meeting of the Midwest Modern Language Association, St. Louis, November 2004.

82. Lee Breuer, "The Two-Handed Gun: Reflections on Power, Culture, Lambs, Hyenas, and Government Support for the Arts," *Village Voice,* 20 August 1991, 90.

83. Ehrlich, "Pop Musicians," 31.

84. Chögyam Trungpa, *Cutting through Spiritual Materialism,* edited by John Baker and Marvin Casper (Boston and London: Shambhala, 1987), 78. The following material is taken from pages 97, 113, 131, and 77–83.

85. Lee Breuer, interview by the author, 15 October 1996.

86. *Doxa,* in Barthes's usage, describes the public attitude that defines the artist solely by means of his or her aesthetics. For more on this, see "Introduction," including note 32.

87. Lee Breuer, "Lee Breuer," interview by David Savran, in *In Their Own Words: Contemporary American Playwrights* (New York: Theatre Communications Group, 1988), 10–11.

88. Frederick Neumann, interviews by the author, 11 and 26 June 1991, respectively.

89. Ross Wetzsteon, "Choices: Mabou Mines," *Village Voice,* 22 May 1990, 112.

90. Arthur Sainer, "The Elite and the Decadent," *Village Voice,* 17 January 1974, 65.

Chapter 3

1. The epigraph is from L. B. Dallas, interview by the author, 14 September 1993. Beckett's works are cited using the following abbreviations.

CSP *The Collected Shorter Plays of Samuel Beckett* (New York: Grove Weidenfeld, 1984)

LO *The Lost Ones* (New York: Grove Weidenfeld, 1972)

P *Play and Two Short Pieces for Radio* (London: Faber and Faber, 1964)

2. Gary Houston, "They Mix Acting and Performing," *Chicago Sun-Times,* 27 April 1975.

3. Ross Wetzsteon, "Wild Man of the American Theater: Lee Breuer Turns His Life and Off-Broadway Upside Down," *Village Voice,* 19 May 1987, 19.

4. Anna McMullan, "Beckett as Director: The Art of Mastering Failure," in *The Cambridge Companion to Beckett,* edited by John Pilling (Cambridge: Cambridge University Press, 1994), 205.

5. Lee Breuer, interview by the author, 14 December 1993.

6. Quoted in Keith Franklin Fowler, "A History of the San Francisco Actor's Workshop," PhD diss., School of Drama, Yale University, 1969, 626.

7. Ruth Maleczech, interview by the author, 8 August 2006.

8. Quoted in Laurie Lassiter, "David Warrilow: Creating Symbol and Cypher," *The Drama Review: TDR* 29, no. 4 (1985): 3. Warrilow, who had been working in Paris as a literary editor, had been considered for roles in two Beckett productions despite his lack of acting experience. First approached to participate in a production of *Endgame* in 1962 (when he met Beckett briefly), he later joined rehearsals for an American production of *Waiting for Godot* for a short time. Although he did not perform in either production, Warrilow was "bitten" by the acting bug and ultimately left the literary life to join Mabou Mines in 1970.

9. Beckett, *P,* 9.

10. Bonnie Marranca, "There, There, and There," *Soho Weekly News,* 23 October 1975.

11. Ellen Stewart, interview by the author, 15 May 2002.

12. Gary Houston, "They Mix Acting and Performing," *Chicago Sun-Times,* 27 April 1975.

13. Ruth Maleczech, interview by the author, 8 August 2006.

14. Beckett inconveniences the actors apparently out of concern for the urns' appearance, which should be tall and slim. Maleczech noted in our conversation that for the restaging Highstein was able to produce the desired visual effect while allowing Akalaitis—who was pregnant with her and Glass's second child, Zachary—to sit (Ruth Maleczech, interview by the author, 8 August 2006).

15. JoAnne Akalaitis, "JoAnne Akalaitis," interview by Sally M. Sommer, *The Drama Review: TDR* 20, no. 3 (1976): 6. The following quote is taken from pages 8–9.

16. Mel Gussow, "Mabou Mines Inhabits Beckett Landscapes on Jane St.," *New York Times,* 23 October 1975.

17. Lee Breuer, interviews by the author, 20 and 22 November 1993. *Come and Go* opened with *Play* at the La Mama Experimental Theatre Club in June 1971. The following year it appeared at the Whitney Museum and the Paula Cooper Gallery and then toured to art galleries and universities around the country in various combinations with *The Red Horse Animation, The B.Beaver Animation,* and/or *Play.* In December 1974 it was staged at the New York Theatre Ensemble with *B.Beaver* but then became part of "Mabou Mines Performs Samuel Beckett," first at Theatre for the New City in April and October, then the following year at the Public Theater. Its final performance may have been at the Beckett Festival at New York University in 1978 or perhaps at the Brooklyn Bridge Centennial in 1983. It is more likely, though, that the Brooklyn Bridge staging took place at a 1971 festival, as reported in the company's 1990 retrospective time line. In any case, this staging of *Come and Go* differed from all others in that the actors were positioned on one pier with the audience seated on another and looking across the water. Although the actors' miked voices seemed close, the distance rendered the sight of the three women very small, thus creating a framing effect similar to that of the mirror (Ruth Maleczech, interview by the author, 8 August 2006).

18. Beckett, *CSP,* 195, 196.

19. Ellen McElduff, interview by the author, 11 February 1994.

20. Ruth Maleczech, interview by the author, 8 August 2006.

21. Philip Glass, *Music by Philip Glass,* edited by Robert T. Jones (New York: Harper and Row, 1987), 19.

22. Lee Breuer, interview by the author, 14 December 1993.

23. Ruth Maleczech, interview by the author, 8 August 2006.

24. Quoted in McMullan, "Beckett as Director," 202.

25. Jack Kroll, "Far from Broadway," *Newsweek,* 7 April 1975, 82.

26. Lee Breuer, interview by the author, 22 November 1993.

27. Gail Merrifield Papp, interview by the author, 9 May 2003. The following material is taken from the same interview.

28. Oskar Eustis, "How Papp Got It Right," *American Theatre,* January 2007, 76.

29. Quoted in Helen Epstein, *Joe Papp: An American Life* (Boston: Little, Brown, 1994), 448.

30. On Akalaitis, see ibid., 447. I was not able to locate Chalisa Gray; reportedly she still lives in New York City.

31. Ellen McElduff, interview by the author, 11 February 1994. The following material is taken from the same interview.

32. Anna McMullan, *Theatre on Trial: Samuel Beckett's Later Drama* (New York and London: Routledge, 1993), 203. The following quotes are taken from page 205.

33. Ruby Cohn, "Mabou Mines' Translations of Beckett," in *Beckett Translating/Translating Beckett,* edited by Alan Warren Friedman, Charles Rossman, and Dina Sherzer (University Park and London: Pennsylvania State University Press, 1987), 176.

34. David Warrilow, "David Warrilow: *The Lost Ones,*" interview by Guy Scarpetta (article in French, source unknown). This interview, which incorporates a discussion of *Dressed Like an Egg,* may have been conducted during Mabou Mines' tour to Lyons in 1979. The article was viewed at the company archive, Mabou Mines office, New York City.

35. Beckett, *LO,* 28–29.

36. I am indebted to Bill Raymond and Linda Hartinian for suggesting this description. They also brought McElduff's silent reaction to my attention (Raymond and Hartinian, interview by the author, 9 August 1996). Here, I situate the silent reaction as following the scream, as it occurs in the videotaped performance. Jaime Caro made the video at the Public Theater on 7 March 1976. Babette Mangolte and William Dolson operated cameras, Terry O'Reilly and Thom Cathcart did the lighting, switching was credited to Christopher Coughlin, and Richard Ryan recorded the sound. "Mabou Mines Performs Samuel Beckett," videotape recording, Mabou Mines Archive, Fales Library/Special Collections, Elmer Holmes Bobst Library, New York University.

37. Beckett, *LO,* 56. The following quote is taken from pages 56–57.

38. Linda Hartinian, interview by the author, 9 August 1996.

39. David Warrilow, interview by the author, 1 June 1993. As elsewhere, Warrilow tells the story of developing the piece in three short weeks of rehearsal. With no money for babysitting, the company needed a third Beckett piece for Warrilow to perform alone. He happened to have a copy of *The Lost Ones* and, although he had no particular liking for the piece, gave it to Breuer to read. Breuer saw its potential and began working with Warrilow on a reading. "In no time at all," Warrilow continued, "I realized I couldn't possibly hold the book and do a reading because there was too much to do. . . . So I started learning it and bingo. It was one of those inexplicable miracles." He gave full credit to Breuer for the production concept and staging choices: "It was Lee. It was always exclusively his vision. All I was doing was trying to realize his ideas."

40. Quoted in Lassiter, "David Warrilow," 10, 11.

41. Jonathan Kalb, *Beckett in Performance* (Cambridge: Cambridge University Press, 1989), 64.

42. Walter Asmus, "Rehearsal Notes for the German Premiere of Beckett's 'That Time' and 'Footfalls,'" in *On Beckett: Essays and Criticism,* edited by S. E. Gontarski (New York: Grove Press, 1986), 344.

43. Kalb, *Beckett in Performance,* 61.

44. Beckett, *LO,* 21.

45. Lee Breuer, letter to Samuel Beckett, 25 August 1975. Viewed at the company archive, Mabou Mines office, New York City.

46. Breuer, interview by the author, 22 November 1993.

47. Deirdre Bair, *Samuel Beckett: A Biography* (New York: Harcourt Brace Jovanovich, 1978), 633–34.

48. Samuel Beckett, note to David Warrilow, 30 April 1978. Viewed at the company archive, Mabou Mines office, New York City.

49. "'Le Dépeupleur'" par les Mabou Mines, au T.N.P.," *Le Progres* (Lyon), 17 January 1979.

50. Ruth Maleczech, letter to Samuel Beckett, 21 February 1986. Viewed at the Mabou Mines Archive, Fales Library/Special Collections, Elmer Holmes Bobst Library, New York University.

Chapter 4

1. Randy Gener, "Mabou Mines: A Love Story," *American Theatre,* April 2007, 51.

2. Lee Breuer, interview by the author, 8 November 1994.

3. Bill Raymond and Linda Hartinian, interview by the author, 9 August 1996.

4. JoAnne Akalaitis, interview by the author, 5 January 1997.

5. JoAnne Akalaitis, "JoAnne Akalaitis," interview by Sally R. Sommer, *The Drama Review: TDR* 20, no. 3 (1976): 5.

6. JoAnne Akalaitis, "Conversation with JoAnne Akalaitis: We Are the Ones," interview by Anne Cattaneo and David Diamond, *Journal for Stage Directors and Choreographers* 10, no. 1 (1996): 9.

7. Ellen McElduff, interview by the author, 11 February 1994.

8. JoAnne Akalaitis, interview by the author, 5 January 1997.

9. Terry Curtis Fox, "The Quiet Explosions of JoAnne Akalaitis," *Village Voice,* 23 May 1977, 77.

10. Roger Copland, "Where Theatrical and Conceptual Art Are Blended," *New York Times,* 1 May 1977.

11. JoAnne Akalaitis, quoted in Jonathan Kalb, *Beckett in Performance* (Cambridge: Cambridge University Press, 1989), 165.

12. JoAnne Akalaitis, "JoAnne Akalaitis," interview by Arthur Bartow, in *The Director's Voice: Twenty-One Interviews,* by Arthur Bartow (New York: Theatre Communications Group, 1988), 5.

13. Erika Munk, "Falling, but into the Month of May," *Village Voice,* 19 April 1976, 113.

14. JoAnne Akalaitis, "In Memory: Meeting Beckett," *The Drama Review: TDR* 34, no. 3 (1990): 11.

15. Munk, "Falling," 113.

16. Bill Raymond, interview with the author, 4 November 1992.

17. Enoch Brater, *The Drama in the Text: Beckett's Late Fiction* (New York and Oxford: Oxford University Press, 1994), 43. The following quote is from the same page.

18. Ruby Cohn, *Back to Beckett* (Princeton: Princeton University Press, 1973), 204.

19. JoAnne Akalaitis, "JoAnne Akalaitis's Passport to Innovation," interview by Barbara Confino, *Theater Week,* 4 July 1988, 26.

20. McElduff, interview by the author, 11 February 1994.

21. David Hardy, interview by the author, 8 July 1994.

22. Terry O'Reilly, interview by the author, 18 September 1997.

23. This and the following quotes are from Mary Overlie, e-mail messages to the author, 14 October and 10 November 1997. I am indebted to Overlie for her assistance with my description.

24. Anne Bogart, "Opening Plenary," panel discussion with Mary Overlie and Wendell Beavers at the conference "Viewpoint Theory and American Performance," New York City, 9 January 1998. In the same discussion Overlie described growing up in Montana across the street from "beatniks" who painted and talked about painting. She decided that dance needed the same sort of language, a way of thinking that would inform practice. This sort of origin story coincided with the conference program's designation of Overlie as the "originator of the Viewpoints." At the same time, both she and Bogart tended to deflect questions of ownership and originality.

25. Lee Breuer, interview by the author, 15 October 1996.

26. Akalaitis, "JoAnne Akalaitis's Passport," 26.

27. Begun in fall 1975, *Cascando* opened at Richard Foreman's loft at 491 Broadway in April 1976 and then toured to Berlin and Geneva in September. In November 1976 it reopened at the Public Theater and appeared again for two weeks at the end of the following February.

28. Arthur Sainer, "Pop America Is Getting to Breuer," *Village Voice,* 9 February 1976, 99.

29. This and subsequent quotes are from Bonnie Marranca, "All the Football Field's a Stage," *Soho Weekly News,* 5 February 1976.

30. This and subsequent quotes are from John Howell, "Sports-Art in Performance: Mabou Mines in *The Saint and the Football Players,*" *Arts Magazine,* September–October 1973, 42.

31. Untitled article in *Sports Illustrated,* 7 May 1973, 73.

32. Mike Steele, "Theater: Mabou Mines," *Minneapolis Tribune,* 27 June 1973.

33. David Hardy, interview by the author, 8 July 1994.

34. John Howell, interview by the author, 8 June 1995. Other participants included Jeffery Bingham, Thom Cathcart, Neal Hanowitz, Jan Campbell, Lady Cecil, Anthony Mascatello, Paul Thompson, Dale Worsley, Cynthia Eardley, and Lynn Spano. "*The Saint and the Football Player,*" Mabou Mines website. Accessed 11 July 2010. www.maboumines.org/productions/saint-and-football-player.

35. Don Shewey, "The Many Voices of Mabou Mines," *American Theatre,* June 1984, 42.

36. Money continued to be scarce, and Mehrten tired of fighting for it. By 1990, when he left the company, he had decided fifteen years with one company was enough; he wanted to work with a variety of people (Greg Mehrten, interview by the author, 19 May 1992). The following quotes are from the same interview. In 2009 Mehrten returned to perform in Breuer's *Porco Morto.*

37. Terry O'Reilly, interview by the author, 18 September 1997.

38. This and subsequent quotes are from Mary Overlie, e-mail message to the author, 14 October 1997.

39. Arthur Sainer, "The Saint and the Football Players," *Voice Centerfold,* 5–11 February 1976, supplement to the *Village Voice,* 9 February 1976, 60–61. The following quote appeared in "Play Ball, America," *Village Voice,* 16 February 1976, 135.

40. Henry Hewes, "The Non-stars of Tomorrow," *Saturday Review,* 20 September 1975, 50.

41. Lee Breuer, quoted in Howell, "Sports-Art," 43.

42. Marranca, "All the Football Field's a Stage," 30, 15.

43. David Hardy, interview by the author, 8 July 1994.

44. Tish Dace, "Mabou Mines: Collaborative Creation," *Soho Weekly News,* 18 May 1978, 23.

45. Lee Breuer, interview by the author, 8 November 1994.

46. Since the mid-1980s Breuer has been remarkably consistent in his vision, although the titles and parts of his epic shift periodically. An author's note in the volume *Sister Suzie Cinema* reads, "In 1970 [Breuer] co-founded Mabou Mines and began the performance poem *Realms,* a work in six parts. Parts I, II and III—the 'animations' *Red Horse, B.Beaver* and *A Dog's Life (Shaggy Dog)*—were published in 1979. Part IV, *A Prelude to Death in Venice,* was published in 1982 and is reprinted here along with sections 1 and 12 of Part V, *A Warrior Ant*" (Lee Breuer, *Sister Suzie Cinema* [New York: Theatre Communications Group, 1987], n.p.). More recently Breuer dropped *Red Horse* from *Caricatura,* while the B.Beaver was still visible in Neumann's performance of Meyerhold in *Ecco Porco* (2002).

47. This and subsequent quotes are from Lee Breuer, interview by the author, 8 November 1994.

48. Ingrid Nyeboe, "*The Shaggy Dog Animation,*" *The Drama Review: TDR* 22, no. 3 (1978): 46.

49. Bonnie Marranca, "Introduction," in Lee Breuer, *Animations: A Trilogy for Mabou Mines* (New York: Performing Arts Journal Publications, 1979), 21. Rose's speech is quoted from page 130.

50. Ruth Maleczech, interview by the author, 28 October 1994.

51. Nyeboe, "*Shaggy Dog,*" 46.

52. This and subsequent quotes are from Lee Breuer, "Lee Breuer of Mabou Mines: Media Rex," interview by Sylvère Lotringer, *Semiotexte* 3, no. 2 (1978): 51, 49, 54.

53. Iris Smith [Fischer], "The 'Intercultural' Work of Lee Breuer," *Theatre Topics* 7, no. 1 (1997): 37–58.

54. Lee Breuer, "Lee Breuer," interview by David Savran, in *In Their Own Words: Contemporary American Playwrights* (New York: Theatre Communications Group, 1988), 12. The phrase "social archetype," mentioned in the same paragraph, is from page 15.

55. Leslie Mohn had begun to work with Breuer during the late 1970s. With the Minneapolis-based Red Eye Collaboration she staged her own version of *The Shaggy Dog Animation* in 1985. While living together (and with their son, Wah Mohn), she and

Breuer codirected *The Wrath of Kali* (1994), and Mohn initiated the role of Sri Moo in *An Epidog* (1996). Mohn died in 2007.

56. Peggy Phelan, *Unmarked: The Politics of Performance* (London: Routledge, 1993), 150.

57. Lee Breuer, interview by the author, 2 November 1992.

58. This and the following quote are taken from Emily Apter, "Acting Out Orientalism: Sapphic Theatricality in Turn-of-the-Century Paris," in *Performance and Cultural Politics,* edited by Elin Diamond (London: Routledge, 1996), 27.

59. Sylvère Lotringer, "Trans-semiotic Analysis: Shaggy Codes," *The Drama Review: TDR* 22, no. 3 (1978): 93.

60. Homi Bhabha, *The Location of Culture* (London: Routledge, 1994), 150. A "metonymic functioning of the actors" was first suggested by Bonnie Marranca as part of the chorus's role as "the structural backbone of the animation." Her use of the word "metonymic" is related to but distinct from my own. See Marranca, "Introduction," 11.

61. Nyboe, "*Shaggy Dog,*" 46.

62. Ross Wetzsteon, "Wild Man of the American Theater: Lee Breuer in the Middle of Life's Passage," part 2, *Village Voice,* 26 May 1987, 34.

63. Gerald Rabkin, "Mirror of a Master's Eye," *Soho Weekly News,* 9 February 1978, 27.

64. Quoted in Charles C. Mann, "Doo Wop Opera and Greek Gospel Tragedies," *Mother Jones,* April 1987, 31.

65. This and the following quotes are from Susan Spector, "Ensemble Design," *Theatre Crafts* 12, no. 3 (March–April 1978): 24, 56–57.

66. Alison Yerxa, interview by the author, 8 July 1997.

67. This and the following material are from Julie Archer, interview by the author, 5 November 1996.

68. Quoted in Gener, "Mabou Mines," 50.

69. Dace, "Mabou Mines," 23.

70. In 1980 Mabou Mines took on Marion Godfrey as director of development. The National Endowment for the Arts had begun to require theaters to stop hiring management services such as Performing Artservices in favor of supposedly cheaper in-house management and bookkeeping. Godfrey's role quickly expanded to that of company manager.

71. Terry Curtis Fox, "Mabou Mines Evolves a Masterpiece," *Village Voice,* 2 August 1976, 89.

72. This and the following material is from Frederick Neumann, interview by the author, 26 January 1995.

73. Akalaitis, "JoAnne Akalaitis," interview by Sommer, 9.

74. Linda Hartinian, joint interview with Bill Raymond by the author, 9 August 1996.

75. JoAnne Akalaitis, interview by the author, 17 August 1993.

76. Greg Mehrten, interview by the author, 21 November 1994.

77. This and the following material comes from JoAnne Akalaitis, interviews by the author, 5 January 1997 and 21 August 1993.

78. Lee Breuer, interview by the author, 8 November 1994.

79. Comte de Lautréamont (pseudonym of Isidore Lucien Ducasse), quoted in Breuer, *Animations,* 150.

80. Michèle Sarde, *Colette: Free and Fettered* (New York: William Morrow, 1980), 273.

81. Quoted in Dana Strand, *Colette: A Study of the Short Fiction* (New York: Twayne, 1995), 108.

82. JoAnne Akalaitis, adapter, *Dressed Like an Egg: Taken from the Writings of Colette,* in *Wordplays 4: An Anthology of New American Drama* (New York: Performing Arts Journal Publications, 1984), 191.

83. Quoted in Mike Steele, "Puzzled Expressions, Scrunched Brows Herald Mabou Mines Arrival," *Minneapolis Tribune,* 5 March 1978.

84. Erika Munk, "Flashes of Astonishment," *Village Voice,* 30 May 1977, 87.

85. Akalaitis, *Dressed Like an Egg,* 197. Subsequent quotes are from pages 193, 220, 200, and 202.

86. Robin Thomas helped to execute this particular idea, building the lights and also finding and installing the circus rigging that kept the half curtain level even on stages that spanned forty feet or more (Robin Thomas, interview by the author, 17 July 1995).

87. Sidonie-Gabrielle Colette, *The Captive* (Harmondsworth, Middlesex, and New York: Penguin, 1964), 74 (originally published in French as *L'Entrave*).

88. Munk, "Flashes of Astonishment," 87.

89. Apter, "Acting Out Orientalism," 15. The following quote is from page 31.

90. This and the following passages are from Akalaitis, *Dressed Like an Egg,* 202–3.

91. Xerxes Mehta, "Notes from the Avant-Garde," *Theatre Journal* 31, no. 1 (1979): 22.

92. Fox, "Quiet Explosions," 79.

93. Akalaitis, *Dressed Like an Egg,* 203.

94. Quoted in Fox, "Quiet Explosions," 77.

95. Wetzsteon, "Wild Man," 26 May 1987, 33.

96. Akalaitis, "JoAnne Akalaitis's Passport," 26. Also see chapter 4, note 19.

97. Mehta, "Notes," 23.

98. Akalaitis, "JoAnne Akalaitis," interview by Arthur Bartow, 3.

99. "Celastic (generic name) is a plastic impregnated fabric which becomes moldable and adhesive when activated by immersion in solvent or with heat. When dry or cool, it is transformed into a light-weight, high impact, weatherproof 'shell,' having excellent shape memory and bonding power. Celastic can be drilled and sanded and will accept many finishing techniques." Schenz Theatrical Supply, "How to Work with Celastic," 1999, accessed 11 July 2010, http://www.schenz.com/fm_celastic.html.

100. Quoted in Strand, *Colette,* 108.

101. B.-St. John Schofield, interview by the author, 30 November 1993. Originally from Minnesota, like Thomas and Archer, Schofield was a doctoral candidate at the

University of Pittsburgh in 1977 when he brought Mabou Mines to perform *The B.Beaver Animation* at the 99-Cent Floating Theatre Festival. He was writing about physiological acting, from the Romans through Delsarte, but he also had extensive technical experience. He joined the tour of *Dressed Like an Egg* in the summer as a full-time technician and designer and moved his family to New York in the fall of 1978. He and L. B. Dallas became members at the May 1979 meeting, during which Warrilow resigned from the company. After working on *Mercier and Camier, A Prelude to Death in Venice,* and *Dead End Kids* (as well as the non–Mabou Mines *Southern Exposure* and *Sister Suzie Cinema*), Schofield performed in *Wrong Guys* and *Cold Harbor.* He developed a project called *Castle Homes* (1984). As his family and professional commitments both grew, though, Schofield left *Cold Harbor* in 1983 and then the company in 1985, with a brief return to work on the film version of *Dead End Kids.*

102. Robert Phelps, *Belles Saisons: A Colette Scrapbook* (New York: Farrar, Straus and Giroux, 1978), 88.

103. Ellen McElduff, interview by the author, 11 February 1994.

104. This and the following statement are quoted in Dace, "Mabou Mines," 23.

105. Robin Thomas, interview by the author, 17 July 1995.

106. This and the following quote are from Overlie's e-mail message, 14 October 1997.

107. This and the following quotes are from Mehta, "Notes," 22, 22, 22, 21.

108. JoAnne Akalaitis, "'Notes by JoAnne Akalaitis,' Scenes from *Dressed Like an Egg:* A Mabou Mines Presentation Based on the Writings of Colette," *Theater* 9, no. 2 (spring 1978): 118.

109. *Dressed Like an Egg* appeared at the Walker Art Center in March 1978 and in June at the New Theatre Festival in Baltimore (where B.-St. John Schofield joined the crew and Xerxes Mehta saw the show). That fall the company toured *Dressed Like an Egg* with *The Lost Ones* and *Cascando* to Paris, Amsterdam, and Rotterdam. In 1980, with *Vanishing Pictures, A Prelude to Death in Venice, Dead End Kids,* "The Keeper" radio series, and *Wrong Guys* in various stages of preparation, the company took *Dressed Like an Egg* to Australia, where it appeared at the Adelaide Festival and the Sydney Opera House and at two venues in Tasmania. It should be noted that *The Shorter Shaggy Dog* toured as well.

110. Wendy Bowler, "Dedication Shows Through," *Saturday Evening Mercury* (Australia), 15 March 1980, 11.

111. Mary Overlie, e-mail message, 10 November 1997.

112. JoAnne Akalaitis, interview by the author, 21 August 1993.

113. JoAnne Akalaitis, interview by the author, 16 April 1991.

114. Quoted in Dace, "Mabou Mines," 35.

115. Breuer, "The Two-Handed Gun: Reflections on Power, Culture, Lambs, Hyenas, and Government Support for the Arts," *Village Voice,* 20 August 1991, 90.

116. Quoted in Steele, "Puzzled Expressions."

117. Quoted in Dace, "Mabou Mines," 23.

118. When Connecticut College technicians could not reproduce lighting reminis-

cent of a "rock-show spotlight" for *Shaggy Dog,* Breuer resorted to the opposite effect, a single, bare, 60-watt bulb, rather than more traditional theater lighting effects (Fox, "Mabou Mines Evolves a Masterpiece," 89).

119. Breuer, *Animations,* 112, 115.

Chapter 5

1. Frederick Neumann, interviews by the author, 6 November 1997 and 5 December 1997.

2. The quoted phrases and following long quotation are from JoAnne Akalaitis, interview by the author, 17 August 1993.

3. In his opinion David Warrilow would have directed if he had stayed with the company. Frederick Neumann, interview by the author, 5 December 1997.

4. Michael McClure, quoted in Ann Charters, ed., *The Portable Beat Reader* (New York and London: Penguin, 1992), xxviii. Henry James is quoted on page xvii.

5. The following information is taken from Frederick Neumann, interviews by the author, 5 December 1997 and 26 January 1995.

6. Frederick Neumann, "Frederick Neumann," interview by Lois Oppenheim, in *Directing Beckett* by Lois Oppenheim (Ann Arbor: University of Michigan Press, 1994), 26.

7. Frederick Neumann, interview by the author, 27 September 1996.

8. I have taken care to be specific about the permissions for *More Pricks Than Kicks* and *Mercier and Camier* since there have been inconsistencies in previous accounts such as Lois Oppenheim's interview with Neumann in ibid. The timing of Beckett's "Please leave the poor little thing alone" is uncertain, but it seems most likely that Neumann received this reply in response to his second inquiry. A total of four months elapsed from the first inquiry about *More Pricks Than Kicks* to the granting of permission for *Mercier and Camier.* Neumann wrote regarding the latter on 19 December 1977, and Beckett, in Paris, responded on 14 January 1978. Compared to the earlier correspondence regarding *The Lost Ones,* this was a fairly rapid series of exchanges (correspondence between Neumann and Beckett viewed at the company archive, Mabou Mines office, New York City).

9. Frederick Neumann, interview by the author, 5 November 1997.

10. S. E. Gontarski, *The Intent of Undoing in Samuel Beckett's Dramatic Texts* (Bloomington: Indiana University Press, 1985), 185.

11. This and the following quote are from Neumann, "Frederick Neumann," 27.

12. Neumann, untitled scenario (probably 1977, photocopy), v, provided by the author from his personal papers, Kingston, New Jersey.

13. This and the following material is from Frederick Neumann, interviews by the author, 26 January 1995 and 23 January 1998.

14. Fergusson worked primarily from home while caring for her and Neumann's two children and, at various times, her father and stepmother, and an elderly friend. She also held part-time jobs. Company financial support, akin to the "babysitting money"

other couples (Akalaitis and Glass and Maleczech and Breuer) received, came the Neumanns' way when Fergusson and the two boys accompanied Mabou Mines on a 1976 tour (Honora Fergusson, interview by the author, 2 June 1994).

15. Frederick Neumann, adapter, "Mercier and Camier," manuscript, version B, 14 February 1979, 1, provided by the author from his personal papers, Kingston, New Jersey.

16. Frederick Neumann, quoted in Barbara Crossette, "Off Broadway Offers Yeats and Beckett," *New York Times,* 12 October 1979, C6.

17. Frederick Neumann, interview by the author, 6 November 1997.

18. Frederick Neumann, manuscript, "Mercier and Camier," 45–46. In the original text the narrator's line reads "A different class, Mercier and Camier, for all their faults" (Samuel Beckett, *Mercier et Camier* [Paris: Minuit, 1970]; *Mercier and Camier,* translated by Samuel Beckett [London: Calder and Boyars, 1974; New York: Grove Press, 1975], 112).

19. Frederick Neumann, untitled scenario, "Mercier and Camier," iv. The following material is from Neumann, interviews by the author, 5 November 1997 and 23 January 1998.

20. Frederick Neumann, interview by the author, 5 November 1997. The following quote is from Neumann, untitled scenario, "Mercier and Camier," i.

21. Philip Glass, interview by the author, 24 May 1993.

22. Frederick Neumann, interview by the author, 6 November 1997.

23. Janice Paran, "Beckett by Baedeker: Mabou Mines' *Mercier and Camier,*" *Theater* (Yale University) 11, no. 2 (1980): 63, 65.

24. William Harris, "Off and On," *Soho Weekly News,* 18 October 1979, 56.

25. Terry O'Reilly, interview by the author, 21 June 1993. The following material, in part, comes from Raymond, interview by the author, 20 November 1997.

26. L. B. Dallas, interview by the author, 14 September 1993.

27. In a 28 December 2009 conversation, Neumann remarked that, while bars and pubs now commonly carry such televisions, the idea was new in 1979.

28. Frederick Neumann, interview by the author, with the following material from interviews of 6 November 1997 and 5 November 1997. *Mercier and Camier* was Hamilton's first Mabou Mines production, but she had earlier assisted with the box office for *The Shaggy Dog Animation* during Festival '77 while working for A Bunch of Experimental Theatres. After serving as assistant stage manager for *Mercier and Camier,* she expanded her participation with *Dead End Kids* and *A Prelude to Death in Venice,* became production manager from 1985 to 1987, and served as director of the internship program. She has worked most consistently with Neumann on the original and touring productions for both *Company* (lighting) and *Worstward Ho* (Sabrina Hamilton, interview by the author, 26 October 1994). Hamilton is now artistic director of the Kō Festival of Performance, held annually in Amherst, Massachusetts.

29. Neumann, manuscript, "Mercier and Camier," 16, 19; subsequent quotes are from pages ii, 29, and 42.

30. Neumann, quoted in Crossette, "Off Broadway Offers Yeats and Beckett," C6.

31. Bill Longcore, letter to the author, dated November 1997. The following material from Longcore is from interview by the author, 26 November 1997.

32. Bill Longcore, letter to the author, 19 January 2010. The following quote and material are from Longcore, interview by the author, 26 November 1997.

33. Bill Longcore, letter to the author, 19 January 2010.

34. Paran, "Beckett by Baedeker," 65. Longcore tested his idea for combining a "large moving projection screen" with two unseen slide projectors by building a small working model. He recalls, "L. B. Dallas then built a practical, full size, chain-driven copy able to gracefully and silently start, revolve, and stop on cue, operated remotely by hand-cranking bicycle pedals. The images, projected from opposing angles onto the slowly wheeling panels, grew larger as they appeared to sweep across and then slip from sight as the following image faded in to sweep up and away in the opposite direction. This gave the illusion of moving images mingling in mid-air as [musician Harvey] Spevak played . . . the bright opening trills of Glass's score. I was dazzled" (Bill Longcore, letter to the author, 19 January 2010). Apparently only one person was needed to operate the bicycle pedals, varying the door's speed or stopping and starting it when needed.

35. Chas Cowing worked with Mabou Mines in the late 1970s and early 1980s. Among other shows, he performed in, assistant-directed, and worked on sound for *Dead End Kids*. Since 1999 he has been president of Access Talent, where he specializes in voice-overs and the spoken word.

36. Frederick Neumann, interviews by the author, 30 January 1993 and 26 January 1995.

37. Mel Gussow, "Vaudeville Labyrinth," *New York Times,* 26 October 1979, C3.

38. This and the following quotes are from Neumann, interview by the author, 5 November 1997.

39. Neumann, untitled scenario, "Mercier and Camier," iv.

40. James Acheson, *Samuel Beckett's Artistic Theory and Practice: Criticism, Drama, and Early Fiction* (Houndmills, Basingstoke, and London: Macmillan; New York: St. Martin's, 1997), 92.

41. Neumann, manuscript, "Mercier and Camier," 42.

42. Eric Levy, "*Mercier and Camier:* Narration, Dante, and the Couple," in *On Beckett: Essays and Criticism,* edited by S. E. Gontarski (New York: Grove Press, 1986), 128. The internal quotation, translated and italicized by Levy, is from Samuel Beckett, "Henri Hayden, homme-peintre," *Documents* 22 (1955), reprinted in *Disjecta: Miscellaneous Writings and a Dramatic Fragment,* edited by Ruby Cohn (New York: Grove Press, 1984), 151.

43. James Leverett, "The Stink of Artifice," *Soho Weekly News,* 1 November 1979, n.p.

44. Gussow, "Vaudeville Labyrinth," C3.

45. Paran, "Beckett by Baedeker," 65.

46. Levy, "*Mercier and Cramier,*" 118.

47. Paran, "Beckett by Baedeker," 65.

48. Bill Raymond, interview by the author, 20 November 1997.

49. Paran, "Beckett by Baedeker," 66.

50. Raymond, interview by the author, 20 November 1997.

51. Frederick Neumann, interview by the author, 6 November 1997.

52. Bill Longcore, letter to the author, November 1997.

53. Ruth Maleczech, "Acting/Non-Acting," interview by John Howell, *Performance Art Magazine*, no. 2 (1979): 12.

54. Jonathan Kalb, *Beckett in Performance* (Cambridge: Cambridge University Press, 1989), 61. See also chapter 3 in this volume.

55. Ruby Cohn, interview by the author, 3 July 1998.

56. Ibid.

57. T. J. Clark, *Image of the People: Gustave Courbet and the Revolution of 1848* (London: Thames and Hudson, 1973; Princeton: Princeton University Press, 1982), 34.

58. Beverly Brown, interview by the author, 29 October 1997.

59. This comparison and subsequent quotes are from Bethany Haye, "Re.Cher.Chez Studio: Pilgrims' Process," *Soho Weekly News*, 4 June 1980, 75.

60. Lee Breuer, "The Funding Game," *Other Stages*, 20 March 1980, 10.

61. Sabrina Hamilton, interview by the author, 26 October 1994.

62. Quoted in Phyllis Lehmann, "Halfway House for the Avant-Garde," *Cultural Post* (National Endowment for the Arts) 6, no. 6 (March–April 1981): n.p. In casting the French term *recherché* as "a bit old-fashioned," Maleczech was passing over other relevant definitions, such as "choice," "refined," and "in great demand." The verb form *rechercher*, which has an identical pronunciation, adds even more interesting dimensions: "to seek again," "to investigate," "to desire," "to aspire to," and "to woo" (*The New Cassell's French Dictionary*, revised by Denis Girard [New York: Funk and Wagnalls, 1962], 621). While Re.Cher.Chez artists may have found high art a bit old-fashioned, in their projects they sought to connect with both past and future, return to the familiar in imaginative ways, and court an audience's desire for the new.

63. Bonnie Marranca, "The Politics of Performance," *Performing Arts Journal* 6, no. 1 (1981): 56.

64. Haye, "Re.Cher.Chez Studio," 75.

65. Mabou Mines, "Re.Cher.Chez Studio for the Avant Garde Performing Arts" (typescript), viewed at the Mabou Mines archive, New York City (probably written by Re.Cher.Chez's executive director, Liza Lorwin, in the fall of 1983).

66. This and the following material is from Lee Breuer, "The Funding Game," 10.

67. Mabou Mines, "The Laboratory—Re.Cher.Chez" (typescript), viewed at the company archive, Mabou Mines office, New York City, n.d., 4. This document appears to have been part of a grant proposal written after 1980. Outside of *The Taud Show*, Mayer and Holms did not participate in Re.Cher.Chez.

68. This and the following material is from Breuer, "The Funding Game," 10.

69. Ruth Maleczech, interview by the author, 22 October 1996.

70. Performing Artservices, untitled press release for *Vanishing Pictures*, n.d., viewed at the company archive, Mabou Mines office, New York City. Beverly Brown spoke with me about the production but did not allow me to view the script. I have reconstructed the events of the play with assistance from Maleczech, Archer, and Rudolph.

71. Among her performances in conventional opera was the lead in *Matrimonio Segreto* by Ciamarosa, a production done at Riverside Church by Opera de Camera. In

1976–77 she performed four roles in Ludlam's *Ring,* followed by a role in *33 Scenes on the Possibility of Human Happiness.* Solo, she performed songs by Granados at Studio 58 and French art songs at La Maison Française (Mabou Mines, "Biographies 2: Beverly Brown," press release, n.d., viewed at the company archive, Mabou Mines office, New York City).

72. Beverly Brown, interview by the author, 29 October 1997.

73. Lee Breuer, "II" (article excerpt), *Other Stages,* 10 March 1980, n.p., viewed at the company archive, Mabou Mines office, New York City.

74. This material and the following quote are from Ruth Maleczech, interview by the author, 22 October 1996. Brown had amassed a huge amount of material on and by Poe. Maleczech insisted, and Brown agreed, that the solo piece should be no longer than forty-five minutes. With feedback from Maleczech and fellow Re.Cher.Chez members, Brown began to make difficult cuts. By the time *Vanishing Pictures* opened on 30 January 1980 at Theater for the New City, then at 162 Second Avenue, they had reduced it to fifty-five minutes. Although Brown recalls feeling uncertain in her role, the run was successful, and *Vanishing Pictures* moved to The Envelope, a space at the Performing Garage on Wooster Street. They revived the show for a single tour, to Oberlin College, in January 1981.

75. Terry Curtis Fox, "Developing Pieces," *Village Voice,* 18 February 1980, 85.

76. Beverly Brown, interview by the author, 29 October 1997.

77. Ibid. The following material and quotes are also from this source.

78. Charles Baudelaire, reply to the critic Théophile Thoré-Bürger, June 1864, quoted in Aaron Scharf, *Art and Photography* (Harmondsworth, Middlesex: Penguin, 1974), 10.

79. Maleczech, interviews by the author, 3 May 1993 and 16 January 1998.

80. Stephanie Rudolph, interview by the author, 20 December 1996. For *Wrong Guys* Rudolph made a short Super-8 film with Mark Daniels, something she had never done before. According to Rudolph, neither *Vanishing Pictures* nor *Wrong Guys* made use of a stage manager; the cast and crew memorized their cues. For *Hajj,* the crews projecting live images from three video cameras developed techniques for cueing in total darkness, as did Maleczech, on whom the cameras were trained.

81. This quote and subsequent material are from Julie Archer, interview by the author, 5 November 1996. Among others involved were L. B. Dallas, Martin Baumgold, Tina Lynch, Robert Kopelson, Mercedes Lois, and Joe Stackell.

82. Detailed descriptions provided during the author's interviews with Brown, Archer, and Rudolph contributed to this account.

83. Edgar Allan Poe, "The Mystery of Marie Rogêt," in *Tales and Sketches,* vol. 3 of *Collected Works of Edgar Allan Poe,* edited by Thomas Ollive Mabbott, with the assistance of Eleanor D. Kewer and Maureen C. Mabbott (Cambridge, MA, and London: Belknap Press of Harvard University Press, 1978), 723.

84. Maleczech, interview by the author, 22 October 1996.

85. The program for the initial run lists four songs: "'Harmonie du soir' and 'La mort des amants,' poetry by Charles Baudelaire, music by Claude Debussy[;] 'Soupir,'

poetry by Stephane Mallarmé, music by Maurice Ravel[;] and 'La diva de l'empire,' words by Dominique Bonnaud and Numa Bles, music by Eric Satie." Piano music was by Louis Moreau Gottschalk (Mabou Mines, program, *Vanishing Pictures,* viewed at the company archive, Mabou Mines office, New York City).

86. Beverly Brown, interview by the author, 29 October 1997.

87. Tony Tanner, "Rub Out the Word," in *William S. Burroughs at the Front: Critical Reception, 1959–1989,* edited by Jennie Skerl and Robin Lydenberg (Carbondale: Southern Illinois University, 1991), 110.

88. Fox, "Developing Pieces," 85.

89. Beverly Brown, interview by the author, 29 October 1997.

90. Stephanie Rudolph, interview by the author, 20 December 1996.

91. Ruth Maleczech, interview by the author, 3 May 1993.

92. See, for example, Bonnie Marranca, "Beverly Brown and Ruth Maleczech, *Vanishing Pictures,*" *Live: Performance Art Magazine,* no. 3 (1980): 42–43.

93. Fox, "Developing Pieces," 85.

94. James Leverett, "In the Works," *Soho Weekly News,* 20 February 1980, n.p.

95. William Burroughs, quoted in Tanner, "Rub Out the Word," 109.

96. John Howell, "Performance in May at Re.Cher.Chez Studio," *Soho Weekly News,* 10 June 1981, n.p.

97. This and the following quote are from Richard Schechner, *The End of Humanism: Writings on Performance* (New York: Performing Arts Journal Publications, 1982), 29–30, 43.

98. Matthew Maguire, "Alive Wire or Vital Signs," *Performing Arts Journal,* no. 16 (1981): 44.

99. Ruth Maleczech, "Am I Dying While I'm Devouring Life?" *Performing Arts Journal* 6, no. 1 (1981): 45.

100. Lorwin joined Re.Cher.Chez in 1981 as executive director and sole staff member. She had found her first full-time job at Performing Artservices in 1979 and thus became familiar with Mabou Mines. As executive director, Lorwin did fund-raising and administration for Re.Cher.Chez, which was incorporated separately from Mabou Mines. Before she left her position, she had already begun producing *Gospel at Colonus.* Lorwin and Breuer have a son, Mojo, born in 1984, who inspired her (as Archer's daughter, Ella Rae, did her) to develop *Peter and Wendy* (Liza Lorwin, interview by the author, 10 December 1996).

101. Breuer, "The Funding Game," 10.

102. Material for this account was taken from Karen Kandel, interview by the author, 19 March 1997; and Don Shewey, "A One-Woman Cast of Many Characters," *New York Times,* 13 January 2002, 24.

103. "Mabou Mines/*Suite* Resident Artists, 2005," Mabou Mines flyer, 2005 (personal copy).

104. The performance and rehearsal space called ToRoNaDa—"no bull"—is named for four individuals whose legacies have continued, despite their deaths, to sustain the company: former managing director Tony Vasconcellos; Ron Vawter, a founding mem-

ber of the Wooster Group and Greg Mehrten's partner; artist Nancy Graves, who helped the company during its first years in New York; and David Warrilow, who died of AIDS in 1995. Mabou Mines *Suite* has been supported by the Jerome Foundation and the New York City Department of Cultural Affairs.

Epilogue

1. Richard Schechner and Richard Foreman, "A Bunch Manifesto," unpublished manuscript, probably July 1977, Richard Schechner Papers and *The Drama Review* Collection, 1943–2007. Department of Rare Books and Special Collections, Princeton University Library.

2. JoAnne Akalaitis, interview by the author, 17 August 1993.

3. Sabrina Hamilton, interview by the author, 26 October 1994.

4. Stephanie Rudolph, interview by the author, 20 December 1996.

5. Randy Gener, "Mabou Mines: A Love Story," *American Theatre,* April 2007, 51.

6. JoAnne Akalaitis, interview by the author, 17 August 1993.

7. Discussed in my Introduction. Julia A. Walker, "The Text/Performance Split across the Analytic/Continental Divide," in *Staging Philosophy: Intersections of Theater, Performance, and Philosophy,* edited by David Krasner and David Z. Saltz (Ann Arbor: University of Michigan Press, 2006), 38.

8. Tony Davies, *Humanism* (London: Routledge, 1997), 27. The following material is from pages 31–33, 38, 131–33.

9. Charles C. Mann, "Doo Wop Opera and Greek Gospel Tragedies," *Mother Jones,* April 1987, 31.

10. Ruth Maleczech and Elizabeth LeCompte, "Two Women: Creating Their Own Worlds," interview by Wanda Phipps, *High Performance* (spring 1990): 32–35.

11. Ruth Maleczech, "Am I Dying While I'm Devouring Life?" *Performing Arts Journal* 6, no. 1 (1981): 45.

Wordplays 4: An Anthology of New American Drama, 191–220. New York: Performing Arts Journal Publications, 1984.

Anderson, Porter. "Teasers and Tormentors: Jettisoning JoAnne." *Village Voice,* 23 March 1993, 94.

Andrew, Dudley. *Concepts in Film Theory.* Oxford: Oxford University Press, 1984.

Apter, Emily. "Acting Out Orientalism: Sapphic Theatricality in Turn-of-the-Century Paris." In *Performance and Cultural Politics,* edited by Elin Diamond, 15–34. London: Routledge, 1996.

Aronson, Arnold. *American Avant-Garde Theatre: A History.* London: Routledge, 2000.

Asmus, Walter. "Rehearsal Notes for the German Premiere of Beckett's 'That Time' and 'Footfalls,' " In *On Beckett: Essays and Criticism,* edited by S. E. Gontarski, 335–39. New York: Grove Press, 1986.

Associated Press. "New York Playwright Wins $355,000 Fellowship." *Kansas City Star,* 17 June 1997, A4.

Bair, Deirdre. *Samuel Beckett: A Biography.* New York: Harcourt Brace Jovanovich, 1978.

Baker, Robb. "Mabou Mines: Animating Art." *Soho Weekly News,* 12 December 1974, n.p.

Banes, Sally. *Greenwich Village, 1963: Avant-Garde Performance and the Effervescent Body.* Durham, NC: Duke University Press, 1993.

Barnes, Clive. "Stage: Trio of 'Red Horse Animation.' " *New York Times,* 20 November 1970, 32.

Barthes, Roland. *Critical Essays.* Translated by Richard Howard. Evanston, IL: Northwestern University Press, 1972.

Barthes, Roland. "From Work to Text." In *Image-Music-Text,* translated by Stephen Heath, 155–64. New York: Noonday Press, 1977.

Barthes, Roland. *The Pleasure of the Text.* Translated by Richard Miller. New York: Hill and Wang, 1975.

Beckett, Samuel. *The Collected Shorter Plays of Samuel Beckett.* New York: Grove Weidenfeld, 1984.

Beckett, Samuel. *Disjecta: Miscellaneous Writings and a Dramatic Fragment.* Edited by Ruby Cohn. New York: Grove Press, 1984.

Beckett, Samuel. *The Lost Ones.* New York: Grove Weidenfeld, 1972.

Beckett, Samuel. *Mercier and Camier.* Translated by Samuel Beckett. London: Calder and Boyars, 1974; New York: Grove Press, 1975.

Beckett, Samuel. *Mercier et Camier.* Paris: Minuit, 1970.

Beckett, Samuel. *Play and Two Short Pieces for Radio.* London: Faber and Faber, 1964.

Bhabha, Homi. *The Location of Culture.* London: Routledge, 1994.

Bigsby, C. W. E. *A Critical Introduction to Twentieth-Century American Drama.* 3 vols. Cambridge: Cambridge University Press, 1985.

Bogart, Anne, Mary Overlie, and Wendell Beavers. Panel discussion at the conference "Viewpoint Theory and American Performance." New York City, 9 January 1998. Personal notes.

Bourdieu, Pierre. "The Field of Cultural Production." In *The Field of Cultural Produc-*

tion: Essays on Art and Literature, edited by Randal Johnson, 29–73. New York: Columbia University Press, 1993.

Bowler, Wendy. "Dedication Shows Through." *Saturday Evening Mercury* (Australia), 15 March 1980, 11.

Brater, Enoch. *The Drama in the Text: Beckett's Late Fiction.* New York and Oxford: Oxford University Press, 1994.

Brentano, Robyn, and Mark Savitt, eds. *112 Workshop/112 Greene Street: History, Artists, and Artworks.* New York: New York University Press, 1981.

Breuer, Lee. "The Actor Evolves." *Soho Weekly News,* 7 July 1977, 42.

Breuer, Lee. *Animations: A Trilogy for Mabou Mines.* Edited by Bonnie Marranca and Gautam Dasgupta. New York: Performing Arts Journal Publications, 1979.

Breuer, Lee. *The B.Beaver Animation. Big Deal 4* (fall 1976): 3–14. Preface by Patricia [Spears] Jones.

Breuer, Lee. "The Funding Game." *Other Stages,* 20 March 1980, 10.

Breuer, Lee. *Hajj: The Performance.* In *Wordplays 3: An Anthology of New American Drama,* 129–44. New York: Performing Arts Journal Publications, 1984.

Breuer, Lee. "How We Work." *Performing Arts Journal* 1, no. 1 (1976): 29–32.

Breuer, Lee. "Lee Breuer." Interview by Michael Goldberg. *Bomb* (summer 1996): 24–29.

Breuer, Lee. "Lee Breuer." Interview by David Savran. In *In Their Own Words: Contemporary American Playwrights,* 3–17. New York: Theatre Communications Group, 1988.

Breuer, Lee. "Lee Breuer of Mabou Mines: Media Rex." Interview by Sylvère Lotringer. *Semiotexte* 3, no. 2 (1978): 48–59.

Breuer, Lee. *A Prelude to Death in Venice.* Work-in-progress script. *Plays in Process* series, edited by James Leverett. New York: Theatre Communications Group, 1979.

Breuer, Lee. *Sister Suzie Cinema: The Collected Poems and Performances.* New York: Theatre Communications Group, 1987.

Breuer, Lee. "The Theatre and Its Trouble—An Essay." In *Sister Suzie Cinema: The Collected Poems and Performances,* 51–53, 66–67, 87–89, 102–3, 123–25. New York: Theatre Communications Group, 1987.

Breuer, Lee. "The Two-Handed Gun: Reflections on Power, Culture, Lambs, Hyenas, and Government Support for the Arts." *Village Voice,* 20 August 1991, 89–90.

Carlson, Marvin. "Semiotics and Its Heritage." In *Critical Theory and Performance,* edited by Janelle G. Reinelt and Joseph R. Roach, 13–25. Rev. ed. Ann Arbor: University of Michigan Press, 2007.

Carroll, Noël. "Mabou Mines, the Performing Garage." *Artforum,* May 1974, 78.

Charters, Ann, ed. *The Portable Beat Reader.* New York and London: Penguin, 1992.

Chaudhuri, Una. "The Future of the Hyphen: Interculturalism, Textuality, and the Difference Within." In *Interculturalism and Performance: Writings from PAJ,* edited by Bonnie Marranca and Gautam Dasgupta, 192–207. New York: Performing Arts Journal Publications, 1991.

Clark, T. J. *Image of the People: Gustave Courbet and the Revolution of 1848.* London: Thames and Hudson, 1973; Princeton: Princeton University Press, 1982.

Cody, Gabrielle. "Behavior as Culture: An Interview with Lee Breuer." In *Intercultural-*

ism and Performance: Writings from PAJ, edited by Bonnie Marranca and Gautam Dasgupta, 208–15. New York: Performing Arts Journal Publications, 1991.

Coe, Robert, and Don Shewey. "Q: Is Mabou Mines Plural or Singular? A: Both." *Soho Weekly News,* 29 April 1981, 9–12.

Cohn, Ruby. *Back to Beckett.* Princeton: Princeton University Press, 1973.

Cohn, Ruby. "Mabou Mines' Translations of Beckett." In *Beckett Translating/Translating Beckett,* edited by Alan Warren Freidman, Charles Rossman, and Dina Sherzer, 174–80. University Park and London: Pennsylvania State University Press, 1987.

Cole, Susan Letzler. *Directors in Rehearsal: A Hidden World.* New York: Routledge, 1992.

Colette, Sidonie-Gabrielle. *The Captive.* Translated by Antonia White. Harmondsworth, Middlesex, and New York: Penguin, 1964.

Copland, Roger. "Where Theatrical and Conceptual Art Are Blended." *New York Times,* 1 May 1977.

Crossette, Barbara. "Off Broadway Offers Yeats and Beckett." *New York Times,* 12 October 1979, C6.

Dace, Tish. "Mabou Mines: Collaborative Creation." *Soho Weekly News,* 18 May 1978, 22–23, 35.

Davies, Tony. *Humanism.* London: Routledge, 1997.

Davis, R. G. *The San Francisco Mime Troupe: The First Ten Years.* Palo Alto, CA: Ramparts Press, 1975.

"'Le Dépeupleur' par les Mabou Mines, au T.N.P." *Le Progres* (Lyon), 17 January 1979.

Diamond, Elin, ed. *Performance and Cultural Politics.* London: Routledge, 1996.

Ehrlich, Dimitri. "Pop Musicians Look to the East, Again." *New York Times,* 28 May 1995, H25, 31.

Epstein, Helen. *Joe Papp: An American Life.* Boston: Little, Brown, 1994.

Eustis, Oscar. "How Papp Got It Right." *American Theatre,* January 2007, 74, 76–79.

Fischer, Iris Smith. "'Abject Idealism' as Ungrieved Loss in Recent U.S. Avant-Garde Performance." Paper presented at the annual meeting of the Midwest Modern Language Association, St. Louis, November 2004.

Fischer, Iris Smith. "C. S. Peirce and the Habit of Theatre." In *Changing the Subject: Marvin Carlson and Theatre Studies, 1959–2009,* edited by Joseph Roach, 118–48. Ann Arbor: University of Michigan Press, 2009.

Fischer, Iris Smith. "The Discipline of Word and Body: Mabou Mines Stage Beckett, 1965–1975." In *Text and Presentation, 2006,* edited by Stratos E. Constantinidis, 43–57. Jefferson, NC: McFarland Publishing, 2007. Published in Italian as "La disciplina di parola e corpo: I Mabou Mines mettono in scena Beckett, 1965–1975." In *Beckett and Puppet: Studi e scene tra Samuel Beckett e il tetro di figura,* edited by Fernando Marchiori, 182–201. Pisa: Titivillus, 2007.

Fischer, Iris Smith. "*Happy Days.*" Review. *Theatre Journal* 51, no. 1 (1999): 86–88.

Fischer, Iris Smith. "The 'Intercultural' Work of Lee Breuer." *Theatre Topics* 7, no. 1 (1997): 37–58.

Fischer, Iris Smith. "*Lear.*" Review. *Journal of Dramatic Theory and Criticism* 5, no. 2 (1991): 197–201.

Fischer, Iris Smith. "Mabou Mines' *Lear:* A Narrative of Collective Authorship." *Theatre Journal* 45, no. 3 (1993): 279–301.

Fischer, Iris Smith. "Wild Dogs: Lee Breuer's New Book of Fiction Runs with the Pack of Literary Avant-Gardists." Review. *American Theatre,* November 2002, 71–73.

Fowler, Keith Franklin. "A History of the San Francisco Actor's Workshop." PhD diss., School of Drama, Yale University, 1969.

Fox, Terry Curtis. "Developing Pieces." *Village Voice,* 18 February 1980, 85.

Fox, Terry Curtis. "Mabou Mines Evolves a Masterpiece." *Village Voice,* 2 August 1976, 89.

Fox, Terry Curtis. "The Quiet Explosions of JoAnne Akalaitis." *Village Voice,* 23 May 1977, 77, 79.

Friedman, Alan Warren, Charles Rossman, and Dina Sherzer, eds. *Beckett Translating/Translating Beckett.* University Park and London: Pennsylvania State University Press, 1987.

Frye, Northrop. *Archetypes of Criticism: Four Essays.* Princeton: Princeton University Press, 1957.

Gener, Randy. "Mabou Mines: A Love Story." *American Theatre,* April 2007, 27–29, 48–51.

Glass, Philip. "Interview with Philip Glass." Interview by Nicholas Zurbrugg. *Review of Contemporary Fiction* 7, no. 2 (summer 1987): 102–7.

Glass, Philip. *Music by Philip Glass.* Edited by Robert T. Jones. New York: Harper and Row, 1987.

Goldman, H. Merton. "Where Conceptual and Performance Art Meet: Mabou Mines Creates Multidimensional Theatre." *Theatre Crafts* 12, no. 3 (March–April 1978): 20–25, 45–49.

Goldstein, Richard. "The Souls of Art Folks." *Village Voice,* 4 June 1979, 49.

Gontarski, S. E. *The Intent of Undoing in Samuel Beckett's Dramatic Texts.* Bloomington: Indiana University Press, 1985.

Gontarski, S. E., ed. *On Beckett: Essays and Criticism.* New York: Grove Press, 1986.

Gray, Spalding, writer and actor. *Swimming to Cambodia.* Directed by Jonathan Demme. Evergreen Entertainment, film 1987, video 1996.

Greene, Alexis. "Mabou Mines Turns Twenty." *Theater Week,* 29 January 1990, 10–14.

Gussow, Mel. "Mabou Mines Inhabits Beckett Landscapes on Jane St." *New York Times,* 23 October 1975.

Gussow, Mel. "Vaudeville Labyrinth." *New York Times,* 26 October 1979, C3.

Harding, James M. "An Interview with Richard Schechner." In *Contours of the Theatrical Avant-Garde: Performance and Textuality,* edited by James M. Harding, 202–14. Ann Arbor: University of Michigan Press, 2000.

Harding, James M., and Cindy Rosenthal, eds. *Restaging the Sixties: Radical Theaters and Their Legacies.* "Introduction" by James M. Harding and Cindy Rosenthal. Ann Arbor: University of Michigan Press, 2006.

Harris, William. "Off and On." *Soho Weekly News,* 18 October 1979, 56.

Haye, Bethany. "Re.Cher.Chez Studio: Pilgrims' Process." *Soho Weekly News,* 4 June 1980, 75.

Hewes, Henry. "The Non-stars of Tomorrow." *Saturday Review,* 20 September 1975, 50–51.

Houston, Gary. "They Mix Acting and Performing." *Chicago Sun-Times,* 27 April 1975.

Howell, John. "Performance in May at Re.Cher.Chez Studio." *Soho News,* 10 June 1981, n.p.

Howell, John. "Some Form to Hold Me." *Art-Rite,* no. 5 (spring 1974): 14–16. Accompanied by "Excerpts: The Red Horse."

Howell, John. "Sports-Art in Performance: Mabou Mines in *The Saint and the Football Players.*" *Arts Magazine,* September–October 1973, 42–45.

Jefferson, Margo. "Fun-House Proportions Turn Dominance Upside Down." *New York Times,* 24 November 2003, B3.

Kalb, Jonathan. *Beckett in Performance.* Cambridge: Cambridge University Press, 1989.

Kaufman, Edward. "Out of La Mama by Le Living." *The Staff* (Los Angeles), 11 February 1972, 18.

Kliewer, Warren. "Artists in Charge: The Revival of the Actor-Manager." *Back Stage,* 14 July 1989, n.p.

Krasner, David, and David Z. Saltz, eds. *Staging Philosophy: Intersections of Theater, Performance, and Philosophy.* Ann Arbor: University of Michigan Press, 2006.

Kroll, Jack. "Far from Broadway." *Newsweek,* 7 April 1975, 80, 82.

Lassiter, Laurie. "David Warrilow: Creating Symbol and Cypher." *The Drama Review: TDR* 29, no. 4 (1985): 3–12.

Lehmann, Phyllis. "Halfway House for the Avant-Garde." *Cultural Post* (National Endowment for the Arts) 6, no. 6 (March–April 1981): n.p.

Leverett, James. "The Stink of Artifice." *Soho Weekly News,* 1 November 1979, n.p.

Leverett, James. "In the Works." *Soho Weekly News,* 20 February 1980, n.p.

Levy, Eric. "*Mercier and Camier:* Narration, Dante, and the Couple." In *On Beckett: Essays and Criticism,* edited by S. E. Gontarski, 117–30. New York: Grove Press, 1986.

Liang, T. T. *T'ai Chi Ch'uan for Health and Self-Defense: Philosophy and Practice.* Edited by Paul B. Gallagher. Rev. ed. New York: Vintage, 1977.

Longcore, Bill. Letter to the author, November 1997.

Longcore, Bill. Letter to the author, 19 January 2010.

"Looking for a Miracle." Featurette. *Mabou Mines Dollhouse,* directed by Lee Breuer. Pour Voir, 2008, DVD.

Lotringer, Sylvère. "Trans-Semiotic Analysis: Shaggy Codes." *The Drama Review: TDR* 22, no. 3 (1978): 88–94.

Lucas, Martin. "Mabou Mines: The First Twenty Years." 1990. Videotape created for the twenty-year anniversary retrospective exhibition of the same name, curated by Tom Finkelpearl, at the Grey Art Gallery and Study Center, New York University, 2–13 January 1991. Funded by the National Endowment for the Arts.

Mabou Mines. *The B.Beaver Animation* [videotape]. Excerpts from performance at the

Walker Art Center, Minneapolis, June 1973. Viewed at the Mabou Mines office, New York City.

Mabou Mines. "Mabou Mines." http://www.maboumines.org. This site contains a complete chronology of productions.

Mabou Mines. "The Work." www.maboumines.org/work.html. Accessed 21 June 2000. The Web site no longer carries this page.

"Mabou Mines." *New York,* 23 February 1981, 30.

Maguire, Matthew. "Alive Wire or Vital Signs." *Performing Arts Journal* 6, no. 1 (1981): 39–44.

Maleczech, Ruth. "Am I Dying While I'm Devouring Life?" *Performing Arts Journal* 6, no. 1 (1981): 45.

Maleczech, Ruth. "Song for New York: An Interview with Ruth Maleczech." Interview by Wendy Weckwerth. *Theater* 35, no. 3 (2005): 53–61.

Maleczech, Ruth, and Elizabeth LeCompte. "Two Women: Creating Their Own Worlds— An Interview with the Wooster Group's Elizabeth Lecompte and Mabou Mines' Ruth Maleczech." Interview by Wanda Phipps. *High Performance* (spring 1990): 32–35.

Maleczech, Ruth, Scott Burton, Michael Smith, Elizabeth LeCompte, and Laurie Anderson. "Acting/Non-Acting." Interviews by John Howell. *Performance Art Magazine,* no. 2 (1979): 7–18. Maleczech's interview appears on pages 10–12.

Mann, Charles C. "Doo Wop Opera and Greek Gospel Tragedies." *Mother Jones,* April 1987, 28–31, 44–45.

Marranca, Bonnie. "The Aging Playwright and the American Theater." *Village Voice,* 16 June 1992, 94.

Marranca, Bonnie. "All the Football Field's a Stage." *Soho Weekly News,* 5 February 1976, 15, 30.

Marranca, Bonnie. "Beverly Brown and Ruth Maleczech, *Vanishing Pictures.*" Review. *Live: Performance Arts,* no. 3 (1980): 42–43.

Marranca, Bonnie. "Introduction." In Lee Breuer, *Animations: A Trilogy for Mabou Mines,* 6-27. New York: Performing Arts Journal Publications, 1979.

Marranca, Bonnie. "The Politics of Performance." *Performing Arts Journal* 6, no. 1 (1981): 54–67.

Marranca, Bonnie. "There, There, and There." *Soho Weekly News,* 23 October 1975.

Marranca, Bonnie, ed. *The Theatre of Images.* New York: Drama Book Specialists, 1977.

Marranca, Bonnie, and Gautam Dasgupta, eds. *Interculturalism and Performance: Writings from PAJ.* New York: Performing Arts Journal Publications, 1991.

Martin, Carol. "After Paradise: The Open Theatre's *The Serpent, Terminal,* and *The Mutation Show.*" In *Restaging the Sixties: Radical Theaters and Their Legacies,* edited by James M. Harding and Cindy Rosenthal, 79–105. Ann Arbor: University of Michigan Press, 2006.

McMullan, Anna. "Beckett as Director: The Art of Mastering Failure." In *The Cambridge Companion to Beckett,* edited by John Pilling, 196–208. Cambridge: Cambridge University Press, 1994.

McMullan, Anna. *Theatre on Trial: Samuel Beckett's Later Drama.* New York and London: Routledge, 1993.

Mehta, Xerxes. "Notes from the Avant-Garde." *Theatre Journal* 31, no. 1 (1979): 5–24.

Munk, Erika. "Art of Damnation." *Village Voice*, 11 April 1977, 81.

Munk, Erika. "Falling, but into the Month of May." *Village Voice*, 19 April 1976, 113.

Munk, Erika. "Flashes of Astonishment." *Village Voice*, 30 May 1977, 87.

Neumann, Frederick. "Frederick Neumann." Interview by Lois Oppenheim. In *Directing Beckett* by Lois Oppenheim, 25–39. Ann Arbor: University of Michigan Press, 1994.

Nyeboe, Ingrid. "*The Shaggy Dog Animation.*" *The Drama Review: TDR* 22, no. 3 (1978): 45–54.

O'Reilly, Terry. E-mail message to the author, 3 January 2010.

Overlie, Mary. E-mail messages to the author, 14 October 1997, 10 November 1997.

Paran, Janice. "Beckett by Baedeker: Mabou Mines' *Mercier and Camier.*" *Theater* 11, no. 2 (spring 1980): 63–68.

Peppiatt, Michael. "Mabou Mines." *Financial Times*, 4 January 1973.

Phelan, Peggy. *Unmarked: The Politics of Performance.* London: Routledge, 1993.

Phelps, Robert. *Belles Saisons: A Colette Scrapbook.* New York: Farrar, Straus and Giroux, 1978.

Piling, John, ed. *The Cambridge Companion to Beckett.* Cambridge: Cambridge University Press, 1994.

Poe, Edgar Allan. "The Mystery of Marie Rogêt." In *Tales and Sketches, 1843–1849.* Vol. 3 of *Collected Works of Edgar Allan Poe.* Edited by Thomas Ollive Mabbott with the assistance of Eleanor D. Kewer and Maureen C. Mabbott, 715–88. Cambridge, MA, and London: Belknap Press of Harvard University Press, 1978.

Rabkin, Gerald. "Mirror of a Master's Eye." *Soho Weekly News*, 9 February 1978, 27.

Rich, Frank. "Opening a Window at a Theater Gone Stale." *New York Times*, 21 March 1993, AL2, 32.

Sabatini, Arthur J. "From Dog to Ant: The Evolution of Lee Breuer's Animations." *PAJ: A Journal of Performance and Art* 26, no. 2 (2004): 52–60.

Sainer, Arthur. "The Elite and the Decadent." *Village Voice*, 17 January 1974, 65.

Sainer, Arthur. "Hot Weather Avant Garde." *Village Voice*, 8 June 1972, 56.

Sainer, Arthur. "Play Ball, America." *Village Voice*, 16 February 1976, 135–36.

Sainer, Arthur. "Pop America Is Getting to Breuer." *Village Voice*, 9 February 1976, 99.

Sainer, Arthur. "The Saint and the Football Players." *Voice Centerfold*, 5–11 February 1976, 60–61. Supplement to the *Village Voice*, 9 February 1976.

Saivetz, Deborah. *An Event in Space: JoAnne Akalaitis in Rehearsal.* Hanover, NH: Smith and Kraus, 2000.

Sarde, Michèle. *Colette: Free and Fettered.* Translated by Richard Miller. New York: William Morrow, 1980.

Sayre, Henry M. *The Object of Performance: The American Avant-Garde since 1970.* Chicago and London: University of Chicago Press, 1989.

Scharf, Aaron. *Art and Photography.* Harmondsworth, Middlesex: Penguin, 1974.

Schechner, Richard. "The Decline and Fall of the (American) Avant-Garde." *Performing Arts Journal* 5, no. 2 (1981): 48–63; 5, no. 3 (1981): 9–19.

Schechner, Richard. *The End of Humanism: Writings on Performance.* New York: Performing Arts Journal Publications, 1982.

Schechner, Richard. *Performance Studies: An Introduction.* 2nd ed. New York and London: Routledge, 2006.

Schenz Theatrical Supply. "How to Work with Celastic." Accessed 11 July 2010. www.schenz.com/fm_celastic.html.

Shewey, Don. "The Many Voices of Mabou Mines." *American Theatre,* June 1984, 4–11, 42.

Shewey, Don. "A One-Woman Cast of Many Characters." *New York Times,* 13 January 2002, 24.

Skerl, Jennie, and Robin Lydenberg, eds. *William S. Burroughs at the Front: Critical Reception, 1959–1989.* Carbondale: Southern Illinois University Press, 1991.

Smith, Iris. See Fischer, Iris Smith.

Sonnier, Keith. "Keith Sonnier: *Send/Receive/Send,* November 29–30." *Avalanche,* no. 8 (summer–fall 1973): n.p.

Spector, Susan. "Ensemble Design." *Theatre Crafts* 12, no. 3 (March–April 1978): 24–25, 56–59.

Sports Illustrated, 7 May 1973, 73. Untitled, unsigned article on *The Saint and the Football Player.*

Steele, Mike. "Puzzled Expressions, Scrunched Brows Herald Mabou Mines Arrival." *Minneapolis Tribune,* 5 March 1978.

Steele, Mike. "Theater: Mabou Mines." *Minneapolis Tribune,* 27 June 1973.

Steinman, Louise. *The Knowing Body: Elements of Contemporary Performance and Dance.* Boston and London: Shambhala, 1986.

Strand, Dana. *Colette: A Study of the Short Fiction.* New York: Twayne, 1995.

Tanner, Tony. "Rub Out the Word." In *William S. Burroughs at the Front: Critical Reception, 1959–1989,* edited by Jennie Skerl and Robin Lydenberg, 105–14. Carbondale: Southern Illinois University Press, 1991.

Towsen, John H. *Clowns.* New York: Hawthorn Books, 1976.

Trungpa, Chögyam. *Cutting through Spiritual Materialism.* Edited by John Baker and Marvin Casper. Boston and London: Shambhala, 1987.

Walker, Julia A. "The Text/Performance Split across the Analytic/Continental Divide." *Staging Philosophy: Intersections of Theater, Performance, and Philosophy,* edited by David Krasner and David Z. Saltz, 19–40. Ann Arbor: University of Michigan Press, 2006.

Warrilow, David. "David Warrilow: *The Lost Ones.*" Interview by Guy Scarpetta. Source unknown.

Weinberg, Mark S. *Challenging the Hierarchy: Collective Theatre in the United States.* Westport, CT: Greenwood Press, 1992.

Wetzsteon, Ross. "Choices: Mabou Mines." *Village Voice,* 22 May 1990, 112.

Wetzsteon, Ross. "Wild Man of the American Theater." *Village Voice,* 19 May 1987, 19–26; 26 May 1987, 33–36.

Witchel, Alex. "On Stage, and Off: A Public Forum." *New York Times,* 22 March 1993.

Yeager, Lynn. "Community Theater." *Village Voice,* 27 May 1997, 82.

Index

Printed and bound by CPI Group (UK) Ltd, Croydon, CR0 4YY

09/06/2025

14685647-0004